SUDBURY
Rail Town
to
Regional Capital

SUDBURY

Rail Town

to

Regional Capital

edited by *C.M. Wallace and Ashley Thomson*

DUNDURN PRESS
Toronto & Oxford

Editing: Freya Godard
Printing and Binding: Gagné Printing Ltd., Louiseville, Quebec, Canada

The writing of this manuscript and the publication of this book were made possible by support from several sources. The publisher wishes to acknowledge the generous assistance and ongoing support of **The Canada Council, The Book Publishing Industry Development Program** of the Department of Communications, **The Ontario Arts Council**, and **The Ontario Publishing Centre** of the Ministry of Culture, Tourism and Recreation.

Care has been taken to trace the ownership of copyright material used in the text (including the illustrations). The author and publisher welcome any information enabling them to rectify any reference or credit in subsequent editions.

J. Kirk Howard, Publisher

Canadian Cataloguing in Publication Data
Sudbury : rail town to regional capital

Includes bibliographical references and index.
ISBN 1-55002-170-2

1. Sudbury (Ont.) – History. I. Wallace, Carl Murray. II. Thomson, Ashley.

FC3099.S84S84 1993   971.3'133   C92-095298-4
F1059.5.S84S84 1993

Dundurn Press Limited
2181 Queen Street East
Suite 301
Toronto, Canada
M4E 1E5

Dundurn Distribution
73 Lime Walk
Headington, Oxford
England
OX3 7AD

Dundurn Press Limited
736 Cayuga Street
Lewiston, N.Y.
14092-1797
U.S.A.

CONTENTS

Maps and Tables

CONTRIBUTORS

Matt Bray is an associate professor of history at Laurentian University.

Dieter K. Buse is a professor of history at Laurentian University.

A.D. Gilbert is an associate professor of history at Laurentian University.

Gwenda Hallsworth is a historical writer and researcher.

Peter Hallsworth was chief librarian at the Sudbury Public Library from 1966 to 1992.

Graeme S. Mount is a professor of history at Laurentian University.

O.W. Saarinen is an associate professor of geography at Laurentian University.

Ashley Thomson is an associate librarian at Laurentian University.

C.M. Wallace is an associate professor of history at Laurentian University.

PREFACE

Though it is tempting to begin a book on Sudbury with some of the well-known clichés, both complimentary and derogatory, in the end there is a good story to tell about Sudbury for its own sake, regardless of its reputation. Sudbury is unique among Canadian resource-based communities in having transcended the limitations of its origins to become the complex metropolitan centre of northeastern Ontario. This history begins with the arrival of the railway in 1883 and carries the reader through the decades into the 1990s. On 1 January 1993 Sudbury reached the hundredth anniversary of its incorporation. This book celebrates that centennial.

Sudbury: Rail Town to Regional Capital has been written by nine colleagues from a wide spectrum of backgrounds. Three come from the Sudbury area, three from other parts of Canada, and three from Europe or Britain. All have connections with Laurentian University of one kind or another. Five are members of the Department of History, one is in the Geography Department, one is a professional researcher, and two are professional librarians, one at Laurentian and one as chief librarian of the Sudbury Public Library. Two of the group are past presidents of the Sudbury and District Historical Society, and others have served on its executive or delivered papers at meetings. Several have written about Sudbury, and all now consider themselves Sudburians.

When the book was conceived about ten years ago, each author was assigned a decade and given guidelines as to topics that might be included. All were asked to comment on population and economic changes during their decade, and all were encouraged to look at municipal government and the physical city, as well as topics such as leisure, social institutions, and significant trends, both internal and external, that had an influence on the community. Finally, all authors were mandated to encapsulate in their own fashion the Sudbury they found in their decade. That is both the strength and the weakness of the book.

Since the authors come from a variety of disciplines or from different branches of history, they all have their own notions of what history should be. As a consequence, each chapter has an individual personality that does not always square with what precedes and what follows. While the editors have imposed some cohesiveness among the chapters, the academic integrity of the authors has not been compromised.

Sudbury: Rail Town to Regional Capital is the work of many people, and as editors we are especially indebted to the other contributors, all of whom share our enthusiasm for Sudbury. This book, naturally, is built upon the work of researchers and scholars who have been assembling the pieces for years, often in isolation. A generation of students at Laurentian first turned our interest to the city. Their theses and essays are identified in the endnotes as well as in the suggestions for further reading that appear in a bibliography at the end of the text. We wish also to express our appreciation to Dr. Frank Peake, a former colleague now living in Ottawa, who supplied invaluable information on the 1890s. Michael Kelly of Cambrian College kindly permitted us to use his material on the first decade of the twentieth century. We owe a special tribute to Peter Krats, a native Sudburian whose 1988 Ph.D. thesis, "The Sudbury Area to the Great Depression: Regional Development on the Northern Resource Frontier," for the University of Western Ontario, offered several insights into Sudbury's first half century.

Several people and institutions offered their assistance with the photographs. Peter Hallsworth spent hours making selections from the excellent collection at the Sudbury Public Library. Nada Mehes of the library staff could not have been more helpful in providing negatives. Mary-Catherine Roche of the Instructional Media Centre at Laurentian University duplicated most of the photographs in this book. Gerry Tapper of the Geography Department took several photographs specifically for this book. Michael Mulloy offered us total access to his own substantial personal file. The Inco collection was also made available to us, and we are especially indebted to archivist Ron Orassi. Most of the maps in this book were prepared by Léo L. Larivière of the Department of Geography at Laurentian University.

We wish to thank Dr. Walter Schwager, dean of social science, for his encouragement and a grant that assisted in the preparation of the manuscript; Joyce Garnett, director of the J.N. Desmarais Library, for her encouragement and a grant; the Institute for Northern Ontario Research and Development (INORD) for generously supporting this work; Rose-May Demoré, the secretary of the Department of History, for good humour and unfailing support throughout; and Freya Godard, whose firm editorial hand saved us from multiple embarrassments.

Finally and above all we express our appreciation to Kirk Howard of Dundurn Press. His confidence in *Sudbury: Rail Town to Regional Capital* typifies his support for historical studies in general and for regional works in particular.

C.M. Wallace
Ashley Thomson

CHAPTER ONE

THE 1880S

C.M. Wallace

A muddy construction camp for the surveyors and labourers building the Canadian Pacific Railway in 1883 marked the beginning of Sudbury. The site had little to recommend it physically, strategically, or aesthetically. Nor were there any known economic advantages to guarantee its survival as more than a watering hole for the steam engines rushing east and west across the Precambrian Shield; yet the urban experience began in Sudbury in that year.

Map 1.1: The Sudbury Basin

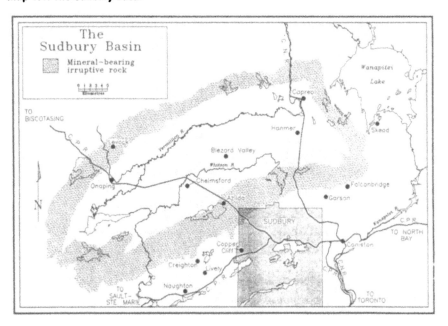

Map 1.2: Territorial Growth of Sudbury, 1883–1993

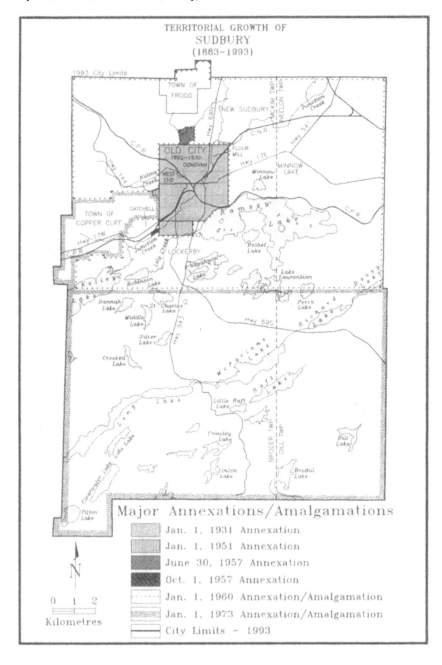

Created north of Lake Ramsey by the Canadian Pacific Railway (CPR) for the company's specific and limited requirements, Sudbury was to be a minor depot like dozens of others every hundred miles or so across Canada. The CPR Syndicate had established its regional headquarters on the "north bay of Lake Nipissing," and a depot to the west was planned near McNaughton on the Sault line running to Algoma Mills on Lake Huron. Late in 1882 the crucial decision was made to build the most economical road possible through Northern Ontario, which meant that Sault Ste. Marie would be by-passed when the line swung northwest through the interior to the top of Lake Superior. From 1882 to 1885 Sudbury Junction at the intersection of the Sault and the main lines became the centre of construction by default. The railway builders had no reason to linger at Sudbury Junction, where the terrain, dominated by gigantic rock outcrops interspersed with extensive swamps and endless lakes, was the most difficult imaginable for railway workers. "Rough and rugged in the extreme" was the way the Provincial Land Surveyor Francis Bolger described it in 1883. "The whole township [McKim] is completely divested of timber, the bush fires having made a clean sweep of every bit of vegetation."[1] That was an exaggeration according to other sources, who said the terrain was not that grim, especially to the west, where the fires had been less devastating. An advantage of those fires was that railway construction was easier through the burned-out areas, where the trees were down and the gravel was exposed.

By 1883 the railway surveyors under W.A. Ramsay had blazed their way to Sudbury from Sturgeon Falls and moved northwest towards Biscotasing. Though they were certainly not among the earliest people in the region, their influence was the most decisive. Over the centuries the area had been populated by several waves of native people, and the French and English fur traders had visited there since the early 1600s, as had missionaries and numerous government agents. The stakes of the railway surveyors, however, marked the way to a city in the wilderness.

Throughout 1883 the railway lines were under construction towards Sudbury Junction from both east and west. Harry Abbott, superintendent of construction for the Sault line, rapidly pushed the Sault line to completion, while James Worthington, the superintendent of construction on the main line, moved west from Sturgeon Falls to the Junction, where the first buildings were erected in March. The tote road had been cut by February

Map 1.3: Railway Lines to Sudbury, 1880s

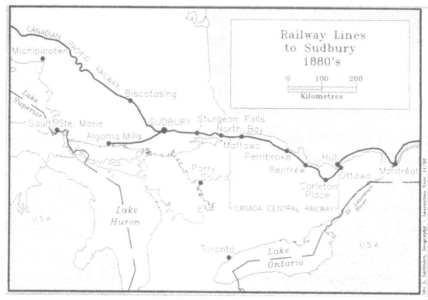

1883, when the equipment and materials were moved into place for the summer push. With about 3,350 workmen on 253 teams in the region that summer, Sudbury became a major construction site and company town.[2] In mid-February Worthington, the senior company official, had named it Sudbury after his wife's birthplace in Suffolk, England.[3] For about twenty-one months activity in the region was hectic.

Law and order was of immediate concern to both company and government, and an effort was made under the Federal Public Works Act of 1 February 1882 to keep liquor out of the area.[4] Worthington was justice of the peace, with first responsibility for the maintenance of law and order, but in May 1883 difficulties in this frontier community led the province to appoint Andrew McNaughton magistrate and Frank Moberly the first provincial constable,[5] and the CPR to station a railway detective, Sam May, in Sudbury. Plans were quickly drawn up for a jail and a courthouse, which by all accounts were much needed, for there was extensive local crime and bootleg liquor puncheons were rolled off the flatcars bound for Sudbury, where a ten-dollar hand flask found ready buyers. The hawkers, peddlers, and prostitutes all competed for the quick money in the hands of the isolated "blanketstiffs" who built the railway.[6]

During the building of the CPR, countless company towns like Sudbury were created and abandoned across the country. Normally the company owned all the property in such towns and provided the facilities it needed for its immediate short-term purposes. In Sudbury it built a company store, a company office, a hospital, a telegraph office, a blacksmith's shop, a carpenter's shop, boarding houses, and a few residences for essential employees such as the doctor and store manager. Those original buildings of rough-hewn logs were thrown up around the junction area. Made from green timber that twisted and cracked in the summer sun, they kept out little rain, less cold, and few bugs, but that was good enough for the "adventurous Finns, swarthy Italians, loquacious French Canadians, and sturdy British navies"[7] who disappeared as the rails moved on. In the meantime, from backpacks, wagons, and tents, the Sudbury merchants hustled for the plentiful dollar.

Over the next few years Sudbury followed a typical pattern of railway development. During the excitement of construction, hundreds, perhaps thousands, of workers were attracted to the community, with a resulting demand for services, which were supplied until the CPR moved its last construction crew out in early 1885.[8] For that short frontier period, Sudbury shared with hundreds of other communities a multitude of legends about bears in back yards, drunks on the main street, hustlers and whores, tragedy, feats of courage, and touching acts of compassion. Sudbury's early chronicler was Florence Howey, the wife of the town's first doctor and the author of *Pioneering on the C.P.R.* (1938);[9] all studies of the era begin with her. On balance, however, the first two to three years of Sudbury's history were typical of most railway company towns and reveal little of what was to follow.[10]

During that turbulent stage, however, the more permanent settlement to be built on the rubble of the construction site was in the planning stage, for in 1883 the Province of Ontario sent its surveyors to divide the region into townships and impose its authority. A form of municipal government was to be implemented, and land, timber, and mineral rights were to be sorted out quickly to facilitate orderly development and exploitation. The representatives of several religious denominations conducted services and planned churches. When the rail head moved on to the northwest, the elements of the new if minor depot were to be put in place. As the winter began to envelop the north in November 1884, the construction phase at Sudbury came to a close. On 28 November, four days after the line to Sudbury was completed, the first train arrived from the east, and on 10 December 1884 freight and passenger service began. The CPR line was already well advanced towards Biscotasing, which became the centre of construction on 21 November. The Algoma branch, no longer in the plans, had been temporarily abandoned a year earlier after all materials and equipment had been moved to the main line. A washout near Naughton had sealed the decision. With North Bay designated as the regional office, Sudbury's importance diminished until only two or three hundred more or less permanent residents were left. The Junction became merely another forgettable whistle stop on the line to the west.

The last spike of the CPR was driven at Craigellachie in British Columbia on 7 November 1885, but the company had already moved into the operations stage. Sudbury continued to provide services as required, but the chaotic activity of the construction phase had ended and was gradually replaced by orderly development. From the beginning the CPR had prohibited "any private buildings being erected within a mile each way of the station."[11] The company had bought the first of two blocks for the townsite from the Crown on 17 September 1884; it acquired the second on 2 January 1886.[12] Though buildings were scattered about the area, most were the temporary shelters that had been abandoned. The company had erected a few permanent structures for its own needs in its mile around the station while attempting to prevent anyone else from building on its property.

The syndicate had made one significant miscalculation. In 1883 it had refused all requests to buy land, including one from the Jesuits, who were building a combined chapel and presbytery within the CPR site to the northeast. Once the survey of McKim Township was complete, the Jesuits as well as the CPR acquired blocks, the Jesuits getting lot 5 in concession IV, to the north and east of the CPR grants. Since the company had several buildings on the Jesuit tract and was intending to construct a branch line through it, negotiations became tangled. Finally in 1886 the Jesuits agreed to sell the CPR the part of its block north of Elm and west of Elgin to Nolin and Junction creeks, and negotiated a large settlement for the Stobie branch right of way.[13]

As a result of the land problems, settlement was scattered widely over the region, giving Sudbury a ragged appearance. A Toronto *Globe* reporter left this description:

> Though Sudbury can boast a court house, gaol, hospital (on a rather diminutive scale), a public alarm in the form of an immense steel triangle, and a host of unlicensed whiskey holes, we have some hesitancy in terming it anything other than a "clearing." The population is transient and uncertain. Picture to yourself an immense camp meeting ground of primitive style, in the centre place three respectable frame buildings, while around the out-

skirts of the woods, in the shadow of the hills, extend a fringe of log houses and tents, leaving an immense open space unoccupied and you will have some idea of Sudbury.[14]

Of the few hundred residents in Sudbury in 1885, well over half were men, most of whom worked for the CPR or its contractors, such as the sawmill operator Leach & Brown Company. Though many lived in boarding houses, family life was becoming more common. The proportion of women and children is always low in the early stages; yet there was schooling for French and English, Protestant and Catholic, and women were prominent in the churches. For most, life was rugged, and their lifestyle earned them a bad name. A typical comment was: "The people of Sudbury are, one might say, as uncouth as their surroundings."[15] Early photographs show primitive buildings scattered among the treeless outcrops, with streets mere wagon tracks that became impassable with the rains. Both Nolin and Junction creeks, which snaked around the town, frequently overflowed into the streets and buildings in the spring run-off.

Map 1.4: Land Grants of Townsite, 1884
   (adapted from Francis Bolger's survey of McKim Township, 1883)

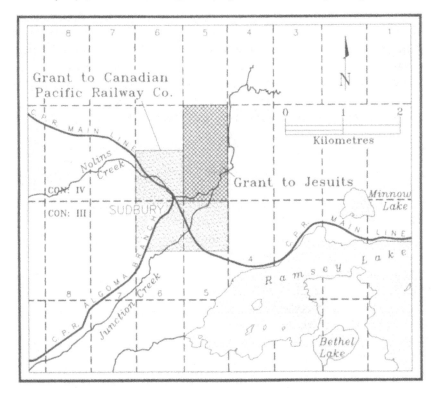

It was obvious that some form of municipal government was required. The Province of Ontario, which of course had been a partner from the early stage of development, began to assume its responsibilities. Northern Ontario, or "New" Ontario, as it was known when Sudbury was created, was administered under a variety of provincial acts. The Baldwin Act of 1849 provided for several levels of municipal government and enumerated their powers, whether it be a city, town, village, or township. In 1857 the Temporary Judicial Act, enacted to improve the administration of unorganized tracts, led to the creation of the "Temporary Judicial Districts of Algoma and Nipissing" on 12 April 1858. Ontario, which had control over the area after Confederation, exempted northern municipalities from the provisions of "The Municipal Institutions Act" of 1873. The north was a treasure chest for the urban-industrial south, a sort of fiefdom that required different political structures. The traditional county system was explicitly rejected with the creation of northern "territorial districts" under the Unorganized Territory Act, and legislation in areas such as land, taxation, public health, and spirits was modified for the northern districts.[16] Municipal government was necessary, of course, and in 1882 North Bay and Kenora became the first incorporated villages in New Ontario. Until the federal Public Works Act for the Sudbury region was rescinded on 1 March 1885, local affairs had been controlled by the CPR. Shortly thereafter the McKim Municipal Township Council was established; the first reeve was James McCormick, though there is some uncertainty about the date because the early municipal records were lost in a fire.[17] While it is possible that the McKim council was not in operation until 1 January 1887, it was sufficiently well organized by 1888 to construct a work road from Sudbury to Copper Cliff.[18] Since Sudbury obviously dominated McKim in that early period, the CPR was in charge, with the consent of the provincial government.

In that winter of 1884–85 not more than a handful of dreamers expected more for Sudbury than the echo of train whistles and the smell of sawdust. The timber trade provided some work for the Sudbury district. Leach & Brown Company, which had set up on Minnow Lake in 1883 to supply lumber to the CPR, was followed by others, such as Potter's mill on Lake Ramsey and McCormick's mill on Junction Creek. The sawmills also turned out finished boards for the houses, stores, and offices that were replacing the bush buildings. The lumber trade expanded for a while, and Sudbury was the centre of a prosperous but seasonal and unreliable industry.[19] In the short term the notoriously transient woodworkers provided customers for the merchants, but neither they nor their employers could create sustained urban growth. "A small lumbering settlement" was the way H.A. Hilyard described Sudbury in the late 1880s, "with but little prospects of importance, as lumber was scanty and transportation difficult."[20]

Dozens of prospectors also drifted in and out of Sudbury village, adding their tales to a fabled list. From as early as the 1630s there had been reports of copper being mined by Indians north of Georgian Bay. Friar Gabriel Sagar had written in 1632, "At about 80 or 100 leagues from the Hurons, there is a copper mine, from which the Interpreter Brule showed me [in 1624] an ingot when he returned from a voyage that he made to the neighbouring Nation."[21] Similar stories had been told over the centuries by fur traders, and even as recently as 1856 there had been official documentation of iron, copper, and nickel in the district, as noted by the *Geological Survey of Canada Report* (1856). Nevertheless, Francis Bolger observed in 1883 that "no economic minerals of any kind were met with" during his survey of McKim, nor did the surveyor Isaac Bowman detect any in Snider to the west.[22] By the summer of 1885, however, the next phase of Sudbury's history was about to begin.

The "discovery" of the Sudbury ores in the 1880s is shrouded in legend. The received version goes like this: "A gossan, a form of iron oxide capping or hat on the top of massive pyrites, was struck by one of the [CPR] workmen, a blacksmith named Thomas Flanagan, while wielding his pick [in August 1883]. When the rest of the gang started digging, a highly mineralized outcrop was exposed."[23] Though it may be true, neither Flanagan nor any of his mates laid a claim and the story is common to several strikes, including Cobalt. Both Dr. William Howey and Magistrate Andrew McNaughton declared they had found valuable ores, which were incorrectly identified by experts. Rinaldo McConnell, a timber cruiser and the most colourful of the prospectors, may have found copper in the early 1880s for he filed several of the most valuable claims over the next few years.[24] Francis Crean, another CPR timber cruiser, claimed to have identified copper in a sample on Worthington's desk in 1883 and to have sent Flanagan out to check.[25] Regardless of the stories, the Sudbury ores were not to be developed by blacksmiths, doctors, or timber cruisers, but by men with enormous amounts of capital and cunning.

The first patent was issued in October 1884 to two brothers from Pembroke, Thomas and William Murray, along with Harry Abbott, the CPR construction boss, and John Loughrin, a businessman who later represented Sudbury in the provincial legislature. They had paid the statutory Ontario rate of one dollar an acre for the rights to 310 acres, which later became the Murray mine, the first claim but not the first in operation.[26] Several other prospectors were scouring the area, and few acres were left unclaimed when the Toronto *Globe* told its readers on 20 September about the new "booming mining city" to the north. McConnell was the most successful, but there were others, including Thomas Frood, James Stobie, Crean, Thomas Cryderman, Henry Ranger, and William McVittie. Some, like McConnell and Stobie, derived considerable wealth from their finds; most, however, got little for their years in the wilderness. Few of those early Sudbury prospectors had had any previous experience, and they were doing little more than scavenge in the difficult terrain for gold, silver, and copper. One of them boarded a train east of Sudbury in 1893

> unshaven, clothing torn, shoepacks worn out from com-
> ing in contact with the rough rocks over which he had
> travelled, with his pack thrown carelessly over his shoul-
> der ... It contains a small cotton tent, a small axe, a
> prospecting pick, perhaps a change of underclothing, a tin
> cup, a small tea pail, and the remnants of his provisions.

After a month in the bush he claimed to have "two rich finds" and a bear skin worth thirty-five dollars.[27] He had come to town for a few nights in a hotel and would be off again. Aeneas McCharles, who discovered the valuable North Star mine, was not in the region long before he learned a hard truth: "The Sudbury district is not a poor man's camp. A few big companies are going to make all the money there is in mining there. It takes large capital to work nickel mines, and if a prospector happens to find a good body of ore, the only thing he can do with it, is to try and sell it."[28]

In 1885 the entrepreneurs entered the scene and began to buy up the mineral rights. News that a "shrewd Yankee [was] on the ground" was circulated in the Toronto *Mail*. "The keen New Yorker is at the present moment laying his fingers on the acres of mineral wealth now manifested to the world by the enterprise of our statesmen and the gentlemen managing the inter-ocean railroad."[29] Abbott and Worthington, among others, were partners in that attempt to extract copper from the Crean-Harwood mine in Drury Township to the west. Soon after a sixty-foot shaft was sunk in May, this first of many mining operations was abandoned,[30] and with it the hope of a mining boom. For about a year the train whistles and the whine of the saw were all that interrupted the melancholy.

Meanwhile the next stage in Sudbury's history was being plotted by another "shrewd Yankee," this one from Ohio. Sam Ritchie had passed through several ventures before arriving in Sudbury in 1885; he had been a marginally successful partner in a carriage business, a pipe factory, a railroad, and a mining operation, the last two in Hastings County, Ontario. The failure of the Coe Hill mine sent him on a new venture to Sudbury in 1885, perhaps with the encouragement of the CPR, which would undoubtedly profit from the transport of ore.[31] That fall he began to acquire mining properties all over the district, assembling thousands of acres before the creation in January 1886 of the Canadian Copper Company (CCC) of Cleveland, Ohio, with Ritchie as president. Capitalized at $2 million, the company moved a small work force onto the western side of McKim in May to develop mines and create another company town in the process. The CPR upgraded the Algoma branch to link with a spur to the Copper Cliff mine, which Ritchie and his associates, several of them relatives, were developing. The local headquarters for the Canadian Copper Company was a rented two-storey CPR office building in Sudbury. Until 1890 the company manager lived in the upstairs apartment and conducted business downstairs.[32] On 25 May 1886 the twenty-five or so workers began blasting at the Buttes or Copper Cliff mine.[33] Throughout the summer the mixed English- and French-Canadian crew worked with some "huge Finlanders" to produce a hand-picked load of ore, 3,307 tons

Map 1.5: Vicinity of Sudbury, September 1886

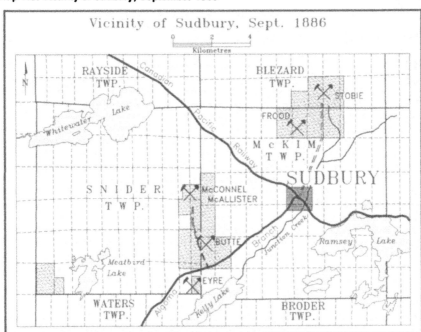

Vicinity of Sudbury, Sept. 1886

Properties – Canadian Copper Company

Open pit mining

of which were shipped to the United States in October.[34] Meanwhile, to the northeast the inaccessible Stobie mine gave promise of high-grade ore. Ever the hustler and needing financing, Ritchie was effectively promoting Sudbury and its hills of copper. The mines, declared the *Montreal Star* on 28 September, have "over 50,000,000 tons in sight, or more copper than will supply the world for years to come." The second great Sudbury boom was on. The CPR advanced its plans to reconstruct the Algoma branch and to build a spur to Stobie across the Jesuit tract, as politicians, prospectors, investors, and the next generation of hucksters rushed to be part of the scheme. That it was a scheme was suspected, especially after the ores proved to be both low grade and to contain nickel, which could not at that time be refined economically. The 1886–87 winter ended in gloom, and Sudbury settled back to its rail yard and the timber trade.

The lazy company town atmosphere had been interrupted, however, by the enthusiasm of 1886 as the rush of people to the region increased the demand not only for goods and services in Sudbury, but for parcels of land controlled by the CPR. This forced the syndicate's hand and a town-site plan was finally drafted at head office in Montreal. The new company

Map 1.6: CPR Plan of Sudbury, 1886

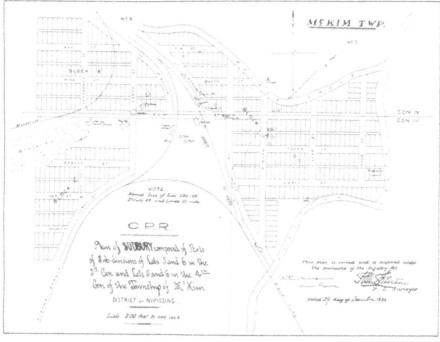

town was to be built around the railway yard in a gridiron design that ignored huge outcrops of rock and twisting creeks. Carrying the signature of William Van Horne, vice-president of the CPR, the plan was registered on 29 December 1886 (see Map 1.6). The mould for Sudbury was set with that design, which was drafted for the company's needs. The railway dominated the centre, as it does to this day, and the Elm Street crossing, the main line trench, and the junction with Algoma branch fixed the urban landscape as permanently as the Shield itself. The north-south streets with their vice-regal names still cross the east-west streets bearing the names of trees, though a Van Horne street intersects Elgin at the station house, which was handsomely decorated on 29 June 1886 to greet the first CPR through train at 2:10 in the afternoon. The sixty-six-foot-wide streets and twenty-foot lanes are flanked by the 50-by-120-foot lots set out in 1886. It was still a wilderness village, but its genetic code was fixed.

By 1887 several other changes had taken place in Sudbury. The Roman Catholic Church was the third constituent, after the CPR and the Canadian Copper Company, in the trinity that was to dominate Sudbury. It had already snatched the Jesuit tract from under the nose of the CPR, and its claim to more than land was extensive. Shortly after the missionary Father Joseph Specht, s.j., conducted the first mass on 30 March 1883, Father Jean-Baptiste Nolin immediately began construction of the mission church and residence. That Christmas the fifty Catholic families celebrated mass in the chapel, named Ste. Anne of the Pines by Nolin. For six years that rustic log structure on the north side of Nolin Creek opposite Durham Street was the centre of the Catholic world, with Father Hormisdas Caron the pastor. By January 1887 there were 376 French- and English-speaking parishioners, who constituted a large majority of the total population. Many of the French Canadians were concentrated on the Jesuit lands to the north and west of the mission in what fast was becoming "French town." The original mission building was no longer suitable, and by 9 September construction of the new church was under way. On 5 May 1889 a tearful Father Caron sang the first mass in the "principal ornament of our town from an architectural point of view," even without its belfry, which was added later.[35] The Catholic presence in Sudbury was unmistakable.

Several other religious denominations were active in Sudbury, though none challenged Ste. Anne's. The Anglicans were served by missionaries like the fabled Archdeacon Gowan Gillmor, who walked the tracks winter and summer from Algoma Mills to North Bay, holding services in boxcars, in shanties, and in the open:

I held services at Sudbury on Sunday, October 7th, 1883.
On November 4th, 1883 at Lorrimers shanty down on the

creek near the present railway station. On 11th November 1883 at Dan Duns. Held service at the new Court House, Sudbury, a frame building standing near the present gaol on 3rd Feb. 1884. Choose the site at Sudbury for Church and Parsonage 20th August, 1886.[36]

Until the end of the decade the small Anglican community was dependent on itinerant preachers. Perhaps having learned something from their land negotiations with the Jesuits, the CPR granted the Anglicans a site, where in 1890 a wooden gothic church was erected, later to be known as the Church of the Epiphany.

The Methodists, who were somewhat more energetic, had a chapel on Beech Street by 1888, and their missionaries had ministered to the railway construction crews since 1884. It was the enthusiasm of Silas Huntington, who arrived in 1887, that resulted in the construction of the chapel and then a parsonage by the two hundred or so parishioners. Similarly, the Presbyterians sent student ministers to the construction camps. Presbyterian services, conducted by Samuel Rondeau, who stayed from 1884 until 1888, were held first in the courthouse and jail, lent by the Presbyterian magistrate Andrew McNaughton, and later in the school-house. The CPR granted the church a site beside the Anglicans on Larch, and in 1889 a frame chapel was in service for the dozen or so families in the congregation.

In the 1880s Sudbury was a predominantly Roman Catholic community, largely "French" and "Irish," but Canadian-born Protestants, plus some Americans, were divided among the three main congregations, of which the Methodists were the largest. Among several others was a small group of Jewish immigrants.[37]

Religion and education in Ontario were interwoven, and during the 1880s Sudbury became part of that system. The first classes for school-children were held in a log building that also served as a Protestant church, a customs office, an insurance office, and a Saturday night dance hall.[38] Because there were so few children, French and English, Protestants and Catholics were taught together, though the girls were segregated from the boys. The private classes, which were not part of either the separate or public system, were taught first by a Miss Smith of Ottawa and then by a Miss Donohue and a Miss Green, all of whom were apparently able to teach in both languages. Separate catechism classes were held for Catholics while Protestants "were given the lessons taught in the public school."[39]

The combined school lasted for two years, but as the *Sudbury Star* astutely observed years later, "It has been one of the characteristics of

Canadian pioneering that the original settlers, whether of French or Anglo-Saxon stock, always took their church and school with them."[40] In 1886 the Catholics organized a separate school, and a public school was established under the Public School Act. These changes may have result- ed from the report of the provincial inspector, R.G. Scott, who had been severely critical of the original school. Separate school classes were con- ducted by Laura Ricard in the house of Steven Fournier until a badly needed four-room school building was opened on Louis Street behind Ste. Anne's in 1888. A four-room public school had been opened a year earlier at the corner of Elm and Lorne with S.E. Wright as the first principal.[41]

As in most Canadian communities in the 1880s, the divisions between Catholic and Protestant were unmistakable in most matters. Catholics, for example, were usually elected to the McKim council, with Fournier, the dominant lay Catholic, as reeve, and there was a sense of religious dissension in the community. This did have class overtones, for the Canadian Copper Company was controlled by a Protestant "elite." By the end of the 1880s the camaraderie of the frontier period was giving way to more traditional attitudes.

The village was also changing physically. The new school and church buildings were part of that reconstruction, and several CPR structures around the rail yard had begun to provide telegraph, freight, and passen- ger services. For accommodation, travellers could choose among the Balmoral Hotel, formerly James McCormick's log boarding house, Mrs. Ross's boarding house (Montreal House), and the Revere House, "a ram- bling frame building" that later became the American Hotel. The gala opening of the new, fully equipped White House on Elm in 1890, which made all others second-class, represented Sudbury's emergence from depot status.

The stores and merchants had also changed. John Frawley was one of the first private businessmen in Sudbury, selling men's clothes from a tent and a packsack in 1884. At the end of the decade Frawley's Outfitting House was one of several stores. Most were concentrated near the Durham-Elm intersection, already considered the centre of town. There was A.B. King's Watches and Jewellery, Martin's Boots and Shoes, Mulligan's Drug Store, Zoellner's Furniture Company, and Frank Cochrane's Contractor Supplies. The Hudson's Bay Company opened a department store, and Max Rothschild had a butcher store beside Rothschild's Liquor Store on Elgin. A.J. Lothian had a photography shop; Purvis Brothers supplied hardware; Turner's, Sweeney's, and Holditch's sold groceries; and Lee Wing ran a laundry.

Professional services were also available. In 1890 the Ontario Bank opened its doors. Among the lawyers was F.F. Lemieux, who became mayor in 1903. Dr. William H. Howey, the original CPR construction doctor, was joined by Dr. R.B. Struthers and Dr. W.H. Mulligan. Dr. Helen E. Ryan, the wife of Court Clerk Thomas Ryan, treated "diseases of women and children" from her office on Durham Street.[42]

Sudbury was by no means a metropolis. Water was still drawn from a spring in the gravel pit to the west, and there were no sewers. The muddy streets were rutted by wagons and became quagmires in the rain. Cattle, pigs, and dogs roamed at will, competing with wild animals that made frequent excursions into the town. Yet Sudbury was not a typical railway town, for the population had grown to almost a thousand and there was an unmistakable sense of an impending monumental industrial change.

Sam Ritchie was not the sort of man to let the poor assay of the first load of ore from Copper Cliff interfere with his new empire. Though the early setback was an inconvenience and production from his mines in 1887 was insignificant, he had moved on to the next stage. If there were difficulties with the extraction technology, modern science would solve the "devil copper" conundrum. If nickel lacked a mass market, then one would be created. If the cost of shipping ore was exorbitant, then initial processing would take place at the mine to eliminate most of the bulk. More mines would be developed, new systems would be introduced, and the world would demand nickel. Ritchie was irrepressible. There was perhaps more of Barnum to him than Carnegie. In the 1880s he promised more than he delivered, but his activity attracted others to the nickel range, and the Canadian Copper Company itself expanded its operations.

When another rush to Sudbury began in the fall of 1887, the more cynical suspected Yankee manipulation. Gold had been "discovered," creating the "wildest excitement,"[43] and for another year or two prospectors and speculators returned to the crowded village. These travellers, who were "almost equally divided between examining specimens, talking of finds and drinking whiskey," forced up the prices of both land and goods in Sudbury. The Vermillion Mining Company under B. Charleton attempted to develop a mine in Denison Township with little success, and by 1889 Sudbury was again "practically at a standstill."[44]

Though many developers still regarded copper as the metal of Sudbury, by the end of the decade copper had been replaced by nickel. In 1889 both the H.H. Vivian Company of Wales and the Dominion Mineral Company of Montreal acquired mining properties on the south rim of the Sudbury basin. Vivian was one of the leading smelting and metal companies in the world and not known for misadventures. The company's decision to set up operations in Sudbury brought international prestige to the district. It acquired the Murray mine, the original strike, and in 1890 blew its first smelter. Dominion Minerals, whose investors included several CPR employees, opened the Blezard mine in 1889, began constructing a smelter, and had over three hundred men on the site by 1891. Neither company claimed profits on its operations in the 1880s, but they had not expected to. Nevertheless, the potential of the Sudbury deposits was considered unlimited, the authority being the 1890 *Report of the Royal Commission on the Mineral Resources of Ontario*.

At the end of the decade Ritchie and the Canadian Copper Company were still struggling, but Ritchie remained optimistic. The task of separating the copper from the nickel was taken on by Robert M. Thompson and the Orford Copper Company of New Jersey, which used tons of ore and spent years experimenting before developing the Orford "tops and bottoms" process, which set an industry standard in the 1890s. Meanwhile Ritchie haunted industry and government on both sides of the Atlantic in his quest for a market. Some officials, it was rumoured, became so offended that he was banned from their offices, and even his backers, who had invested huge sums with no return, began to manoeuvre against him. With thousands of tons of unsalable matte piled up in Copper Cliff, the situation became desperate by 1889. In May of that year, at a meeting of the Iron and Steel Institute of Great Britain, James Riley of the Steel Company of Scotland delivered a paper entitled "The Alloys of Nickel and Iron," which turned the tide.[45] Nickel-steel, according to Riley's research, was the best material for armour and armour plate and would be indispensable to the military. An elated Ritchie rushed to see General Benjamin F. Tracey, the American secretary of the navy, who agreed to pursue the matter. In 1890 the Canadian Copper Company launched its future with American warships.

While all of this was going on, the Canadian Copper Company's operations in Copper Cliff had been altered dramatically. The solution to the third problem, high shipping costs, was the elimination of as much waste as possible at the site, which was done by smelting the ore. A trial heat roast in December of 1886 proved its practicality, and in 1888 the operational yard was started. The process was described in the 1890 *Royal Commission Report*:

> The ore is run through crushers at the Copper-cliff mine and is graded according to size, after which it is loaded on cars and taken over an elevated track to the roasting yard, located about three hundred yards from the smelting furnace. The beds of the yard have been made with layers

of clay and gravel, for the want of better material, and shallow drains have been cut for the purpose of drawing off water in the event of a heavy rainfall during the roasting operation. About thirty beds have been prepared in this way, and each heap when finished contains from 400 to 600 tons of ore. In building a heap a layer of fine ore is spread upon the bed to the depth of six inches, and over this a layer of wood to the depth of eighteen inches. The fuel used is dry pine – the remains of an extensive forest fire which swept over this country about fifteen years ago. It is laid with frequent openings for draughts along the sides and ends, while sticks are set on end at intervals throughout the heap to serve as chimneys. The wood is covered with coarse ore to the depth of two or three feet, and this in turn by fines to prevent a too rapid combustion, the whole when completed making a pile about six feet high. The fire is set to kindling material in the draught openings, and as it spreads and the heat increases the sulphur of the ore adds to the fuel, sending up a heavy, yellowish cloud of acrid smoke. The heap burns from thirty days to seven weeks.[46]

At the end of the burn the roasted ore was taken to the smelter furnace to be combined with America coke, delivered by the CPR from the port at Algoma Mills. Once fired, or "blasted," it produced a molten mass that separated into layers. The heavier metal at the bottom was drawn off, cooled, and, since there were no refineries in Canada, shipped abroad on the CPR for processing. The remaining slag went to a waste heap between Copper Cliff and Sudbury.

In 1890 the Canadian Copper Company moved its offices and officers out of Sudbury and into the new industrial village it was building at Copper Cliff. Its workers were already living in segregated campsites typical of company towns. South of the Copper Cliff mine a shantytown had arisen in 1886 to house the ethnically mixed work force. Starting with one boarding house, it had grown erratically along a twisting work road. Meanwhile, growing to the north was a second, planned community, which housed the English-speaking elite, including management and technical personnel. The segregation within was combined with the separation from outside. The company sought control of its total operation on its wholly owned territory and divorced itself from Sudbury. The roast heaps and smelter that were built between Sudbury and Copper Cliff created not only a wasted landscape but also a barrier of misunderstanding and mistrust.

The acrid yellow smoke that began to drift over Sudbury from the roast heaps in the summer of 1888 carried more than the smell of the future. Prosperity arrived in an odious cloud; yet the one was unavailable without the other. As the vegetation withered and the rains washed the unprotected topsoil away, the rocks turned from grey to black; even the houses darkened. From the beginning there were fears of dire consequences for the health of the residents, especially the children, but the price of progress was high, and what could be done when the decisions were beyond Sudbury's control? The power was held in Cleveland, Montreal, and Toronto; from the beginning Sudbury was at the mercy of external finance, industry, and government.

The 1891 Canadian census revealed that 2,354 people were living in the district. No separate figures were provided for Sudbury, but it is unlikely that there were more than a thousand. The majority of the population were probably in the several mining camps about the district, Copper Cliff, Stobie, Blezard, and Murray, and practically all were men. The only ethnic group of any size was the Finns, though there was a smattering of others who worked the mines with the English- and French-Canadian majority. In the valley to the north, perhaps as many as a hundred people were farming, mostly French Canadians, and there were clusters of population at the CPR sites at Azilda, Chelmsford, Levack, and Cartier.[47]

Few people connected with the mining industry lived in Sudbury itself, which was also still predominantly male. The only large employer was the CPR, and though the census of 1891 lists a wide variety of occupations, there was a predominance of labourers and construction workers. A very small white-collar group and an even smaller number of professionals and employers substantiate the picture of the rugged working-class community described by contemporary reporters. Even the prominent Sudburians had little claim to status. Most were from poor backgrounds and were in the frontier to make their fortune. Sudburians were a dependent people.

As the last decade of the nineteenth century began, the future of Sudbury was set as firmly as the nickel-steel ingots. In the mid-1880s both Sudbury and nickel had bad reputations and poor prospects. By 1890 both had unlimited if uncharted futures, and they would travel together. While the railway had planted the design of the town, nickel had imposed its personality on the people as firmly as it had on the landscape. The company town mentality was already fixed in the minds and lives of the inhabitants.

1   Francis Bolger, "District of Algoma, Township of McKim," Annual Report of the Commissioner of Crown Lands for 1883: Appendix 31, *Ontario Sessional Papers*, no. 34 (1884): 46–47.

2   *Ottawa Free Press*, 4 May 1883, cited in Peter V.K. Krats, "The Sudbury Area to the Great Depression: Regional Development on the Northern Resource Frontier" (Ph.D thesis, University of Western Ontario, 1988), 78. Krats states that the total in the area rose to about six thousand in 1884 (p. 80). The Krats study was especially useful in the preparation of this chapter.

3   *Montreal Star*, 16 February 1883.

4   The temporary act applied to the area from Callender to Algoma Mills. See *Canada Gazette*, 4 March 1882, 1314. It was cancelled in 1885.

5   E.G. Higgins, *Twelve O'Clock and All's Well: A Pictorial History of Law Enforcement in the Sudbury District, 1883–1978* (Sudbury: Sudbury Regional Police Association, 1978), 3.

6   Gilbert A. Stelter, "Origins of a Company Town: Sudbury in the Nineteenth Century," *Laurentian University Review* 3, no. 3 (February 1971): 10. In 1883 alone there were 110 convictions (Krats, "The Sudbury Area to the Great Depression," 107).

7   *Globe* (Toronto), 15 April 1884.

8   The size of the transient construction population is an estimate, for it varied from week to week and month to month. It may have been as high 2,000, though 1,500 is the most widely used figure. It is to be doubted that all 3,350 mentioned by Krats were there at one time.

9   Florence R. Howey, *Pioneering on the C.P.R.* [Ottawa: Mutual Press, 1938]. Reprinted as *Sudbury Minus One* (Sudbury: Sheridan Technical School, 1968).

10 Those interested should read Howey. E.G. Higgins and F.A. Peake in *Sudbury Then and Now: A Pictorial History of Sudbury and Area, 1883–1973* (Sudbury: Sudbury and District Chamber of Commerce, 1977) concentrate on this era and owe much to Howey. Stelter, "Origins of a Company Town," provides the best analysis.

11 *Ottawa Free Press*, 2 May 1884. Provincial surveyor Bolger said the claim was "one mile in every direction from Sudbury Junction." See his "Report and Field Notes: McKim Township," 26 October 1883, Crown Lands "Surveys," Book 20, no. 1548, reel 50, quoted in Krats, "The Sudbury Area," 114.

12 The CPR had applied for property to the commissioner of Crown lands in 1883 but had to wait until the survey of McKim was complete. The first purchase consisted of the northern sections of lots 5 and 6, concession III, and the southern section of lot 6, concession IV. This sold for the statutory $470. The second purchase, for ten dollars, was in lot 5, concession XIV, north of Elm to Nolin Creek (Stelter, "Origins of a Company Town," 7, as well as Higgins and Peake, *Sudbury Then and Now*, 21).

13 Stelter, "Origins of a Company Town," 6–9; Higgins and Peake in *Sudbury Then and Now*, 21, have a slightly different version.

14 *Globe*, 13 September 1884.

15 Quoted in Krats, "The Sudbury Area," 107.

16 Oiva Saarinen, "Municipal Government in Northern Ontario: An Overview," *Laurentian University Review* 17, no. 2 (February 1985): 12; and *Revised Statutes of Ontario*, 1877.

17 In *Biographies de la Région de Sudbury / Biographies of the Sudbury Region*, Version préliminaire/Preliminary edition (Sudbury: Département d'histoire, Université Laurentienne/Department of History, Laurentian University, 1980), McCormick and Jean-Étienne Fournier are both credited with being first. Fournier certainly served as reeve, though McCormick is usually considered to have preceded him. Louis Ashman wrote Ritchie on 16 December 1886 that the McKim council was about to be organized, which may suggest it was not in place until 1 January 1887. See Inco Files, Box 929-53.

18   Ontario, *Sessional Papers*, no. 22, 1890, "Report of the Superintendent of Colonization Roads," in Appendix 39 of the "Report of the Commissioner of Crown Lands for the Year 1889."

19   See Gwenda Hallsworth, "'A Good Paying Business': Lumbering on the North Shore of Lake Huron, 1850–1910 with Particular Reference to the Sudbury District" (M.A. thesis, Laurentian University, 1983).

20   H.A. Hilyard, "The Nickel Region of Canada," *Canadian Magazine*, June 1893, 313.

21   Quoted in Olga Jurgens, "Étienne Brûlé," *Dictionary of Canadian Biography*, vol. 1 (Toronto: University of Toronto Press, 1966), 133.

22   Bowman said there were "no valuable minerals" in the Snider, which included much of the western part of the Sudbury Basin (Isaac L. Bowman, "District of Algoma, Township of Snider," Appendix 32 of "Annual Report of the Commissioners of Crown Lands for 1883," Ontario, *Sessional Papers*, no. 34 [1884], 48). Bolger's statement is in Appendix 32, 46.

23   F.B. Howard-White, *Nickel: An Historical Review* (Toronto: Longmans, 1963), 64.

24   See John F. Thompson and Norman Beasley, *For Years to Come: A Story of International Nickel of Canada* (Toronto: Longmans, 1960), 33–34; Eileen Goltz in "Genesis and Growth of a Company Town: Copper Cliff, 1886-1920" (M.A. thesis, Laurentian University, 1983), 21, notes that McConnell told S. Ritchie of a "gossan-stained cliff located in the northern part of lot 12, concession II, McKim Township." This would have been after Bolger submitted his survey, possibly in 1884.

25   Years later Crean claimed that Henry Abbott, his superior, took over and threatened to fire him unless he abandoned the field (Francis C. Crean, *Northern Miner*, 2 October 1930, letter to the editor, 2).

26   Royal Ontario Nickel Commission, *Report* (Toronto: King's Printer, 1917), 30. Abbott was the supervisor on the Sault line and replaced Worthington on the main line in 1884.

27   Hilyard, "The Nickel Region of Canada," 309–10.

28   Aeneas McCharles, *Bemocked of Destiny* (Toronto: William Briggs, 1908), 102.

29   E. Odlum, "The Mineral Wealth of Ontario," *Mail* (Toronto), 26 June 1886, quoted in Krats, "The Sudbury Area," 3

30   Krats, "The Sudbury Area," 100.

31   Ritchie's "discovery" of Sudbury ore is, like all others, hidden in fog. He may have got his sample from the Ottawa Museum or from the office of William Van Horne, general manager of the CPR. He certainly read the newspapers and knew about the "boom" in 1884 and the Crean-Harwood operation in 1885. The CPR encouraged a wide range of projects across Canada, including farming and lumbering as well as mining.

32   Goltz, "Genesis and Growth of a Company Town," 25.

33   The mines in the district went through several name changes. The Copper Cliff mine, discovered by Thomas Frood, was originally called the Buttes. The McAllister and McConnell claims were renamed Lady Macdonald and Number Four respectively. The Eyre mine became the Evans mine.

34   Matt Bray, who is writing a book on the Canadian Copper Company, provided the details on these early years of the company.

35   F.A. Peake and R.P. Horne, *The Religious Tradition in Sudbury, 1883–1983* (Sudbury: Downtown Churches Association, 1983), 10–12. The description of Father Caron is from the *Sudbury Star*, 2 August 1930. The quotation of St. Anne's is from the *Sudbury Journal*, 22 March 1894.

36 Quoted in Peake and Horne, *The Religious Tradition in Sudbury*, 1–2, but see R. Frank Mason, "The Vulnerable Gowan Gillmor: St. Paul of Algoma" (honours essay, Department of History, Laurentian University, 1988).

37 Manuscript census, 1891, microfilm.

38 Charles Dorion, *The First 75 Years: A Headline History of Sudbury, Canada* (Ilfracombe: Stockwell, [1958]), 228.

39 *Sudbury Star*, 2 August 1930.

40 Ibid.

41 The records are contradictory on dates. The special edition of the *Sudbury Star*, 2 August 1930, has been used here, though it gives both 1886 and 1887 as the division date between Catholic and public. While 1888 is given for the new separate school, 1892 is the date used by Charles Dorion, *The First 75 Years*, 228.

42 *Sudbury Journal*, 1891, *passim*.

43 *Globe*, 3 September 1887.

44 *Globe*, 21 August 1888; and *Mail*, 25 July 1889.

45 *Report of the Royal Commission on the Mineral Resources of Ontario* (Toronto, 1890), 383.

46 Royal Ontario Nickel Commission, *Report*, 379. Edward Peters, the general manager, also described the process in "Nickel Ores of Sudbury," United States Geological Survey, *Mineral Resources of the United States* (1888), 113–14.

47 Manuscript census, 1891, microfilm.

CHAPTER TWO

THE 1890s

Ashley Thomson

Baikie, Fournier, Howey, McCormick, Ryan, Struthers, Cochrane, Mulligan, Rothschild, Purvis, and Lemieux: these and others of the 1880s, the pioneering members of Sudbury's business and professional elite, continued to influence the town's development in the 1890s. During the decade, others joined their ranks: James Orr, the owner and editor of the *Sudbury Journal*, is the best example. They were the men who sought Sudbury's incorporation as a town, ran for council, implemented an ambitious program of public works, founded the board of trade, served on the school boards, and directed the social and recreational affairs of citizens during the 1890s and into the decade beyond. Their successes were many, and by the turn of the century the town had grown steadily enough to become, in Krats's words, the "metropolitan centre of the Nickel Belt."[1] Most of its leading citizens, however, had larger visions than this. For them, Sudbury was destined to become the nickel capital of the world. By 1901 the stage was set for this vision to become a reality.

An analysis of the growth of Sudbury's population during the 1890s must be tentative because the 1891 census listed the village as part of McKim Township. A review of this census in manuscript suggests that 1,000 is as good a number as any to assume as the population in that year. As the decade wore on, the *Sudbury Journal* occasionally reported increases to that figure. In 1893, for example, the paper quoted the assessor, Mr. Anctil, as saying that the town's population was "close to 1,400." In 1895 James Purvis, a local hardware merchant, claimed that the population had risen to 1,800. In 1897 the *Journal*

---

reported, "Our population is slowly but steadily increasing."[2] In 1901 the new census recorded that the town had 2,027 inhabitants.[3] During the 1890s, therefore, Sudbury's population about doubled.

It appears that the town was predominantly British (including Irish) and French in origin, with a smattering of other ethnic groups. A Wing Lee owned a laundry but is reported to have left for China in 1893, "having made his pile."[4] In 1896 Ste. Anne's was the scene of a Polish marriage with about "75 Poles in attendance,"[5] but just as the officiating priest was from out of town so too might have been many of the guests. Relations between the English and French appear to have been good, primarily because the French accepted English as the working language of the community. In 1894, though, as a harbinger of things to come two decades later, the *Journal* received a letter, signed by "Parlez-vous Français," complaining that francophones were not keeping their French.[6] The religious composition of the town is as indeterminate as its ethnic composition. Roman Catholics were a significant presence; both French and English worshipped, in separate services, at Ste. Anne's. But the major Protestant denominations – Anglican, Presbyterian, and Methodist – had their own churches in town, although between 1896 and 1901 the Methodists were so few in number that they were unable to support a full-time pastor.[7] There were a scattering of Jews and a few members of the Salvation Army after it arrived in 1895;[8] if there were other denominations, none of them left much mark on the historical record.

For the most part, relations between Catholics and Protestants were as amicable as those between French and English, although in the very early years, as the town was getting established, religious divisions surfaced. This was, of course, most evident in the school system. The Catholics had their own school; Protestants and everyone else attended the public school. Because of the growth of the population, overcrowding was a problem in both schools during these years. In 1894 the Catholics enlarged their school from four to six rooms, and in 1896 the public school added an extra room. Even though the school system was divided by religion, each system tolerated the other. Occasionally, there were flashes of intolerance at the political level, but these appeared to have been few. More typical was a report in the *Sudbury Journal* that Catholics attended Orange demonstrations and even helped pay for prizes, and that Protestants attended picnics organized to raise money for the reconstruction of Ste. Anne's Church.[9] In general, Sudburians were more interested in building their community than in fighting among themselves.

In 1892, by virtue of place and population, Sudbury dominated the affairs of McKim Township. Stephen Fournier was, as usual, the reeve, and his council that year consisted of four Sudburians. Shortly after the election, Gus Harwood, the man Fournier had defeated, contested the legitimacy of the council on the basis of election irregularities, and in November the case was finally settled in his favour.[10] At a new election on 8 December, the old council, with the exception of Joseph Anctil, who had been convicted of bribery, was returned by acclamation to serve the rest of the month.[11] That there was not more interest, even from Harwood himself, may in part be explained by the fact that on 1 January 1893 the system of governing McKim Township was to be changed. Sudbury was about to become a town[12] because its leading residents became convinced that the community would advance faster if it could spend its taxes on itself instead of dispersing them throughout a wider area.

The movement to incorporate had been led by Reeve Steven Fournier and by three aldermen, Joseph Anctil, Andrew Gallagher, and James McCormick, and was supported by a "company of 100 associates" who petitioned the provincial legislature for incorporation.[13] In the light of James Orr's reputation as a town booster, it is interesting that his name was not on the petition. Indeed the *Journal* carried little of the story, and one can only speculate that as the owner of a newly founded newspaper wishing to serve not only Sudbury but McKim Township and beyond, Orr did not want to offend readers and businesses in the township by telling them that Sudbury would be better off without them.

In 1892 the provincial Municipal Act provided that any village wishing to be incorporated as a town must have at least two thousand inhabitants.[14] Even though Sudbury's population was at most fourteen hundred, the provincial legislature passed the bill of incorporation in April 1892, and royal assent was given shortly afterwards.[15] The act did at least three things for the new town: first, it expanded its boundaries; second, it established a new electoral system; and third, as will be seen, it made it possible to finance major new developments in town services.

Until incorporation, Sudbury consisted of lots 5 and 6 in concessions III and IV, or roughly 1,280 acres.[16] After incorporation, the town approximately doubled to include lots 4 and 7 of the same concessions, III and IV – approximately because part of its territory included Lake Ramsey. This was the first time that Sudbury had expanded its borders and it had plenty of room for development, since by 1894 only 380 acres had been subdivided.[17] By that year the shape of the town had already been set. There was a central business district, bounded on the northeast by "French Town" and on the southeast, near Lake Ramsey, by an enclave where

Map 2.1: Township Survey and Mining Claims, 1890s

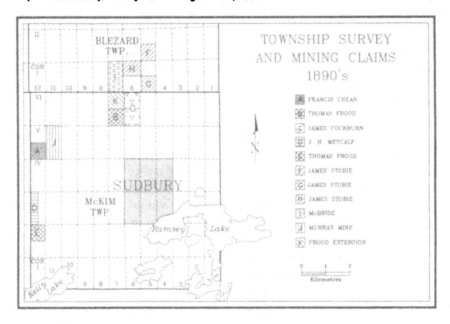

Map 2.2: Downtown Sudbury, 1894

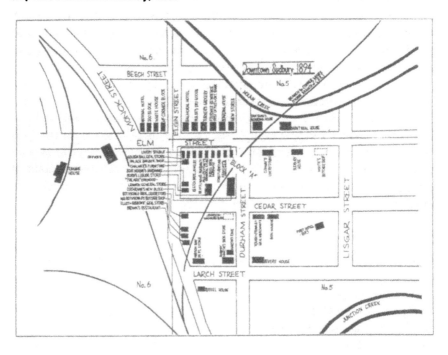

wealthier Sudburians of Anglo-Saxon descent lived in privileged comfort. (See maps 2.1 and 2.2.)

The second result of incorporation was a new electoral system. The town was to be run by a mayor and a council made up of three representatives from each of the three wards that were created by the act (Fournier, McCormick, and Ryan). The terms were to be one year, with elections to take place in early January of each year. It has been suggested that the original ward system proposed by Fournier and others in the petition of incorporation was designed to give an electoral advantage to the French-Catholic population, but that this plan was scuttled after the intervention of two English Protestants, Dr. Robert Struthers and Alexander Paul, whose case was endorsed by the largely Protestant Mowat government.[18] Though it is true that in the early nineties Catholic-Protestant divisions were strong in certain parts of the country, in Sudbury such divisions did not seem to affect the community at the municipal level. During the decade the mayors of Sudbury were Stephen Fournier (1893 and 1896), Dan O'Connor (1894), Murray C. Biggar (1895), Frank Cochrane (1897 and 1898), and Thomas Ryan (1899–1901). That is, a French Catholic was followed by an Irish Catholic, who was followed by three Protestants. At council level, English Protestants predominated under the ward system. However, by 1899 the provincial government had reduced the number of councillors from nine to six and made it a requirement that they, like the mayor, be elected at large, rather than by ward.[19] Despite the fact that by 1901 Catholics made up 54.02 percent of the population, the council continued to be dominated by English Protestants.[20]

A more credible explanation of town governance during the 1890s depends less on religion or language than on class. As Donald Dennie has shown, during the decade the vast majority of mayors and councillors came from the merchant and professional class, and a person's success in municipal politics was largely determined by his socio-economic status (see Table 2.1).

In any case, the problems facing the town did not turn on religion or language, for Sudbury was a municipality, not the provincial or federal government, and though religion or language may have been relevant at more senior levels of government, in this decade they were largely irrelevant locally. An examination of the development of town services during the 1890s demonstrates that the merchant and professional class used town council to promote a better climate for business in the town.

Throughout the decade town councils did what they could to enhance the appeal of the town. By-laws were passed, town constables were hired to enforce the by-laws, and generally the community began to take on an air of solid permanence that it might have lacked at the beginning. During

Table 2.1
Occupations of Council Members, Sudbury, 1893–1900

Occupation	Position on Council	
	Mayor	Councillor
Merchant/businessman	2	19
Lawyer	1	2
Physician	-	3
Insurance agent	1	2
Contractor	-	2
Barber	-	1
Publisher	-	1
Liveryman	-	1
Dairyman	-	1
Mason	-	1
Unknown	-	4

Source: Donald Dennie, "Sudbury 1883–1946: A Social Historical Study of Property and Class"
(Ph.D. thesis, Carleton University, 1988), 44.

the decade the wooden sidewalks were considerably extended, and in 1900 when S.N. Doyle of the American Hotel wished to lay 120 feet of granolith in front of his hotel, council agreed to pay half the cost.[21] An important matter for the council elected in 1893 was the state of the community's health, but before long it also acted in the areas of waste disposal, water, and lighting. Improvement in all these services was essential if the town was to progress.

In 1887 the original CPR hospital had been moved to Dufferin Street and converted to a private home. Still without a hospital in 1891, the citizens petitioned the province to set up a facility to serve not only the community but "the large mining and lumber industries in operation in this part of the province." When the province failed to respond quickly enough, Dr. J.W. Hart purchased the original hospital building from its private owner and refitted it as a hospital. The Sudbury Hospital, as it was known, changed ownership again in 1894 when Dr. J.S. Goodfellow of Toronto took it over, but it continued under its original name until 1905.[22]

In 1894 a second hospital, the Algoma and Nipissing, was established on nearby Elm Street West by a group led by Dr. Struthers. The following year it was renamed the Sudbury General Hospital, and in 1896 it was leased to the Grey Nuns of Ottawa, who renamed it St. Joseph's General Hospital. In 1897 the contents of the building were seized by the town for unpaid taxes, inspiring the Grey Nuns to build a new hospital on Mount St. Joseph. The new St. Joseph's, which opened on 1 December 1898, was described by a patient from Hull, Quebec, who was treated in it shortly thereafter, as "a beautiful establishment whether you be a Catholic or a Protestant." Meanwhile, after the tax case was settled in its favour in 1900,[23] the Sudbury General continued in operation until 1913.[24]

In spite of the doctors and hospitals, infant mortality was common; so too were sickness and death, especially from typhoid fever. Though Sudbury was not untypical of communities of its day,[25] its problems were a cause for concern to its municipal leaders. In 1891, as required by the Public Health Act, McKim Township appointed a board of health, consisting of Dr. W.H. Mulligan, John Frawley, and A. de Grange.[26] Its job was to enforce the act, for example, the provision "no hogs may be kept in the municipality except in pens 70 feet distant from any house." In 1893, as one of its first by-laws, the new town council appointed its own board of health, and two weeks later Dr. William Howey became the town's first medical officer of health. The council also decided to take up the matter of animals in the streets because strays not only posed a health hazard, but offended the aesthetic sensibilities of more refined citizens, especially the ladies, who had to navigate their way around the droppings. The *Sudbury Journal*, which had long complained of this problem, was able to report on 13 July 1893 that council had passed a by-law which stated, "No horses, cows or other animals are permitted to run at large within the improved section of town." But the sudden change in traditional practice did not find favour with voters, and two weeks later the *Journal* reported, "In accordance with a petition signed by about 100 ratepayers, the Council on Monday night repealed that portion of the by-law which prevents cows from running at large ... and these animals are again free commoners."[27] For the rest of the decade and into the next, Sudbury was beset by strays in the streets.

If animals were one source of health problems, disposal of waste, both garbage and sewage, was another. During the period, citizens were responsible for getting rid of their own refuse – they were supposed to take it to the dump on the western outskirts of town – but most of them left it for their animals. As with the animals, garbage was not only a health but an aesthetic problem, as the *Journal* noted as early as 1892: "The practice many of our businesses have of sweeping paper and other refuse onto the streets should be stopped. It gives the place an untidy appearance." In response, the new board of health sponsored clean-up days, and under the circumstances, this was about the best that could be done[28] until 1915, when a later council made garbage pickup mandatory. The second aspect of the waste disposal problem, far more serious than the first, was sewage. Not only were the outdoor privies that dotted the landscape unsanitary and smelly, but they contributed a less than citified look to the community. It quickly became apparent to the new council that a new sewage system was only one of three public works projects that needed to be undertaken.

The second was a new waterworks system. Almost from the beginning, the citizens obtained their drinking water from a spring near a gravel pit (which in 1939 became Queen's Athletic Field), "a spot absolutely unprotected from cattle and dogs, and we have been informed that women sometimes go … there to rinse their clothes in our drinking water." Some householders arranged to have water delivered from the spring at fifteen cents a barrel, but this arrangement was hardly satisfactory in a growing community. As the decade began, a number of businesses elected to drill artesian wells for themselves. In 1891 the Russell House hotel sank such a well 106 feet,[29] but everybody knew that this too was only a short-term solution and not a practical one for most ratepayers.

Part of the urgency of improving the supply of water arose from two other difficulties the town was facing. The less important was the problem of keeping dust down on the unpaved streets during the summer. The manual sprinkler system then in use was cumbersome and ineffective. If strong streams of water could be obtained from hydrants, the dust problem might resolve itself – at least until the town could think about paving. Of greater importance was the problem of fire. As the decade opened, there were only two brick buildings, one house and Ste. Anne's Church. The rest were made of wood, and fires were a regular feature of town life. As the decade wore on, brick structures began to replace wood, particularly after 1895, when J.C. McCormick began manufacturing bricks in town and selling them for about half of what they had previously sold for. Among the first of the new brick buildings put up was the town jail, an early casualty of fire. Others followed, most noticeably the Cochrane Block[30] in 1894. But even brick buildings were not immune from fire. On "Good Friday, March 23 [1894] Ste. Anne's Church, was destroyed by fire. The fire engine failed to shoot a stream far enough to save the fire, though the intake was in the creek at Beech Street 100 feet away."[31] To minimize the possibility of fire, councils tried to impose safety regulations on all buildings. In its first year council amended the building code to compel "all persons building houses to put in brick chimneys. A stove pipe sticking out through the roof won't answer in the future."[32] It also regularly supported the town's volunteer fire brigade by making sure its equipment was of good quality. But whatever was tried, the fire insurance companies were not impressed. For a town that wished to attract new business, high insurance premiums were hardly an inducement. Obviously an improved water supply was a first step in the fight against fires.

If, after a new sewage system the town needed a new waterworks system, it was also clear that it needed an electrical system. At the turn of the decade the citizens had to rely on candles and gasoline. In February 1893 "Mr. Veach [put] up a handsome lamp opposite his restaurant lighted with gasoline. It lights up the street for a long distance," the *Journal* reported.[33] These methods of securing light obviously did nothing for the fire problem in town, besides being inconvenient and inefficient.

Realizing, even in its first year of existence, that something had to be done, the town council commissioned Willis Chapman, a civil and sanitary engineer, to investigate sewage, waterworks, and electric light for the town. Chapman visited the town in August 1893, and in October his report was presented to a public meeting. The *Journal*, which was delighted to see these developments, put its finger on the one obvious drawback to big plans. "Is this place wealthy enough to undertake such a large expenditure?" it asked. Noting that the town's population was still under fourteen hundred, it observed, "It is an undeniable fact that neither the town nor its prospects as a whole have improved during the past three years; rather they have apparently been getting worse." Could Sudbury afford to build expensive sewer, light, and water systems? Could it afford not to? As the debate wore on, it became clear to many that the new utilities would save the ratepayers money and should in the long run pay for themselves. By the following year, council, deciding to canvass the ratepayers' opinions on the matter of the proposed public works, submitted two by-laws to a referendum. The first, for $30,000, payable over thirty years, was to cover the cost of waterworks; the second, for $10,000, payable over twenty years, the cost of sewers and electric light. On 15 August 1894 both by-laws passed with strong majorities. The vote clearly showed the confidence that the council and the community had in its future. In contrast, two years later Sturgeon Falls, a longer-established town to the east, defeated similar by-laws.[34]

In the latter part of 1894, after passage of the by-laws, council engaged two engineers, J.R. Gordon and L.V. Rorke, to supervise the installation of the projects. In 1895 the new council under Mayor Biggar awarded the contract for the projects to M.N. McCarthy of Sherbrooke, Quebec, and to W.H. Plummer of Sault Ste. Marie.[35] Work began in June and was to have been completed in October 1895, but whereas the sewage system was finished on time, McCarthy and Plummer had serious difficulty completing the other parts of their contract. On 1 August, "a number of workmen in the waterworks struck for higher wages" – Sudbury's first recorded strike.[36] Later that month, the cost of the project had jumped $10,000, and the town was obliged to go back to ratepayers before it could spend this extra sum. Then, without consulting the engineers, council unilaterally arranged for an extension of time for completion of the contract until the end of November, thereby voiding the penalty clause for non-fulfilment of the contract. Taking advantage of the voiding of the penalty, the contractors made no special effort to hurry the work through, with the result that early in the summer of 1896 the work was taken out of their hands and finished under the direction of the engineers. In the meantime, in October of the preceding year, Gordon and Rorke had warned that McCarthy and Plummer were installing an inferior electrical generator, but council ignored this advice and allowed the contractors to proceed. A year later, when the engineers were proved correct, the town was forced to replace the generator and the overhead wires used to transmit the electricity. By December 1896, a waterworks and an electric light system were operating in the community.[37]

Sudbury's was the first municipally owned and operated electrical system in the province, and the early difficulties should not detract from that achievement. Nonetheless, these early projects were not a complete success. As far as sewage was concerned, the new system did not succeed in eliminating health hazards or bad smells because, for many years, the effluent was dumped raw into the two creeks, Nolin and Junction, that ran through the centre of town.[38] In the spring, when these watercourses flooded, matters got worse.[39]

The new water system certainly improved the lives of individual citizens and made possible, among other things, improvements in home heating,[40] but it failed to solve the town's dust problem. As early as July 1898, the *Journal* complained, "The plan of watering the streets adopted by ... Council has been freely criticized ... If they intend to continue the system, more hose should be procured at once, so that the whole of the street between hydrants can be watered. As at present, portions of each street are not watered, and many merchants and businessmen are receiving no benefit."[41] There is no record of whether the additional hose was obtained. There is, however, a record of further complaints about summer dust well into the next decade.[42]

The new water system also failed to improve the fire problem noticeably. To be sure, there were some successes, and in 1899 council decided to improve the chances of the brigade by erecting "a telephone line from [the centre of] town to the power house, so that in case of a serious fire, the pumps could at once be utilized."[43] But the water pressure was erratic, and often not good enough to save all buildings from flames. In 1898 the *Journal* reported that the firemen had failed to save Mr. Gallagher's shops because the "water pressure from the tank was not very good." Not surprisingly, fire insurance rates did not go down; indeed, shortly after the new waterworks went into operation, insurance rates in the town were raised some 20 to 50 percent, provoking outrage in the *Journal*. The reason appeared to be that most buildings were still of wooden construction.[44]

Even the electrical system was imperfect. When the first lights went on, the *Journal* noted that the system "continue[d] to give the best of satisfaction,"[45] but as Gwenda Hallsworth, the historian of the Sudbury Hydro notes, there were problems almost immediately: "The initial capacity soon proved to be inadequate, operating costs were high and revenue small, which resulted in deficits. Service was poor by today's standards, with frequent breakdowns, and power was shut off over night ... Additional requests for service by customers had to be refused."[46]

There were further, probably unintended, political consequences of the town's ambitious construction projects. In 1896 Mayor Biggar and most of the council who had bungled the contract with McCarthy and Plummer were defeated in the town election.[47] That the new mayor was Stephen Fournier had less to do with the fact that Biggar was an English Protestant and Fournier a French Catholic than with the fact that the voters had confidence that the seasoned Fournier would straighten things out. More important than Biggar's fate[48] was that of town finances. Simply put, as a result of its projects, the town became "deeply in debt,"[49] a situation that had serious implications for the projects the town's councils could undertake.

Since during those years the income of the town was largely dependent on taxes raised from property owners, in the 1890s Sudbury town councils devised various strategies for obtaining as much money as they could from property taxes. In 1896, shortly after it was forced to add an additional $10,000 to the municipal debt, council threatened property owners who failed to pay their taxes with the loss of the franchise in the upcoming municipal elections. Later, it offered those who paid their taxes in full before 15 December a 5 percent discount on the amount owing; those who waited until after 1 January were subject to a 5 percent penalty.[50] Of course, this was mere tinkering. What council needed to do was to identify new properties for assessment or jack up the value of existing properties.

The former strategy was used by the hard-pressed council of 1896 against the Sudbury General Hospital, which was owned by Dr. Struthers. Ignoring an opinion given the preceding year by Mayor

Biggar, who was a lawyer, that the hospital was exempt from municipal taxation because it, like churches and schools, served a "public purpose," the council, as mentioned above, seized the building, forcing Struthers to fight back (successfully) in court. Council was equally unsuccessful in its interminable fights against the CPR, the largest landowner in town. In 1894, reasoning that the CPR held nearly six hundred acres that were appreciating in value while the town grew around it, the town raised the company's assessment from $25,000 to $38,000. On appeal, the courts decided in favour of the railway and dropped the assessment to $28,000.[51] The fight against the railway continued into the next decade.

All these endeavours did not substantially relieve the town's debt, with the result that council was forced to be frugal throughout much of the period. This was most evident in council's approach to social services. Shortly after Sudbury was incorporated as a town, council decided to establish a poor and indigent, or relief, committee. An examination of municipal financial statements reveals that the committee sporadically awarded small amounts of money to persons in need. On 14 February 1894 it paid sixteen dollars to Sudbury's first foster parent, Mrs. Joseph Levesque, for boarding Margaret Ranger's children. Mrs. Ranger had been charged with murder (the first in Sudbury) for shooting William T. Warren, a local butcher and one of her husband's friends. When Mrs. Ranger was acquitted on the grounds that the shooting was accidental, her children were returned to her and council was spared further expense. In addition to stepping into a situation like this, the relief committee occasionally lent a helping hand to others. In 1897 it decided to pay three dollars a week each to Mrs. Jones and Mrs. Dion, presumably because they had lost their husbands, although the specific reason is not recorded. Even though these were hardly princely sums, there were occasional grumbles that the council was too generous. In 1897 the *Journal* wrote, "Up to the present season, Sudbury has been comparatively free from tramps, but they have become so numerous of late that they are a perfect nuisance. The fact appears to be that those who came here first, and by their own peculiar system, have notified all the others that Sudbury is a good place to stop at." A year earlier it had observed happily that David Dion had been cut off from further assistance.[52]

That Sudbury was so much less generous to "indigents" at this time than it was a hundred years later may be explained, not only by the condition of the town finances, but also by the prevailing philosophy of the day that welfare relief should be left to private organizations, especially the churches. In 1899 the *Journal* noted with regret that Father Lussier of Ste. Anne's Church was leaving town; and one of the reasons for its sorrow was that Lussier had been very successful in "relieving the poor."

A second social service that did not fare very well at the hands of the town fathers was the library. At the beginning of the decade, when Sudbury was still a village, some enterprising citizens determined to provide a small library on their own. In November 1892 the *Journal* called for the establishment of a Mechanics' Institute so that a library could be set up "as in Chapleau ... With a good library and reading room, our young men and old ones too, would have a place to spend their evenings and be kept out of bad company and temptations of various kinds." Two weeks later, the paper reported the establishment of the Sudbury Literary Institute ("the first step towards the establishment of a Mechanics' Institute"), with W.A. Quibell (the police magistrate) as president, John Frawley (merchant) as vice-president, and L.V. Rorke (surveyor) as secretary-treasurer; and a board consisting of T.J. Ryan, A.J. Macdonnell, J.B. Hammond, Dan Baikie, and James A. Orr. A week after that, the *Journal* reported, "The free reading room has been nicely fixed up and supplied with daily papers, the leading magazines, chess and other innocent games. Citizens have contributed most liberally towards carrying out the project. The rooms are open every afternoon and evening and the public are invited to avail themselves of the privileges it affords."

It appears from the description of the new library that the guiding spirit behind the reading room was James Orr, the editor of the *Journal*. During the next four years, there is no further mention of the reading room in the pages of the *Journal*, and it seems reasonable to conclude that after the first enthusiasm, the Sudbury Literary Institute, the sponsor of the room, died a natural death as its members became involved in other important activities.

By 1895 the town council had time to turn its attention to the matter of the public library, and it may not be a coincidence that James Orr, the guiding spirit behind the earlier reading room, was on the council at the time as a representative of Ryan Ward. A by-law was drafted, and in early 1896 the ratepayers voted in favour of establishing a public library. Shortly thereafter T. Fournier was appointed librarian and a room was obtained in the Johnson-Washburn Block. The library's collection included a gift of books from the prospector Aeneas McCharles, as well as other titles purchased with its own funds. Despite the citizens' support, council seemed to feel that the library was a luxury the town could ill afford. In March 1896 the finance committee recommended against a grant to the library. In January of the following year the secretary of the library board, F.F. Lemieux, a lawyer and future mayor, complained that council had failed to authorize taxes (one-half mill on the dollar) to help pay for the library – that is, that council had "refused to pay for a service wanted by the voters." The result, he said, was that the library board was in debt for rent and other expenses. Since it was clear that a library was not a priority for the town council, it is not surprising to read that three years later library services had again been privatized. "A library of over 800 volumes has been placed in the Rectory of Ste. Anne's Church for free use by the public," the *Journal* reported. In fact, Sudburians had to wait until 1912 before another group of citizens, Dan Baikie among them, got public library service under way in the community on a permanent basis.[53]

In 1896, as part of a necessary fund-raiser for the public library, a recital was given in the library by Miss Daisey Torrey, one of many speakers who came to town during the decade. Probably the most famous was Pauline Johnson, the "celebrated Indian poet reader," who performed for an appreciative audience in 1894. Others included politicians such as Wilfrid Laurier. It was the railway that allowed such entertainment to come to town, and it was also the railway that citizens turned to each summer to escape from town, beginning in 1895. That year, Sudburians were invited to take a pilgrimage to Ste. Anne de Beaupré and a short excursion to the Sault. Such expeditions became annual events for many years to come.[54]

There were other, home-grown pleasures, such as the local bars. Sudbury had always been a "wet" community, and in the two referendums on the topic held during the decade, prohibition lost hands down both times. Sometimes, the drinking got out of hand. "A sorrowful looking sight on our streets Tuesday was a mother trying to lead along a young lad about 15 years of age, so drunk he could scarcely walk," the *Journal* reported. In 1899 the more refined ladies of the town, lead by Mrs. R.B. Struthers, formed a local branch of the Women's Christian Temperance Union (WCTU) to promote temperance.[55]

In the summer Sudburians liked to camp, canoe, fish, and swim at Lake Ramsey. At other times of the year they could join a chess club organized by James Orr or attend theatrical performances or band or orchestra concerts. And of course there were always the fraternal societies. The local St. Jean Baptiste Society was formed in 1891, and by 1894, according to Orr, "Sudbury had more lodges than any other Canadian town of its size."[56]

As in municipal government, leadership in leisure and recreation was frequently provided by the merchant and professional class. This was certainly true in the fraternal societies, and even more so in sports. From the beginning Sudbury was an enthusiastic sports community, and the 1890s was the decade that many sports organizations were set up. One of the prerequisites, of course, was proper facilities, and this explains why the town rejoiced in January 1892 when Martin's new rink was opened. Almost simultaneously, with the prodding of the *Journal's* James Orr, the Sudbury Curling Club was formed. By the end of the year, the club reported thirty-five members, which the paper described as a "remarkable showing ... for a small town like Sudbury." Throughout the decade, the *Journal* covered curling events with almost more enthusiasm than it covered anything else. A new rink also made hockey possible, and that same year saw the formation of a local club. Also created in 1892 was a rifle association, to which some of the best shots in town belonged. Its first executive consisted of J.R. Gordon, James Orr, L.V. Rorke, and W.A. Quibell, all of whom were active in other civic activities. Like Orr, the jeweller A.H. Beath was also an organizer. In 1891 he started a baseball club and a year later a lacrosse team. The latter proved to be very popular during the 1890s, so much so that in 1899 the club needed and got a new field on CPR grounds immediately across from Junction Creek, which is where the Sudbury Arena now stands.[57]

Another new sport of the nineties was bicycling, which was particularly popular because it could be practised without a team. In 1893 the *Journal* spotted Albert Picard riding Sudbury's first bicycle; a year later it recorded the first lady bicyclist. By 1897 several merchants were carrying bicycles and there were so many riders in town that a club was organized by one of the merchants, Dan Baikie, who also happened to own the bookstore. Beginners favoured the Junction Creek bridge, which was about a hundred yards long and had a railing, but in the spring this was a popular spot for many, since the streets were too muddy for passage. In 1897, possibly as a result of club lobbying, a bicycle path, about a third of a mile long, was set up by the CPR.[58]

The 1890s, unlike the 1880s, was a decade in which the CPR was to be less decisive in the town's development than was nickel. The railway remained the town's largest employer during this period, but everybody knew that in the long run it could never compete with the nickel industry. Writing in the inaugural issue of the *Sudbury Journal*, James Orr spelled out a vision for his town:

> We recognize the fact at the outset that Sudbury is unique, that there is no other place like it in the world. We have here the bull's eye of a great new district of Canadian territory, a district for long neglected because of its

supposed poverty, but now the centre of potential wealth. Nickel, one of the precious metals hitherto drawn in small quantities by mere laboratory process from refractory ores, is found here in masses, whose value none can state, because the most conservative estimate looks like wild exaggeration. Though not yet an incorporated village, Sudbury has already attracted greater attention ... than almost any other place in Canada outside of our largest cities. It is the meeting place of two great railway lines and the objective point of others that are to be built within a short time. It may be predicted with reasonable *certainty that Sudbury, as the centre of the greatest nickel district in the world has a splendid future before it.*[59]

It was not long before such great optimism gave way to crashing disappointment. By 1894 the Vivian Company and the Dominion Mineral Company had closed their operations; in 1891 Drury Nickel opened, and by 1894 it was also closed.[60] Only the Canadian Copper Company survived to see another day.[61] Though the real culprit was a depressed world market, the townspeople blamed these developments on the new provincial royalty on mining lands, and regularly they and their board of trade and their councils implored the provincial government to remove it.[62] At various times later in the decade, both the federal and provincial governments also tried to impose an export duty on nickel matte with the intention of providing companies like Canadian Copper with an incentive to refine the matte in Canada.[63] Most Sudburians, who saw these duties as a threat to their livelihood, agreed with Canadian Copper that it should be removed.[64] In the meantime, the citizens looked on with hope as new minerals were found in the area – copper, gold,[65] even coal,[66] but none of these led to anything profitable.

It is no wonder that throughout the 1890s the local economy seemed lethargic, at least by the standards of Orr's editorial. "Things have been so dull in town this summer that many of the businessmen have taken to playing quoits as a past-time [sic]," noted the *Sudbury Journal* in 1893. The next year it observed, "Our anticipation of three years ago, as regards either the *Journal* or the town or the mining district have not been realized." In 1895 the newspaper recorded, "The times are about as dull in Sudbury as at any previous period in its history." "Hard times [are prevailing] in Sudbury," it observed in 1897. As evidence of the general malaise, a number of businesses abandoned the community to seek their fortune elsewhere. The most notable was the Hudson's Bay Company, which pulled up stakes in 1897.[67]

The truth was that though the town's economy was hardly booming, it grew steadily throughout the decade. According to Krats, the number of businesses in town doubled during the 1890s, from about fifty in 1890 to about a hundred ten years later.[68] In 1891 Richard Dorsett and Charles Labelle set up shop as painters and decorators. In 1897 T. Evans and Son opened a carpentry and building shop. In the professional area, Dr. Lewis Leduc, a veterinary surgeon from Montreal with twelve years' experience, chose to settle in town in 1900. As new businesses and professionals came into town, existing firms expanded. In 1892 Messrs. A. and C. Paul started the community's first dairy, promising to supply milk for eight cents a quart. In 1894 Frank Cochrane, relying upon his affiliations with the Canadian Copper Company, erected a new brick block at the corner of Cedar and Durham. By the end of the decade almost any good or service could be purchased locally.[69]

Among several factors that promoted the expansion of the town's business was the *Sudbury Journal* itself, which published its first issue 5 March 1891. Although the *Journal* was not Sudbury's first paper, or its only paper during the period,[70] it was undoubtedly the most influential. For it was the *Sudbury Journal*, whose masthead proudly proclaimed it "devoted to the mining interests of Nipissing and Algoma Districts," that gave voice to the aspirations of the town and to the town's significance in Northern Ontario. Its success depended on the growth of the town, and as the town grew, so too did the *Journal*. Even after the arrival of the *Sudbury Star* in 1908, the *Journal* continued to fill a gap in the community until 1918, when upon Orr's retirement at the age of seventy, his former partner and the new owner, W.J. Cressey, decided to close the *Journal* down and concentrate on the successful printing business, which survives to this day.

In 1895 Orr became a founding member of the new board of trade. Almost from its first issue, the *Journal* had editorialized about the need for such a body, but it was only in 1895 that the first meeting was called to organize a board. The fact that the town did not have the necessary population (2,500) to set up a board did not deter the organizers, and by February 1895 thirty-four names had been secured as charter members. As with the incorporation of the town itself, local enthusiasm seemed to count for more than the necessary numbers, and by 31 October 1895 the board had been incorporated and had chosen Frank Cochrane as its first president. The board's history has not always been smooth, but the organization founded in 1895 continues to the present, although since 1941 it has been known as the chamber of commerce.

Local businessmen were interested in the board because it promised to lobby beyond the community for a number of changes that would improve town business, such as lower rates for fire insurance and better regulations for the depressed nickel industry. During the rest of the decade, the board worked hand in hand with the town council to promote these causes. For some years, the board met in the council chambers above the fire hall, and more importantly, there was a considerable overlap in membership. In 1897 and 1898 the former president of the board, Frank Cochrane, became the mayor.[71]

Of all the causes undertaken by the board of trade and the town council, perhaps the most important for the long-term economic health of Sudbury was the improvement of the local transportation network, for obviously without efficient transportation goods and services could not travel to and from their markets. In 1896 the "mayor and the council petitioned the provincial government for $2,000 to complete the road from Sudbury to the Lake Wahnapitae gold fields." In 1897 a deputation travelled to Toronto to lobby the provincial government for the Parry Sound to Sudbury Railway. During the decade, Sudburians were very conscious of the fact that "the Ontario government [had] taken $3,000,000 out of this district in the past few years from mineral lands, and millions of dollars for timber, but not one percent [had] been spent here."[72] The board and council were determined to get back some of that money for the region.

Such efforts were not without success. Though the Sudbury businessmen did not obtain everything they had asked for, they did begin to enjoy the benefits of improvements and additions to the road network, which were due in part to government grants. In February 1891 a winter road was completed between Sudbury and Wahnapitae, thanks largely to a government grant of $500. In April 1893 the provincial government's estimates contained funds for improvements to the roads from Sudbury to Blezard, Sudbury to Murray mine, and Sudbury to Neelon. In March 1896 the government announced a $500 grant for the road between Sudbury and Whitefish.[73]

By the end of the decade it was clear that the town had become a service centre for the Nickel Belt, a status that was symbolized by the arrival of the Trader's Bank (later the Royal) in 1899. The *Journal* noted, "A large extent of country is tributary to this place as there is no other [bank] branch between here and Port Arthur on the main line [of the CPR] or between here and Sault Ste. Marie on the Soo line."[74] The town's growing importance within the district was seen not only in the establishment of the bank but also by the creation by Sudbury firms of branch outlets. In 1893 A. Paul opened a branch store in North Bay and the next year, one in Little Current. In 1899 J.S. Gill, a watchmaker and jeweller, opened a branch store in Copper Cliff.[75] In the professional area, beginning in 1897

Dr. Mulligan visited Chelmsford professionally every Tuesday, no doubt taking the stagecoach that had begun running daily between Sudbury and Chelmsford the previous November.[76]

At this point one might well ask what markets kept Sudbury businesses going when the mining industry was in a slump. The answer appears to have been agriculture and forestry. Agriculture was not a large force in the region in the 1890s, but there were signs of better things to come. The industry had begun in the late 1880s as farmers moved into the Blezard Valley in search of good land, and by 1891 the valley boasted eighty-one farms. Agricultural settlement was encouraged by the provincial government, which wished to open up "New Ontario" for farming; it was made possible by the presence of an urban market newly accessible by road. In an interview in a Toronto paper in 1895, a local hardware merchant, James Purvis, commented that "agriculture was looking up." He said that there was "good land in Algoma," especially for potatoes, peas, oats, and hay. The next year, on a drive out to Chelmsford through the townships of Rayside and Balfour, Orr saw "as fine crops of oats, peas, barley and potatoes as we have seen in any other portion of Ontario." As evidence of the increasing importance of agriculture to the local economy, in 1895 an Agricultural Society was formed. Although designed to promote the products of area farms, it is indicative of Sudbury's importance in the region that its officers were from Sudbury itself: D. O'Connor, T. Fournier, and Frank Cochrane. In 1897 Lockerby and O'Sullivan, general blacksmiths, also in Sudbury, started catering to the market by selling farmers "everything they require[d] in the way of wagons, plows, harrows, etc."[77]

Forestry was another matter. The removal of the federal export tax on woodstuffs in 1890 was followed by a "full-fledged lumber boom." Indeed, throughout the 1890s the great stands of "pine, spruce and the boreal tree species were the steadying force in the local economy."[78] By 1901 the *Journal* was able to report:

> This place is the main business centre of an immense lumbering district that stretches from 50 miles north of us to the Georgian Bay from 40 miles east on the main line of the CPR to 200 miles north-east on the same line, and 125 miles south-east of the Soo branch of the same railway. In this territory over 5,000 lumbermen have been working this past winter in camps from 25 to 100 men. Nearly all pass through here or take the trains from here for their homes in various parts of the province when the season's work is over.[79]

Even though much of the surrounding region had been burned over by great fires that had devastated the landscape, leaving large outcroppings of bare rock, McKim Township still contained harvestable trees, and in 1895 the Canadian Copper Company acquired harvesting rights in the township and turned to a Sudburian, John Frawley, for the work it needed. That same year, Messrs. Booth and Gordon "commenced lumbering operations in the Township of Snider." It was reported that they expected to employ about a hundred men from Sudbury. In addition to contracting with local Sudburians for work in the forests, lumber firms regularly purchased large amounts of food and equipment in town. And of course, visits by shantymen provided seasonal injections of cash into its economy – particularly the hotel business. In 1894 the new owners of the American Hotel completely renovated their premises, "showing unlimited faith in Sudbury's future." To keep up with business in 1900, the same hotel rushed through a new addition to its premises, completed in two months.[80]

However important forestry was in tiding the community over, Orr was right: nickel was what mattered, and throughout most of the 1890s, nickel was going nowhere. But by 1898 the Spanish-American War gave new hope when it became clear that the metal would find its market in the armaments industries of large nations. That year the Canadian Copper Company added a fourth furnace to its smelting plant. "A fifth furnace is to be started right away, which is the best proof of the greatly increased demand for nickel that has sprung up within the last 12 months."[81] In England, Ludwig Mond saw possibilities, and possessed of a different method of refining nickel ores that he could not sell to anyone, he decided to acquire property himself in the Sudbury area. In 1899 the prospector Rinaldo McConnell sold Mond his stake, "the best news we have [had] to report for several years," the *Journal* commented. The Canadian Copper Company did not take this development lying down. Using Major Leckie as its agent, the company contested McConnell's right to sell his properties, but to no avail. When the legal dust had cleared in 1900, there were two main companies in the region. The fascinated Sudburians who read of these developments in the pages of the *Journal* could see that they boded well for the community. As early as 1899, the *Journal* was declaring the "depression over."[82]

Some statistics tell the story. In 1897, the year before the boom, the Canadian Copper Company allocated $197,000 to pay its Sudbury labour force; by 1901 that figure had more than tripled to $677,000.[83] Meanwhile, by 1900 Mond, which had no one in the region in 1897, employed three hundred men in its nickel mines.[84] Though both companies settled their work forces near their sites of operations, it was Sudbury that reaped the benefit. As Eileen Goltz has shown, the mining companies wished to control their workers and had no desire to encourage the creation of local businesses that would compete for their workers. Situated at the centre of the district, with improving transportation facilities and owing allegiance to no one company, Sudbury was the inevitable beneficiary of those policies.[85]

In Sudbury's history, the 1890s have occasionally been seen as a wasted decade.[86] Internally, the extensive public works projects failed to meet the expectations of their promoters and created large municipal debt that had to be carried into the future. Externally the economic environment was unpromising, a reflection of the world-wide depression.

Yet in many ways the 1890s were a crucial decade in the town's history. The decision to incorporate in 1892 made possible a new municipal government that was quickly used by the town's business and professional leaders to create an environment hospitable for town growth. Even though the public works projects were not as successful as expected, they were still an important foundation for the future. Also in place for the future were the expanded public and separate schools, and numerous other important buildings and institutions, such as a business block, the skating rink, and especially St. Joseph's Hospital.

In the 1890s the population of the town almost doubled, as did the number of businesses. By the end of the decade there was hardly any need to shop outside the town. An added benefit was that Sudbury became the destination for many people from the hinterland who needed goods and services. Their trips to town were made possible by the continually improving transportation network.

By the end of the decade the world-wide depression was over and the economic environment, particularly in the mining sector, looked more promising than it ever had. As the year 1901 dawned upon them, citizens, and especially Mayor Ryan, Frank Cochrane, James Orr, and the others, could be forgiven for thinking that the twentieth century belonged to Sudbury.

---

1   Peter V.K. Krats, "The Sudbury Area to the Great Depression: Regional Development on the Northern Resource Frontier" (Ph.D. thesis, University of Western Ontario, 1988), 206.

2   *Sudbury Journal*, 20 April 1893, 29 August 1895, and 18 February 1897.

3   *Census of Canada*, 1901.

4   *Sudbury Journal*, 5 October 1893. A more sinister explanation for Wing Lee's departure may have been racism. The previous year, a group of young men were brought up

before Magistrate Quibell for "disturbing Wing Lee"; Quibell was lenient with them, since it was their first time before him. See *Sudbury Journal*, 28 July 1892.

5 *Sudbury Journal*, 29 October 1896.

6 Ibid., 10 May 1894. The explanation for amicable French-English relations offered here is supported by Gail Cuthbert Brandt, "The Development of French-Canadian Social Institutions in Sudbury, Ontario, 1883–1920," *Laurentian University Review* 11, no. 2 (February 1979): 5–22.

7 Graeme S. Mount and Michael J. Mulloy, *A History of St. Andrew's United Church, Sudbury* (Sudbury: The Church, 1982), 7. Note that Krats incorrectly claims it was the Presbyterians who had mission status. See Krats, "The Sudbury Area to the Great Depression," 198.

8 *Sudbury Journal*, 28 May 1895.

9 *Sudbury Star*, 2 August 1930, and *Sudbury Journal*, 7 July 1892, 28 December 1893, 30 August 1894, and 21 May 1896.

10 *Sudbury Journal*, 17 November 1892.

11 See ibid., December issues as well as D.M. LeBourdais, *Sudbury Basin: The Story of Nickel* (Toronto: Ryerson Press, 1953), 77–81.

12 Afterwards, of course, Copper Cliff "held a monopoly of the Township Council for years" (*Sudbury Journal*, 28 December 1899).

13 Charles Dorion, *The First 75 Years: A Headline History of Sudbury, Canada* (Ilfracombe, Devon: Stockwell, [1958]), 3–4.

14 *Revised Statutes of Ontario*, 1877, chap. 174. Higgins and Peake observe, "It is interesting to note that the Municipal Act of 1892 stated that 'an incorporated village of 2,000 inhabitants may be erected into a town provided the census is certified to the Lieutenant governor.' Either the petition for incorporation antedated the Municipal Act or someone in the village had strong political connections." In fact, as noted above, the *Revised Statutes of Ontario*, 1877, contain the same language on numbers as the 1892 act, and so it is clear that the citizens were not trying to pull a fast one. Strong political connections are a more likely possibility. See E.G. Higgins and F.A. Peake, *Sudbury Then and Now: A Pictorial History of Sudbury and Area 1883–1973* (Sudbury: Sudbury and District Chamber of Commerce, 1977), 49.

15 "An Act to Incorporate the Town of Sudbury," *Statutes of Ontario*, 1892, chap. 88.

16 Lebourdais reminds us that "townships varied somewhat in size, but were usually six miles square, each subdivided into 72 lots ranged in six tiers, called 'concessions,' of twelve lots each, and each lot was therefore one mile long (north and south), by half a mile wide, containing approximately 320 acres" (Lebourdais, *Sudbury Basin*, 38).

17 Krats, "The Sudbury Area to the Great Depression," 217.

18 John Lawrence Kesik, "A Linguistic and Religious Study of the Sudbury Town Council, 1893–1900" (B.A. honours essay, Laurentian University, 1985), 9ff.

19 *Sudbury Journal*, 25 February 1897.

20 *Census of Canada*, 1901, and Kesik, "A Linguistic and Religious Study of the Sudbury Town Council," 18. Note that in this matter, Stelter has written, "Of the twenty-six men who served as mayors and aldermen between 1893 and 1900, at least eighteen were Roman Catholic (nine French Canadian and nine Irish)" (Gilbert A. Stelter, "The Origins of a Company Town: Sudbury in the Nineteenth Century," *Laurentian University Review* 3, no. 3 [February 1971]: 22). While Stelter is correct, he is double-counting people. If one examines the 74 positions available between 1893 and 1900 (10 each year between 1893 and 1898, and 7 each in 1899 and 1900), Protestants were in a majority on council in six of those years, Protestants and Catholics tied in 1896, and Catholics were in the majority only once, in 1893. See Kesik, 59. That said, Stelter's fun-

damental conclusion that "it would appear that occupation was a more significant factor in determining political leadership" (p. 22) is correct.

21 *Sudbury Journal*, 11 October 1900.

22 Ibid. 5 November 1891, 18 February 1892, and 26 July 1894. See also Krats, "The Sudbury Area to the Great Depression," 194.

23 *Sudbury Journal*, 25 November 1897, 19 January 1899, and 29 March 1900.

24 Krats, "The Sudbury Area to the Great Depression," 194–95. There is a great deal of confusion in the literature about town hospitals in the 1890s. Among those who have the story wrong are Higgins and Peake, *Sudbury Then and Now*, 61, who have the Grey Nuns renting Dr. Hart's log hospital, and Jeannette Bouchard, who has the nuns renting from Dr. Goodfellow. See Jeannette Bouchard, *Seven Decades of Caring* (Sudbury: Laurentian University Press, 1984), 14.

25 As late as 1900, the *Journal* was complaining that "typhoid fever is more prevalent in this place and generally throughout Ontario this season than at any other time." See *Sudbury Journal*, 22 November 1900.

26 Ibid., 2 April 1891. See also Bouchard, *Seven Decades of Caring*, 13.

27 *Sudbury Journal*, 14 May 1891, 13 April 1893, 27 April 1893, 13 July 1893, and 27 July 1893.

28 Stelter, "The Origins of a Company Town," 20; and *Sudbury Journal*, 12 May 1892, and 25 May 1893.

29 *Sudbury Journal*, 2 April 1891 and 28 May 1891.

30 E.G. Higgins, *Twelve O'Clock and All's Well: A Pictorial History of Law Enforcement in the Sudbury District, 1883–1978* (Sudbury: Sudbury Regional Police Association, 1978), 5; and *Sudbury Journal*, 9 June 1892, 27 December 1894, and 6 June 1895.

31 Dorion, *The First 75 Years*, 210.

32 *Sudbury Journal*, 13 July 1893.

33 Ibid., 9 February 1893.

34 Ibid., 26 October 1893, 26 July 1894, 16 August 1894, and 7 January 1897.

35 Ibid., 9 May 1895.

36 Ibid., 1 August 1895. Note that Stelter, "The Origins of a Company Town," 27, incorrectly sets the date as 1899 when some workers in Copper Cliff withdrew their service.

37 Ibid., 19 September 1895 and 31 October 1895; Gwenda Hallsworth, *A History of Hydro in Sudbury* (Sudbury: Sudbury Hydro-Electric Commission, 1985), 3, and *Sudbury Journal*, 10 December 1896.

38 *Sudbury Journal*, 7 July 1907.

39 And not just because of smell. On 21 April 1904, the *Sudbury Journal* reported, "The body of Mr. Patterson's little boy which had fallen in Nolin creek last fall ... [had been] recovered." The paper added that the body "was not very badly decomposed considering the long time it had been in the water."

40 "Purvis Bros. has just completed the installation of a very fine hot water system of heating in the residence of W.A. Quibell, our P[olice] M[agistrate] ... This is the first residence in town to be heated by this system" (*Sudbury Journal*, 12 January 1899).

41 *Sudbury Journal*, 14 July 1898.

42 On 28 April 1904, the *Sudbury Journal* carried this ditty:

> How fine to have the snow all gone,
> How fine to have the sidewalks bare.
> How fine to have the dust clouds,
> In one's nose and eyes and ears and hair.

43 *Sudbury Journal*, 18 May 1899. This was the first telephone in town. In June, when R.J. Heller of Bell Telephone analysed the possibilities of expanding the phone service, he

concluded that at the time there was not enough interest. But the *Journal* concluded that there would be "in the near future" (*Sudbury Journal*, 15 June 1899).

44 Ibid., 7 January 1897, 21 April 1898, and 4 May 1899.

45 Ibid., 17 December 1896.

46 Hallsworth, *A History of Hydro*, 4.

47 *Sudbury Journal*, 9 January 1896.

48 In 1896 Biggar himself mysteriously vanished, leaving behind his law practice, his wife, and his home. At the time, everybody thought he had drowned in Lake Ramsey, but in 1898 Gus Harwood, Fournier's challenger in 1891, came across the former mayor in San Francisco, where he had repaired after failing to strike it rich in the Klondike. Later, Biggar was alleged to have gone to South America. See Dorion, *The First 75 Years*, 49.

49 *Sudbury Journal*, 22 March 1900.

50 Ibid., 11 October 1896 and 6 January 1898.

51 Ibid., 1 February 1894 and 16 August 1894.

52 Ibid., 14 January 1897, 4 February 1897, 2 September 1897, and 30 April 1896.

53 *Sudbury Journal*, 17 November 1892, 1 December 1892, 8 December 1892, 9 January 1896, 12 March 1896, 2 April 1896, 7 January 1897, 16 February 1899, and 24 August 1899; and Dorion, *The First 75 Years*, 203.

54 *Sudbury Journal*, 1 January 1894, 30 August 1894, 25 July 1895, 8 August 1895, and 9 April 1896.

55 Ibid., 6 February 1893, 4 January 1894, 29 September 1898, and 18 May 1899.

56 Ibid., 11 June 1891, 26 November 1891, 24 December 1891, 7 December 1893, 20 August 1896, 21 January 1897, and 21 June 1900; and Krats, "The Sudbury Area to the Great Depression," 200.

57 *Sudbury Journal*, 23 April 1891, 9 July 1891, 7 January 1892, 14 January 1892, 17 November 1892, 1 December 1892, 8 December 1892, 17 December 1892, and 1 June 1899.

58 Ibid., 27 April 1893, 24 May 1894, 22 April 1897, 27 May 1897, and 29 July 1897. At one point, the *Journal* complained that the mud on Durham Street was over seventeen inches deep! See *Sudbury Journal*, 11 April 1895.

59 *Sudbury Journal*, 5 March 1891.

60 See Krats, "The Sudbury Area to the Great Depression," 137ff, for an explanation of the demise of these two companies.

61 See Stelter, "The Origins of a Company Town," 25, for reasons the CCC survived. In 1898 the *Journal* noted that the CCC had "a monopoly on the production of nickel" (*Sudbury Journal*, 28 April 1898).

62 *Sudbury Journal*, 28 January 1897; and Krats, "The Sudbury Area to the Great Depression," 145.

63 Krats, "The Sudbury Area to the Great Depression," 145.

64 Orr was an exception. See *Sudbury Journal*, 24 February 1898.

65 When gold was reported near Wahnapitae, the *Journal* celebrated: "Whoop 'er up boys! Let's have some gold, and plenty of it, as we cannot do much with nickel just now." *Sudbury Journal*, 25 August 1892.

66 *Sudbury Journal*, 20 April 1893 and Krats, "The Sudbury Area to the Great Depression," 156.

67 *Sudbury Journal*, 27 July 1893, 1 March 1894, 11 April 1895, 20 May 1897, and 8 July 1897.

68 Krats, "The Sudbury Area to the Great Depression," 218. Though it is not entirely clear where Krats gets his figures for the beginning of the decade, he bases his figure for the

end of the decade on his analysis of Dyn and Wiman's *Reference Book*, January 1901, 250, and the *Ontario Gazetteer and Directory*, 1901–1902, 922–24.

69 *Sudbury Journal*, 23 April 1891, 26 May 1892, 14 January 1897, and 22 November 1900; and Stelter, "The Origins of a Company Town," 19.

70 The honour of being Sudbury's first paper belongs to the short-lived *Star*, edited by J.J. Barton, which lasted for a couple of weeks in 1890 (Dorion, *The First 75 Years*, 201). During the 1890s, the *Journal's* competition was the *Sudbury News*, begun in 1894 and edited by a series of men until 1899 when it closed after a bad fire. See ibid., 202.

71 *Sudbury Journal*, 19 March 1891, 7 February 1895, 28 February 1895, and 5 April 1900.

72 Ibid., 13 July 1893, 17 December 1896, and 25 February 1897.

73 Ibid., 23 February 1891, 27 April 1893, and 12 March 1896.

74 Ibid., 23 March 1899 and 16 May 1899.

75 Ibid., 9 November 1893, 21 June 1894, and 19 February 1899.

76 Ibid., 26 November 1896 and 16 December 1897.

77 See interview with James Purvis, a local hardware merchant, in the *Sudbury Journal*, 29 August 1895, as well as Krats, "The Sudbury Area to the Great Depression," 162. See also *Sudbury Journal*, 18 April 1895, 25 April 1895, 29 August 1895, 6 August 1896, and 29 April 1897.

78 Krats, "The Sudbury Area to the Great Depression," 157. See also *Sudbury Journal*, 6 October 1892.

79 *Sudbury Journal*, April 18, 1901.

80 Ibid., 6 October 1892, 20 July 1894, 22 August 1895, 28 November 1895, 24 August 1899, and 30 August 1900. See also Krats, "The Sudbury Area to the Great Depression," 158.

81 *Sudbury Journal*, 7 July 1898; and Krats, "The Sudbury Area to the Great Depression," 147.

82 *Sudbury Journal*, 23 February 1899, 3 August 1899, and 14 September 1899.

83 "Canadian Copper Company's Preliminary Reports for Year-End," available from Inco Archives Sudbury, boxes 927–55 (1897) and 936–50 (1901). I wish to thank Dr. Matt Bray for making these documents available.

84 *Sudbury Journal*, 5 November 1900.

85 Eileen Goltz, "The Exercise of Power in a Company Town: Copper Cliff, 1886–1980" (Ph.D. thesis, University of Guelph, 1989). Note that the title of Stelter's "The Origins of a Company Town," meaning Sudbury, is in fact misleading!

86 Kelly, "By Divine Right," 1.

CHAPTER THREE

1900–1910

Ashley Thomson

During the first decade of the twentieth century the town of Sudbury built on its earlier successes. As in the previous decade, much of the direction came from a small group of merchants and professionals who led the community. In the 1900s, many of the town's original "Old Boys" continued their civic work, men like Dan Baikie, the well-known owner of the Sudbury Book Store who did double duty as collector of inland revenue; Frank Cochrane, former mayor who represented the community in the provincial legislature and since 1905 also sat in Premier Whitney's cabinet as minister of lands and mines; Stephen Fournier, the town's first and fourth mayor; John Frawley, the area's first merchant; W.H. Howey, the town's first doctor; W.H. Mulligan, a physician and pharmacy store owner who specialized in diseases of lumbermen; James Purvis, a prominent hardware merchant; and James Orr, editor of the *Sudbury Journal*, the town's weekly newspaper. In the decade, as might be expected, new men took their place alongside the community's founders. In 1899 Larry O'Connor, a merchant and saloon owner, began a distinguished and colourful career as town councillor that continued until 1905, when he became mayor. He served again in that position in 1906, 1907, 1910, and 1911. There were others like him.[1]

But the first decade of the twentieth century was not an exact replica of the one that had preceded it. The external political and economic climate was significantly healthier than in the 1890s, with the result that in Sudbury's history, these years saw the community cementing its position as a regional metropolis that dominated the Nickel Belt, and at the same time extending its influence beyond.[2]

During this decade Sudbury's population overtook Copper Cliff's for the first time. In 1901 the census found Sudbury's population to be 2,027 and that of the Sudbury Basin to be about 7,500, a figure that included about 2,400 who lived in Copper Cliff.[3] Ten years later Sudbury's relative position within its immediate hinterland had changed. The town's population had climbed to 4,150, an increase of 104.7 percent, while the Basin's had risen only to about 12,500, an increase of 66 percent. The 12,500 included Copper Cliff, which had grown to a more modest 3,082.[4]

Population figures can be analysed in many different ways. In ethnic composition, Sudbury did not change much through the decade, for people of British or French ancestry continued to predominate, as in the preceding decade.[5] (See Table 3.1.) In religious composition there was also very little change between the two census periods. As in the 1890s, Roman Catholics predominated.[6] (See Table 3.2.)

Like the previous decade, the years 1900–1910 saw little strife between English and French. When Dr. R.H. Arthur was nominated for mayor in 1903, he demurred on the grounds that it was time for a Frenchman to hold this office, and as a result, F.F. Lemieux, a lawyer,

Table 3.1

Sudbury, Ethnic Composition, 1901 and 1911

	1901		1911	
Ethnic Origin	N	%	N	%
British	1,139	55.19	2,218	53.45
French	702	35.63	1,518	36.58
German	39	1.92	74	1.78
Italian	48	2.37	78	1.88
Jewish	73	3.60	87	2.10
Netherlands	1	.04	3	.07
Polish	-	-	14	.34
Russian	1	.04	6	.15
Scandinavian	14	.69	14	.34
Ukrainian	-	-	-	-
Asiatic	3	.15	28	.67
Aboriginal	-	-	-	-
Other	-	-	-	-
Total population	2,072		4,150	

Source: Census of Canada, vol. 1, 1901 and 1911.

Table 3.2
Sudbury, Religious Composition, 1901 and 1911

Religious Denomination	1901		1911	
	N	%	N	%
Anglican	277	13.66	677	16.31
Baptist	29	1.43	81	1.95
Jewish	71	3.50	85	2.05
Lutheran	10	0.49	12	0.27
Methodist	193	9.52	379	9.13
Presbyterian	330	16.28	666	16.04
Roman Catholic	1,095	54.02	2,155	51.93
Salvation Army	-	-	3	0.07
Other	22	1.08	92	2.22
No religion	-	-	-	-
Total population	2,072		4,150	

Source: Census of Canada, vol. 1, 1901 and 1911

began a two-year term. The reasons for this amicability were varied. In part it had to do with the fact that French Canadians did not go out of the way to assert themselves. The French and English lived apart from each other, the French being concentrated in the northern and eastern parts of town on lands purchased largely from the Jesuits. French-Canadian social life revolved around the parish.[7]

A second reason for the amicability between the French and the English was leadership. "The evidence suggests that before 1910, the priests of Ste. Anne's, although French Canadians for the most part, did not champion the use of French ... for fear of alienating their English-speaking parishioners or incurring the displeasure of their Irish Bishop [Mgr. Scollard]." Towards the end of the decade, however, there were ominous rumblings of things to come. In January 1910, local French Canadians attended the first meeting of the Congrès de l'Association d'Éducation, newly formed in Ottawa. That organization was to play an important role in promoting French rights during the next decade.[8]

If leadership explains why French Canadians between 1900 and 1910 did not challenge the English, it also helps explain why the English did not go out of their way to bait the French. French leaders like Lemieux and Fournier could speak English and were seen to be contributing to the town's growth. That was enough for the English, whose goodwill towards the French was symbolized by Dr. Arthur's renunciation of the mayoralty.

The attitude of the English majority towards most ethnic groups other than French Canadians can be described as indifference. In 1904 the *Journal* reported an explosion on the CPR line that killed "three Finlanders, three Austrians and the walking boss, Mr. H. Poole." In 1905 it reported, "A foreigner with an unpronounceable name was killed instantly on the CPR yard here Tuesday a few minutes before noon."[9] If the reporting in the *Sudbury Journal* is at all representative, English-speakers referred to immigrants by their ethnic origin rather than by their name, not because of an innate dislike of them but out of frustration at being unable to understand them. Classes in English as a second language did not appear in Sudbury until the 1940s.[10] Before that time foreigners were left on their own to pick up English, or if they were lucky they used the services of any available interpreter or translator. Unfortunately, unlike the French Canadians, these interpreters or translators did not have access to the English-speaking boosters who formed the town elite.[11] Inevitably, the "foreigners" tended to stick together in groups where they could be understood, but by so doing they reinforced the tendency among English-speakers to lump them together.

In the first decade of the century, the Chinese in Sudbury appear to have been at the greatest disadvantage. Among all the immigrants they stood out, not just because they could not speak English or were of a different colour, but because Sudburians believed that they failed to boost town business. At that point indifference changed to hostility. In 1903, for example, Sudbury Steam Laundry, founded in 1901, placed the following advertisement in the *Sudbury Journal*:

> To the residents of the town of Sudbury who patronize the Chinese: Consider that you are giving your good cash to a class of people who send every cent to their native land and invest nothing in the towns in which they do business. On the other hand, Sudbury Steam Laundry has invested over $6,000 and we are paying out in wages over $7,000 annually all of which is spent in the town and helps materially to build the town. Ring up Tel. 155 and we will do the rest."[12]

Like people everywhere in Ontario at that time, most Sudburians in the first decade of the twentieth century were church-goers, and as their numbers grew, their churches grew with them. Throughout the period, all Catholics continued to worship at Ste. Anne's. The English part of the congregation did not branch off on its own until 1917, when it began to worship in Jubilee Hall, which had been opened in 1905 as a parish hall for the Ste. Anne's congregation.

The main Protestant denominations were a different matter. In 1900 there were three churches in town; in 1902, four, since in that year the Salvation Army barracks, which had been destroyed by fire a couple of years earlier, was completely rebuilt to seat three hundred.[13] At the turn of the century the Anglicans, the largest Protestant denomination, worshipped in a frame church on Larch Street originally opened in 1900; the Presbyterians, with mission status, worshipped at St Andrew's, also on Larch; and the Methodists, also with mission status, were in a small church on Beech Street. By 1910 the Anglicans began thinking about building new quarters; by 1913 they did so in what continues as the Church of the Epiphany.[14] In 1901 the Presbyterians had formed a self-supporting congregation, and by 1907, when they found that their old quarters were too small, they moved temporarily to the local opera house; then in 1908 they decided to build a new church, which opened in 1910. Meanwhile, in 1901 the Methodists also formed a self-supporting congregation,[15] and by 1908, after exchanging properties with T.J. Ryan,[16] they moved to a new church at the corner of Cedar and Lisgar, which seated five hundred and contained fifty-five electric lights, quite an accomplishment for the time.[17]

At the turn of the century, there was no Baptist congregation in Sudbury – the town was a mission field visited first by W.C. Norton in 1901. By 1907 the Baptists had become numerous enough to form a congregation. At first the congregation worshipped at the Palace Rink and held its baptisms in Lake Ramsey, but as winter approached, they decided to rent the former Methodist church on Beech Street. In 1911 the congregation purchased the church and moved it to the corner of Larch and Minto.[18]

Much of the leadership in the churches came from the clergy themselves. The Reverend E.S. Logie, the Presbyterian minister who oversaw the construction of St. Andrew's, was described as "a builder by instinct and a forceful leader."[19] But as one might expect, members of a congregation who were self-employed business or professional men were also active in church expansion. J.H. Clary, the lawyer, served on the building committee of the new Presbyterian church,[20] and the Honourable Frank Cochrane laid the cornerstone for the new Methodist church in 1907.

During the decade the churches were involved in more than expansion. They were also active in promoting community recreation that they regarded as wholesome, unlike some of the other forms available. In 1901 St. Andrew's Presbyterian Church hosted W.J. Carnahan, a baritone singer. Each year, as it had since 1895, Ste. Anne's Church sponsored a pilgrimage to Ste. Anne de Beaupré. With the construction of Jubilee Hall in 1905, that church also sponsored plays and "healthy" music. In 1909 the town's first Knights of Columbus Council was organized. Known as Sudbury Council 1387, it was headed by Dr. W.H. Mulligan.[21]

In the meantime, other citizens were indulging in worldlier pursuits.

> Sudbury was noted as a "show town" much in advance of others of its size. In 1902 George H. Lennon converted a three-storey brick building on Cedar St, midway between Durham and Elgin Streets into an "Opera House," capable of staging any of the companies which came to town. It had a stage 20' x 10' and the auditorium had seating for 650, with provision for another 200 in the gallery.[22]

In 1909 a second, even larger, hall opened its doors on Elgin Street – the Grand Opera House, whose shareholders included many prominent local businessmen, such as W.J. Bell (lumber), W.A. Evans (building supplies), and Larry O'Connor, who was soon to resume the mayor's chair. To these stages, in addition to plays, came singers like A.H. Bewell, elocutionists like Margaret Dunn, and cartoonists like J.W. Bengough. Sudburians of the decade were also exposed to Dowker's Wild West Show, the Lemon Brothers' Circus, Mrs. Louise Mitchell, a psychic scientist, Dr. J. Gerste, a champion billiard and pool player, and lastly, a boxing kangaroo.[23]

It would be a mistake, however, to assume that Sudburians were entertained only by imported performers. In fact, the townspeople were very accomplished at making their own fun. Such activities were even more important to town life than they are today, since the possibilities for private recreation were more limited then in the days before radio and television. Many joined lodges or service clubs like the Masons, the Orangemen, the Odd Fellows, and the Independent Order of Foresters. Much to the discontent of some clergy, dancing was a popular recreation. On 13 February 1908 the "Lonely Lasses of the Upper Classes" sent out heart-shaped invitations to a fancy-dress ball to be held at Lennon's Hall. Also available, albeit irregularly, during these years were a choral society, an amateur orchestra, and an amateur dramatic society. Many Sudburians of the age also got together for friendly games of progressive euchre.[24]

As the announcement of the dance at Lennon's Hall suggests, a good number of the local entertainments were designed by and for the better-off members of the community.[25] The one form of entertainment that appealed to everybody, churchgoer and non-churchgoer, men and women, rich and poor, was sports. Lacrosse, a popular sport of the 1890s, appeared to be on the wane during this decade partly because the lacrosse field was taken over by the new public school in mid-decade, and completely suitable alternative arrangements were never made.[26] A second reason was Copper Cliff's practice of importing star players for its teams and offering them "so many inducements" that the enthusiastic local amateurs who played for other teams in the district could not compete enjoyably. A final explanation for the decline of lacrosse was the increasing popularity of other sports. As in other areas, the merchant and professional class was often instrumental in getting such activities under way.

A serious competitor to lacrosse was baseball, which became popular in the town after a new club to promote it was organized in 1902 by Frank Cochrane and Dr. W.H. Howey.[27] Later, cricket[28] and soccer became popular. In 1902 Cochrane (as mayor) also presided over the formation of the Sudbury Boating Club. Restricted in membership to forty-two, the group subsequently built a clubhouse on the lake and sponsored regattas open to all who qualified.[29] By the end of the decade, the town had a golf club, a relatively late development but "not surprising considering Sudbury's terrain."[30] In the fall and spring, hunting and fishing continued to be popular. In 1902 the Onaping Fishing and Hunt Club was incorporated, with Dr. Howey as the first president. Apparently being a good shot was not a prerequisite for joining this club. In November, the Sudbury Journal reported that "one of the members of the Onaping Hunt Club while out hunting the other day got sight of a deer and fired 21 shots without wounding it."[31] In the winter, curling, hockey, and skating continued as the local favourites. On 1 January 1904 a group of local entrepreneurs, including James Purvis and James Orr, opened a new town rink that, in addition to providing a temporary meeting place for local Baptists three years later, also served the community well as a centre for winter sports. Unfortunately the rink burned to the ground in 1910 and was not replaced because of the expense.[32] Of all winter sports, hockey appears to have been the most popular. In 1904 even the women of the community organized a team, which had some success, and four years later the new high school organized two teams that competed against each other.[33]

The appearance of high school hockey teams, in their distinctive garnet and pale blue uniforms,[34] dramatized the most important change that occurred in the field of education during this decade. Because of the town's growth, one would of course expect some significant changes in education during the period under review. The least dramatic were in the separate school, still located near Ste. Anne's Church. Since 1899 the Grey

Nuns had been responsible for education in the school, and though the board had been forced to expand the school by adding more classrooms,[35] students were still instructed largely in English; French was merely an extra subject. In 1909 Felix Ricard arrived back in town to establish a hardware store, and at the time few had an inkling that this man would revolutionize French-language separate education in Sudbury before the next decade was out.[36]

In the public school, located since 1887 at the corner of Elm and Lorne, the changes were more dramatic. In 1906 the school moved into new quarters on CPR grounds where the arena now stands. In 1909 the school was expanding so fast that the kindergarten had to be held in the basement of the school, but after an inspection by government officials, that location was deemed inadequate, and in 1910 the school was forced to dispense with kindergarten. In 1904 the principal of the public school, Mr. Lowe, began continuation classes, that is, grades 9 and 10, which even Roman Catholic children could attend, for a modest fee; in January 1908 high school classes began in the new Jubilee Hall; in September 1909 Sudbury High School was opened on CPR property; and in 1910 H.G. Carmichael joined its staff as director of the first mining program in Canada.[37]

As with growth in many other areas of the community, members of the business and professional class were instrumental in the expansion of the school system. The chairman of the first high school board, John Frawley, was a Catholic who had tired of sending his children to Loyola College in Montreal,[38] and the secretary-treasurer, Dan Baikie, was the owner of the stationary store (who of course also stood to benefit from the expansion of local education).[39] The decision to build a high school was a controversial one that split the local leadership. Everybody recognized that the idea was one whose time had come, and not just because, like Frawley, they did not want to send their children out of town. They also knew that the failure to have a high school meant that Sudbury might not be able to attract or keep the kind of citizens the town needed. As early as 1903 the *Sudbury Journal* noted the departure to Brockville of the family of W.L. Connolly, the manager of the Toronto Bank, because "some members of the family wish to attend high school and our town is not advanced far enough to have such an institution."[40] That said, not everyone was pleased with the decision to build Sudbury High School. James Orr of the *Sudbury Journal* would have preferred a less expensive alternative to the one proposed. In his view, the town could not afford to do everything, and improvements to Sudbury's sewage system were needed more urgently. Nonetheless, when the decision was made to proceed, he supported it.[41]

Despite the lack of a high school throughout much of the decade, in the years 1900–1910 a good many entrepreneurs took advantage of Sudbury's hospitable atmosphere. One of the most enduring types of businesses was the hotel industry. At the beginning of the decade, the town had six hotels: the Balmoral, the American, Montreal House, the National, Russell House, and the White House. Except for the National, which burned to the ground in 1904, they were all renovated and expanded during these years. Two new hotels, the Queen's and the King Edward, were built, the latter on the lot formerly occupied by the Russell House, which had also been destroyed by fire. By 1910 the hotels could accommodate at least sixty guests apiece, in rooms renting for between $1.00 and $1.50 a day. All had large dining rooms. The expansion of the hotels, in facilities, if not in numbers, responded to the need of a transient population, not only for accommodation but also for a drink.[42] Another group of businesses as successful in their own way as the hotels were those specializing in real estate and construction, especially in brick. Many other firms also continued to expand both in size and in number: grocery stores, hardware stores, and clothing and footwear stores.

During the decade, as the population grew to support them, new types of firms joined those that had already been established. One was a photo studio. A second was Sudbury Steam Laundry, established in 1901 by the Bissets. A third, the New Ontario Bottling Works, which opened in 1905, supplied soft drinks to thirsty Sudburians. A fourth, and one of the most welcome, was the Sudbury Brewing Company, which set up operations on Lorne Street in 1907. Its owners included J.J. Doran, previously of the English Chop House in Toronto, who had liquidated his assets there for $40,000 and had used the proceeds on this new venture.[43] Until then beer drinkers had had to be satisfied either with home brew or with imported brands, such as Pabst.[44] After 1907 they could drink the hometown favourite, Silver Foam, pronounced "A No. 1" by connoisseurs.[45]

Sustaining much of the town's growth, as well as reflecting its "increasing importance," were its financial houses. As the decade opened, branches of the Trader's Bank and the Ontario Bank were established in Sudbury. The town council did most of its business with the latter, but when the head office of the Ontario Bank collapsed in scandal in 1906, its business was taken over by the Bank of Montreal at no loss to the creditors. The Bank of Toronto came to town in 1902, and the Sterling Bank (later the Bank of Commerce) in 1909. That same year both the Bank of Montreal and the Trader's Bank moved into new premises, followed in

1910 by the Bank of Toronto.[46] These were good years for both banking and business.

As businesses grew, so too did the labour force. Unions had been legal in Canada since 1872, but Sudbury did not get its first real union until 1906, when sixteen bartenders formed Local 237 to protect their jobs, which seemed endangered by recent changes in provincial law requiring that they be licensed.[47] It is a wonder that not more workers unionized. In those days teachers, for example, were particularly ill paid, no matter how good or experienced they were.[48] In 1910 the high school board refused to raise the pay of its principal, Mr. John Davidson, despite general acknowledgment that he was doing excellent work, and he was lost to another position elsewhere. Other public school principals before him left teaching entirely. The teaching profession was not atypical. That there were so many options available to people dissatisfied with their line of work may help explain the reluctance of most workers to challenge their employers with unions.

During the decade, business was able to expand in Sudbury partly because of population growth and the presence of financial institutions and possibly because costs could be kept down by scrimping on employees' salaries. But an important factor in this expansion was the efforts of the local business class, who, as individuals, promoted town business. In 1904, for example, the *Sudbury Journal* reported:

> Messrs Begg and Co, who purchased the bankrupt stock
> of E. Baskin, Sudbury and North Bay ... reckoned without
> their landlord, Messrs Baikie and Gill. The owners of their
> store, believing it would be an injustice to the regular mer-
> chants of the town to have such a large stock of bankrupt
> goods sacrificed here, refused to lease the store, and the
> firm, being unable to obtain another place, removed their
> goods elsewhere.[49]

The *Sudbury Journal* was also instrumental in promoting local business. Distributed to over a thousand homes and businesses,[50] not only in town but within fifty miles of Sudbury,[51] the *Journal* played up the advantages of the town and of doing business there. It was also a standing policy of the paper to refuse advertising from firms, such as Eaton's, that competed with city merchants but whose profits failed to stay in Sudbury.[52] This loyalty to advertisers was repaid when the *Sudbury Daily Star* went looking for such business in 1909. Most local merchants refused to patronize the paper, with two results. First, the *Star* began to accept advertisements from outsiders like Eaton's,[53] and second, it cut back its production schedule to twice a week. After 30 March 1910, the *Sudbury Daily Star* became the *Sudbury Star*. As the decade closed, it was only Orr's advancing age that might have led a perspicacious observer to imagine that a mere eight years later, the upstart would see its rival go out of business.

During the decade, the mayors were T.J. Ryan (1901), Frank Cochrane (1902), F.F. Lemieux (1903–1904), Larry O'Connor (1905–1907), John McLeod (1908–1909), and Larry O'Connor (1910–11). Contests for the mayoralty occurred only in 1902, 1904, 1908, 1909, and 1910, and modest contests for council seats took place in 1902, 1903, 1904, 1906, 1908, 1909, and 1910. Although these elections have been interpreted by some observers as struggles between the French and the English, the Catholics and Protestants,[54] the evidence, as was the case in the preceding decade, suggests otherwise. The fact is that the contests were relatively few, an indication of underlying consensus, and the candidates, almost without exception, were in favour of growth and business, their contests generally being over method, not result.

An economic interpretation of town councils during the period helps explain the agenda they set for themselves.[55] During the decade, the councils did not touch library services, which had been established with a flourish in 1896 but allowed to die shortly thereafter.[56] Moreover, the councils were not very interested in the welfare of the indigent. True, there was a relief committee that operated sporadically,[57] but for the most part the councils seemed to feel that responsibility for the down-and-out belonged to the Salvation Army, the ladies' aid of local churches, or the Children's Aid Society, established in town in 1907.[58] What was particularly significant, however, was that the councils did not concern themselves with the dangers posed by big companies if to do so might discourage the companies from doing business in Sudbury. The councils' indifference to these dangers was never a deliberate policy, but rather arose from unstated fears about what might happen if the town started to bite the hand that fed it. During the period there is no recorded challenge to the International Nickel Company about the dumping of sulphur throughout the district, nor is there any known attempt by council to discipline the CPR for its blasting practices. On one occasion, a fifty-pound rock crashed through the roof of Mr. B. Savage's house, destroying part of his floor and the corner of his piano stool.[59]

It would, of course, be unfair to suggest that Sudbury's town councils were different from most others in the province. As the preceding chapter has shown, the councils of the period were hampered by the limitations on their revenues. In the years 1900–1910 Sudbury councils were saddled with a heavy debt from the preceding decade, from which it was difficult to escape. In 1904 a proposal for a debenture to raise fifteen thousand dollars to extend the sewers and water mains did not succeed because the citizens who had this service outnumbered the ones who were to receive it and saw no reason why their taxes should rise to help others. More understandably, in 1910 the town fathers rejected a proposal from the Westermete Company of Brantford to pave the streets, in spite of the fact that the first "automobilly," as it was called, had appeared in town in 1906 and by 1910 there were three.[60]

Within the financial restraints imposed upon them, the Sudbury councils were clear about their first goal: to create or improve those services deemed essential if business was to operate in a favourable climate: health (sewage), water, fire protection, and policing. It is worth examining in more detail the Sudbury council's role in the expansion of each of these services during the decade.

Judged by the standards of the 1990s, Sudburians, like the citizens of other towns of the period, were not particularly healthy. In 1901 Sudbury suffered a smallpox epidemic brought in from the lumber camps, and throughout the decade there were frequent cases of typhoid.[61] One reason for these problems was the state of the town sewage system. In Sudbury, as elsewhere, council had very little interest in sewage treatment; rather, it was interested in continuing the program begun the previous decade of replacing unsightly and inconvenient town outhouses with pipes that carried human waste to the town's creeks.[62]

Equally inconvenient was the system of obtaining water, either from the spring located to the west of town off Elm Street or from wells that had to be dug. In the 1890s the town had set up a system of waterworks that served the central business district, but the system needed to be expanded. In 1907 the town decided to enlarge the intake pipe and extend it into Lake Ramsey to allow for a better and more abundant supply of water.[63] Aside from the desire for convenience, an improved water system was essential for the efficient operation of the fire brigade. During this period the town had a volunteer brigade equipped with a steam-operated pump and hoses that could be attached to hydrants around town.[64] Until 1908 the Ramsey Lake section, which was not hooked up to the water system, was essentially unprotected. By that year, however, council had authorized the purchase of a reel and five hundred feet of hose for the area.[65] For the most part, the brigade was deemed? efficient, and during the 1890s only a few premises were seriously damaged by fire,[66] usually because the brigade was not notified in time.[67] In spite of the efficiency of the fire brigade, in 1911 over sixty-two insurance companies were doing business in town.[68]

Police protection appeared as efficient as fire protection; certainly offenders seemed to get caught. The *Sudbury Journal* contended that most crimes were committed by transients and that residents generally obeyed the law. There appears to be some truth to this claim, although Sudburians were not perfect. In 1902 Ayer and Meyer Silverman got into a fight with each other and were fined $20 plus costs. In 1909, in one of the more colourful cases of the period, Isadore Bourassa was charged with dynamiting the home of former mayor F.F. Lemieux. Although he was acquitted, as he was leaving the witness box he was rearrested on a charge of bigamy. This time Bourassa was not so lucky. When he next appeared before the judge, he was sentenced to three years in Kingston Penitentiary.[69] Most crimes were of a petty nature, drunkenness being the most common, and robbery and forgery running a distant second and third. Interestingly enough, there appears little evidence, at least in the paper, that prostitution was a serious problem. For some businessmen, of course, prostitution was no problem at all, since it was a way of attracting potential customers to town. But even Orr, however anxious he was to boost local business, frowned on using prostitution for that purpose. Better that people patronize Sudbury businesses because of ads they had seen in the *Sudbury Journal*. Orr's attitude may, of course, explain the absence of stories on prostitution, for as his refusal to accept ads from businesses outside Sudbury proves, he was known to censor what he published.[70]

Whatever the success of the local constabulary in tracking down offenders, they did not keep everyone happy. The town clergymen in particular felt that far too many drunks escaped punishment. In one celebrated instance, the ministers of the Anglican, Methodist, and Presbyterian churches joined forces to ensure that town hotels observed the 7:00 p.m. closing by-law. On arriving at the last establishment and noticing that a light was on, they entered and charged the proprietor with a violation of the by-law. When the case went to court, they were astonished when the accused pleaded innocent. They then asked for an adjournment so that they could obtain a lawyer, but their request was refused. When the owner explained to the judge that though he had been open, he was not serving, he was found not guilty, and the clergymen were awarded all costs.[71]

It was obvious that a service that the town could secure at little cost or that would save it money would be attractive to council. This helps to explain the advent of two important (privately owned) utilities during this period: Bell Telephone and Wahnapitae Power. In 1901 the town had a modest phone system, with few connections, run by W.A. Evans. In 1902 Bell Telephone proposed to take over the service, with the right to erect the necessary poles. The town agreed, subject to the condition that it be allowed two free extensions, one to the fire chief and one to the power-house.[72] Even with these two included, Bell's head office needed twenty-five subscribers, and as they were still short by two, the local manager arbitrarily assigned numbers to John Doe and Richard Doe.[73] The manager's confidence was not misplaced. At the beginning, "Central" was H.S. Young's Drug Store, where an operator received calls from phones with a crank on their side. To call Central, it was necessary to "wind them up," because the electricity needed for a call was generated by a magnet. At first, service was available for only twelve hours a day, but as the demand increased, twenty-four-hour service was introduced.[74] During the decade, as Sudburians came to realize the utility of the telephone,[75] increasing numbers came to use it. The town was connected by phone to Copper Cliff, which was separated from it by an unincorporated section of McKim Township. Later, long-distance service was made available between the town and Chelmsford at twenty-five cents for a three-minute call.

A second utility that was of equal significance to the development of the town was the electrical system. In 1895, in recognition of the importance of electrical power, the town council had installed a wood-fired generator at its David Street substation, the first municipally owned and operated electricity plant in the province. The problems with the system became immediately apparent, not the least being unreliable service. As the cost of wood continued to mount, council decided to install meters on town homes, effective 1 January 1903, thereby abandoning the old flat-rate system, which was not only unfair to lighter users, but uneconomical as well.[76]

But everybody agreed that something more had to be done, for with electricity, homes and businesses could be lighted and so could streets, an important safety factor. A good electrical system also made equipment run more efficiently. The wire service at the *Sudbury Journal* needed the product. Finally, electricity ensured that the water system operated year-long. Winter freeze-ups caused untimely inconveniences in homes and businesses and, of course, created unfortunate problems for the customers of town firemen. With electricity – and, in particular, after 1904, thanks to the ingenuity of the new town engineer, R.H. Martindale – frozen water pipes were thawed out quickly.[77]

The first proposal to improve the system came from Major J.R. Gordon, an engineer who had been involved in setting up the system in 1895, but whose technical advice had been ignored by council.[78] Gordon offered to sell power to the town from a station he was building on the

Vermilion River, at a lower price than the town was then paying. Though initially in favour, the mayor, T.J. Ryan, opposed Gordon's scheme "on the grounds that it had the potential of trapping Sudbury into a long and unfriendly relationship." Ryan managed to have the decision postponed, partly because a smallpox epidemic hit town about the same time and forced council to turn its attention to more pressing matters. One of the members of council who had supported Gordon's bid for power was Cochrane, but when the bid failed, Cochrane and William McVittie incorporated the Wahnapitae Power Company in 1902.[79] Two years later, in response to the town's request for bids, this company submitted a proposal, as did the Huronian Power Company (a subsidiary of the Canadian Copper Company) and the Sudbury Power Company (the successor to Gordon's company, and still headed by him). Cochrane and McVittie, who offered the town the best deal, were successful in their bid. What made their scheme particularly attractive was that it got the town out of the electrical business and saved it money as well. Indeed, as early as 1907, two years after the Wahnapitae plant began operating, council was able to offer a 10 percent rate reduction to its customers, all its expenses having been paid.[80]

The appearance of telephone poles and the extension of the power lines were not the only physical evidence that Sudbury was expanding during the decade. The architecture was also changing, as frame buildings gave way to brick.[81] There have been several explanations for the increasing use of brick, a popular one being that brick expressed a new sense of permanence among the townspeople during the decade.[82] One must, however, dismiss this explanation out of hand, since there were many in the town who had always thought the place was a permanent settlement. The increasing use of brick can be understood better as an economic phenomenon: brick grew in popularity largely because wood was becoming more expensive as the stands of lumber receded.[83] It must of course be acknowledged that a plank of lumber was still cheaper than a row of bricks. But lumber burned and brick did not. And, as has been noted, in the interests of fire protection, a council by-law passed in 1910 demanded brick construction within the city core. Moreover, wooded buildings needed to be painted regularly, particularly when exposed to corrosive sulphur fumes; brick did not. Finally, frame buildings did not retain heat as well as brick, an important consideration in a place with long, cold winters.[84]

New buildings demanded architects. Though it has been suggested that "the architectural profession in the Sudbury area is not very old, P.J. Gorman being recognized as the pioneer architect of northeastern Ontario (1919 to 1959)," the fact is that the first professional architect in the area was Russell Halton, who arrived in town in 1903.[85] Later that decade, the town attracted W. Harland of the W.H. Angus firm (North Bay). Before leaving the area to become the assistant architect of the Parliament Buildings in Toronto, Harland designed a new wing on St. Joseph's Hospital, the Jacobs Block, and, his crowning achievement, the Grand Opera House.[86]

As the town continued to grow, its physical boundaries also expanded. Particularly after 1907, when direct links with Toronto were established by the CPR and Canadian Northern, there was a building boom of sorts. New subdivisions were established: one in Donovan, just south of the garbage dump; a second, the Morin subdivision, to the east of Elm Street, near Keziah; and a third, the McLeod subdivision, to the immediate west of the new brewery and settled by many who worked there. The planning of these subdivisions consisted simply of laying out the streets and lots.[87]

It has been claimed by Lola Dubé-Quibell that town planning in this period suffered because of the presence of five hundred acres of land held by the CPR in the centre of town, as well as the holdings of Frédéric Romanet du Caillaud. The mysterious *comte*, a French businessman and charter subscriber to the *Sudbury Journal*, after sensing that the town would boom, in 1902 purchased property on the north side of Lake Ramsey extending east from the Nelson Street railway crossing about three and a half miles. It was on this land that the devout *comte* erected the grotto honouring Notre-Dame de Lourdes that exists to this day.[88]

While Dubé-Quibell is correct in suggesting that large holdings within the town's boundaries affected its growth, one might question whether the *comte*'s lands, at the edge of town, were anywhere near as significant as the CPR's in the centre. The problem with the CPR was that it held on to its lands for speculative purposes, and it asked such high prices that people tended to build elsewhere. In 1901 a ratepayers' meeting passed a motion that included the following preamble:

> That whereas the inner portion of the town site of Sudbury, comprising about 500 acres, was originally granted to, and is still owned by the CPR; that the prices at which building lots are being held by said company are simply prohibitive, and no poor man can afford to buy a lot on any of the company's lands; that even at such exorbitant prices the company refuses to sell lots except in special cases; that as a natural result of this incomprehensible policy, the growth of the town has been seriously kept back for over ten years, and while the greater part of the

company's lands is still in a vacant, wild unimproved state, many of the citizens have been obliged to go outside on other lands and build homes at inconvenient distances for their children to get to school, and especially in the winter time. The company has also managed to get out of paying its fair share of municipal taxes to the town.[89]

Though there is a bit of hypocrisy in this motion, since nobody objected when a local Sudburian made a considerable profit in real estate,[90] it is possible that if the CPR had not had so much control, the town's growth might have been more orderly. While Dubé-Quibell is misleading about the significance of the *comte*'s lands, she is fundamentally wrong in concluding that had these large landholdings not existed, town planning would have been more rational. The fact is that town planning, at least as it is known today, would still not have taken place. People could build whatever they liked with few restrictions on either purpose or quality. Houses could appear next to businesses, and services would be available or not, as economics demanded. As one old-timer recalled, "You didn't have to bother with permits and regulations, then, but just built where you fancied. I built one house, got tired of living in it and began erecting another. It went on like that over the years until I made building a full time job."[91] In fact, after the CPR finally relinquished its lands in 1927, Sudbury failed to exert much control over its development until the mid-1950s.

On 2 August 1930, in the city "Inaugural edition" of the *Sudbury Star*, Charles McCrea, minister of mines for Ontario, claimed that the election of the Conservative government in 1905 was a turning-point in the town's development, though he acknowledged the crucial part played by Sudburians in the town's growth: "[With] the coming to power of Sir James Whitney, Sudbury and the district took on new life, and a new spirit inspired all."[92]

In some ways, McCrea was right. Certainly during this decade, the federal government of Sir Wilfrid Laurier appeared to have little influence on the daily lives of Sudburians, other than agreeing in 1909 to spend twenty thousand dollars to build a new post office. And between 1899 and 1905, when the province had been governed by the Liberals under George W. Ross, even though Sudbury was represented in the legislature by a member of that party, the town formed a small part of the constituency of Nipissing, and its interests usually appeared to be ignored.

After the election in 1905 of the Conservatives under the leadership of James Whitney, the constituency of Nipissing was divided into East and West. As a result, Sudbury got its first representative into the cabinet, Frank Cochrane.[93] Seemingly, things began to happen. In 1907 the new government passed the Metal Refining Bounty Act, which was intended, like the old Mines Act, to encourage the establishment of copper, nickel, silver, and cobalt refineries in Ontario. But instead of penalizing companies with an export tax, as the Ross government had done, the new act provided, as Nelles has pointed out, a modest bounty of "six cents per pound upon the refinement within the province of metallic nickel, nickel oxide, metallic copper, and cobalt oxide to be limited in any one year to $60,000 for copper and nickel, and $30,000 for cobalt."[94] The new act, like the one it replaced, failed to achieve the desired result, primarily because the bounties were too small; nickel refining in the province had to await the events of the First World War.

In 1907 the provincial government made Sudbury a judicial district, with the result that people with legal business no longer had to travel to North Bay; instead, people near Sudbury had to travel there! As a judicial district, the town soon got a registry office and courthouse. The provincial government also assisted in the expansion of the school system. In 1907 John Frawley, the chairman of the high school board, met Frank Cochrane in Toronto, and shortly thereafter, the province agreed to assist in the construction of the new school. Two years later, after a visit from the minister of education, Dr. Pyne, Sudbury High School was allowed to offer its new mining program. Throughout this period, Frank Cochrane was a provincial minister.[95]

In a larger sense, McCrea's interpretation of Sudbury's development appears misleading, if not inadequate. It is true that the town's business and professional class was a significant factor, and it is true that government policies were generally helpful, and yet the most satisfying explanation is that the region's three resource-based industries – lumbering, agriculture, and mining – boomed during the period and the community grew as it supplied services to the people in those industries.

The oldest industry was lumbering. Even though Sudbury later gained a reputation as the city with no trees, and even though in this period the trees within the immediate vicinity had receded, there was still an active lumbering industry in the region. "Lumbering continued to be the "first line of defence" throughout the decade, and indeed, until the 1920s.[96] In 1907, for example, "a timber limit embracing about 93 square miles located near Killarney on the north side of Georgian Bay was purchased in Toronto last week by W.J. Bell of this place, who it is understood has some associates with him in the deal."[97] Lumbering was a seasonal activity, fall to spring, and as in the preceding decade, Sudbury firms supplied equipment, food, lodging, and entertainment to those who worked in the industry.

Second to lumbering was agriculture. As the forests of white pine vanished from the immediate area around the town, especially to the northeast, farms began to take their place. By 1911 there were over five hundred in the Blezard Valley, and over 90 percent of them were larger than fifty acres.[98] The fertile land in the valley earned a reputation as a source of vegetables and roots, such as potatoes, turnips, and cabbages, but dairy farming remained the backbone of the industry.[99] Like the lumbermen, farmers needed supplies, which Sudbury merchants attempted to provide. In 1903 G.A. Lockerby announced that he had just received "a carload of farm wagons and implements." In 1910 the Ontario and Manitoba Flour Mill was constructed in the "French quarter" of town, which eventually came to be known as the "Flour Mill." Consisting of a seven-storey brick mill and six adjoining grain silos, the mill symbolized the growing importance of agriculture in the district. Not surprisingly, the town's businessmen did what they could to promote their link with agriculture. Their primary vehicle was the newly revived Sudbury and District Agricultural Society, which, among other activities, held a fall exhibition that brought farmers into town. Lockerby served as a one of the first directors, but what is even more interesting is that other members of the town's business and professional class who normally had nothing to do with agriculture were also active in the society. In 1903 its president was D. Baikie, its second vice-president, T.J. Ryan, and one of its auditors, James Orr.[100]

If agriculture was the second source of business for the town, the third was of course the mining industry. This decade saw considerable expansion in that sector as nickel began to be demanded for domestic and military uses. These were the years when European and American navies were preparing for the conflict many feared was inevitable. By 1900, as the previous chapter noted, Ludwig Mond, a Swiss investor then living in England, began operations in the area in earnest. The other main company during the decade was the Canadian Copper Company. In 1902 the capital available to Canadian Copper was considerably enhanced by its merger, under prodding from the wealthy American banker J.P. Morgan, with the Orford Copper Company, the American Nickel Works, the Société minière Caledonienne, the Anglo-American Iron Company, the Vermilion Mining Company of Ontario, the Nickel Corporation, and, shortly after, the Huronian Company to form the International Nickel Company. Mond and Canadian Copper, still operating under that name, were the most important companies in the region, but there were others as well.[101] Like lumbering and agriculture, the mining industry had needs that Sudbury was only too eager to fill, particularly when miners came to town in search of some excitement.

The main problem merchants had in serving their customers was that there was no easy method of transporting goods and people back and forth to market. This helps explain the preoccupation in the period with road and railway building. Locally, both council and the board of trade lobbied for a Sudbury, Copper Cliff, and Creighton electric railway that would "greatly promote material development in the municipalities through which the road [would] pass."[102] During the decade the project never materialized because of opposition from the Copper Cliff Town Council, which was concerned that town merchants might suffer from the competition with Sudbury.[103] But everyone knew that there was a second reason that council killed the project. The Canadian Copper Company, afraid that such a railway would diminish its control over its workers, ensured that the Copper Cliff Town Council voted the company's wishes.

Both Sudbury Town Council and the board of trade made regular representations to the provincial and federal governments concerning other forms of transportation.[104] In 1907 the board recommended that the province give grants to the "Sudbury, Blezard and Hanmer trunk road; to the Sudbury and Wahnapitae road; to the road leading south from Sudbury to Broder and Dill Townships; [to the] the Garson and Neelon Road; the bridge over Junction Creek on Pilon Settlement, and [to] the road from Sudbury to Chelmsford."[105]

Of even greater importance were railways to Toronto and to the northern parts of the province. For the first seven years of the decade, Sudbury was linked indirectly to Toronto via North Bay, a total distance of 350 miles; a more direct link, the *Sudbury Journal* calculated, would shave off about 106 needless miles. As early as 1900, Mayor Ryan, Frank Cochrane (the former mayor), A. McCharles, W.A. Quibell (town magistrate), J. McCormick, and J.S. Gill (jeweller) made up a deputation to Ottawa to hasten the building of a railway from Toronto to Sudbury. In 1903 the board of trade reinforced this plea by authorizing Dan Baikie and William McVittie to go to Ottawa. In 1907 council voted to send Mayor Larry O'Connor and William McVittie to explain to Donald Mann (of the Canadian Northern) why the new line from Toronto should pass through Sudbury instead of by-passing the town, as was rumoured that it would. In 1909, as enthusiasm for silver in the Gowganda area developed, Mayor John McLeod, former mayor Larry O'Connor, and Charles McCrea lobbied Premier Whitney and Frank Cochrane for railways to these resources.[106]

It would be difficult to assess the effect of these representations. It is true that in June 1908 both the CPR and the CNR came in from Toronto and that in 1909 the Canadian Northern opened a line to Gowganda. Not only did Sudbury benefit from supplying these companies during construction, but these lines made it easier for the town to serve its ever-expanding hinterland. And yet the CPR came in its own good time, and the CNR did not build its line exactly where town merchants wanted, claiming engineering difficulties. What does seem clear is that all this lobbying tended to have the greatest influence on the government, for during the decade, the Whitney government seemed to pour money into roads, enhancing the communication between the town and its neighbours. By 1910, "most of the farming communities [in the basin] were linked to Sudbury by road or rail."[107]

Of course, for some town boosters, nothing the government did was good enough. This explains the curious "separatist movement," one of whose strongest proponents was James Orr of the *Sudbury Journal*, who referred regularly to the failure of the provincial government to give back to "New Ontario" what it was taking out. In 1908 some fifty Sudburians turned out to a meeting addressed by J.R. Gordon (of Sudbury Power fame, more recently in the mining business in Cobalt). At Gordon's urging the meeting endorsed the creation of a separate province, much to the disgust of Dr. Howey, who commented later, "If the silly, ridiculous and nonsensical speeches of these secessionist agitators ever reach Toronto, we shall likely see in the supplementary estimates a large appropriation for a mammoth lunatic asylum in new Ontario."[108]

Sudbury's "Oldest Old Boy" was right. However far Sudbury had come by the end of the decade, one really has to question whether a town that was still so beholden to outside economic forces had what it took to succeed as a new province.

In Sudbury's history the decade before the Great War was a time of consolidation of trends evident in the 1890s. As in the earlier decade, the town's population doubled – and yet, as earlier, its basic English-French character did not change. The population growth was reflected in the growth of churches and schools. Sudbury High School, for example, was built during this decade. In the political arena, town council continued to be dominated by the merchant and professional class, who used their positions to promote town growth. Though this decade saw some modest improvement in municipal services, the town was unable to do more, partly because of the large debts run up the previous decade and partly because the assessment base was so low. This explains why the council happily turned to private enterprise to improve its electrical system.

What was different about this decade was a more vibrant economy. Unlike the 1890s, which had suffered through a world-wide depression, the years 1900–1910 saw a global economic recovery. Nowhere was this more evident than in the mining sector, as nations began to arm for war. During these years, Mond and the Canadian Copper Company, now part of International Nickel, did well. Sudbury's economy was not, however, dependent solely upon mining. As in the previous decade, forestry was a stabilizing force, although by 1910 the stands of harvestable lumber had moved far beyond the Nickel Basin. In their place and growing in importance was agriculture. In 1891 there had been eighty-one farms in the valley; in 1911 there were more than five hundred. Though never as significant as mining, farming still provided strong support for the town's economy.

Businesses continued to expand and to be established to serve these developments, and they were aided by an increasingly sophisticated transportation and communications network. Not only was the regional road system substantially enhanced during the decade, but the rail network improved as well. In 1908 the town was linked to Toronto for the first time, a development whose importance to the community's future cannot be underestimated. In 1902 Bell Telephone arrived in town, and by the end of the decade communication was about to be established by phone with other parts of the country. The result of all this was that by 1910 Sudbury had cemented its position as a regional metropolis that dominated the Nickel Belt and was poised to expand its influence beyond. These were good years for most townspeople, and as the next decade approached, they had every reason to believe that their situation would only improve.

---

1   *Biographies de la région de Sudbury/Biographies of the Sudbury Region* (Sudbury: Dépt d'histoire, Université Laurentienne/Dept. of History, Laurentian University, 1980).

2   Michael Kelly suggests that by the end of this decade the town dominated "much of Ontario's northland." This claim seems a bit grandiose, considering that Sudbury, with a population of about 4,000 by 1910, was still much smaller than either North Bay to the east (population 7,737) or Sault Ste. Marie to the west (population 10,984). See Michael Kelly, "By Divine Right: Sudbury as a Regional Metropolis, 1900–1910" (M.A. thesis, University of Toronto, 1984), 7.

3   *Census of Canada*, 1901, vol. 1. See also Eileen Goltz, "Copper Cliff: The Pioneer Period," in *Industrial Communities of the Sudbury Basin: Copper Cliff, Victoria Mines, Mond and Coniston* (Sudbury: Sudbury and District Historical Society, 1986), 14. Goltz reminds us that in 1901 Copper Cliff was as yet an unincorporated town, and thus its population has to be abstracted from the population of McKim Township, of which it formed the most important part. In 1901 McKim's population was 2,939, and in 1902, following incorporation, this had fallen to 498.

---

4   *Census of Canada*, 1911, vol. 1.

5   The growth in the Catholic population had one unintended effect. During the summer of 1909, the congregation of Ste. Anne's Church, the only church in town, had to move the bodies in the Catholic cemetery (then at the town limits) to a new cemetery on the sixth concession of McKim Township (then part of J.H. Morin's farm). See *Sudbury Journal*, 7 July 1909.

6   The census data notwithstanding, there is all kinds of evidence that the Salvation Army had been active in town since 1895. See F.A. Peake and R.P. Horne, *The Religious Tradition in Sudbury 1883–1983* (Sudbury: Downtown Churches Association, 1983), 33ff.

7   *Sudbury Journal*, 1 January 1903; and Gail Cuthbert Brandt, "The Development of French-Canadian Social Institutions in Sudbury, 1883–1920," *Laurentian University Review* 11, no. 2 (February 1979): 10.

8   Brandt, "The Development ... Sudbury," 14; and *Sudbury Journal*, 16 December 1910.

9   *Sudbury Journal*, 7 July 1904 and 5 August 1905.

10 Interview with George W. Thomson, 31 July 1986. Thomson, a former director of education with the Sudbury Board, was a young English teacher for that program.

11 On 29 July 1909, the *Sudbury Journal* reported that Charles Ellul, the well-known Italian interpreter, had died in the district jail the preceding Tuesday. "Through over-indulgence in intoxicants Charles was *non compos mentis* for some months past, and had to be confined to the gaol prior to removal to an asylum. Deceased was a British subject, born at Malta, was well-educated and spoke six languages. The Italian community here will miss him as he translated a good deal of business for them."

12 *Sudbury Journal*, 5 February 1903. Sudbury Steam did not succeed in driving the Chinese out of business. As late as 18 March 1909, the *Sudbury Journal* carried an ad for the Hop Sing Hand Laundry.

13 *Sudbury Journal*, 29 May 1902, not 1901, as claimed in Peake and Horne, *The Religious Tradition in Sudbury*, 35.

14 Peake and Horne, *The Religious Tradition in Sudbury*, 22–31.

15 Graeme S. Mount and Michael J. Mulloy, *A History of St. Andrew's United Church, Sudbury* (Sudbury: The Church, 1982), 7.

16 The exchange took place in 1905 and was made possible by a welcome decision by the CPR to remove a restriction on the land Ryan obtained from the Methodists, namely that it could only be used for church purposes (*Sudbury Journal*, 21 September 1905). Obviously Ryan did not want to set up his own church, intending the property for other purposes.

17 *Sudbury Journal*, 9 January 1908. Frank Cochrane, a prominent member of the congregation, at least when in town, also happened to be part owner of the Wahnapitae Power Company, which supplied Sudbury with electricity. There is no direct evidence linking Cochrane with these lights.

18 Ibid, 8 August 1901, 17 June 1907, and 24 October 1907; and Peake and Horne, *The Religious Tradition in Sudbury*, 37.

19 *Sudbury Star*, 23 June 1926. Quoted in Peake and Horne, *The Religious Tradition in Sudbury*, 32.

20 Peake and Horne, *The Religious Tradition in Sudbury*, 32.

21 *Sudbury Journal*, 25 April 1901, 2 August 1900 to 21 July 1910, 22 June 1905, and 22 April 1909.

22 D.M. LeBourdais, *Sudbury Basin: The Story of Nickel* (Toronto: Ryerson, 1953), 104.

23 *Sudbury Journal*, 9 August 1900, 23 August 1900, 1 November 1900, 1 April 1901, 28 August 1902, 11 December 1902, 24 March 1903, and 8 April 1909.

24 Ibid., 6 April 1905, 31 October 1907, 13 February 1908, 17 July 1909, and 16 December

1909. Euchre was as popular in this decade as bridge became in the 1930s.

25 For further confirmation that workers had little organized social life, see *Sudbury Star*, 20 May 1959. The issue contains reminiscences of three city pioneers.

26 *Sudbury Journal*, 21 June 1906.

27 Ibid., 17 April 1902.

28 Ibid., 30 August 1906. A club was formed the next year. See *Sudbury Journal*, 6 June 1907.

29 Ibid., 17 April 1902.

30 LeBourdais, *Sudbury Basin*, 104.

31 *Sudbury Journal*, 7 August 1902 and 13 November 1902.

32 *Sudbury Star*, 29 September 1910.

33 *Sudbury Journal*, 4 February 1904 and 30 January 1908.

34 Ibid., 13 February 1908.

35 Ibid., 13 August 1903.

36 *Sudbury Star*, 24 June 1933.

37 *Sudbury Journal*, 18 August 1904, 15 March 1906, 30 August 1906, 31 October 1907, 28 June 1910, and 1 September 1910.

38 *Sudbury Star*, 2 August 1930.

39 *Sudbury Journal*, 15 August 1907.

40 Ibid., 19 March 1903.

41 Ibid., 6 August 1908. Orr claimed that the high school board wanted an expensive school so that it could get bigger grants from the provincial government.

42 Ibid., 12 October 1905 and 10 February 1910. This issue carries a report on Sudbury hotels by an admiring reporter from the *Toronto World*.

43 Ibid., 6 December 1900, 24 October 1901, 15 May 1905, and 31 October 1907.

44 Ibid., 1 May 1902. On sale at the National Hotel before it burned to the ground in 1904.

45 Ibid., 20 February 1908.

46 Ibid., 30 October 1902, 21 January 1909, 28 January 1909, 11 February 1909, and 15 December 1910.

47 Ibid., 3 May 1906 and 6 December 1906.

48 Ibid., 18 September 1902.

49 Ibid., 21 January 1904.

50 *Sudbury Star*, 4 June 1910.

51 *Sudbury Journal*, 1 August 1901.

52 Ibid., 4 April 1904.

53 The *Sudbury Daily Star* was the successor to the *Northern Daily Star* (NDS), which existed between 14 January and 24 June 1909. The editor of the NDS, Douglas Patterson, was a former actor who in April 1909 became the manager of the town's new opera house. It is hard to determine whether Patterson's new job contributed to the demise of his paper, or whether he took it because he saw the writing on the wall. In any event, when the successor paper appeared, William Edge Mason, and not Patterson, was in the editor's chair.

54 See for example John Lawrence Kesik, "A Linguistic and Religious Study of Sudbury Town Council, 1893–1930" (B.A. honours essay, Laurentian University, 1985). See also *Sudbury Journal*, 7 January 1907, which reports the contest in Catholic-Protestant terms.

55 For further confirmation of the thesis advanced here, see Donald Dennie, "Sudbury 1883–1946: A Social Historical Study of Property and Class" (Ph.D. thesis, Carleton University, 1989).

56 *Sudbury Journal*, 8 December 1904. On 18 May 1910 the *Sudbury Star* editorialized in favour of a "real" public library, open to all instead of the paying few [sic], as was the case with the one established in 1896.

57 See Lola Dubé-Quibell, "Le Conseil Municipal de Sudbury, 1893–1914" (Thèse de Maîtrise ès Arts, Université Laurentienne, 1983), 62. Dubé-Quibell has read and analysed the minutes of the town council's meetings during the period of her thesis and provides much useful information on their activities during the period.

58 *Sudbury Star*, 2 August 1930. See also *History of the Children's Aid Society of the Districts of Sudbury and Manitoulin* (Sudbury: n.p. 1982).

59 *Sudbury Journal*, 16 July 1903.

60 Ibid., 7 April 1904 and May 31, 1906; and *Sudbury Star*, 15 March 1910. In retrospect, the decision not to pave might have been a good one, since there might otherwise have been pressure on council to increase the speed limit beyond fifteen miles an hour, scaring town horses out of their wits! See *Sudbury Star*, 11 June 1910.

61 *Sudbury Journal*, 19 July 1900 to 9 September 1909.

62 Ibid., 25 April 1907.

63 Ibid., 29 August 1907.

64 Ibid., 2 May 1901.

65 Ibid., 17 September 1908.

66 Ibid., 6 June 1901.

67 Ibid., 24 October 1901. See also *Sudbury Journal*, 23 December 1909. In the first instance, the fire bell was not strong enough to be heard; in the second, the power was out, so that the bell did not ring at all. The worst tragedy of the decade, or at least the most embarrassing, occurred in 1907, when Marion Frances Fowler perished in a fire. Mrs. Fowler was the wife of Joseph Fowler, a town lawyer who did double duty as fire chief. See *Sudbury Journal*, 27 June 1907.

68 Kelly, "By Divine Right," 19.

69 *Sudbury Journal*, 9 January 1902, 5 April 1906, and 14 October 1909. Bourassa was let out early, and one cannot help wondering whether it was because he had somehow made friends with his jailer's wife.

70 Ibid., 1900–1910. See especially 17 October 1901 for Orr's (only) coverage of the prostitution problem.

71 Ibid., 31 May 1900. The troubles that befell the Reverend A.B. Johnston, the Methodist clergyman involved in this incident, were not over. A year later, as he was preparing to leave town for a charge elsewhere, he was run over by a buggy and a bone in his leg was broken. See *Sudbury Journal*, 20 June 1901.

72 *Sudbury Journal*, 30 January 1902. Later (in 1907), the chief of police was added to this list (ibid., 7 March 1907).

73 *Sudbury Star*, 2 August 1930.

74 *Sudbury Journal*, 2 April 1903. This issue also commented, "Sudbury has a larger list of subscribers than any other place of its size in the Dominion."

75 One woman saved her pies by using the new gadget. She had put them in the oven one Sunday morning and then headed off to church, forgetting to turn down the heat. A quick call to a neighbour from Central during the service saved her desserts. See *Sudbury Journal*, 14 December 1905.

76 For a concise review of these early years, see the preceding chapter or Gwenda Hallsworth, *A History of Hydro in Sudbury* (Sudbury: Sudbury Hydro-Electric Commission, 1985), 2ff. On meters, see *Sudbury Journal*, 1 January 1903.

77 *Sudbury Journal*, 25 February 1904. In 1907 council purchased an electric thawing machine and offered the use of it free of charge to anyone who needed it (ibid., 28 February 1907 and 7 March 1907).

78 Gordon was one of the most interesting souls to touch the pages of Sudbury's history. His father was a distant cousin of General Gordon, known as "Chinese Gordon," and one of his brothers was the author "Ralph Connor." Another brother was a "distinguished" professor at the University of Toronto (*Sudbury Journal*, 5 July 1906). After Gordon's ventures in Sudbury turned sour, he headed north, to the Cobalt area, where he met with greater success.

79 Kelly, "By Divine Right," 28–34. Kelly suggests that Cochrane was against Gordon and influenced Mayor Ryan on this matter. Not so. See *Sudbury Journal*, 3 January 1901.

80 *Sudbury Journal*, 11 April 1907. The Wahnapitae Company was to supply the town's growing electrical needs until 1928, when the Cochrane family sold its shares to the Hydro-Electric Commission of Ontario (now Ontario Hydro) for $1,059,000. McVittie held on to his for another two years, selling the balance to the provincial utility for $1,030,000. See Scott Young and Astrid Young, *Silent Frank Cochrane: The North's First Great Politician* (Toronto: Macmillan, 1973), 36.

81 Kelly, "By Divine Right," 18, claims that brick was made locally after 1901. In fact, J.C. McCormick had begun manufacturing brick in town back in 1895 (*Sudbury Journal*, 6 June 1895).

82 E.G. Higgins and F.A. Peake, *Sudbury Then and Now: A Pictorial History of Sudbury and Area 1883–1973* (Sudbury: Sudbury and District Chamber of Commerce, 1977), 64.

83 *Sudbury Journal*, 17 May 1900.

84 *Sudbury Daily Star*, 20 April 1910; and Kelly, "By Divine Right," 19.

85 G.S. Mount, *The Sudbury Region* (Burlington: Windsor, 1986), 153, as contradicted by Charles Dorion, *The First 75 Years: A Headline History of Sudbury, Canada* (Ilfracombe, Devon: Stockwell, [1959]), 26. The *Sudbury Journal* claims that the first architect in town was Grayson Brown, representing the Angus firm in North Bay (*Sudbury Journal*, 8 February 1906).

86 *Sudbury Journal*, 22 April 1909.

87 On the building boom, see Higgins and Peake, *Sudbury Then and Now*, 64; on Donovan, see the *Sudbury Journal*, 26 March 1908. See also the history of the Donovan in the *Sudbury Daily Star*, 23 June 1950; on Morin, see the *Sudbury Journal*, 2 April 1908; on McLeod, the *Sudbury Journal*, 2 April 1908, and *Sudbury Star*, 9 January 1962.

88 Dubé-Quibell, "Le Conseil Municipal de Sudbury," 86; on the size of the CPR land, see Peter V.K. Krats, "The Sudbury Area to the Great Depression: Regional Development on the Northern Resource Frontier" (Ph.D. thesis, University of Western Ontario, 1988), 284; and on the *comte* and his landholdings, see Gilbert Stelter, "The Origins of a Company Town: Sudbury in the Nineteenth Century," *Laurentian University Review* 3, no. 3 (February 1971): 30; and Lorenzo Cadieux, *Frédéric Romanet du Caillaud: "Comte" de Sudbury* (Montreal: Éditions Bellarmin, 1971).

89 *Sudbury Journal*, 1 January 1903.

90. Ibid., 12 April 1906. In this instance, the *Journal* congratulated John Price, who later (in 1907) became a town councillor, for his wisdom in buying a piece of downtown property for $1,100 and letting it go for $7,000.

91 *Sudbury Daily Star*, 20 May 1959.

92 *Sudbury Star*, 2 August 1930; and *Sudbury Journal*, 25 November 1909. The post office opened in 1915. By that time, Cochrane was minister of railways at the federal level in Borden's Conservative government.

93 Although Cochrane had tried for elective provincial office in 1902, he had failed. In the general election of 1905 he did not run, but when the Conservatives won and Cochrane was appointed to the cabinet, the sitting member in Nipissing East stepped aside for

him. Interestingly enough, for his first three years in provincial politics, Cochrane represented Nipissing East, rather than West, where Sudbury was located. Sudburians still thought of him as their representative, and so he became in 1908, when the new provincial riding of Sudbury came into existence.

94   H.V. Nelles, *The Politics of Development: Forests and Hydro-Electric Power in Ontario, 1849–1941* (Toronto: Macmillan, 1974), 132.

95   On the creation of the new judicial district, see *Sudbury Journal*, 21 November 1907; for more on the origins of Sudbury High School, see *Sudbury Star*, 2 August 1930; on the mining program, see *Sudbury Journal*, 9 December 1909.

96   Kelly, "By Divine Right," 11.

97   *Sudbury Journal*, 9 May 1907.

98   Kelly "By Divine Right," 9–24. In their article on agriculture and settlement in Northern Ontario, Brozowski, Topps, and Rees claim, "In the Sudbury area, both the number of farms and the number of acres under cultivation steadily increased until 1921, when a consolidation of landholding began to occur. Many of the farmers were French Canadians who had followed the lumbering industry into the district, as well as Finns and Ukrainians who immigrated to Canada in the years preceding World War I" (Roman Brozowski, Keith Topps, and David Rees, "Agriculture and Settlement," in *A Vast and Magnificent Land* [Sudbury: Laurentian University, 1984], 121).

99   On the types of farming, see *Sudbury Journal*, 8 October 1903; and Kelly, "By Divine Right," 23.

100 On Lockerby, see *Sudbury Journal*, 9 July 1903; on the Flour Mill, see Michael C. Kelly et al., *Inventory and Guide to Historic Buildings in Sudbury* (Sudbury: Dept. of History, Laurentian University, 1978); and on the revival of the Agricultural Society, see *Sudbury Journal*, 24 June 1902.

101 Interestingly enough, one of the might-have-beens in the town's history occurred in 1901, when Thomas Edison came to town, inspired by its possibilities after seeing them displayed at the PanAmerican Exhibition in Buffalo (sponsored, incidentally by the Ross government). Edison failed to find much and retired from the scene. Certainly the state of the town's electrical system in 1901 would fail to keep him. In 1929, when Falconbridge Nickel was formed, it developed deposits just metres away from the area Edison had examined. See LeBourdais, *Sudbury Basin*, 62–63.

102 *Sudbury Journal*, 14 May 1903.

103 Ibid., 22 February 1900.

104 Of course, it was not just Sudburians who wanted better transportation. In 1906, for example, "Mr. Joseph Pilon circulated a petition among the farmers of Blezard, Hanmer and Capreol, and the north end of Rayside ... asking the Government to make a grant of $6,000 for a road through the township of Blezard to the north" (*Sudbury Journal*, 18 January 1906).

105 Ibid., 7 January 1907.

106 On the distance to Toronto, see ibid., 3 September 1903; on the deputation in 1900, see Dorion, *The First 75 Years*, 8; on the one in 1903, see *Sudbury Journal*, 3 September 1903; on the one in 1907, see Kelly, "By Divine Right," 66; and on the one in 1909, see *Sudbury Journal*, 18 March 1909.

107 On the arrival of branch lines from Toronto, see LeBourdais, *Sudbury Basin*, 108-9; on the branch of the Canadian Northern to Gowganda, see *Sudbury Journal*, 30 December 1909; on engineering problems, see *Sudbury Journal*, 21 June 1906; and on the state of transportation in 1910, see Kelly, "By Divine Right," 23.

108 The first call for a separate province was made by James Stobie in a letter to the *Journal* in 1891. In it he argued that the provincial mining laws were inimical to the region and that since the province was not about to change its laws, the solution lay in the creation of a new province. At the time Orr was not as sympathetic as he was later to become: "Even talking on such a grand subject may help to keep us cool during the sultry weather," he editorialized (*Sudbury Journal*, 25 June 1891; on Howey's reaction, see *Sudbury Journal*, 9 April 1908).

CHAPTER FOUR

1910–1920

Matt Bray

For Sudbury the decade from 1910 to 1920 was indelibly imprinted with the mark of the Great War, that so myopically mislabelled "war to end all wars." Like other Canadians, Sudburians assumed that the British declaration of war on 4 August 1914 included Canada, and they greeted it enthusiastically. Their zeal persisted long after the illusions about the superiority of the Allied armies and the consequent expectation of a brief struggle had been dashed. Still, as Canadian resources of men and matériel became taxed to unforeseeable limits, differences of opinion began to surface about the justifiability of an unrestricted Canadian war effort, differences that profoundly affected the ethnic ambience of the community.

An important measure of Sudbury's support for the war effort was its response to the minister of militia's call for volunteers for the hastily organized Canadian Expeditionary Force (CEF). By 20 August 1914, only a few days after Sam Hughes's appeal had been received by the local militia commander, Major W.J. Cressy, 255 men – twice the number asked for – had enrolled in the 97th Algonquin Rifles and boarded a special Canadian Pacific Railway troop train for Valcartier, Quebec. Sixteen-year-old Effie Stewart of Sudbury noted the headiness of the young men on those trains, singing as they left:

> We're on our way to Germany;
> Under Kaiser's roof we mean to stay;
> We'll drink his beer and give a cheer,
> For Canada far away.[1]

In Valcartier these first Sudbury units merged with Toronto's 48th Highlanders to form the 15th Overseas Infantry Battalion. Almost 75 percent of the "Originals" were casualties in their first military action, the German gas attack at St. Julien in April 1915. Little wonder, then, that when the 15th Battalion finally returned to Canada four years later, only Pte. Joseph McGuire still remained with it.[2]

The transformation of what was expected to be a quick and easy Allied victory into a stalemated war of attrition during the winter of 1914–15 meant that this first recruiting venture, rather than standing out as a unique, memorable experience, became simply one in a series of local manpower mobilizations. The 97th Algonquin Rifles enlisted further regiments until it reached battalion strength in August 1915, at which point it was followed by the 159th Battalion, mustered by April 1916, and then by the 227th "Men O' The North," assembled by August of the same year.[3] Thereafter the recruiting efforts concentrated on getting much-needed reinforcements, until the summer of 1917, when Prime Minister Borden abandoned the voluntary system for compulsory military service.

For the most part, recruiting was carried out with dispatch. Indicative of this was that the Sudbury and District Civilian Recruiting Association, whose purpose was to bolster the flagging efforts of the military authorities, was not formed until April 1916, a step taken fully one year earlier in other parts of Canada. Yet there were difficulties. Sudburians found it galling that the 227th "Men O' The North," whose official name was the Algoma, Manitoulin and Sudbury Battalion, should be popularly known as the "Soo" Battalion because its headquarters were in Sault Ste. Marie, one of Sudbury's chief regional rivals. Such local jealousy was placated and the town's place of importance in the region acknowledged in February 1917 with the creation of the Sudbury Mobilization Centre, to which henceforth all recruits from Northern Ontario went for examination and induction.[4]

Because the population of the Sudbury district was highly transient, it is impossible to determine precisely how many Sudburians served with the CEF. Certainly not all of the men recruited locally were native Sudburians, or, for that matter, residents of the town. Even the *Sudbury Star*, never reluctant to boast about the community's patriotic fervour, admitted with respect to one group of volunteers, "From the list of names, it is apparent the cosmopolitan and floating population is largely represented in the quota, with some addresses from Vancouver to Quebec."[5] It is equally impossible to provide an accurate ethnic breakdown of the recruits from the region, although an impressionistic survey of the volunteer lists published by the *Star* suggests that in Sudbury, as elsewhere, it was the British, by birth or by heritage, who volunteered first. On the other hand, Sudbury may not have been typical of Canada at large in so far as French Canadians appear to have been represented more on those lists than in the country as a whole.

According to the official register of the Sudbury branch of the Royal Canadian Legion, eighty-five men from Sudbury and Copper Cliff, including locally familiar names like Belanger, Ferry, Morrison, and Tuddenham, made, in that depressingly accurate contemporary phrase, "the supreme sacrifice," thus creating a permanent bond between their friends and families and far-away plots of land in France and Belgium.[6] In addition, countless others returned from Europe bearing physical impairments or psychological scars not fully comprehensible to anyone who had not shared their experiences.

Though the most dramatic act of patriotism open to Sudburians was enlistment, it obviously was not an option for most people. For those remaining on the "home front" – the physically unfit, the old, the young, women, and the occupationally essential – there were other outlets for patriotic expression.

Within a week of the declaration of war, the Sudbury chapter of the Imperial Order of the Daughters of the Empire collected eight hundred dollars for the national association's project to establish overseas hospitals. An equally spontaneous outburst of war enthusiasm occurred in the summer of 1915 when Sudburians, swept up in the nation-wide hysteria over rumours that the CEF did not have enough machine guns, embarked on a highly successful campaign to collect funds for the purchase of five weapons for the Department of Militia.[7]

Throughout the Great War, the main recipient of Sudburians' generosity was the local branch of the Patriotic Fund, a national voluntary association set up to provide financial assistance to the wives and dependents of men serving in the CEF. Formed on 8 September 1914 under the presidency of District Court Judge J.J. Kehoe, the Sudbury Patriotic Society over the next four and a half years raised slightly more than $125,000, half of which was spent on 185 local families and half of which was remitted to the national organization in Ottawa for use elsewhere. Assisted by Le Fonds de Secours Canadien Français de Sudbury, the society at first relied primarily on grants from the Sudbury Town Council and the Mond Nickel Company. (The Canadian Copper Company supported the Copper Cliff Patriotic Society.) When the town fathers balked at this annual call on the public purse in 1917, the society embarked on a highly successful financial campaign whose objective of $25,000 was easily surpassed in less than a week, an experience repeated in 1918.[8]

By all conventional measurements, Sudbury's response to the Great War was affirmative and continuous. Yet because roughly 50 percent of

Sudburians were of British origin and 35 percent of French-Canadian origin, the town could not escape the divisive conscription crisis that erupted in Canada during 1917. Like their *confrères* in Quebec, French Canadians in the town argued that the Canadian war effort must remain strictly voluntary, a view that by 1917 was increasingly challenged by many English Canadians who demanded that the country's contribution become more systematic and compulsory.[9]

The first open manifestation of the local division over conscription came in mid-May 1917, when Bishop Scollard, head of the Roman Catholic diocese of Sault Ste. Marie, announced that a new English-speaking pastorate, St. Joseph's, would be carved out of the formerly bilingual Ste. Anne's parish, leaving it unilingually French. Admittedly, the conscription issue was not the only factor in this decision. As early as 1914 complaints had been voiced by Father Paquin of Ste. Anne's about overcrowding and the difficulties of holding bilingual services.[10] As well, since 1912 English and French Roman Catholics had been in conflict over the extent to which French should be used as a language of instruction in their schools, a local variation of the Ontario-wide dispute revolving around the Department of Education's controversial Regulation 17.[11]

Yet there can be no doubt that it was conscription that finally made it impossible for the two groups to continue sharing the same religious facilities, and from October 1917 onward, the three hundred English-speaking families met separately across the street from Ste. Anne's in Jubilee Hall, until their own church, Christ the King, was constructed in the 1920s.

The English-French conflict over conscription was also demonstrated during the federal election campaign of December 1917. The riding of Nipissing, of which Sudbury was a part, witnessed a two-way fight between Charles R. Harrison, an Independent Labour candidate from North Bay, who carried the Union Government banner, and Edmond R. Lapierre, a commercial traveller from Sudbury who ran as a Laurierite Liberal. The campaign was an acrimonious one, in which the supporters of Harrison accused their Liberal opponents of stabbing Canada's soldiers in the back by refusing to endorse conscription. In Sudbury such tactics worked, and Harrison, relying mainly on the predominantly English-speaking wards of Ryan and McCormick, outpolled Lapierre, whose strength was concentrated in the largely French-speaking Fournier ward, by more than 150 votes. In the constituency at large, on the other hand, Lapierre won a 1,300 majority of the civilian votes, only to see Harrison finally declared the victor on the basis of an additional 1,500 ballots supposedly cast on his behalf by soldiers overseas.[12]

Inevitably this English-French split carried over into the municipal arena. Traditionally, at least one and occasionally two of the town council seats were held by French Canadians, a result guaranteed by their nominating only one or two candidates and then concentrating their support behind them in the town-wide elections. In 1918 this tradition was set aside with the formation of the French Canadian Citizen's Association (FCCA), which endorsed four candidates, including the English-speaking M.W. Terrell. Tactically this approach failed in the face of the united English-speaking majority. As there were only nine candidates running for six positions, one of the FCCA's nominees had to be elected, and one was – Terrell – leaving council without a French-speaking member.[13]

The acrimony continued in 1919, when council demonstrated its English bias by "forgetting" to invite seventy-five French-Canadian veterans to a civic banquet held in October to honour Sudburians who had served in the CEF.[14] Such pettiness was finally brought an end in 1920 with the election of O.A. Lauzon as councillor and J.A. Laberge as mayor, the first French Canadian to hold that position in over a decade.

The English-French relationship was not the only aspect of Sudbury's ethnic character to be adversely affected by the war. Although the "foreign" – meaning non-British and non-French – component of the town's population was only about 15 percent during these years, this group made up approximately 30 percent of the population in the surrounding townships. Even before the war there had been some expressions of nativistic discontent about the ethnic heterogeneity of the district. In 1913, for example, the Canadian Copper Company made a concerted effort to hire what it called "white men" from Michigan and Nova Scotia because it distrusted the non–English-speaking element in the area.[15]

Because of its inherently xenophobic nature, the war intensified such prejudices, and for a while Sudbury became a less open and tolerant place in which to live. Indeed, in 1918 the all–English-Canadian town council enacted part of that intolerance into municipal law when it imposed a special wartime licence, payable to the Sudbury Patriotic Fund, on all businesses operated by non-British subjects. That same bias was also demonstrated in the 1919 council's decision to reinforce the British image of Sudbury by renaming a number of streets, especially those with German and other "unpronounceable" – mostly French – names; du Caillaud Street, for example, was changed to Howey Drive.[16]

Given the direct and personal ways in which Sudburians had been affected by the Great War, it was not surprising that they greeted the news of the armistice, flashed along the telegraph lines at 3:00 a.m. on 11 November 1918, with day-long celebrations and services of prayer – scenes, according to the *Star*, "such as Sudbury has never seen and may never see again."[17] Though few could realize it at the time, in one sense the war would never be over for Sudbury because its impact would shape the community for decades to come. In particular, by stimulating an unprecedented demand for nickel and copper and thereby vastly expanding the economic substructure of the district, the war was directly responsible for transforming Sudbury's urban environment and its status in northeastern Ontario.

Economically the immediate pre-war years were prosperous ones for Sudbury's mining industry, as production levels of nickel rose from 34 million pounds in 1911 to 49.9 million pounds in 1913, while those of the area's other metallic staple, copper, increased from 18 to 25.8 million pounds. During the winter of 1913–14 a world-wide recession temporarily halted this growth, but the downturn was reversed by the demands of the war. From 1914 to 1918 nickel extraction in Ontario jumped from 45.5 to 92.5 million pounds a year, and copper from 28.9 to 47 million pounds. Financially the chief beneficiaries of these increases were Canadian Copper and Mond Nickel, whose profits climbed dramatically, but so, too, was the British America Nickel Corporation, which in 1916 became the third mining firm active in the Sudbury Basin. Because its smelting facilities at Murray mine did not go into production until January 1920, British America failed to take advantage of the economic opportunities generated by the war and thus became a victim of the severe post-war depression that reached its nadir in 1922, when only 17.5 million pounds of nickel and 10.9 million pounds of copper were extracted.[18]

Predictably, Sudbury's economic fortunes followed closely those of the mining industry. With regard to employment, for example, the years from 1911 to 1913 witnessed a steady growth in jobs. As elsewhere in Canada, this growth slowed measurably during the winter of 1913–14 (although as late as February 1914 the *Star* continued to maintain that the main barrier to Sudbury's expansion was not a lack of jobs but a shortage of housing), and by the summer of 1914 there was a large pool of unemployed in the area. About four hundred of these men, described in the press as dissatisfied "foreigners," were forced to live in unsanitary, squalid conditions in abandoned boxcars near Old Stobie mine. On June 29, the date of the provincial election, many of them marched through the streets of Sudbury in a protest demonstration that was "distinctly new and novel" to the town. This brought swift action from all levels of government, and within a week the "colony" was dispersed, its occupants given the choice of taking work and wages that they had previously refused as inadequate or leaving the community.[19]

Paradoxically, the outbreak of war initially aggravated this bleak employment picture. The Canadian Copper Company immediately laid off 550 workers at its No. 2, No. 3, Crean Hill, and Dill mines and at the Copper Cliff smelter, explaining its decision in the following manner:

> As was to be expected with a commodity so closely allied to Armageddon the nickel industry is one of the first to feel the direct result of the great conflict in Europe. The demand for nickel in the construction of the engines of war is practically suspended, while the demand in the remaining avenues of commerce in which the commodity is used is more or less affected by the general trade conditions. A temporary retrenchment is to be expected.[20]

In addition to the depressed "general trade conditions" referred to, the fact that in the pre-war years the International Nickel Company's (INCO's) second-largest customer had been Germany, a market that was lost for the duration, must also have had a bearing on the company's decision. Mond, on the other hand, because of its British orientation, not only maintained normal production levels at its newly established Coniston plant, but in December 1914 increased those levels by one-third.[21]

By April 1915 the market had improved to the extent that Canadian Copper not only rehired the men it had let go but began to expand its smelting facilities. For the next three and a half years, labour was at a premium, and workers were in a much better position to improve their wages and conditions of employment. As of 1 November 1915, for example, both Canadian Copper and Mond Nickel reduced the work day of all surface employees from twelve to eight hours, bringing it into line with that of the underground workers.[22] As this was done without any reduction in pay, hourly wages were effectively increased by one-third; the companies also enlarged their above-ground work forces by one-third.

As the war dragged on and the military and industrial sectors of the country increasingly competed for limited manpower, labour shortages became the norm and wage increases more frequent. In 1916, for example, Canadian Copper, with the assistance of the federal government, began to bring hundreds of "enemy aliens," mostly Austro-Hungarians, to the region to work in its mines and smelter. In February 1917 the company temporarily closed two mines – No. 2 and Vermilion – in order to transfer men to more essential work elsewhere. That same month saw the announcement of a 10 percent bonus for all Canadian Copper hourly workers. A year later the story was the same, for in April 1918 Canadian Copper raised the daily wage of all employees by fifty cents. These incentives were effective. By 1918 Canadian Copper was employing approximately 3,200 men in its various Sudbury operations, and Mond more than 1,800.[23]

In the same communiqué of 8 August 1914 in which Canadian Copper announced layoffs, it also predicted, "With the cessation of hostilities ... the nickel industry will undoubtedly experience the greatest boom in its history." That too turned out to be a complete miscalculation of the situation, because the cessation of hostilities brought "bust," not "boom." Within six months Canadian Copper reduced its work force to 1,000, and that of Mond fell to 750. For Sudbury workers this trauma was compounded by the fact that during that same period the community was being flooded by men from southern Ontario, many of them returned soldiers, looking for jobs. Unemployment soared and wages fell. The response of labour was much the same here as elsewhere in Canada during these years – a determination to organize collectively. Within the individual companies these efforts led to nothing, although 1919 did see the formation of the Sudbury Trades and Labour Council, which at last gave labour a voice in community affairs.[24]

Apart from the war, which was of an entirely different order, Sudbury's most significant achievement in the decade from 1910 to 1920 was its emergence as a leading metropolitan centre in northeastern Ontario. The boundaries of its regional hinterland gradually expanded in ever-widening concentric circles, eventually overlapping those of its chief rivals, Sault Ste. Marie and North Bay. Of the reasons for this development, none was more important than Sudbury's central position in the transportation and communications networks so vital to the area. As the point of departure for the railway's "Soo" branch, it had always had a pivotal place in Canadian Pacific's transcontinental system. Its centrality had been strengthened in 1908 with the completion of the Canadian Pacific and Canadian Northern direct lines to Toronto, which had diminished North Bay's role as gateway to Northern Ontario. The completion of the Algoma Eastern in 1913 drew Manitoulin Island and points in-between into Sudbury's orbit.[25]

Highways then followed railways. In 1911 the provincial government located the route for a trunk highway from Sault Ste. Marie to Sudbury to North Bay. The first section was completed in the summer of 1914, but the war slowed construction so that not until 1917 were Sudburians able to travel all the way to Toronto by car.[26] Sudbury thus became the hub of a complex transportation network that connected it with the two largest cities in Canada, Montreal and Toronto, and gave it a vital intermediary position on the way west.

Along with this network came a revolution in communications. New telegraph services accompanied the railways to Toronto. Even more important was the expanded telephone system. Before 1911 there were only about two hundred telephones in Sudbury and Copper Cliff combined, and it was impossible to communicate with any other place in the province. This changed in November 1911 when long-distance service to points east via North Bay and west via Sault Ste. Marie was introduced; the Bell subscription list for Sudbury alone climbed to approximately eight hundred in 1914 and double that number in 1921.[27]

Sudbury's status as the dominant urban centre in the Nickel Basin was also strengthened during the decade. In 1910 places like Garson, Creighton, Frood, Levack, and Coniston, if they existed at all, were simply residential groupings at mine and smelter sites. By 1920 they were a little larger or, in some cases, a little smaller but essentially unchanged. In 1910 only Copper Cliff and Sudbury could be fairly classified as urban in the functional sense of the word, and even then Sudbury's advantage was evident. By the end of the decade, certainly, there was no question as to which was uppermost.[28]

The clearest measure of Sudbury's paramountcy was demographic. According to the 1911 census Sudbury's population was 4,150, compared to 3,082 for Copper Cliff. In total numbers the difference between them was not great, although the fact that Sudbury had over 850 more women and three hundred more families than Copper Cliff suggests that even then its urban function was considerably more diversified. By 1921 the two were no longer even moderately close in size, for Sudbury's population had risen to 8,621 while that of Copper Cliff had actually declined to 2,597. Sudbury had also made significant demographic gains in relation to the region as a whole. Whereas in 1911 its population constituted 13.9 percent of the census district, by 1921 the figure was 20 percent.[29]

Urban dominance arises out of more than simple demographic supremacy, although the sheer weight of numbers alone does give a community a decided advantage over its smaller rivals. Yet in most instances that advantage must be compounded by superiority in business, commercial, and financial activities. Here, too, by 1921 Sudbury had completely outdistanced its chief competitor. In banking, for example, Sudbury had branches of seven major institutions, Copper Cliff only one. Similarly, there were 131 retail and wholesale establishments in Sudbury at a time when there were only 26 in Copper Cliff. Of those in Sudbury, 33 were grocery stores, as compared to one in Copper Cliff.

The story was much the same with respect to the service sectors of the two towns. Whereas a variety of recreational, legal, medical, artisanal, and educational services were offered by 142 Sudbury firms, only 17 such businesses existed in Copper Cliff. Most surprising of all, perhaps, was the fact that Copper Cliff, a company-owned mining town, contained no establishments that catered specifically to the mining industry, whereas Sudbury had 7. In total, Sudbury had 342 businesses of various sizes; Copper Cliff had only 51.[30]

What marked the demise of any lingering pretensions by Copper Cliff of competing with Sudbury was perhaps the construction of the Sudbury–Copper Cliff Suburban Electric Railway. Indeed, it may be argued that in granting the necessary rights of way, the Canadian Copper Company implicitly acknowledged Sudbury's claim to commercial primacy in the region. Such recognition had always previously been denied: in 1906 an earlier venture, the Sudbury, Copper Cliff and Creighton Electric Railway Company, was refused those rights of way because of opposition from Copper Cliff merchants. When the subject again arose in 1910, those same merchants, led by the owner of the bus service between Copper Cliff and Sudbury, John Thomson, continued to be decidedly hostile. Yet all such opposition was later overridden, first by the rights-of-way agreement signed between the railway and mining company in May 1914 and then by a popular vote of the Copper Cliff ratepayers in October of that same year.[31]

According to the *Sudbury Journal* in 1913, the railway would "mean a great commercial development, and the establishment of a closer relationship between the Hub of the North and adjoining business centres."[32] Conceiving the idea and bringing it to fruition proved to be two very different matters, for more than three years passed between the incorporation of the company in April 1912 and the running of the first trains in 1915. There were several reasons for the delay. Negotiations between Sudbury Town Council and Charles McCrea, local lawyer and MPP for Nipissing West, who was acting on the company's behalf, lasted from January to June 1913, and then the requisite agreement-in-principle by-laws had to be ratified by a vote of the ratepayers on 4 August.[33]

Thereafter the details of site location and financing remained to be worked out, so that actual construction did not begin until 30 May 1914, the last date permissible under the terms of the franchise. Some progress was made during the summer of 1914, but in August the outbreak of war dashed the company's hope of floating a crucial bond issue. All activities were suspended and not resumed until June of the following year, when

Sudbury taxpayers approved a plan whereby the town itself guaranteed a series of twenty-year company bonds.[34] Hence, only on 11 November 1915 did the long-awaited hourly train service between Sudbury and Copper Cliff finally begin.

During its first five years of operation, the Sudbury–Copper Cliff Suburban Electric Railway Company was not a particularly successful business venture. It was not a losing proposition, since it managed, though just barely, to meet all operating expenses, but it did not generate enough profits to pay dividends on its common stock. In 1920, therefore, the shareholders proposed that the town buy them out and run the railway as a municipal enterprise. After lengthy consideration, council voted four to two against the proposal for the philosophical reason that it was better that the system be owned privately and for the practical reason that if the company ever went bankrupt, the terms of its franchise permitted the town to acquire its properties for much less than the $190,000 being asked.[35]

Council might have been somewhat more sympathetic to the company's plight, since during its short existence the railway had served the community well. Most important, it had done pretty much what the *Sudbury Star* had predicted it would, that is, "make Sudbury, Copper Cliff, [and] Creighton Mine ... all but one community, only separated by steel rails, efficient and uninterrupted service and a CHEAP FARE."[36]

From the beginning the use of the Sudbury to Copper Cliff section of the line was relatively heavy, averaging over nine hundred fares a day in the first year alone. Unfortunately, it is impossible to determine how many of those fares originated in Sudbury and how many in Copper Cliff, although the *Star* did report that whereas in 1915 only about twenty Sudburians had commuted to Copper Cliff to work, a year later the figure was more than two hundred.[37] In any event, in both cases Sudbury was clearly the beneficiary.

Sudbury's local dominance was also reinforced by the network of roads and highways constructed during the decade. In 1912 the Ontario legislature adopted the Northern and North Western Ontario Development Act, which authorized the Whitney government to borrow up to $5 million (amended in 1916 to $10 million) for the construction of essential roads and public works in the area. Sudbury benefited from this act, particularly in the immediate pre- and post-war years, when roads were built or upgraded between the town and the outlying communities of Garson, Coniston, Copper Cliff–Creighton, Hanmer-Capreol, Azilda-Chelmsford, Frood Mine, and Nickelton (Murray mine).[38]

The automobile did not fully come into its own until the 1920s, but still the number of "horseless carriages" in the district increased from

The Canadian Pacific Railway created Sudbury. Shown here is the town's first station, erected shortly after 1883. The train was heading east.

Courtesy: Sudbury Public Library.

A group of Canadian Copper Company executives and Ontario government authorities at the Frood claim site in 1886. The burnt terrain of McKim Township is clearly visible in the background.

Courtesy: Inco Archives

On 15 June 1891, at the village centre in front of the Balmoral Hotel, a celebration
was held to honour Samuel J. Ritchie, founder of the Canadian Copper Company –
this in spite of the fact that he had just been manoeuvred out of the company.
Ste. Anne of the Pines Church is under construction on the left.

Courtesy: Inco Archives.

In the early 1890s Sudbury was a modest village nestled between Ste. Anne's on the
right and the railroad on the left. Vegetation was sparse.

Courtesy: Inco Archives.

The railroad and Ste. Anne's dominated Sudbury at the end of the century. The CPR
station is on the left; Junction Creek flows under the tracks and the south end of
Durham Street. Ste. Anne's rises above the bare rock formation at the back.

In this 1898 photograph old men and young boys can be seen using shovels and
picks at what would become Clarabelle Open Pit mine. Hughie Dixon, with his
hands in his pockets at the rear, was the boss. His son stands beside him,
holding a pick.

Mining in the Sudbury district required massive excavations in hard rock, as revealed at Creighton mine. The foreman is at the top, workers at lower right, and rail line enters mine at lower left.

Three prominent early Sudburians: (left to right) Dr. William F. Howey, the first CPR doctor who stayed; Francis Charles Crean, a prospector; and Stephen Fournier, the town's first mayor and a leading French Canadian in the area.

Frank Cochrane was one of Sudbury's earliest hardware merchants and three times mayor (1898, 1899, 1902). He expanded his interests to include lumbering, mining, and industrial holdings. Serving as a Conservative in both provincial and federal politics, he was minister of railways and canals in the Borden cabinet (1911–17).

Elm street, looking east in 1910. The Balmoral Hotel with its distinctive
pyramid tower is on the left, fronted by wooden sidewalks beside a muddy street.
Hydro and telephone lines have been installed, as have water mains.
Note the fire hydrant at left.

Elm Street, looking east about 1919. Horses and wagons are still dominant, but Elm
Street is paved, streets are lighted, and the automobile and streetcar have moved in.
The Nickel Range Hotel is the large building on the left.

Sudbury had moved north, east, and south by 1910, crossing Junction Creek, which is the valley from the lower left to upper right. Ste. Anne's is hidden in upper left.

Courtesy: Inco Archives.

Erected in 1915, shortly before this photo was taken, the post office building at the corner of Elm and Durham served as Sudbury's centrepiece until it was demolished in 1957.

Firemen show off their new station, about 1914, with the old building in the rear.
The sleighs were standard winter equipment in Canada at the time.

Courtesy: Sudbury Public Library.

While horses remained in use into the 1930s, this first fire truck in the 1920s and
others like it made them obsolete. The Grand Theatre is in the background.

Courtesy: Sudbury Public Library.

Copper Cliff in 1915, looking southeast. The general manager's house is middle-right, with the rock house and Copper Cliff mine behind it. The workers' "Shantytown" is on the right in the distance; the spire of the Polish/Ukrainian church is visible. On the left, on the road towards Sudbury, is the roast-heap.

Courtesy: Inco Archives.

A French-Canadian marriage in Sudbury in 1921. Stephen Fournier is fifth from the right, front row.

Courtesy: La Société Historique du Nouvel-Ontario.

George Wandziak, driving, and Dymtro Prydanik, both of Coniston and both bachelors, show off a car in the early 1920s. Coniston was linked to Sudbury by a road beside the CPR line. Hydro and telephone lines also followed the tracks.

Courtesy: Mike Solski.

The Snow White Restaurant on Durham Street South was a gathering spot for local
Finns in 1926–27. Nestor Puska, the owner, is on right front beside Ensti Kallio.
Beginning sixth from left at back: Eino Kautiainen, Vaino Jarvi, Kusti Kolppanen,
Lily Hill (later Jussila), and Toivo Kolpaanen.

The public school ball team at Burwash in 1926. Back row, from left: Jim Kidd, Peter
Johnson, Colin Soule, and J.T. Kidd. Front row, from left: Garnet Simms, Elmer
Stewart, Harold Sinclair, Harry Cresswell, and Ron Duncan.

By the end of the 1920s Sudbury was at the centre of a highway network that linked all regional communities to the town. This fleet of busses carried passengers on regular service to and from places like Coniston, Capreol, Copper Cliff, Creighton, Frood Mine, Azilda, and Long Lake.

Courtesy: Inco Archives.

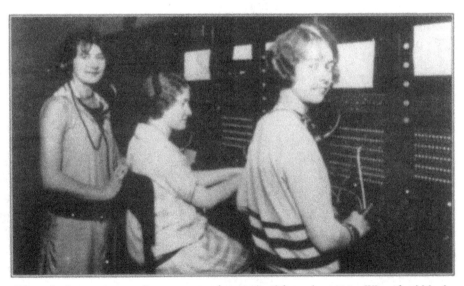

The telephone operator became part of everyday life in the 1920s. Winnifred Heal, Annabelle Lee, and Winnifred Ade (left to right) operated the Bell Canada Copper Cliff switchboard in 1929.

Courtesy: Bell Canada, Telephone Historical Collection.

When Sudbury became a city in 1930, this was its sixteen-man police force, under Chief David Louden. Back row, from left: Sgt. Dave McNabb, Stan Wilson, Horatio Walker, Jack Adams, Wilfred Leclair, Bert Light, Patrick McVey, Emile Lafond, George Brown, and Sgt. Leo Campeau.
Front row, from left: Alex McLaren, Sgt. Frank Scott, Chief Louden, Deputy Chief Edward Pyle, Sgt. Fred Davidson, and Robert Greggor.

Courtesy: *Sudbury Star.*

Bell Park on Lake Ramsey was donated to Sudbury by lumber magnate William Bell. Both the lake and the park have been the centre of summer and winter recreation activities for decades. This 1930s photograph shows swimmers and change houses in the foreground and canoeists in the distance.

Courtesy: Michael J. Mulloy.

Junction Creek overflowed its banks and inundated Sudbury on an annual basis until the 1960s, when flood control measures were finally put in place. From the water tower hill, this photo looks southwest. The first east-west street is Elm; the skating rink is at top right.

Courtesy: Sudbury Public Library.

Although Sudbury escaped the Depression relatively unscathed, the early 1930s were difficult years. With the improvement after 1934, Sudbury became a destination city for job seekers, some of whom are shown here in front of the Employment Service of Canada office.

Courtesy: Ray Thoms.

William Edge Mason, a central figure in Sudbury from the day he started the *Northern Daily Star* in 1909 until his death in 1948. He was involved in businesses, entertainment, sports, hospitals, charities, school boards – virtually everything. He was the quintessential "city booster," though he made enemies among several groups, especially the labourers and unionists.

Courtesy: *Sudbury Star.*

William "Bill" Beaton, a world champion canoeist and sports enthusiast, is shown here at Lake Ramsey in the 1920s. He built a successful insurance business and local political career on that athletic background.
Mayor of Sudbury continuously from 1941 to 1951, a record, he symbolizes Sudbury's infatuation with sports heroes.

Courtesy: Gwen Whissell.

only twelve in 1910 to nearly a thousand in 1921. As early as June 1913, traffic was sufficiently heavy that town council passed a by-law directing all vehicles to drive on the right-hand side of the road, and the province instituted a mandatory driver's test on 1 December 1914.[39]

Though Sudbury's central position in the communications network of the region was crucial to its rise to urban prominence, another contributing factor was the town's class composition, unique in the Nickel Basin. The great majority of people in the industrial towns of Coniston, Creighton, Copper Cliff, and Garson fell into the category of working class, whereas those in the Valley – the townships of Balfour, Rayside, Blezard, and Hanmer – were largely farmers. Sudbury alone had a highly diversified social structure headed by a growing entrepreneurial class, which, as it had done from the beginning, played a leading role in the community's development.[40]

Predominantly British but partly French-Canadian, this class, following the demographic pattern of the town itself, doubled in size in the decade from 1911 to 1921.[41] For example, in 1921 there were eleven legal firms, ten medical doctors, and seven dentists, whereas in 1911 the numbers had been six, five, and three respectively. There was similar growth in the number of retail outlets: in 1921 there were eighteen clothing stores compared to only seven in 1911; four agricultural implement dealerships compared to one; five bottling companies compared to three; sixteen confectionaries compared to five; seven furniture stores compared to three; thirty-three grocery stores compared to twenty-three; ten jewellers compared to two; and sixteen tobacconists compared to four. The numbers of hardware stores (seven) and lumber dealerships (nine) remained relatively constant over the decade, but there was considerable growth in real estate (twelve firms in 1921 and five in 1911), contracting (twenty-six companies in 1921 and fourteen in 1911), and insurance (thirteen agents in 1921 and six in 1911).

A characteristic of Sudbury business that did not change over the decade was its essentially commercial nature. The only real attempt at industrial diversification, the Ontario and Manitoba Flour Mill operations, which dated from 1910, faltered in February 1914, a casualty of the recession that winter. It reopened under new ownership in April 1915 and was sustained by the wartime demand until 1919, when it closed for good.[42] Sudbury then, as for much of its history, was a commercial entrepôt heavily dependent upon the mining sector for its economic well-being.

Socially Sudbury's entrepreneurial group was prominent in a variety of quasi-elitist organizations. One of the most important was the Sudbury Club. This exclusive club – its membership was limited by its act of incorporation to a restricted number of shareholders – came into existence in the summer of 1914. Over the next three and a half years its clubhouse, purchased from Dr. W.H. Howey, served as a private meeting place for the community's businessmen. The club had barely become established when it was faced with the Sudbury Temperance Alliance's campaign for prohibition, chaired by the mining entrepreneur J.F. Black. In December 1915 its members voted to abide by the eight o'clock closing regulations imposed by the provincial Licence Commission on taverns, although technically it did not fall into that category. The provincial adoption of prohibition on 20 September 1916 left the club high and dry, and in October 1917 it went into receivership. The idea was revived in 1919, the new Sudbury Club taking on such projects as sponsoring the formation of the men's branch of the Canadian Club in January 1920.[43] By 1922 it had evolved into the Idylwylde Land Syndicate, developer of the Idylwylde Golf and Country Club.

Institutionally the most visible expression of the town's business-professional elite was the Sudbury Board of Trade. Presided over by such men as J.F. Black, lumber magnate W.J. Bell, the real estate and insurance agent P. Gorman, and the furniture dealer and funeral director J.G. Henry, the board attempted to boost the business climate of Sudbury in various ways. One was by petitioning the federal government for better postal service. In May 1913 letter boxes were distributed throughout the town, and in November 1915 a new post office was opened at Elm and Durham. The board of trade also succeeded in getting Sudbury declared a chief port of customs entry, effective April 1913. Copper Cliff was made a sub-port. The fact that the federal minister of railways was a former mayor, Frank Cochrane, obviously worked to the board's advantage on issues such as these, although even that did not result in the construction of the rail link between Sudbury and the National Transcontinental via Timmins for which the board also lobbied.[44]

On most questions, however, the board looked for assistance, not to Ottawa, but to provincial authorities in Toronto. Annually it forwarded resolutions to Queen's Park pleading the north's case for expanded highway and railway services, with reasonably good results. One campaign that quickly bore fruit was that begun in January 1913 to have a prison farm established in the area. Members of the board argued that such an institution was vital because of the increased crime in the district, a phenomenon they attributed to the growing "foreign" element in the community. Whatever the validity of that claim, in September 1914 a temporary prison camp for minor offenders was opened to the south of the town, although the permanent industrial farm at Burwash was not ready until February 1916.[45]

A project central to the board's aspirations for Sudbury was the development of a cheap source of hydro-electricity, which was essential if Sudbury was to be more attractive to industry. To that end, board representatives, along with delegates from town council, met first in November 1916 and again in April 1920 with Adam Beck, chairman of the Ontario Hydro-Electric Commission; both times they came away full of optimism that the commission was prepared to meet its request by damming the Chaudière Falls on the French River.[46] Unfortunately that optimism proved to be unfounded, and the decade ended with nothing accomplished.

In the summers of 1912 and 1913, the board of trade was the chief booster of the community when, with financial assistance from town council, it held exhibitions of Sudbury's great potential at the "New Ontario Days" in Toronto. The local board also took the lead in the establishment in April 1913 of the United Boards of Trade of New Ontario, an association composed of affiliates from North Bay, Sturgeon Falls, Callendar, Blind River, Thessalon, and Sault Ste. Marie as well as Sudbury, and dedicated to broadcasting the virtues of the north far and wide.[47]

This campaign was helped immeasureably by the Great War, which drew national attention to the vast mineral wealth of the region. Paradoxically, though, the war nearly destroyed the Sudbury Board of Trade because it raised several very serious questions about the policies and practices of the two mining companies, Canadian Copper and Mond, and in responding, often unwillingly, to those questions, the board members found themselves in divisive situations.

The first such perplexing issue arose in October 1914 from the fact that because of American neutrality laws, the International Nickel Company, the American parent to Canadian Copper, was not legally subject to Canadian orders-in-council prohibiting the export of nickel to enemy countries. Since Germany had been an important INCO customer before the war, rumours spread that this trade was continuing and that the German war effort was benefiting from nickel extracted from Sudbury mines. The rumours were false. In late October INCO officials had negotiated an agreement with Sir Robert Borden that in effect gave the British government a veto over the company's export sales.[48] On 21 December 1914 the federal government assured the Canadian people that with the full co-operation of INCO nickel exports were being carefully monitored. Three days later the Sudbury Board of Trade also expressed its confidence in the company.[49]

The ubiquitous J.F. Black was not so sure. In his capacity as president of the board of trade, Black wrote the British Board of Trade conveying his suspicion that International Nickel was indeed supplying Germany via South America.[50] This was not Black's first confrontation with INCO, nor would it be his last, but it was certainly the most controversial. At an unusually well attended meeting on 12 January 1915, the general membership overwhelmingly repudiated his action by a vote of one hundred to one and reiterated its position of the previous December. For the board, the short-term consequence of this controversy was organizational confusion, as Black, unintimidated and unrepentant, first failed to forward the censure motions to local politicians as he had been directed to do, and then, exercising his presidential prerogative, refused to call an annual meeting to elect the 1915 executive. Elections finally did take place on 11 February, but by then serious damage had been done to the board's reputation.[51]

At the same meeting that censured Black, the Sudbury Board of Trade firmly identified itself with the interests of International Nickel on another matter. It carried unanimously a lengthy motion in favour of refining nickel matte in Canada, but with the qualification that this should only be done "if the same [was] economically practicable and ... without injury to Canadian trade." The motion also recommended that "no action should be taken by the Government by placing an export duty on nickel matte, without first making a thorough investigation of the matter, as this Board of Trade and this community do not wish large industries such as the Canadian Copper Co. and Mond Nickel Co. jeopardized by misguided patriotism or rival interests."[52]

During the summer of 1915 the pressure on the Ontario government to take action vis-à-vis the nickel industry built up steadily, leading to the appointment of the Royal Ontario Nickel Commission on 9 September.[53] During the next eighteen months the commission carried out an extensive study, and on 19 March 1917 it produced a voluminous final report. One of the crucial issues it addressed was the economic viability of refining in Ontario, but by the time its recommendations appeared, the question had largely been settled by other events. Of particular importance was the revelation in July 1916 that a German cargo submarine, the *Deutschland*, had, without INCO's knowledge, transported Sudbury nickel from the United States to Germany. Faced with an outburst of popular protest, International Nickel suddenly found that, like the fledgling British America Nickel Corporation, it too could refine profitably in Ontario.[54]

The *Deutschland* scandal rather unfairly tarnished INCO's image, and that reflected badly on the Sudbury Board of Trade, which had so completely placed its trust in the company. Other consequences, the construction of the refinery at Port Colborne and the transformation of the Canadian Copper Company into the International Nickel Company of Canada in 1918, also affected the Sudbury district adversely. The Canadian headquarters of the new company were located not in Copper Cliff as before, but in Toronto, thereby diminishing the prestige of the area, at least in the view of some Sudburians.[55]

The reputations of International Nickel and Mond were both blackened somewhat during these years by another issue of vital concern to the community, the question of sulphur pollution. Though the heart of the matter was a dispute between the farmers and the mining companies over the effect of sulphur fumes on crops, the town was also drawn into the debate. The matter first came before the board of trade in 1912, when the newly formed Sudbury Horticultural Society was forced to cancel its inaugural show because most of the plants in town had been severely injured by sulphur fumes.[56] The society, presided over by none other than J.F. Black, who also owned the Buena Vista Conservatories, located in downtown Sudbury, was badly divided on the issue but finally resolved to enlist the support of the board and of town council in censuring the main culprit, the Canadian Copper Company. Nothing of the sort happened, and instead the society itself disintegrated, not to reappear until 1920.[57]

The enormous increase in wartime mining production brought with it a corresponding growth in the volume of sulphurous gases released from the roast-beds, resulting in a series of lawsuits against the companies. Leading the fight was the irrepressible J.F. Black, but this time he was not alone. In fact, so many suits were launched that the Supreme Court of Ontario selected six – four against Canadian Copper, of which one was Black's, and two against Mond Nickel – which collectively became a single test case on the issue of sulphur pollution. Begun in March 1916, the trial before Justice J.J. Middleton lasted over fifteen months, judgment not being rendered until 31 May 1917.

In the meantime the farmers sought the assistance of the Sudbury Board of Trade, which, predictably, was reluctant even to comment on the sulphur question, let alone range itself against the companies. In March and April of 1916 the board was urged to speak out by three separate deputations from the farming community, but typically, when it finally did so on 14 April, its remarks were directed less to Canadian Copper and Mond Nickel than to the provincial government. Of the three resolutions then adopted, one requested the appointment of a provincial commission to assess damage by sulphur smoke to crops in the region, the second petitioned the Hearst government to supply Sudbury farmers with much-needed seed grain for 1916, and the third asked the mining companies to roast their ore during the winter rather than the summer.[58]

The Ontario government responded quickly to these suggestions, agreeing both to appoint a special sulphur fumes investigator for 1916 and to assist farmers in purchasing seed grain. Meanwhile Mond Nickel switched its roasting schedule to the winter for 1916–17.[59] For its part, Canadian Copper attempted to alleviate the problem by moving its main roast-beds to the more remote part of O'Donnell to the west of Copper Cliff.

These small victories for the farmers in 1916 were more than offset by the defeat explicit in the Supreme Court ruling on the sulphur fumes test cases handed down at the end of May 1917. In essence, Mr. Justice J.J. Middleton found that the mining industry, with its unfortunate but unavoidable side-effect of sulphur pollution, must take precedence over farming in the Sudbury Basin. In each of the six cases on which he heard evidence, the judge, in order to discourage farmers from taking similar legal action in the future, awarded compensatory damages less than those offered out of court by the mining companies.[60] From this perspective the decision was a failure, for the question reappeared regularly in the judicial and parliamentary arenas of Ontario for the next half century.

The cumulative effect of the various controversies related to the mining industry was to drain the Sudbury Board of Trade of its active supporters. Attendance fell off steadily during the war years, and successive board presidents apologetically accounted to their annual meetings for its relative unproductivity.[61] In February 1919 the newly elected president, J.G. Henry, acted to reverse this trend by embarking on a recruiting drive that within a few weeks raised its membership from fewer than sixty to nearly two hundred. To help the campaign, the board voted on 24 March to enlarge its constituent boundaries from Sudbury and McKim Township to encompass the whole of the Sudbury judicial district, a measure of jurisdictional self-aggrandizement that symbolized perfectly the new metropolitan-hinterland relationship that had evolved between Sudbury and the outlying communities.[62]

The post-war world that faced the Sudbury and District Board of Trade was considerably different from that of the pre-war years, so much so, in fact, that one of its members, the jeweller A.H. Beath, urged it to depart from its traditionally non-political stance and run a slate of business candidates for municipal council. Beath's proposal, prompted by the successful candidature of a representative of Sudbury labour circles, D. Burbidge, in the 1919 elections, was seriously debated but then rejected by his fellow board members on the grounds that such a step was not in keeping with the organization's *raison d'être*.[63]

More to the point, such a move was entirely unnecessary because town council, just as throughout its history, continued to be controlled by the same entrepreneurial and professional class of men as the board itself. Between 1911 and 1921 there were five occupants of the mayor's chair – Lawrence O'Connor, mining and real estate agent (1911, 1914, 1915); J.G. Henry, furniture dealer and funeral director (1912, 1913); Thomas Travers, diamond driller contractor (1916); Percy Morrison, master electrician and shop owner (1917, 1918, 1919); and J.A. Laberge, lumber dealer (1920, 1921) – all of whom fell into this category. Similarly, of the thirty-two councillors who served one or more terms during these years, a large majority were businessmen of one sort or another.[64] From that perspective, Burbidge's election was obviously an aberration, but it was a measure of the hysteria in post-war Sudbury over the so-called socialist threat that Beath even made the proposal.

In addition to working with the board of trade to make Sudbury the economic hub of the north, Sudbury's municipal authorities also were responsible for guiding the internal changes to the town's urban environment. Certainly that environment was visibly different in 1920 from what it had been in 1910. As a result of its doubled population, for example, the town grew spatially in several directions, tending to reinforce the established ethnic and class patterns of settlement. The Ramsey Lake region to the southeast continued to be populated by middle- and upper-middle-class English-speaking residents, while English Canadians of more modest means gravitated towards the Lorne Street district to the west and southwest. At the same time, French-speaking Sudburians of all social ranks moved steadily northeast into the Flour Mill district, and immigrant groups of various backgrounds expanded in the northwestern Donovan district.[65]

An important determinant in the shaping of Sudbury's physical layout was its internal transportation network, which, because of both demographic pressures and technological change, was markedly improved during the decade. The appearance of the automobile meant that Sudbury streets required a good deal more attention than they had received in the past. Periodically the *Sudbury Star* complained about their condition, but only in the summer of 1914 did town council inaugurate a paving program, which was continued in subsequent years and supplemented in 1915 by the oiling of other streets. Pedestrians also received consideration. Street paving was accompanied by the construction of cement sidewalks and, in 1914, the installation of new street lighting.[66]

The town's internal lines of communication were affected most radically by the building of the street railway. By December 1916, streetcars ran to the downtown Elm and Durham business core from the Lake district via Nelson and Station streets, from the Flour Mill via Notre Dame Avenue, and from Copper Cliff via Copper Cliff Road and Lorne Street. Along all of these routes, new streets opened up and old ones became more densely settled. This was especially true in the Flour Mill, where the improved transportation system facilitated the development of an entirely new residential subdivision known as O'Connor Park.

Many municipal services expanded to meet the needs of the town's burgeoning population, although interestingly enough, the number of town officers did not increase proportionately. Whereas in 1911 there were eight officials (clerk and treasurer, assessor and collector, town engineer, town solicitor, medical health officer, police magistrate, police chief, and fire chief), in 1921 there were only eleven (the above eight plus building inspector, superintendent and collector of water and light, and the market clerk), and two of those, the building inspector and the market clerk, worked part time.[67]

Even before this moderate bureaucratic growth, Sudbury was badly in need of a new municipal building. In 1910 serious consideration was given to purchasing the financially troubled Grand Opera House for this purpose, but the idea was dropped. Council finally decided to build a new structure on Elgin Street, and construction began in August 1912. When completed in July 1913, the building housed not only the municipal offices but also the fire hall, the jail, and the police department.[68] The police department in particular needed new quarters, inasmuch as during the decade its full-time strength had risen from three to nine men, although the number dropped temporarily in 1916, when, apparently because of the introduction of prohibition, petty crime fell quite dramatically.[69] The decline was temporary. Within a year an increase in arrests, many of them related to violations of the Ontario Temperance Act, required the hiring of additional policemen.[70]

A constant problem facing town council was how to exercise administrative control over the police force without interfering with its work. One solution came in May 1911, when it appointed a board of police commissioners consisting of the mayor, the police magistrate, and the district court judge, but that did not work satisfactorily either – judicial and police functions proved not always to be compatible – and in December 1916 the board was abolished and direct council supervision reimposed.[71]

In contrast to the attention paid to police matters, municipal councillors showed relatively little concern about Sudbury's fire-fighting ability. Throughout the decade the town's fire department remained only a voluntary force headed by a permanent fire chief and his assistant. Apart from the distribution of a series of fire alarm boxes around town in May

1913, a move prompted by a record high $134,000 worth of fire losses the year before, not much else was done, and as late as April 1919 council rejected a proposal for a paid fire brigade "as prohibitory in cost and far in advance of the needs of Sudbury."[72]

As finances permitted, council extended municipal sewer and water lines into new residential districts and improved those in older districts. A new sewer trunk line was in place by the autumn of 1913, but because of difficulties with the site chosen for the projected sewage disposal plant (it turned out to be mainly quicksand) it was not built, and as a result the system was only half functional and drained directly into Junction Creek on the outskirts of town.[73]

The lack of proper sewage treatment played havoc with Sudbury's water supply. Tests taken in November 1914 showed Lake Ramsey to be generally polluted, and the residents were advised to boil or chlorinate their drinking water. By the end of April 1915 a new municipally financed chlorination plant was in operation, and the board of health reported that all samples of the water were pure and potable once again. In 1917 the town's water system was further modernized with the construction of a new steel water tower, at a cost of nearly $50,000, to replace the old wooden tower, which dated from 1895.[74]

The years 1910 to 1920 also brought Sudbury other municipal services that it had previously lacked. In 1913 it adopted uniform house numbering. Before then, guidebooks such as *Vernon's Directory* could identify buildings only by reference to each other or to cross streets.[75] In the same year town council took up the question of garbage disposal, the responsibility for which had formerly been left to individual householders, with less than sanitary consequences. Under pressure from the board of health as well as from the press, on 6 August council authorized the establishment of a voluntary, user-pay garbage collection system for an experimental six-month term. When that period expired, the system was adopted permanently. Because many residents failed to subscribe to the service, health problems persisted, so in July 1915 the municipal authorities made the system comprehensive by dropping the fee and funding the service out of general tax revenues.[76] The increased use necessitated the construction of a new incinerator at the garbage dump that summer.

Another vital urban amenity to appear in Sudbury during these years was a summer market. First proposed by the board of trade and approved in principle by town council in June 1913, the market only then became a real possibility because of agricultural expansion in, and improved transportation ties to, the surrounding districts. From Sudbury's point of view, the idea had much to recommend it, for it was assumed that locally grown produce would be cheaper than imported food.[77] By general consensus the best site for the market was on Borgia Street, between Beech and Louis, on land owned by the Canadian Pacific Railway. In April 1914 Mayor O'Connor reached an agreement with the railway making the land available on a temporary, annual basis. The town then erected a set of buildings as shelters, and the market officially opened on 12 August.[78] Unfortunately, expectations of lower prices were dashed by the inflationary impact of the war. The provincial Department of Agriculture representative recorded that from August 1915 to August 1918 the market price of cream jumped from 20 cents to 50 cents a quart, of beef from 12–18 cents to 20–25 cents a pound, of pork from 15–17 cents to 35–38 cents a pound, and of butter from 30 cents to 45 cents a pound.[79]

Along with officials in many other parts of Ontario during this era, Sudbury's municipal leaders came to recognize the value of carefully planned parklands. The town was certainly in need of recreational parks, especially after September 1913, when Victoria Park was reclaimed by its Jesuit owners as the campus of the newly created Sacred Heart College. Temporary arrangements were made in the spring of 1914 to use the grounds of Sudbury High School for athletic events, but this still left the community without a public park.[80] During the next few years the question was much discussed in the press, but nothing was done until February 1917, when council created the Sudbury Parks Board, chaired by W.J. Bell. The board's first act was to approve on 2 April the purchase of four acres of land next to the skating rink from the CPR for $10,000. The acquisition of the future Memorial Park was greeted sceptically in some quarters. The *Sudbury Journal*, for example, commented derisively that the site was good only for a "spud patch."[81]

In July of 1917 the parks board arranged for Thomas Adams, the British town planning adviser to the federal Commission of Conservation, to visit Sudbury and assess the town's potential. Adams's brief report was highly laudatory in many respects, but particularly so vis-à-vis the board's plans to acquire further parkland on Ramsey Lake. Those plans came to fruition on 31 October 1917, when an agreement was reached with La Corporation du Collège de St. Marie à Montréal, which allowed the town to purchase seven acres of lake-front property for $15,000. Much of this land was being rented by cottagers who had to be given the requisite notice, a process not completed until the spring of 1919. When opened that summer, however, the park proved to be immensely popular; on Sunday, 1 June, in the midst of a heat wave, an estimated four thousand people took advantage of its beach. Later that month, W.J. Bell proposed to double the size of the park by donating four and a half acres of adjacent

Ramsey Lake property to the town in return for the right to close several streets surrounding his house. The idea was warmly received, although the exchange did not actually take place until 1926.[82]

One long-standing institution in Sudbury that was revitalized during these years, partly because of the efforts of town council, was the public library. Originally established in 1896, it had collapsed in the intervening years. In April 1912 a group of citizens headed by the district police magistrate, D.M. Brodie, revived the idea by founding the Sudbury Public Library Association. In May, armed with a grant of $1,000 from the local branch of the Council of Women, the association asked town council to provide free space for a private lending library. This request was eventually agreed to, and on 9 November 1912 a library room was opened to the public in the Huron Chambers.[83]

Like its predecessor, the library association was constantly faced with financial difficulties, and in October 1916 it was forced to recommend that the library be taken over and operated as a municipal service. This step was approved by Sudbury ratepayers in a by-law vote on 29 December 1916; the organizational meeting of the Sudbury Public Library Board was held on 12 February 1917.[84] For the rest of the decade the new board fared considerably better than had the old. A stable financial base permitted it to expand the library's holdings regularly, and that in turn guaranteed a steady growth in the number of its patrons.

Like the municipal services, a variety of social institutions also had to adapt to the changing needs of the population during the decade. For example, the number of churches increased from five to eight, with the addition of the Salvation Army Citadel in 1911, the Jewish synagogue, Sharey Shamaen, in 1914, and the English-speaking Roman Catholic parish of St. Joseph's in 1917. As well, two of the original five required larger premises. The new Anglican Church of the Epiphany was opened in late April 1913, constructed on the same Larch Street site as its 1890 predecessor, and in the spring of 1919 Sudbury's Baptists moved from their original Beech Street location to a partially completed building on Larch Street.

The town's schools underwent a similar growth. In 1913 there was only one public school, Central, with a student population of 373. By 1920 there were three – Central, Elm Street, and College Street – with a combined student enrolment of approximately 950. Attendance at Sudbury's two separate schools also grew dramatically, from 460 in 1914 to over 1,000 in 1920, while that of the high school rose from 70 to about 200 during the same years.[85] For French-speaking Sudburians, the most notable educational event of the decade, apart from the continuing struggle against Regulation 17, which limited Franco-Ontarians' right to public education in the French language, was the establishment by the Society of Jesus of the private Sacred Heart College in September 1913. Notable also was the graduation of the first class of student nurses at St. Joseph's Hospital in 1913.[86]

Health services also expanded during the decade, the number of doctors rising from five to ten. The closure of the General Hospital, on the other hand, left the eighty-five-bed St. Joseph's as the only hospital in the town. Between 1910 and 1920 its patient days increased by a third.[87] By far the most serious challenge to Sudbury's health services was the outbreak of the Spanish influenza in October 1918. The suddenness of the outbreak was startling. On 11 October Sudburians were told that there was no particular danger. Four days later a joint meeting of the board of health, town council, and local doctors banned all public gatherings. Between five hundred and eight hundred cases of "flu" had been reported, 15 percent of them severe and almost all in Sudbury itself; Copper Cliff, Coniston, Garson, and so on were spared the worst of the attack.[88]

Over the next few weeks the Sudbury Emergency Committee that was set up to deal with the situation was badly overworked as the number of new cases reached the thousands. The inoculation of five thousand people in the area helped, as did self-imposed quarantines. Sacred Heart College, for example, which went into virtual isolation, suffered no cases. The threat receded only gradually. On 6 November the ban on meetings was lifted, except for the library and schools, which reopened on 18 November. By the beginning of December, life had returned to normal, with only a few mild cases a day being reported. Still the toll was heavy. Sixty-five Sudburians as well as an unreported number of outsiders who had been brought to the town for treatment had died.[89]

For many Sudburians a decade that had started on such a promising note in terms of economic growth and prosperity turned all too quickly into one better forgotten. Still, behind the trials of war, disease, and hardship was a glimmer of hope in the solid economic foundations of the regions' nickel-copper industry. Optimists, too, could take heart from the very significant place Sudbury was assuming in the metropolitan networks of northeastern Ontario. Fortuitously located at the intersection of the Montreal and Toronto hinterlands, it drew strength from both and parlayed that strength into a regional hinterland of its own. Although

Sudbury was far from being the dominant urban place in the region, the foundations were firmly laid in the decade of the Great War for that eventuality.

1 Effie Stewart Diary, 20 August and 26 August 1914. I must acknowledge my debt to the late Mrs. Helen Stewart and her daughter, Mrs. Anadel Hastie, for access to this diary, now in the latter's possession. See also *Sudbury Star*, 22 August 1914.

2 *Sudbury Star*, 10 May 1919. By far the most important source for this study has been the *Star*, and this was possible only because of the *Index to the Sudbury Star, 1910–1949* prepared by Laurentian University's Department of History in the summer of 1980 with the assistance of a Summer Youth Employment Program Grant.

3 *Sudbury Star*, 31 October 1914, 15 December 1915, 5 April 1916, and 16 August 1916.

4 Ibid., 5 April 1916 and 1 March 1917.

5 Ibid., 14 July 1915.

6 For example, see *Sudbury Star*, 6 May 1916. According to the records of Branch 76, Royal Canadian Legion, Sudbury, twenty of the eighty-five Sudburians killed in the conflict had French-Canadian names.

7 *Sudbury Star*, 12 August 1914 and 21 August 1915.

8 P.H. Morris, *The Canadian Patriotic Fund: A Record of Its Activities, 1914–1919* (Toronto: The Fund, 1919), 207. Mond Nickel was the British family-owned company whose local headquarters were in Coniston. Canadian Copper, based in Copper Cliff, was the mining subsidiary of the International Nickel Company of New Jersey. See also the *Sudbury Journal*, 15 February 1917. Other war-related organizations were also active in the area, including the Belgian Relief Fund and the Canadian Red Cross Society, but in financial terms their operations were relatively minor compared to the work of the Patriotic Fund.

9 *Sudbury Star*, 23 May 1917.

10 Ibid., 16 May 1917 and 21 March 1914.

11 In 1912 the provincial Whitney government issued Department of Education Regulation 17, which severely curtailed the use of French as a language of instruction in Ontario schools. In Sudbury, a community with a large French-speaking population, the regulation was highly contentious and divided the town bitterly along linguistic lines. See, for example, Margaret Prang, "Clerics, Politicians and the Bilingual Schools Issue in Ontario, 1910–1917," *Canadian Historical Review* 41, no. 4 (December 1960); and Victor Simon, "L'application du Règlement XVII dans les écoles bilingues de l'Ontario" (B.A. honours essay, Department of History, Laurentian University, 1981).

12 *Sudbury Star*, 21 November 1917, 8 December 1917, 9 December 1917, and 2 March 1918. Because of the highly irregular manner in which the soldier vote was taken and then distributed amongst the various constituencies, it is impossible to verify the accuracy of this result.

13 Ibid., 5 January 1918; and *Sudbury Journal*, 10 January 1918.

14 *Sudbury Star*, 8 October 1919.

15 These percentages are based on statistics prepared by the author covering the twenty townships in the immediate Sudbury area drawn from the Census of Canada *Reports* for 1911 and 1921. See also Inco Archives, Sudbury, Inco Letter Book #14, John Lawson vice-president, to W.A. Bostwick, 2nd vice-president, Canadian Copper Company, 18 March 1913; and Lawson to Bostwick, 20 March 1913.

Sudbury was far from being the dominant urban place in the region, the foundations were firmly laid in the decade of the Great War for that eventuality.

1   Effie Stewart Diary, 20 August and 26 August 1914. I must acknowledge my debt to the late Mrs. Helen Stewart and her daughter, Mrs. Anadel Hastie, for access to this diary, now in the latter's possession. See also *Sudbury Star*, 22 August 1914.

2   *Sudbury Star*, 10 May 1919. By far the most important source for this study has been the *Star*, and this was possible only because of the *Index to the Sudbury Star, 1910–1949* prepared by Laurentian University's Department of History in the summer of 1980 with the assistance of a Summer Youth Employment Program Grant.

3   *Sudbury Star*, 31 October 1914, 15 December 1915, 5 April 1916, and 16 August 1916.

4   Ibid., 5 April 1916 and 1 March 1917.

5   Ibid., 14 July 1915.

6   For example, see *Sudbury Star*, 6 May 1916. According to the records of Branch 76, Royal Canadian Legion, Sudbury, twenty of the eighty-five Sudburians killed in the conflict had French-Canadian names.

7   *Sudbury Star*, 12 August 1914 and 21 August 1915.

8   P.H. Morris, *The Canadian Patriotic Fund: A Record of Its Activities, 1914–1919* (Toronto: The Fund, 1919), 207. Mond Nickel was the British family-owned company whose local headquarters were in Coniston. Canadian Copper, based in Copper Cliff, was the mining subsidiary of the International Nickel Company of New Jersey. See also the *Sudbury Journal*, 15 February 1917. Other war-related organizations were also active in the area, including the Belgian Relief Fund and the Canadian Red Cross Society, but in financial terms their operations were relatively minor compared to the work of the Patriotic Fund.

9   *Sudbury Star*, 23 May 1917.

10   Ibid., 16 May 1917 and 21 March 1914.

11   In 1912 the provincial Whitney government issued Department of Education Regulation 17, which severely curtailed the use of French as a language of instruction in Ontario schools. In Sudbury, a community with a large French-speaking population, the regulation was highly contentious and divided the town bitterly along linguistic lines. See, for example, Margaret Prang, "Clerics, Politicians and the Bilingual Schools Issue in Ontario, 1910–1917," *Canadian Historical Review* 41, no. 4 (December 1960); and Victor Simon, "L'application du Règlement XVII dans les écoles bilingues de l'Ontario" (B.A. honours essay, Department of History, Laurentian University, 1981).

12   *Sudbury Star*, 21 November 1917, 8 December 1917, 9 December 1917, and 2 March 1918. Because of the highly irregular manner in which the soldier vote was taken and then distributed amongst the various constituencies, it is impossible to verify the accuracy of this result.

13   Ibid., 5 January 1918; and *Sudbury Journal*, 10 January 1918.

14   *Sudbury Star*, 8 October 1919.

15   These percentages are based on statistics prepared by the author covering the twenty townships in the immediate Sudbury area drawn from the Census of Canada *Reports* for 1911 and 1921. See also Inco Archives, Sudbury, Inco Letter Book #14, John Lawson vice-president, to W.A. Bostwick, 2nd vice-president, Canadian Copper Company, 18 March 1913; and Lawson to Bostwick, 20 March 1913.

Sudbury was far from being the dominant urban place in the region, the foundations were firmly laid in the decade of the Great War for that eventuality.

1 Effie Stewart Diary, 20 August and 26 August 1914. I must acknowledge my debt to the late Mrs. Helen Stewart and her daughter, Mrs. Anadel Hastie, for access to this diary, now in the latter's possession. See also *Sudbury Star*, 22 August 1914.
2 *Sudbury Star*, 10 May 1919. By far the most important source for this study has been the *Star*, and this was possible only because of the *Index to the Sudbury Star, 1910-1949* prepared by Laurentian University's Department of History in the summer of 1980 with the assistance of a Summer Youth Employment Program Grant.
3 *Sudbury Star*, 31 October 1914, 15 December 1915, 5 April 1916, and 16 August 1916.
4 Ibid., 5 April 1916 and 1 March 1917.
5 Ibid., 14 July 1915.
6 For example, see *Sudbury Star*, 6 May 1916. According to the records of Branch 76, Royal Canadian Legion, Sudbury, twenty of the eighty-five Sudburians killed in the conflict had French-Canadian names.
7 *Sudbury Star*, 12 August 1914 and 21 August 1915.
8 P.H. Morris, *The Canadian Patriotic Fund: A Record of Its Activities, 1914-1919* (Toronto: The Fund, 1919), 207. Mond Nickel was the British family-owned company whose local headquarters were in Coniston. Canadian Copper, based in Copper Cliff, was the mining subsidiary of the International Nickel Company of New Jersey. See also the *Sudbury Journal*, 15 February 1917. Other war-related organizations were also active in the area, including the Belgian Relief Fund and the Canadian Red Cross Society, but in financial terms their operations were relatively minor compared to the work of the Patriotic Fund.
9 *Sudbury Star*, 23 May 1917.
10 Ibid., 16 May 1917 and 21 March 1914.
11 In 1912 the provincial Whitney government issued Department of Education Regulation 17, which severely curtailed the use of French as a language of instruction in Ontario schools. In Sudbury, a community with a large French-speaking population, the regulation was highly contentious and divided the town bitterly along linguistic lines. See, for example, Margaret Prang, "Clerics, Politicians and the Bilingual Schools Issue in Ontario, 1910-1917," *Canadian Historical Review* 41, no. 4 (December 1960); and Victor Simon, "L'application du Règlement XVII dans les écoles bilingues de l'Ontario" (B.A. honours essay, Department of History, Laurentian University, 1981).
12 *Sudbury Star*, 21 November 1917, 8 December 1917, 9 December 1917, and 2 March 1918. Because of the highly irregular manner in which the soldier vote was taken and then distributed amongst the various constituencies, it is impossible to verify the accuracy of this result.
13 Ibid., 5 January 1918; and *Sudbury Journal*, 10 January 1918.
14 *Sudbury Star*, 8 October 1919.
15 These percentages are based on statistics prepared by the author covering the twenty townships in the immediate Sudbury area drawn from the Census of Canada *Reports* for 1911 and 1921. See also Inco Archives, Sudbury, Inco Letter Book #14, John Lawson vice-president, to W.A. Bostwick, 2nd vice-president, Canadian Copper Company, 18 March 1913; and Lawson to Bostwick, 20 March 1913.

67 *Vernon's Directory*, 1911 and 1921.

68 *Sudbury Star*, 19 March 1910 and 26 July 1913.

69 Ibid., 15 November 1916. Chief Lyle reported that in October 1915 there were 166 cases, whereas a year later there were only 63.

70 *Sudbury Star*, 20 June 1917, 2 September 1917, and 9 March 1918.

71 Ibid., 24 May 1911 and 16 December 1916.

72 Ibid., 23 April 1919.

73 Ibid., 13 September 1913.

74 Ibid., 21 November 1911, 8 May 1915, and 9 June 1920.

75 Ibid., 19 July 1913.

76 *Sudbury Journal*, 7 August 1913; and *Sudbury Star*, 18 February 1914 and 2 August 1915.

77 *Sudbury Star*, 11 June 1913.

78 Ibid., 29 April 1914 and 29 July 1914.

79 Archives of Ontario, MS597, reel 59, eighth annual report of the Sudbury Branch of the Ontario Department of Agriculture, 1918–19, 54–55.

80 *Sudbury Star*, 30 August 1913 and 6 May 1914.

81 Ibid., 7 February 1917 and 4 April 1917; and *Sudbury Journal*, 5 April 1917.

82 *Sudbury Star*, 26 July 1917, 3 November 1917, 4 June 1919, and 18 June 1919.

83 *Sudbury Journal*, 18 April 1912, 16 May 1912, and 7 November 1912.

84 *Sudbury Star*, 25 October 1916 and 14 February 1917.

85 Ibid., 1 April 1914, 28 August 1920, and 2 September 1920.

86 Ibid., 28 August 1913 and 19 November 1913.

87 Sudbury Public Library, Sudbury Room, Sudbury and District Hospital Council Brief, 1966, 10.

88 *Sudbury Star*, 12 October and 16 October 1918.

89 Ibid., 23 and 26 October 1918, 2 November 1918, 9 November 1918, 20 November 1918, and 7 December 1918.

CHAPTER FIVE

THE 1920S

A.D. Gilbert

"What is Sudbury?" enquired the bold headline of an advertisement in the *Sudbury Star* in May 1927. "Ten Thousand thrifty, industrious and contented people," ran the answer. "With the certain growth of mining operations, Sudbury's future is assured."[1] Such complacency and optimism were not entirely typical of the years between the Great War and the Great Depression. For Sudbury, the Roaring Twenties were ushered in by disastrous conditions in the mining industry, followed by bouts of serious unemployment throughout most of the decade. During these years Sudbury became more completely a mining town, with its fortunes tied ever more tightly to a single resource-based industry, which was itself undergoing dramatic reorganization. Despite uneven economic conditions, the twenties witnessed significant growth and development, and at the end of the decade the necessary formalities were begun to achieve for Sudbury the legal status of a "city."

The metamorphosis from town to city reflected the continuing high growth rate in a population that again more than doubled during the decade, increasing from 8,621 in 1921 to 18,518 ten years later, at a time when the provincial population was increasing by only 17 percent.[2] Nor was the town typical of its region, which, excluding Sudbury, grew by only 15 percent during this period. The result, of course, was that Sudbury became even more pre-eminent in the region. Whereas the town constituted one-fifth of the total population in 1921, it accounted for almost one-third a decade later, probably because improved transportation facilities now permitted the mining work force to live in Sudbury and commute to the mines and smelters.[3] As the town became more closely linked occupationally to the mining industry, one might have expected its population to have a high proportion of young single men in search of work, as is thought to be common in mining towns. Such, however, was not the case. Although males slightly outnumbered females in 1921 and by a greater margin at the end of the decade, the proportion of single men was in fact less than the provincial average in 1921 and only slightly greater in 1931. This preponderance of married workers was also reflected in the increase in residential dwellings and households which faithfully mirrored the growth in population.

In other ways, however, Sudbury was a quite untypical Ontario town, particularly in its ethnic and religious composition. The French-Canadian proportion of the population remained constant during the twenties at slightly more than one-third, while the British proportion declined from 50 percent to 36 percent, just fractionally higher than the French, and this in a province where the British constituted three-quarters of the population, and the French only 9 percent. This dramatic decline in the British preponderance in Sudbury was matched by the increase in the "other" category, which doubled to 28 percent by 1931 while the number of foreign-born jumped from 9.3 percent to 19.5 percent. The "others" consisted of a long list of western and eastern European as well as Asiatic peoples, including Finns, who increased from 2.3 percent of the town's population in 1921 to 7.4 percent in 1931, Italians, from 3.2 percent to 3.4 percent, and Ukrainians, from 0.15 percent to 4.1 percent.

This distinctive ethnic profile was visible in the town's religious leanings. During the decade the Roman Catholics, who had accounted for rather more than half of the population in 1921, rose to almost 60 percent, whereas in the province as a whole the corresponding figure was about 20 percent. Although the various Protestant denominations increased their numbers, their share of the total population declined; that was particulary true of the Presbyterians, who lost many of their adherents to the new United Church of Canada, born out of church union in the middle of the decade. If the census data are to be believed, Sudbury was a religious-minded community, with only two self-declared atheists in 1921 and none ten years later, while those professing no religion declined from forty-six to twenty-seven.

What it all added up to was a town that lacked the homogeneity of the province as a whole. The town, in fact, was beginning to take on the appearance of a cluster of communities, each with a distinctive ethnic, religious, and occupational atmosphere. Nevertheless, there was surprisingly little evidence of animosity between the various groups of which the town was composed. In 1920 the board of trade was moved to protest strongly against the new provincial forms for registering births and deaths, objecting in particular to the inclusion of "racial origin" and the directive that "Canadian" was not a satisfactory answer.[4] The board believed that "the regulation would tend to promote and keep alive differences due to a racial origin, instead of promoting the idea that citizens of Canada ... were in the truest sense of the word Canadians."[5]

Despite this laudable sentiment, however, there were a few ugly incidents. "Has Sudbury Yellow Peril?" inquired a heading in the *Sudbury Star* in 1921 over a report of a council meeting at which a long-time Sudbury resident requested that Chinese restaurant licences be restricted to two.[6] "If this thing continues we'll soon be working for the Chinamen," he said. "In my opinion they are a menace to Sudbury." This was not an isolated incident. Over the next few years the council engaged in a running battle with the proprietors of Chinese cafés, which were thought to be hotbeds of vice and in which "white" waitresses were not safe from "molestation" at the hands of the Chinese. At one point council decided to ban women from working in these restaurants and to order the removal of all stalls and partitions so as to preclude any private or semi-private dining areas. The owners responded by seeking legal advice and an injunction from the courts. An uneasy truce was called in 1922 under the terms of which the restaurants would refrain from hiring women and would not press any further legal action. Council, for its part, would allow the stalls to stay and would drop the closure order it had passed against several of the restaurants. If this did not entirely close the issue, at least the issue ceased to occupy so prominent a place on the front page of the *Sudbury Star*.[7]

More sensational were the trial and conviction in 1929 of Arvo Vaara, editor of the local Finnish newspaper, *Vapaus*, on a charge of seditious libel. Although ostensibly the charge resulted from derogatory remarks in the newspaper concerning King George V, the issues went much deeper than that. *Vapaus* was the organ of the Finnish Organization of Canada, a component of the Communist Party of Canada (CPC) that provided over half of that newly formed party's membership during the twenties; the party claimed as many members in the Sudbury region as in all of southern Ontario.[8] Published three times a week, *Vapaus* early in the decade reached a circulation of 2,700, larger than that of the *Worker*, the main party organ.[9] Although little was known about the CPC, communism, in the twenties, was believed to be un-Canadian, un-British, immoral, and un-Christian. *Vapaus* was even more suspect because it was published in Finnish, and lurking just beneath the surface of the *Vapaus* affair was the nativistic fear of an unassimilated immigrant group.

The leading spokesman in the anti-*Vapaus* crusade was the Reverend T.D. Jones of the All-People's Mission of the United Church, also described as "director of non–Anglo-Saxon work in the Sudbury

District."[10] At a meeting of clergy, both Protestant and Roman Catholic, and members of "patriotic and public spirited organizations" held on 22 January 1929, before the charge against Vaara had come to trial, *Vapaus* was assailed as "subversive of morals and good Canadian citizenship."[11] According to Reverend Jones, the Finnish community was "living in terror," isolated by language and intimidated by a small group of communists. Children were being indoctrinated with seditious ideas, and the sanctity of marriage was being undermined, since Finns were encouraged to live common-law. The newspaper was also accused of printing salacious advertisements. "Vapaus," claimed Jones, "seeks to undermine marriage just the same as the Russian Soviets did years ago."[12] At the meeting, suspicion was also directed at the loyalty of the Ukrainian community, which constituted the other main language group within the CPC. Jones called for the suppression of *Vapaus* or, failing that, a requirement that all material be published in English as well as Finnish.

Despite an able defence by Arthur Roebuck, a future provincial attorney-general, Vaara was convicted and sentenced to six months plus a $1,000 fine, subsequently upheld on appeal. This did not quite close the matter. In April 1929 a petition calling for the suppression of *Vapaus* was endorsed by most of the town's religious and patriotic organizations.[13] Within the Ukrainian community, smarting under accusations of disloyalty, the members of the new parish of St. Peter and St. Paul of the Greek Catholic Church signed a resolution affirming their loyalty to Canada and repudiating "all forms of Communism and Bolshevism."[14] That summer police broke up a communist demonstration in Bell Park, and in December the *Sudbury Star*, in an article dripping with sarcasm, reported on renovations being carried out at Liberty Hall, where the floor had been weakened "by the stampings of thousands of proletariat hobnails" and the walls stained "by the smoke of cheap tobacco." According to the *Sudbury Star*, the portraits of Lenin, Stalin, and Trotsky had been temporarily removed.[15]

The dissension between the English-speaking and French-speaking groups, which had emerged during the war, was largely quiescent during the twenties. That it had not entirely disappeared, however, was demonstrated in 1925 when a group of three hundred French Canadians from Quebec, headed by Henri Bourassa, editor of *Le Devoir*, included Sudbury in their tour of the province and were given a civic reception. The purpose of the visit, which followed a similar one to the Maritimes, was to re-establish links between Quebec and francophone minorities in the other provinces, although the *Sudbury Star* chose to interpret it as the imposition of Quebec ideals on the rest of the country.[16] At a stormy council meeting after the reception, a complaint was made about the excessive use of French at the function. According to one councillor, he and others there were "a captive audience and had to listen to all that French." Tempers were not cooled when Alderman Lauzon responded in kind. Many French Roman Catholics, he pointed out, resented the Orangemen being given the use of Lakeside Park for their annual regatta. If Catholics wished to use the park on that day, they would be subjected to speeches which "no Catholic would want to listen to or hear."[17]

These same tensions were evident in a struggle for control of the local branch of the Children's Aid Society. When, after a year of controversy, English-speaking Protestants used their majority position to replace the francophone inspector with an anglophone, the French and Catholic members of the board resigned.[18] Although peace was finally restored and the board reorganized on a more representative basis, the issue was indicative of the social difficulties inherent in an ethnically and religiously fragmented community.[19]

Despite these periodic outbreaks of intolerance and mutual suspicion, the decade was a period of social and institutional consolidation, as the community moved further from its pioneer and frontier origins. This phenomenon had a physical manifestation in the building of churches and schools. The parish of St. Joseph's, for example, which had been created in 1915 for English-speaking Roman Catholics, built a basement in 1923 to be used as an interim church. The rest was completed later in the decade, and the first mass was celebrated on 23 December 1928.[20] During that same year St. Mary's Ukrainian Catholic Church was built with the financial assistance of the International Nickel Company.[21] In January 1924 the town's Baptist congregation held its first service in its new church building on Larch Street, the south side of which became a Protestant stronghold during the twenties. By the end of the decade the Baptist church, the Anglican Church of the Epiphany, and the new Salvation Army Citadel, built in 1922, had as neighbours the Presbyterians and the new United Church of Canada. Although Cedar Street Methodist Church had been rebuilt after being destroyed by fire in 1923, the result of the 1925 church union was the absorption of the Cedar Street congregation by St. Andrew's United Church in 1927. Those members of St. Andrew's who were not prepared to accept the fact of union joined in 1927 with their like-minded brethren from the former Knox Presbyterian Church in Copper Cliff to build the new Knox Presbyterian Church on Larch Street.[22]

For no apparent reason, schools, like churches, showed a tendency to cluster together geographically, particularly in the Mackenzie-College-

Lansdowne district. In the case of the new Mining and Technical School, which opened its doors in the fall of 1921, the location was natural enough, since it was built beside Sudbury High School on Mackenzie Street, and the two schools were administered by a single principal throughout the decade, although the Department of Education was quite firm that the two schools must be separate: "A student must either go to the Technical School or the High School – one or the other."[23] In creating a technical school, Sudbury was in tune with the times. From the war had come a belief that Canadians needed more practical skills, leading the federal government to introduce the Technical Education Act, which appropriated $10 million for this purpose. Despite this and despite the fact that at about the same time the province raised the school-leaving age to sixteen, enrolment in the new school proved disappointing for the first few years, reaching only a hundred by 1924.[24] This may have resulted from a belief that vocational education was a dead end. Certainly, by 1924 the high school board was entering into negotiations with the University of Toronto and McGill to gain admittance into their science programs for graduates of Sudbury's mining program.[25]

Given the religious and ethnic composition of the community, it is not surprising that elementary school enrolment was fairly evenly divided between public and separate schools, although the latter had a definite edge. The town had three public schools in 1920 – Central, College, and Elm – and in that year the Elm Street School was enlarged to eight rooms. By 1929 bulging classrooms led to the construction of a new eight-room school at the corner of Lansdowne and Baker, not far from the existing College Street School, the two secondary schools, and two separate schools – Central and St. Aloysius. Three other separate schools were built during the twenties – St Mary's and Nolin in the Flour Mill area, and St. Thomas on Van Horne Street.[26] Although the hopes of the English-speaking community for a junior college or university in the north – and preferably in Sudbury – did not materialize in this period, in 1927, after several years of fund raising, the Collège du Sacré-Coeur opened a new wing, and a small, but significant number of nurses graduated each year from St. Joseph's.[27]

These manifestations of a maturing community were due, of course, to the expansionary economic conditions of the twenties, which, in the case of Sudbury, were characterized by an increasingly symbiotic relationship with the nickel industry. This was symbolized by International Nickel's announcement in March 1926 that the development of the enormous

Frood deposit, not only would begin that year, but would not be accompanied by a townsite. In the past, inadequate transportation facilities had obliged the mining companies to provide housing at their mine sites, but, in future, International Nickel, according to J.L. Agnew, its head of Canadian operations, would prefer to see its work force housed in Sudbury.[28] Three days later, Mond Nickel confirmed that it too had decided against the construction of a townsite in connection with its developments at Frood.[29] The *Sudbury Star* was understandably ecstatic about what it interpreted as "a wonderful stimulant to the business community and a reassurance ... that Sudbury was due for a new era of prosperity ... from which it would eventually emerge a city, of greatly increased population and enhanced importance."[30] Although these prophecies were true enough, they ignored the less attractive aspects of depending on economic development that was based on the extraction and processing of a single resource and that left the community at the mercy of a volatile international marketplace over which it had no control.

For Sudbury the twenties proved to be an extreme example of the boom and bust syndrome in mining. The war had encouraged a great increase in productive capacity, but the enormous demand for nickel as a strategic material had masked the fact that significant peacetime uses for the metal had yet to be developed. In 1919 International Nickel's ore production was only a quarter of that of the previous year. In 1920 better times seem to have returned, as output more than doubled.[31] Then disaster struck. A severe downturn in the American economy, on which International Nickel depended for its markets, led to an announcement early in November 1920 that production would be cut back by one-quarter and between two and three hundred men laid off. Three weeks later there was a further production cut of one-third together with additional layoffs. In March an announcement of a 15 percent wage cut was accompanied by assurances that no further cutbacks were foreseen.[32] This was followed, in November 1921, by the complete shutdown, until the following September, of International Nickel's mines in the region.[33] As luck would have it, the fledgling and ill-fated British America Nickel Corporation began production in 1920, only to have to suspend operations in February 1921 and lay off about seven hundred men.[34] Only Mond, with its more stable European markets, its better research and development, and its willingness to stockpile during hard times, remained in operation, although on a much reduced scale and with a wage cut for all employees. The summary of metal production for 1922 by the Dominion Bureau of Statistics showed nickel at its lowest level since 1904.[35]

The result, for the town and the district, could be little short of disastrous. In October 1921, foreseeing a hard winter ahead, the town council decided to help create jobs by extending the trunk road to Coniston, with provincial assistance. By January it was necessary to open an unemployment register at the town hall, so that unemployed men could be used in public works on three-day stints at thirty-five cents an hour. Towards the end of that month the council approved the issuing of meal tickets, which had first been used in the hard times of 1914. Two weeks later the increasing demand for relief led to the appointment of a relief officer for the town. In an effort to reduce its costs, council slashed the salaries of all civic employees by a minimum of 10 percent, eliminated some positions, and decreed that half of its weekly relief payment of $1,000 would be used to hire men to straighten Nolin's Creek.[36] Worse was to come, as men from the lumber camps, put out of work temporarily by the spring break-up, began arriving in town. Although the police station could accommodate seventy-two transient guests and the district jail another sixty, this proved inadequate, and the CNR made several boxcars available for overnight accommodation.[37]

At a mass meeting of the unemployed at the Finnish Liberty Hall, two hundred were turned away for lack of room. The lucky four hundred who could be accommodated listened to an appeal for labour solidarity and the overthrow of capitalism by the Manitoba organizer for the Workers' Party of Canada, a front organization for the still clandestine Communist Party. According to the Sudbury Star, fifty-nine men joined up.[38] A further meeting was called for four days later, but by then the unemployed had taken matters into their own hands. On 29 March 1922 a crowd, estimated at between three and four hundred, marched to protest council's decision to discontinue the meal-ticket relief system for transients. They entered ten Chinese cafés and demanded meals. Although very little damage was done, the police, reinforced by officers from Copper Cliff and the provincial force, arrested the apparent leaders of the mob, and after a hastily summoned council meeting, the chief of police informed the crowd that meal tickets would be issued the following morning.[39] With that, the "riot" was over – except that three men were arrested and quickly convicted of unlawful assembly and property damage.[40]

Within several weeks the Sudbury Star was reporting that jobs were opening up all over the north, particularly on the railways and in the lumber camps; only eighty men were left on the bread line.[41] International Nickel resumed production in September 1922, but only at one-third of wartime production. British America did not reopen until the following June and, ironically, by August was faced with a severe labour shortage. In

September International Nickel announced an "entirely voluntary" wage increase that would bring rates for those working underground from thirty to thirty-seven dollars a week.[42] The rest of the decade witnessed a steady and spectacular increase in demand for nickel, until, in 1928, production surpassed the previous record level attained during the war, only to reach an even higher peak the next year.[43] This was partly a result of the buoyant economic climate of the twenties, but it also owed much to the aggressive search for new products and new markets by Mond and by a reorganized International Nickel under the leadership of Robert Stanley. The Canadian government, after being lobbied by the Canadian Mining Institute, supported by the Sudbury Board of Trade, announced the introduction of a new five-cent nickel coin.[44] Engineers, searching for light, high-strength materials, made increasing use of nickel alloys in heavy machinery, mining equipment, aircraft, and, above all, in the automobile, which by 1926 was devouring over one-third of American nickel consumption.[45] Small wonder that the *Sudbury Star* rejoiced at the news in 1928 that the dividends paid to date by the nickel industry in Canada now surpassed those of both gold and silver.[46]

Despite the strength of the nickel industry, however, Sudbury had not seen the last of economic difficulties. In the spring of 1925, for example, the *Sudbury Star* reported that there were eight hundred transient unemployed in town looking for work in the mines, on the railways, or in the lumber camps. An attempt at a public demonstration was unsuccessful, but once more municipal relief was necessary.[47] A much more serious problem, and one that demonstrated the hazards facing a community dominated by a single industry, had occurred the previous July when, without any warning, the British America Nickel Corporation went into liquidation and its seven hundred employees were laid off.[48]

Possessing lower-grade ore but a superior refining process than its rivals, British America had been left in a precarious position by the cancellation of contracts by the British government and the shutdown of 1921. It was also crippled by high energy costs, since, unlike its competitors, it had no hydro-electric generating facilities and had to rely on steam instead. Forced into direct competition with Mond and International, which controlled prices and had divided the world market between them, British America attempted to undercut International's prices on the crucial American market, only to be caught in a full-scale price war. In the end, British America went on the auction block not because of the price war, but because of its own precarious financing.[49]

For a time it appeared that no buyer would be found for the company's mines and plants, which the receiver was hawking around Europe and the United States. Finally, in May 1925, it was announced that an unknown corporation, the Anglo-American Mining Company, had purchased British America for $5 million. For several months Sudbury buzzed with speculation as to the identity of the new owners of the property, amid denials by Mond and International Nickel that they were in any way involved.[50] Then at last it became clear that Anglo-American was simply a dummy corporation created by International and Mond for the purpose of this sale.

The absorption of British America by its rivals proved to be only a prelude to a more far-reaching reorganization of the mining industry in the Sudbury area. For years now International Nickel and Mond had co-existed harmoniously. Their active properties were geographically separated; each had its own refining facilities. Mond looked mainly to Europe for its markets, while International had the lion's share in North America. Together they had a virtual monopoly of the world's nickel supply, particularly after the elimination of British America, and Mond, as the much smaller company, was content to allow International to set the world price. Even the hard times of the early twenties did not lead to competition for each other's customers.[51]

This situation might have continued indefinitely had it not been for two events. One was the decision by both companies in the mid-twenties to develop their adjacent Frood properties. The other was a reorganization of the Mond company that made its Sudbury interests much less important in its overall operations. International's decision to develop Frood apparently resulted from pessimistic forecasts – later proved untrue – about the remaining reserves in the Creighton orebody.[52] In any event, the absorption of Mond Nickel by International, or the "fusion" as Mond preferred to describe it, was only logical given the difficulty of developing a huge orebody, the centre of which was owned by Mond and the rest by International.[53] After months of rumours and the usual ritual denials by both companies, the merger was confirmed in October 1928, and at almost the same time, allegedly to avoid the application of American anti-trust legislation, International Nickel underwent a technical reorganization to emerge as a "Canadian" corporation owning subsidiaries in Great Britain and the United States.[54] As it turned out INCO was not to enjoy a complete monopoly in the nickel trade. Little more than a week after the merger was announced, the *Sudbury Star* reported the formation of Falconbridge Nickel Mines Limited, which had acquired the nickel-copper deposit in Falconbridge township first staked by Thomas Edison more than twenty-five years previously.[55]

This restructuring of the nickel industry necessarily had important ramifications for the town and the surrounding communities. Although they were undoubtedly better served by the presence of two mining companies than by that of one, they were still overwhelmingly dependent on a single industry, a fact to which little heed was paid during the heady optimism that followed the hard times of the early twenties. Much of this optimism resulted from the prospect of further mineral development in the district. "Watch your step," the *Sudbury Star* warned in 1928. "Guard against being carried away in a wave of excitement, and keep one foot on the ground."[56] A lesson might have been learned from the Larchwood coal deposit near Chelmsford. The initial enthusiasm following its discovery was somewhat dampened by the report of the provincial geologist, who confirmed that the deposit was indeed coal, but added that it had one unfortunate characteristic: it would not burn.[57] More encouraging was the development of the Errington mine near Chelmsford to exploit the lead-zinc deposits discovered there. Although the operation was brought to a halt by the Depression, in the twenties it generated a rash of claim staking and prompted the Sudbury Town Council to offer a vacant lot on Pine Street as a site for a smelter, an offer that fortunately came to nothing.[58]

Despite the suggestion that the Errington mine be renamed the "Billion Dollar Mine,"[59] the town's prosperity in the later twenties was derived almost entirely from the healthy state of the nickel and copper industry, which led to large-scale expansion. The development of the Frood deposit was followed by the construction of a new smelter at Copper Cliff with a 510-foot stack – "the highest in the British Empire" – which spelled the end of the O'Donnell roast yard. "It is hoped in this way," commented the *Sudbury Star*, "that the hot fumes escaping into the rarer atmosphere 500 feet from the surface of the earth will be disseminated to such a degree as to nullify the injurious effects they would have on the vegetation of the district."[60] A new copper refinery was begun in 1929, also at Copper Cliff, where, at the same time INCO was constructing a new flotation mill, and CIL a new sulphuric acid plant. Simultaneously Falconbridge was sinking its first shafts and erecting a smelter. Although all of these developments were physically removed from the town, they were to have a profound effect on it. At a joint meeting of the town council and the board of trade in April 1929, a representative of INCO pointed out that the company's construction and development activities at Frood and Copper Cliff would employ 2,865 men temporarily and 3,100 permanently. Since the company did not plan to build or expand townsites at either location, Sudbury would be faced with a severe housing shortage.[61]

In the event, the company decided that it would have to take steps to alleviate the housing problem, and in July 1929 it announced the creation of a special fund from which employees could borrow for the purpose of buying a house. The loans would be repaid through payroll deductions.[62] The plan was probably made redundant by the downturn in the economy later that year. In any case, the twenties witnessed a very substantial increase in the town's residential accommodation, for two unrelated reasons. Under the authority of the post-war provincial Housing Act, the town established a housing commission that financed about eighty houses a year during the early twenties.[63] Then, in 1927, the CPR put most of its remaining townsite property – some four hundred lots – on the market at bargain prices.[64]

Much of the new residential construction was in the west end, now accessible by street railway, and the town was spreading towards what would become known as Gatchell. There was also, however, considerable building in the Flour Mill, the Donovan, and the city core.[65] In 1929 council passed a by-law to establish residential zoning, requiring that any future non-residential use in a designated area would need council approval.[66] The business district was also expanding, although it remained firmly based on Elm and Durham streets. The Frawley Block at the corner of Elm and Durham, which was destroyed by fire in 1926, was rebuilt. Across the intersection J.J. Mackey, president of the Sudbury Brewing and Malting Company, constructed a five-storey building to house stores, offices, and apartments. On Durham Street, the Bank of Toronto put up a new building, as did Bannon Brothers for a furniture store and F.M. Stafford for a department store.[67]

These developments necessarily accentuated the town's metropolitan dominance over its region, which had been clearly established by the beginning of the decade. During the twenties Sudbury's business establishments increased from 342 to 515, while those of Copper Cliff, for example, actually declined. Other changes, characteristic of the age, were noticeable. The T. Eaton Company opened a mail-order store. The town's three livery stables had disappeared by 1930, to be replaced by numerous businesses selling or servicing cars.[68] The railways, of course, were still vital to the town, and their operations received close scrutiny from the town council, which hoped for better service, particularly from the new Canadian National Railways, whose main line skirted the town. It was suggested that Sudbury could have a "union station" if the CNR would either build a new line into the town or share the CPR right-of-way from Coniston.[69] But there was also an awareness that the railways could open new markets for the town's business community, for example in the growing tourist industry on the French and Pickerel rivers, which was being served from Parry Sound.[70]

Increasingly, however, Sudburians wanted roads and better roads. This was only natural given the phenomenal increase in the number of motor vehicles. In the first seven months of 1928 local dealers sold 560 new cars, and in the following year the *Sudbury Star* could boast that one person in ten drove a car and that there were almost 3,000 motor vehicles registered in Sudbury, comprising forty-eight different makes, although the two most popular by far were Ford and Chevrolet.[71] Automobiles carried new problems with them. The exhilaration of speed brought threats from the bench that over forty miles per hour would mean licence cancellation. More frightening was the increasing incidence of traffic accidents and fatalities, which led to the realization that roads designed for horses and buggies were not adequate for motorized traffic.

At the same time, of course, there were obvious advantages to the town from this new and more convenient means of transportation, which made Sudbury's businesses and services easily accessible to people living outside the town. The board of trade urged that roads outside the town be kept open all winter because open roads meant more business. Pressure began to build too for better roads, particularly hard-surfaced roads. The first concrete road in the north, between Sudbury and Coniston, which was completed in 1924, was claimed to reduce the travelling time between Coniston and Copper Cliff by one-half.[72] The most urgent need – according to successive councils and the almost moribund board of trade – was a paved road to Frood, urgent because there was always the chance that poor roads would lead the mining companies to change their minds and develop a townsite, thereby frustrating Sudbury's dreams of expansion. The difficulty was that between Sudbury and Frood lay the township of McKim, which would not or could not pay its share of a hard surface for the road that the province had already constructed. In the end a cost-sharing arrangement was reached between the town, the mining companies, and the province, and work was begun in June 1928.[73] Although the most pressing need was for improved roads in the immediate vicinity of the town, the board of trade occasionally had visions of a larger empire and lobbied for a road south to Burwash or, better yet, to Noelville, before North Bay managed to extend its grasping tentacles to that area. To the north lay the possibility of a highway to Shining Tree, Gowganda, and Timmins. "Sudbury gets cold feet," remarked a member of the board of trade, "and is afraid to ask for too much."[74]

It was perhaps only natural that the increased use of motor vehicles should pose a threat to the street railway. Although the street railway maintained a monopoly on the Copper Cliff route, bus service to Coniston and Garson began in 1923, and to Frood in 1925. After an abortive attempt in 1920 to sell the system to the municipality, the street railway company had struggled along, presumably with better revenues from higher use, but with no attempt to repay the first mortgage on its property held by the town. This situation might have continued indefinitely had it not been for a campaign launched by the *Sudbury Star*, attacking the level of transit service, and the formation of a rival, the Sudbury Transit Company, one of the directors of which was W.E. Mason, who also happened to own the *Sudbury Star*. The new company proposed to use buses on the Sudbury–Copper Cliff route. Stung into action, the street railway petitioned the provincial government for a monopoly on the route. The Sudbury Transit Company responded immediately:

> A couple of hours after Mayor Charles A. Bibby walked into Jerry's Cigar Stand and requested that the street railway petition be posted for signatures, another petition was filed, similar in many respects but lacking the sanction of the Chief Magistrate, who, it so happens, is general manager of the Sudbury–Copper Cliff Suburban Electric Railway and, accomplishing most of his travels by automobile, is well qualified to speak for all those who ride the street cars.

Map 5.1: Sudbury Streetcar System, 1920s: Sudbury–Copper Cliff Suburban Electric Railway (SCCSER)

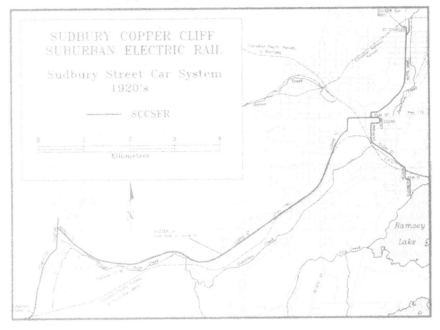

The counter-petition was tongue-in-cheek, but barbed:

> Whereas 800 ... Copper Cliff residents have petitioned for a bus service, many others have purchased cars of their own and numerous commuters would sooner board a bicycle or peregrinate on roller skates than be pummelled into berry baskets by the street cars; ... whereas ... nobody has the right for one moment to think of any such thing as endeavouring to provide adequate transportation facilities since the same thought has never occurred to the Sudbury–Copper Cliff Suburban Electric Railway.[75]

For the moment the street railway survived, although its position had not been strengthened by the controversy.

A more novel form of transportation was introduced to the town in 1925, when, after a year's trial, the provincial government announced the establishment on Lake Ramsey of a permanent air base for forestry work. During that year experiments with short-wave radio were carried out by the Department of Lands and Forests, and for the first time air-to-ground radio was used successfully to report a forest fire. Using a sending key strapped to a board on his knee, the pilot was able to inform the base on Lake Ramsey of a fire in Scotia Township.[76] The town's merchants, quick to grasp other uses of aircraft, arranged to have the forestry planes drop leaflets advertising Sudbury's "Dollar Day" sale of 19 June 1925 on "every town and village" in the area.[77] When it was learned in 1929 that Dominion Airways was considering locating an airport at Whitewater Lake, town council immediately wrote to the company requesting that any airport in the area be near Lake Ramsey. Combined land and water landing facilities could be secured if a landing field were built on the east side of the lake.[78]

A novelty of a different form was provided by the newest sensation – the radio. In March 1922 the *Sudbury Star* published an enthusiastic report of a new radio receiving set recently set up at the Mining and Technical School, where programs from various stations in the United States could be heard over the "wireless telephone." Within a year the newspaper had established a regular radio feature by T.K. Rodger, a local enthusiast who had recently broadcast a report of the Sudbury-Sault hockey game over his transmitter. The audience must have been small, since there were only about a hundred radio sets in the town.[79] The first radio station was CFTR, curiously enough run by the forestry service when its equipment was not needed for its own work.[80]

Another advance in communications came with the announcement in 1928 that Sudbury was to be the eastern terminal in a trans-Canada telephone network that would eliminate the necessity of routing calls to western Canada through Chicago.[81] Sudbury in fact was beginning to think of itself as essential to northeastern Ontario. In 1924 the *Sudbury Star* boasted that its circulation of sixty-five hundred made it the largest newspaper in the north, with subscribers throughout the northeast. With the demise of the *Sudbury Mining News* in 1922, the *Sudbury Star* had a monopoly in the town, and in 1927 its management took over the *North Bay Nugget*.[82]

In local politics the decade was a dull period, and there was an extraordinary degree of apathy among voters. Acclamation became the rule rather than the exception, with mayoralty contests only in 1924 and 1926. The entire council was acclaimed four times. Mayors continued to serve their traditional two terms, and the local political elite continued to be dominated by professional and business people and monopolized by the British and French, the latter now becoming somewhat more active, presumably at the expense of the Irish Roman Catholic representation, which lessened somewhat. The dramatic growth in other ethnic groups revealed by the census was not reflected in municipal politics, where the names of those nominated for office do not suggest any desire to break into this exclusive preserve. Nor is there any indication of any attempt by women to exercise their recently won right to enter the arena of municipal politics.[83]

The revitalization of the board of trade by J. Henry proved to be short-lived. Within two years attendance was down to a handful, meetings were sporadic, and the treasury reduced to nine dollars. Despite the efforts of men like W.E. Mason and L. O'Connor, who was elected president in 1922 "after considerable persuasion" at an annual meeting attended by seven members, to inject the spirit of boosterism into the board, the organization continued to have difficulty in attracting active members and was not a significant force in the town's development.[84] If there was a lack of excitement in civic affairs, the decade nevertheless witnessed a steady, if unspectacular, evolution of municipal services. Water and sewers are prosaic affairs, but necessary all the same, and they were gradually extended through the residential parts of the town. In 1925 work began in the west end, with the installation of sanitary sewers on Douglas Street, and four years later the residents of the Kingsmount district successfully petitioned for water and sewers. Doubts about the adequacy of Lake Ramsey as the town's sole source of drinking water led council to seek the water rights on what was then called Trout Lake, later renamed

Nepahwin. Though the demand for sidewalks and paved streets far exceeded the money available, each year a mile or two was completed, even if only the worst hills, in the downtown, the Flour Mill, and the Donovan.[85]

Electricity too was fast ceasing to be a luxury. At the beginning of the decade the town itself sold electric ranges from a showroom in the town hall in order to encourage their use. In his annual report for 1921, Superintendent R.H. Martindale boasted that Sudbury had over two hundred of these appliances in use, each bringing in an average monthly revenue of $3.84. Five years later the town gave up selling appliances, since there were other businesses in town doing so.[86] The town purchased its electricity from the privately owned Wahnapitae Power Company until the Cochrane estate sold its controlling interest in that company to the Hydro-Electric Power Commission of Ontario (now Ontario Hydro) in 1929. A year later the commission announced the construction of a 110,000-volt transmission line to Sudbury from the Abitibi Canyon.[87] Increased consumption meant more unsightly overhead wires in the streets, although an agreement with the telephone company in 1929 for the shared use of poles somewhat improved the situation.[88]

Growing pains were also evident in the provision of fire and police services. The decade was punctuated by a series of serious fires, particularly downtown, where many of the earliest buildings had been thrown up quickly with little heed for safety. The Frawley Block at the corner of Elm and Durham was gutted in 1926, and another fire six months later heavily damaged four businesses located in the New American Hotel.[89] In the same year the town decided to purchase a new motorized fire truck, thereby freeing up two teams of horses for other town work – except during the winter, when it was felt that heavy snow might prevent the use of the new truck.[90] If modern equipment was important, trained personnel was even more so, but it was not until 1928 that the town began to enlarge its complement of full-time firemen.[91]

The town fathers displayed equal parsimony in their dealings with the police department. During the early twenties economic conditions resulted in a reduction from eleven to seven men. When Chief John Fyvie requested an increase in manpower in 1923, painting a picture of rampant prostitution and vice, he was refused until outraged public opinion forced council to relent and agree to an increase of two.[92] There then ensued a struggle for control of the force. Since the disbandment of the police commission in 1916, council had exercised direct control through its police committee. Because of impropriety on the part of one councillor in his dealings with the police, or so the newspaper report implied, a divided council, at its last meeting in 1923, passed a by-law re-creating a police commission. Almost exactly two years later, council voted to abolish the police commission and resume direct control of the force. Little more than a month later a new council once again, and for the last time, created a police commission to oversee the force.[93]

Despite a report in 1928 that Sudbury was second only to Toronto in the province in the number of its citizens who were jailed, most of the crimes were of the petty variety. The police undoubtedly breathed a sigh of relief when Ontario's experiment with prohibition ended, but the new Liquor Control Act and the Highway Traffic Act gave them plenty of work. In 1928, for example, 1,800 of the 2,300 charges laid in the town were either under one of these two acts or for vagrancy. Either because of its location on the main rail lines or its role as an employment centre for lumbering, mining, and the railways, the town had difficulties with a transient population throughout the decade.[94]

Since Sudbury had a resident district court judge, it necessarily became the law enforcement and legal centre for the region. In 1923 lawyers joined forces in the Sudbury District Law Association to secure a common-law library in the courthouse to which the Law Society of Upper Canada would contribute. The town's central role, together with its own growing population, put a severe strain on the judicial facilities available. The courthouse was considered inadequate, and successive grand juries condemned the jail with monotonous regularity. A jury in 1926 reported, "We visited the gaol and, in common with many former Grand Juries cannot say anything in its favour. It is old, out of date, dilapidated, dangerous and entirely unfit." The law association and the board of trade combined to lobby the provincial government for a new district jail and an addition to the courthouse, as did council, but it was not until 1929 that the province called for a new jail.[95]

The town's hospital also proved inadequate for the growing community. Early in the decade the board of health considered building an "isolation hospital" beside St. Joseph's, to be used for cases of communicable diseases, such as diphtheria and scarlet fever, which were very difficult to control before the discovery of antibiotics and before impure water supplies had been eliminated. There was some consideration given to building a new "general hospital" in the Kingsmount district, but in the end it was decided to add a large new wing to St. Joseph's.[96] In 1923 the Victorian Order of Nurses, which had a staff of one, began making home visits. Two years later, with a thousand-dollar grant from council, a second nurse was hired.[97]

The town had good reason to be worried about public health, for at one point in the twenties it had the second-highest rate of infant mortality in the province, as well as a general mortality rate almost double the provincial average.[98] Although the latter phenomenon was attributed by the medical officer of health, Dr. J.B. Cook, to the fact that there was a large number of deaths in the town of non-residents, the board of health was convinced that one necessary reform was the compulsory pasteurization of milk. A survey by the province in 1925 of the town's twenty milk producers found that between 60 percent and 70 percent of the milk-producing cows were tubercular, a fact that jolted council into passing a by-law requiring that all milk sold in the town be pasteurized. It was more than ten years before the province enacted similar legislation. If a 1928 news report that Sudbury residents drank four thousand quarts of milk a day – 50 percent more per capita than any other Canadian centre – was true, they could at least do so without apprehension.[99]

The lively debates preceding the various referenda on the Ontario Temperance Act suggest that milk was not the only beverage in demand in Sudbury. As in the rest of the province, the battle was fought by organized groups. In 1921 the issue on the ballot was the prohibition of imported alcohol, and in Sudbury a referendum committee, dominated by Protestant clergy, joined forces with the local WCTU to support prohibition and to oppose the demand for government-controlled sale of liquor and beer espoused by the rival Citizens' Liberty League. "Some believe the working man is entitled to his glass of beer," remarked a spokesman for the latter group. "Some believe he should be imprisoned if he takes it, and so we are having an election to try and make the country so dry that a man can't even spit." The Roman Catholic Church remained largely aloof from the controversy. When pressed by the *Sudbury Star* for an opinion, Father Trainor of St. Joseph's responded only, "I will depend upon guidance from on high in casting my vote."[100]

Whether acting under divine influence or not, Sudbury, like most of Northern Ontario but unlike the south, voted resoundingly "wet" both in 1921 and 1924. During the latter year more than $30,000 in fines for breaches of the Temperance Act was collected in the Sudbury district. There must, therefore, have been a sigh of relief in certain quarters when Premier Ferguson announced in 1925 the introduction of "4.4" beer, that is, beer containing 4.4 percent alcohol. Certainly there were more than three hundred applications from the Sudbury district for licences to sell this novel beverage, although some apprehension was voiced over the ability of "Fergie's Foam" to satisfy the raging thirst of the north, "where men are men and drinkers are critical."[101] The answer was perhaps provided by two headings in the *Sudbury Star* in 1926: "874 Homes in Sudbury and District Brewing Their Own" and "Rayside Township is Scene of Big Booze Industry."[102]

The referendum device had largely removed prohibition as an issue in provincial elections, and perhaps this was one reason why those were such tame affairs in Sudbury during the twenties. The other reason, of course, was that Charles McCrea, who held the Sudbury seat for the Conservatives, appeared to be so strongly entrenched that elections became more like coronations, particularly after his elevation to Howard Ferguson's first cabinet in 1923 as minister of mines, certainly an appropriate post for Sudbury's representative. A former town councillor and Frank Cochrane's protégé and political heir, McCrea had held the seat since Cochrane's departure to the federal government in 1911. After a solid victory in the election of 1923, McCrea was returned unopposed in both 1926 and 1929.[103] His appointment to the cabinet was celebrated with a mammoth parade of over three thousand followed by a picnic at Lakeside Park, complete with fireworks and a dance. In Sudbury, as well as in other communities in the area, the day was declared a civic holiday. According to the *Sudbury Star*, which had impeccable Conservative credentials and gave McCrea its unwavering support, the gathering was the largest in the town's history, with the possible exception of the Armistice Day Parade.[104]

As northern Ontario's acknowledged Conservative chieftain and leading organizer both provincially and federally, and the only representative of the province's Roman Catholics in the cabinet, McCrea was a major Ontario political figure. As minister of mines and a good friend of the mining companies, he quickly secured tax concessions as well as the repeal of the special tax on nickel, measures that possibly contributed to the large expansion of nickel mining during the decade.[105] Not even McCrea's influence, however, or the *Sudbury Star*'s scathing denunciations of a continuing Liberal exploitation of the conscription issue was sufficient to elect the federal Conservatives in Nipissing Riding, in which Sudbury was located. Although it probably did no harm to be represented by a member on the government side, on the whole the federal government had much less direct influence than Queen's Park on the life of the town. One exception occurred when the Post Office announced, in August 1929, that twice-daily home delivery of mail would be introduced in Sudbury the following year, provided that the town number all houses, place street signs at all intersections, and extend the sidewalks.[106]

Gradually, Sudbury was acquiring the amenities of a city. In 1926, satisfied that the parks commission was in a financial position to proceed with improvements, W.J. Bell handed over the deed for 110 acres of land beside Lakeside Park on the west side of Lake Ramsey. Although his dream of a grandstand and athletic field complete with baseball diamond, football field, grass tennis courts, bowling greens, a new pavilion, and a community hall in the enlarged park proved impractical, Bell was nevertheless instrumental in preserving a large piece of waterfront property for the enjoyment of the general public.[107] At about the same time, work began on Central Park, beside the skating and curling rink and the Central Public School. It was also decided to change its name to Memorial Park and to erect there a war memorial, for which Rudyard Kipling was asked to compose an inscription. The cenotaph was unveiled on 20 August 1928, the fourteenth anniversary of the day on which the first Sudbury troops had left for the war.[108]

Sudbury was sports-minded, with teams that competed in leagues for baseball, curling, lacrosse, football, basketball, bowling, and, of course, hockey, where the senior team, the Wolves, played in the Northern Ontario Hockey Association (NOHA) and the Cub Wolves in the Junior NOHA. Those less interested in team sports could avail themselves of the Idlewylde golf course, completed in 1924, the Sudbury Canoe Club, organized the following year, or – the latest rage in Sudbury in the twenties – skiing.

Parks and sports were not the only diversions available to the townspeople, although the answer was unclear when the *Sudbury Star* posed the daring question: "Do Sudbury Girls Pet?"[109] Statistics from the Public Library showed a steady increase in members and an overwhelming preference for fiction, and by 1929 there was talk of constructing a library building.[110] The Grand Opera House, in an acknowledgment that times were changing, was renamed the Grand Theatre and began offering silent movies in 1922, although it continued with live performances as well. It received stiff competition from a revitalized Regent Theatre, relocated in a spanking new building – "the finest theatre in Canada for its size" – on Elm Street. The era of silent movies, however, was short: in 1929 the Grand invested twenty thousand dollars in new equipment, which enabled it to advertise "the first 100% natural colour, talking, singing and dancing picture" from Warner Brothers.[111]

One casualty of the era was Chatauqua, the American movement with the mission of bringing cultural enrichment to isolated communities. Chatauqua's one-week summer tours offered entertainment of high quality and were backed by a financial guarantee from local sponsors. The failure to secure this guarantee meant that Chatauqua gave its last performance in Sudbury in 1925. The town, however, still retained its place on the North American entertainment circuit, and the Grand continued to book travelling shows and visits by such attractions as John Philip Sousa and his band.[112]

If the decade did not quite live up to its reputation as the Roaring Twenties, still it was a happy interlude between the Great War and the Great Depression. Nothing in the 1920s could equal the traumatic impact of those events. It was a decade, not of new beginnings, but of solid and impressive consolidation, which both contributed to and resulted from a substantial increase in the population. In all but name, Sudbury grew from town to city and, in the process, strengthened its dominance over the region. Within the community there was consolidation of the physical and social infrastructure. Houses were built, services were extended, the business community expanded. Simultaneously, educational, cultural, and recreational opportunities became richer and more diverse. The most obvious consolidation of the decade was in the nickel industry itself, where INCO absorbed its two competitors and enormously strengthened its dominance of the industry. More than ever before the fortunes of Sudbury depended on nickel.

1   *Sudbury Star*, 28 May 1927.
2   Unless otherwise indicated, these and the following population statistics are from the *Census of Canada*, 1921 and 1931.
3   G.A. Stelter, "Community Development in Toronto's Commercial Empire: The Industrial Towns of the Nickel Belt, 1883–1931," *Laurentian University Review* 6, no. 3 (June 1974): 7.
4   *Sudbury Star*, 12 January 1920.
5   Ibid.
6   *Sudbury Star*, 18 May 1921.
7   On this issue, cf. *Sudbury Star*, 28 January 1922, 4 February 1922, 8 February 1922, 22 February 1922, 18 March 1922, 29 March 1922, 15 April 1922, 5 September 1923, and 3 December 1924.
8   William Rodney, *Soldiers of the International: A History of the Communist Party in Canada, 1919-1929* (Toronto: University of Toronto Press, 1968), 34–35; Ivan Avakumovic, *The Communist Party in Canada* (Toronto: McClelland and Stewart, 1975), 35. It should be noted that the total party membership was small, ranging from 2,500 to 5,000 during this period.
9   Rodney, *Soldiers of the International*, 69; and Avakumovic, *Communist Party*, 39.
10 *Sudbury Star*, 23 January 1919 and 2 February 1929.
11 Ibid., 23 January 1929.
12 Ibid.; see also 15 December 1928 and 12 January 1929.
13 Ibid., 1 May 1929.
14 Ibid., 23 February 1929; see also 22 May 1929.

15   Ibid., 3 August 1929 and 14 December 1929.
16   Robert Rumilly, *Henri Bourassa: La vie publique d'un grand Canadien* (Montreal: Éditions de l'homme, 1953), 661–63; and *Sudbury Star*, 8 August 1925 and 19 August 1925.
17   *Sudbury Star*, 19 August 1925.
18   Ibid., 15 July 1922, 21 November 1923, and 19 December 1923.
19   Ibid., 13 February 1924 and 15 October 1924.
20   F.A. Peake and R.H. Horne, *The Religious Tradition in Sudbury, 1883-1983* (Sudbury: Downtown Churches Association, 1983), 16–19.
21   Ibid., 71.
22   Ibid., 43–45.
23   *Sudbury Star*, 21 May 1921.
24   J. Donald Wilson et al., eds., *Canadian Education: A History* (Scarborough: Prentice-Hall, 1970), 362; *Sudbury Star*, 5 September 1923 and 3 September 1924.
25   *Sudbury Star*, 13 September 1924, 8 October 1924, and 7 January 1925.
26   Ibid., 3 April 1929, 8 February 1925, and 25 August 1928; and *Vernon's Sudbury and Copper Cliff Directory*, 1921–22 and 1930.
27   Ibid., 26 April 1924, 24 January 1925, 22 April 1925, 26 March 1927, 5 June 1926, 25 June 1927, and 8 May 1929.
28   Ibid., 31 March 1926.
29   Ibid., 3 April 1926.
30   Ibid., 31 March 1926.
31   O.W. Main, *The Nickel Industry in Canada: A Study in Market Control and Public Policy* (Toronto: University of Toronto Press, 1955), 101.
32   *Sudbury Star*, 6 November 1920, 27 November 1920, and 16 March 1921.
33   John F. Thompson and Norman Beasley, *For the Years to Come: A Story of International Nickel of Canada* (Toronto: Longmans, 1960), 178–79.
34   Main, *Nickel Industry*, 92; and *Sudbury Star*, 26 February 1921.
35   Main, *Nickel Industry*, 100–101; and *Sudbury Star*, 26 February 1921 and 28 July 1923.
36   *Sudbury Star*, 25 January, 8 February, 19 February, and 22 February 1922.
37   Ibid., 19 October 1921, 14 January 1922, and 1 April 1922.
38   Ibid., 29 March 1922. On the WPC and its relationship to the CPC, cf. Avakumovic, *Communist Party*, 27–30, and Rodney, *Soldiers of the International*, chap. 4. The Manitoba organizer was Thomas Bell, who had played an active role in the formation of the CPC.
39   *Sudbury Star*, 1 April 1922.
40   Ibid., 5 April 1922.
41   Ibid., 19 April 1922.
42   Ibid., 2 September 1922, 6 June 1923, 11 August 1923, and 12 September 1923.
43   Ibid., 12 December 1928; and D.M. LeBourdais, *Sudbury Basin: The Story of Nickel* (Toronto: Ryerson, 1953), 133.
44   *Sudbury Star*, 13 March 1920 and 16 April 1921; and Main, *Nickel Industry*, 91.
45   Lebourdais, *Sudbury Basin*, 132; and Main, *Nickel Industry*, 91.
46   *Sudbury Star*, 11 July 1928.
47   Ibid., 1 April 1925.
48   Ibid., 23 July 1924.
49   On the history of the British America Nickel Corporation, see Main, *Nickel Industry*; and H.V. Nelles, *The Politics of Development: Forests, Mines & Hydro-Electric Power in Ontario, 1849-1949* (Toronto: Macmillan, 1974).
50   *Sudbury Star*, 21 March 1925, 9 May 1925, 3 June 1925, 25 July 1925, and 29 July 1925.
51   Main, *Nickel Industry*, 94–102.

52 Thompson and Beasley, *For the Years to Come*, 204.

53 *Ibid.*, 199–206; and Main, *Nickel Industry*, 104–05.

54 *Sudbury Star*, 23 June 1928, 8 August 1928, and 24 October 1928; Jamie Swift and the Development Education Centre, *The Big Nickel: Inco at Home and Abroad* (Kitchener: Between the Lines, 1977), 24; and Main, *Nickel Industry*, 106.

55 *Sudbury Star*, 3 November 1928; and Thompson and Beasley, *For the Years to Come*, 216.

56 *Sudbury Star*, 14 March 1928.

57 On Larchwood, cf. *Sudbury Star*, 12 August 1922, 18 October 1922, 30 January 1924, 28 February 1925, 10 February 1926, 13 March 1926, and 19 March 1927.

58 *Ibid.*, 1 August 1925, 12 February 1927, 23 February 1927, 30 April 1927, and 4 June 1927; and D.M. Lebourdais, *Metals and Men: The Story of Canadian Mining* (Toronto: McClelland and Stewart, 1957), 281–82, 291.

59 *Sudbury Star*, 30 April 1927.

60 *Ibid.*, 17 October 1928 and 17 August 1929.

61 *Ibid.*, 27 March 1929 and 20 April 1929; and Lebourdais, *Sudbury Basin*, 146–47, 154, 162.

62 *Sudbury Star*, 10 July 1929.

63 *Ibid.*, 17 December 1921.

64 *Ibid.*, 27 July 1927.

65 *Vernon's Sudbury and Copper Cliff Directory*, 1921–22 and 1930; and Bruce Eldridge, "The Sudbury-Copper Cliff Suburban Streetcar System – A Study of Urban Transit" (graduate essay, Department of History, Laurentian University, 1980).

66 *Sudbury Star*, 20 March 1929.

67 *Ibid.*, 5 June 1920, 17 July 1926, and 18 September 1926; and *Vernon's Directory*, 1921–22 and 1930.

68 Judith Topham, "Sudbury: Growth and Development, 1920–1940" (honours essay, Department of History, Laurentian University, 1981), 55, 66–67; and *Sudbury Star*, 14 May 1927.

69 *Sudbury Star*, 29 April 1925, 12 June 1929, and 11 December 1929.

70 *Ibid.*, 24 September 1924 and 24 January 1925.

71 *Ibid.*, 8 August 1928 and 25 May 1929.

72 *Ibid.*, 6 June 1925, 20 November 1929, 15 November 1924, and 25 January 1928.

73 *Ibid.*, 28 January 1925, 28 March 1925, 18 April 1928, 12 May 1928, 13 June 1928, and 27 June 1928.

74 *Ibid.*, 29 April 1925, 28 March 1928, 28 January 1925, and 27 April 1927.

75 Topham, "Sudbury: Growth and Development," 67; and *Sudbury Star*, 8 May 1929.

76 Richard S. Lambert and Paul Pross, *Renewing Nature's Wealth: A Centennial History of the Public Management of Lands, Forests and Wildlife in Ontario, 1763–1967* (Toronto: Department of Lands and Forests, 1967), 243–45.

77 *Sudbury Star*, 8 April 1925 and 10 June 1925.

78 *Ibid.*, 6 November 1929.

79 *Ibid.*, 29 March 1922, 20 January 1923, and 18 April 1923.

80 *Ibid.*, 15 September 1923, 29 March 1924, 30 July 1924, and 1 October 1924.

81 *Ibid.*, 4 August 1928.

82 *Ibid.*, 15 July 1922, 31 May 1924, and 2 August 1927.

83 John Kesik, "A Linguistic and Religious Study of Sudbury Town Council, 1893–1930" (honours essay, Department of History, Laurentian University, 1985).

84 *Sudbury Star*, 5 February 1921, 16 November 1921, 18 February 1921, 2 March 1927, and 30 January 1929.

85 Ibid., 19 June 1929, 13 January 1926, and 18 April 1928.

86 Ibid., 11 February 1922 and 8 December 1926.

87 Ibid., 3 April 1920, 24 November 1928, and 27 February 1929; and Merrill Denison, *The People's Power: The History of Ontario Hydro* (Toronto: McClelland and Stewart, 1960), 192.

88 *Sudbury Star*, 8 June 1929.

89 Ibid., 14 April 1926 and 27 October 1926.

90 Ibid., 3 March 1926.

91 Ibid., 18 January 1928 and 13 February 1929.

92 E.G. Higgins, *Twelve O'Clock and All's Well: A Pictorial History of Law Enforcement in the Sudbury Area* (Sudbury: Sudbury Regional Police Association, 1978), 25–27; and *Sudbury Star*, 9 May 1923.

93 *Sudbury Star*, 19 December 1923, 9 December 1925, and 13 January 1926.

94 Ibid., 17 October 1928, 16 January 1929, and 23 July 1921.

95 Ibid., 5 June 1920, 23 February 1921, 17 November 1923, 5 March 1924, 6 April 1927, 27 February 1929, and 11 May 1929.

96 Ibid., 24 July 1920, 8 December 1920, 23 October 1926, and 4 May 1929.

97 Ibid., 10 November 1923 and 22 April 1925.

98 Ibid., 21 May 1924 and 16 December 1925.

99 Ibid., 6 June 1925, 9 September 1925, and 3 November 1928.

100 Ibid., 16 April 1921.

101 Ibid., 20 April 1921, 25 October 1924, 5 November 1924, and 20 May 1925.

102 Ibid., 10 March 1926 and 26 June 1926.

103 Ontario, Chief Election Officer, *Centennial Edition of a History of the Electoral Districts, Legislatures and Ministries of the Province of Ontario, 1867–1968*, 364.

104 *Sudbury Star*, 15 August 1923 and 18 August 1923.

105 Peter Oliver, *G. Howard Ferguson: Ontario Tory* (Toronto: University of Toronto Press, 1977), 206–7; and *Sudbury Star*, 14 November 1923.

106 *Sudbury Star*, 2 August 1929.

107 Ibid., 3 December 1921, 7 December 1921, and 17 February 1926.

108 Ibid., 23 January 1926, 28 April 1928, and 18 August 1928.

109 Ibid., 9 February 1929.

110 Ibid., 2 September 1922, 7 April 1923, 8 January 1927, and 6 November 1929.

111 Ibid., 26 November 1924 and 13 November 1929; and Dorothy M. Forster, "Entertainment in Sudbury, 1920–1930" (undergraduate essay, Department of History, Laurentian University, 1985).

112 *Sudbury Star*, 8 August 1925, 5 September 1928, and 5 August 1925.

CHAPTER SIX

THE 1930S

C.M. Wallace

"Sudbury is important, really important, though it may not be famous outside the mining circles," wrote British journalist Julian Duguid, who visited the region in the depths of the Depression in 1933. The reason, he continued, was nickel, an essential component in "transformers, motor and generator plants, struts and auto engine pistons, thermostatic metals, tanks for holding chemicals, electric machines, castings, jewellery mountings in white gold, die castings, electric furnace castings." Duguid was worried about the strategic importance of Sudbury in case of a confrontation. "It is a sobering thought. For American capital and enterprise are largely responsible. In the event of opposing interests between the United States and ourselves, Sudbury might figure in the headlines."[1] That eventuality never took place; yet as the article was being written, the world demand for nickel began an upward spiral directly related to "opposing interests." Nickel was the reason Sudbury was the first city in Canada to emerge from the Depression.

The Great Depression devastated most of Canada in the 1930s, but its shadow over Sudbury was pale and short. Sudbury had become a city on 4 August 1930, and over the next ten years, while much of Canada shuddered in misery, Sudburians were prosperous without parallel at the time in the country. The world came for Sudbury nickel, and Canadians rushed to Sudbury for work, increasing the population by almost 74 percent over the decade and more than stretching the inadequate services such as housing, roads, and utilities. Numerous expedients were attempted, but the difficulty of collecting taxes during the early part of the decade all but crippled the city in the later 1930s. The four years of heady prosperity that began in 1933 gave way to disturbing signs of stagnation in 1937 and 1938, but they evaporated with the outbreak of the Second World War in the late summer of 1939.

In the 1930s Sudbury was a destination city. Job seekers and others from across the country took the train to Sudbury, increasing the population from 18,518 to 32,203,[2] or 73.95 percent, over the decade, a growth rate three times greater than that of any other Canadian city. By 1941 Sudbury had overtaken such well-established places as Kingston and St. Catharines to move to the twenty-second position in Canada. The only resource-based city in the twenty-seven cities chosen for extensive analysis in the 1941 census, Sudbury was a mining town with a difference, and an overcrowded one at that. Since the city had only slightly more than four square miles within its limits, the density rose in the 1930s from 4,115 to 7,667 people per square mile, many of them living in substandard housing with poor municipal services.

By national standards it was a young city. About half the growth was from natural increase, a reflection of that young population with a startling birth rate of fifty per thousand population over the decade. The other half was from migrants, largely from Ontario, although over 850 were immigrants, a majority of them women.[3] The result was a slight change in the composition of the population. Those of British origin rose from 36.7 percent of the total to 41.5 percent, while most other groups fell: French from 35.9 to 33.5 percent, Finns from 7.4 to 3.9 percent, and Italians from 3.4 to 3 percent. The Ukrainians went up from 4.1 to 5 percent. The same trends occurred in the surrounding region. In the 1930s Sudbury had a fragmented and astonishingly diverse population. At the top, in control of business, government, and the professions, was thought to be an "English" elite, though the leaders were neither homogeneous nor exclusively English. They were divided among several church congregations, Protestant and Catholic, and among them were some prominent francophones. Sudbury, like practically all others in the province, was an "English" city that conducted its affairs in English, fought for the honour of the Union Jack, and celebrated jubilantly when King George VI and Queen Elizabeth visited in 1939. Queen's Athletic Field received its name in honour of that visit.

While most ethnic groups tended to be concentrated in separate districts, those of British origin were spread throughout the whole city and region, though they were always an overwhelming majority in the city core. The Flour Mill remained predominantly French and Roman Catholic, as did the Valley communities like Hamner, Chelmsford,

Balfour, and Rayside. Capreol was English. Finns were clustered in the west and northwest of Sudbury and in Copper Cliff. The Italians in Copper Cliff were even more densely concentrated, though they moved into the new western suburb of Gatchell in the 1930s. It was this spatial segregation around churches and ethnic clubs rather than the actual percentages that gave Sudbury its flavour, which was captured by the *National Geographic*'s Ontario issue of July 1932:

> In mining towns like Sudbury, group after group may pass you in the Saturday night parade, their talk a language riddle such as fell on ancient Babylon ... [In Sudbury there are] still more Finns, a "Finnlandia" café, and Finns buying talking-machine records of Finnish songs, and Finns squatting about shoe shops and cigar stands, playing more Finnish tunes on mandolins and singing boisterous Finnish songs in a "beverage bar."[4]

That was an exaggeration, no doubt, for the actual number in each ethnic group was not large, and in a sense Sudbury's multicultural diversity became less pronounced during the 1930s. Yet Sudbury was not like Kingston or St. Catharines. This ethnic diversity was to find expression in several aspects of the social and political life of Sudbury. Especially during the difficult early years of the Depression, there were instances of anti-foreign sentiment on the one hand and ethnic estrangement on the other.

As the decade opened, the "boisterous" Finns were highly visible and profoundly divided. "Some of the best miners, most progressive farmers and finest citizens" in the region was the description in the *Sudbury Star*,[5] but the Finns were splintered into several clubs, congregations (Lutheran, Pentecostal, and Presbyterian), societies, and warring ideologies, largely imported from Europe. In 1931 the two main groups were the communist Finnish Organization of Canada (FOC), which published *Vapaus* in Sudbury, and the Conservative Loyal Finns of Canada; the two groups were known respectively as "the Red Finns" and "the White Finns." The Reds, who had a political goal, provided leadership in the attempts at industrial unionism, whereas the Whites concentrated on social and cultural activities. In the depths of the Depression the minority Reds became the target of official repression and of aggression by the White Finns, which hastened the departure of hundreds of the Reds to Soviet Karelia, beginning in 1932.[6] The Whites consolidated their position around the Finnish Hall on Antwerp Street, which was dedicated in December 1935.[7]

The situation among the Ukrainians was similar, though they were regarded less favourably. The Ukrainian Labour Temple Association, which was pro-Soviet, had opened its temple at 189 Spruce Street in the mid-1920s. It was opposed by the Ukrainian Catholic Church, which had been erected on Beech Street in 1928, and by the ultra-conservative Ukrainian War Veterans' Association (established on 9 February 1930) and the Ukrainian National Federation, which set up its headquarters in the middle of the community at 130 Frood Road in 1933. The federation inspired the Ukrainian Grocery Cooperative (1938) and the erection of the Orthodox Church of St. Volodymyr on Baker Street, which held its first service on Christmas Day, 9 January 1940.[8]

The political activity of the radical Ukrainians in the early 1930s was most controversial. Not only had they antagonized the Ukrainian nationalists in Canada by denouncing their claim for an independent Ukraine, but they fought for a socialist order in Canada. A demonstration on May Day 1930 began at the Ukrainian Labour Temple, moved on to a scuffle at a police blockade, and ended in a rally at Bell Park attended by about a thousand people.[9] In February 1931 seven "Parading Communists," all Ukrainians, disrupted a city council meeting and ended up in jail.[10] Another celebrated demonstration, which began at the Ukrainian Labour Temple on 1 May 1932, nearly resulted in a riot: "Spectators Attack Communists When Union Jack Ignored; Stones, Clubs and Fists Fly." Eighteen were arrested that day – six Ukrainians, five Finns, four Slavs, and three Poles. Among those arrested were Mike Kostaniuk, the leader, and one woman, Annie Kinchuk, who was alleged to have assaulted the mayor.[11] With the Depression at full tide, the demonstrators had legitimate demands, but there was little tolerance of such agitators. That fall the deportation of foreigners, mostly "Finns, Ukrainians, Serbs and other Slavs," began in earnest.[12] The conservative forces in the Ukrainian community were left to run their clubs and churches and control their image.

Despite appearances, open conflict within ethnic groups was rare, since most, like the Poles and the Italians, clustered together around their churches and favourite corners for comfort and guidance in a new land. The Poles settled in the Donovan area, organized their Polish Club in 1934, and, on 25 October 1936, opened their "Polish House," where they married, celebrated, and taught their language. The Italians went to Adolfo Pianosi's butcher shop on Domenico Street in Copper Cliff for both food and passage to a job in the Copper Cliff plants. This was near the centre of "Little Italy" with its *piazza* and *bocce*. Wanting their own centre, the Italians founded the Societa Italiana di Copper Cliff in 1934 with the intention of converting the abandoned Roman Catholic church on Craig Street into a clubhouse.[13] The activities of Mussolini in Italy, however, and the support for him by the Italian Fascio of Sudbury apparently raised suspicions and inhibited the club's activities. When Italy invaded Ethiopia in October 1935, Dr. Luigi Pancaro of the local Fascist organization declared, "Well, we do not talk about it very much because we are in a delicate position, but show me the Italian who does not love his own native Italy, and I will show you a bad Canadian."[14] After the outbreak of the Second World War four years later, followed by the Italian-German alliance on 10 June 1940, many of these Canadians were treated as enemy aliens.

The working-class French Canadians began the decade enthusiastically with the establishment of Saint-Jean-de-Brébeuf parish in 1930. A large new church, in Gothic Revival style, was to be built in the Flour Mill district on Notre Dame between Collège du Sacré-Coeur and L'École Nolin and was to be a showpiece and a community centre. All that was built until 1957, however, was the basement, which served as church and hall. Many French Canadians, especially the elite, continued to attend Ste. Anne's in the city core.

The decade also began well for the Irish Catholics, though English-speaking Catholics had become a more correct term. The congregation of St. Joseph's, beside Ste. Anne's, finally moved out of its basement and into a new church, which was dedicated in September 1929; in 1935 the name was changed to Christ the King. But the new church was too small to accommodate the incoming Catholics wanting an English parish, and for this reason St. Clements was created in 1936, Holy Trinity in 1937, and All Saints' in 1938. Overall, Roman Catholics made up 57 to 58 percent of the total population, increasing from 10,785 in 1931 to 18,466 in 1941.

The several Protestant denominations also grew during the 1930s. Members of the United Church increased from 2,184 in 1931 to 5,685 in 1941, making St. Andrew's the largest Protestant congregation in Northern Ontario.[15] Rather than build a new church, the congregation enlarged the old one at the end of the decade. The Presbyterians, who had stayed out of church union in 1925, built Knox and increased their numbers from 1,380 to 1,723. The Anglicans were up 60 percent from 1,901 to 3,094, all accommodated at the Epiphany. The Baptists almost doubled their numbers, from 273 to 596, after building their new church in 1930. By the middle of the decade, however, there was a split among the Baptists, and in 1939 the Sudbury Baptist Church became "First Baptist" to distinguish itself from the Union of Regular Baptists.[16] Certainly the most colourful denomination was the Pentecostals, who, in the summer of 1937, began their ministry in a large tent at the corner of Larch and Minto, across the street from the Salvation Army, which fed, clothed, and housed the destitute throughout the Depression.

Two images of the Depression economy have survived in Sudbury. Some recall the misery and the soup lines, but the majority remember the "good times" and the sports championships. Both views have validity, for there was poverty, and yet compared to the nation as a whole Sudbury thrived. Though the local economy almost collapsed in 1931 and 1932, it recovered dramatically from 1933 to 1937 before stumbling into the war. The pace was set by the global demand for nickel.

In 1929 and 1930 nickel and copper production were at record levels. The decade opened with the claim that in Sudbury "greater and more outstanding progress was registered during the year [1929] than in any other metal mining area of similar size on the North American Continent."[17] Both International Nickel and the new Falconbridge Nickel Company were constructing plants and opening mines. Expansion at Copper Cliff alone created twelve hundred jobs on the gigantic concentrator and smelter that went into operation in 1930. Falconbridge was building not only a modern plant but also a model town with "every modern facility provided for citizens" from the "village pump to a modern hospital."[18] As a consequence, building permits for the district in 1929 were at a record value of $2,311,000, a total never equalled again in the 1930s. Even the $1,252,000 spent in 1930 was more than double any year until 1937.

The momentum from this construction masked the impact of the Depression throughout most of 1930, and there was a notion that Sudbury would avoid the calamity. Prominent stock analysts maintained that "nickel seemed to be unaffected" by the Crash, an opinion echoed in the November issue of the prestigious New York Engineering and Mining Journal, which devoted a full issue to "the INCO enterprise." In March 1931 Maclean's magazine published a feature entitled "Sudbury Looks to the Future," in which Mayor Peter Fenton was quoted with approval: "Sudbury can't miss."[19]

That optimism crumbled during the long winter of 1931–32. The drastic curtailment of both construction and mining put thousands out of work. Layoffs, bankruptcies, and default of mortgage payments and taxes became commonplace. The nadir was the winter of 1932–33. Nickel production and value for 1932 were a mere one-quarter of 1929 levels. Falconbridge had temporarily shut down at the end of 1930, and International Nickel began a series of slowdowns and closures. Coniston was reduced from two furnaces to one in September 1931, and both Creighton and Garson mines had their production slashed. Six months later work at Copper Cliff slowed to trickle. On August 1932 Coniston was shut down completely, leaving only Frood mine in production.

Employment at International Nickel had dropped from 8,839 in February 1930[20] to about 2,000 full- and part-time employees in July 1932.[21] In the meantime, a reorganized Falconbridge was able to put 250 men to work for a few months. Having a lean operation and a secure European market, it even began a small expansion at the end of the year, though it ceased production before resuming operations on 17 April 1932. That expansion was the only bright spot in a very dreary winter. Only welfare prevented starvation among the unemployed.

No dramatic change was expected, and yet "four years of almost continuous 'braking' on the wheels of industry came to an end in the Sudbury district" by 17 June 1933, according to the *Sudbury Star*. International Nickel reopened Creighton mine, expanded Frood, and refired the Coniston smelter. Nickel and copper were essential for cars, electrical components, stainless steel, and shells, and the world nickel inventory was exhausted. Production for 1933 rose by 275 percent, and the records of 1929 were surpassed in 1934. The peak was in 1937, when 224,791,404 pounds of nickel were produced compared to 30,327,969 in 1932, almost an eightfold increase. Copper production more than doubled in the same period. International Nickel opened a $1-million converter in April 1934, and in December of 1935 a $6-million expansion of the smelter was announced. In 1937 the Levack and Garson mines were reopened, and the next year a $10-million crusher was added at Frood. Two and a half million dollars was spent to upgrade Garson mine.[22] Until 1938 both mining companies had record year after record year, and thousands of men found work in Sudbury both during construction and in the mining operations. No place in Canada could match the money spent on materials and steadily rising wages. In the last two years of the decade, however, an unhealthy malaise settled over the industry as production outstripped demand, at least until the outbreak of war.

In 1933 Eysten Berg, representing IG Farbenindustrie of Frankfurt-on-Main, had been in Sudbury purchasing nickel to "test [their] new process" with no application for "military use." "We work very closely with the International Nickel Company, and our relationships are very friendly."[23] This did not convince the Reverend Percy Frank Bull, rector of the Church of the Epiphany, who in 1933 warned of war. "All nations are talking peace and preparing for war," he said. "It may come this month. It may come next April, but it's coming."[24] Mr. Bull, a former officer of the British Army, in which he had served as a chaplain, might easily have been ignored had he not hit a raw nerve. R.C. Stanley, president of International Nickel, personally denied there were abnormal shipments of nickel to Germany and insisted that sales were for "peace time use."[25]

This was a theme repeated by Stanley and the *Sudbury Star* continu-

ously until the war. "There is no nickel at all in rifle or machine gun bar-
rels or even in bayonet steel," Stanley argued in 1935. "Heavens," he said
to the suggestion that war benefits industry, "it would be disastrous.
Industry depends on peace."[26] Statistics were published showing that the
United States received most of the nickel, though no indication was given
of where it went next.

Much of this debate was a response to a resolution by J.S.
Woodsworth in the House of Commons on 21 March 1934 that "Canada
be requested to forbid the export of nickel to be used for war purposes."[27]
He mentioned Germany and Japan among other countries, and called on
the members to support the ideals of the League of Nations. Few were lis-
tening to Woodsworth and most of those who were rejected the suggestion that nickel could be used for war materials. Dr. Joseph-Raoul
Hurtubise, who represented the Sudbury region in the Commons, was
especially upset that an embargo might be considered on the sale of nickel. The debate was closed when the minister of mines, W.A. Gordon,
insisted it would be folly for the government to interfere with the private
enterprise system.

Variations on this debate were repeated every year until the war. On
20 May 1935 Prime Minister R.B. Bennett dismissed Woodsworth's
arguments as tiresome. The next year Italy invaded Ethiopia, but
Woodsworth's exhortations were still to no avail. When Tommy Douglas
took up the battle for an embargo in 1937 and 1938, Minister of Trade and
Commerce W.D. Euler said the suggestion was irrelevant, since there was
no longer "a war demand for their product."[28] With hostilities on the
horizon in 1939, the government finally acted, but not before Douglas had
delivered some hard truths on 3 April:

> Our exports of nickel, which is the basic commodity in
> the manufacture of war materials, have increased since
> 1932 between 200 and 800 per cent. Our exports to
> Germany in that period have increased 1,000 per cent, or
> tenfold, and there are indirect exports to Germany
> through Norway and the Netherlands, increasing the
> exports by a larger percentage. The exports to Japan, car-
> rying on as she has been in the last few years a campaign
> of piracy in China, have increased 5,000 percent or fifty-
> fold.[29]

By then it was too late. Woodsworth, Douglas, and others had obviously expected too much in 1930s. Sudbury's vibrant economy was
almost unique in Canada at the time, and any suggestions that production

be curtailed were naturally greeted with disdain or, in the case of the *Sudbury Star*, near hysteria. Only when the stacks were belching full blast, no matter what the costs, could the economy be kept humming, and who could question that in the 1930s?

The long-term importance of this mining activity was the spill-over effect on Sudbury. Businesses supplying the mining companies, like Cochrane-Dunlop, Felix A. Ricard, and Fowler Hardware, naturally expanded their activities, but it was the increase in the number of stores and services for the enlarged population that stands out. The number of retail outlets rose from 236 in 1930 to 366 in 1941, while net sales jumped from $10 million to more than $20 million during the same period. The number of grocery stores, for example, rose from twenty-nine to forty-nine, restaurants from twenty-four to forty, drug stores from ten to six-teen, tobacco stores from four to twenty-six, and building materials out-lets from seven to twelve.[30]

Automotive sales and service businesses were also multiplying. The twelve dealerships in 1941 were up from seven in 1930, and there were thirty-two garages in total, up from seventeen. Early in the 1920s the taxi was the most common form of motorized transport for citizens; by the 1930s private cars, buses, and trucks took over the roads. In 1932 the Sudbury region had the highest number of vehicles per capita in Northern Ontario. This included 3,914 cars and 400 commercial vehicles, a ratio of one vehicle to every 7.3 persons.[31] Three years later the ratio was one to four, compared to a North American average of one to six. In addition, Sudbury had the highest per capita sales of new cars in Ontario.[32] Sudbury also had a bad reputation. A report in the *Sudbury Star* of 17 July 1935 named Sudbury as the "worst city in North America" for automobile accidents and stated that speeding on very poor roads was considered epidemic. The most serious "bottle neck" in the city was the Elm Street crossing.[33]

This increase in cars stimulated its own expansion. Percy Gardner, who sold and serviced Chrysler cars and trucks, more than doubled his space at the corner of Elm and Lorne in 1934 by adding a second floor and putting an addition on the back.[34] The next year McLeod Motors opened its new sales and service facility for Fords on Larch Street. Imperial, BA, and White Rose, among others, acquired strategic corners for gas stations, equipped with hand pumps and grease pits. By 1938 Canadian Tire had brought its counter service for the home mechanic to town.

Like many other service industries, car and life insurance companies grew in response to increased demand. Arne Ritari took advantage of a need by broadening his insurance business into A.R.M. Ritari Insurance and Travel Agency, the first in the city. The prosperity also attracted several dentists, druggists, physicians, chartered accountants, and lawyers. The new professionals, however, while significant, were not numerous, nor did they have large businesses. In 1941 about 90 percent of all employed men were hourly wage earners. In the mining industry the percentage was even higher. Virtually all women working in Sudbury were hourly workers.[35] Men who worked in Sudbury were the highest paid in Canada, with an average yearly income of $1,391. Women, on the other hand, were the lowest paid in the country, with an average annual income of $484 a year.[36]

During the 1930s, despite strenuous efforts by various union organizers, no unions were organized in the mining industry. In fact, Sudbury was the least unionized city in Canada in that period.[37] The few that did exist were mostly locals of nationals or internationals, such as electricians, railway employees, and letter carriers. None were connected with mining or smelting.[38] The high wages for men go far in explaining the relative failure of unions in Sudbury, but there were others. The unions met with vigorous opposition, especially from the large mining companies and from W.E. Mason, the publisher of the *Sudbury Star*, who attacked union organizers relentlessly. When Noranda union organizers held a meeting in June 1934, for example, Mason wrote, "Loud mouthed agitators ... inspired by the Communists to stir up strife in the Sudbury mines and plants will be given short shift by the workers."[39] A few months later he declared it was "happy days for miners" in Sudbury. "The average workman employed in the mining industry is too well satisfied with his lot to be led astray by paid radicals fermenting disturbances."[40]

In 1933 the Communist Workers' Unity League had established a local of the Mine Workers Union of Canada, with Neilo Makela of *Vapaus* as secretary, but it disappeared within a year.[41] More successful was Local 239 of the International Union of Mine Mill and Smelter Workers, which began to organize Copper Cliff workers in March 1936, though it also was considered communist. George "Scotty" Anderson, a Falconbridge worker, became a full-time organizer, and his brother Hugh edited *Union News*, formerly the *Nickel Bullet*. Local 239 picked up several of the members of the defunct Mine Workers Union "on transfer" and attempted to build on them. A public information meeting of over six hundred at Ste. Anne's Parish Hall on 7 April 1936 was addressed by Mayor Bill Cullen, who welcomed the union to Sudbury. Local 239 lasted for three years, reaching a high of 325 members in 1936–37, after which it declined rapidly when financial support from the international union was withdrawn. The local was disbanded in 1939. Falconbridge Local 361, chartered in July 1937, had even less success.

The mining companies, with the encouragement of Premier Mitchell Hepburn, did much to make union membership unattractive. On the one hand, they used part of their record profits to raise wages regularly, 5 percent in 1936, and 10 percent in March 1937, making Sudbury miners the highest-paid in the country. International Nickel then established a company union, and Falconbridge started a "workman's council." At the same time, the companies punished any worker who dared to participate in real union activities. Workers who were found to belong to a union were fired instantly, a private detective agency was used to place industrial "spies" among the workers, and the distribution of union publications was banned in company towns such as Copper Cliff and Frood Village.[42] The Mine Mill people also claimed that "goon squads" were used regularly to terrorize organizers and workers. "Scotty" Anderson was "molested by thugs and the union office wrecked."[43] Anderson has left this description of an attempted meeting:

> During the organizational campaign in the "hungry thirties" we had a meeting in the Grand Theatre in Sudbury. INCO threw a free booze party in the afternoon, transported over 300 intoxicated potential goons to the meeting. We didn't get a chance to speak. We were howled and booed beyond any opportunity to convey the union message to the workers of Sudbury. The city police stood by and laughed, ignoring the most foul and filthy language being screamed at us, no matter that many women were in the audience.[44]

The suppression of the unions left a legacy of bitterness that was to harden during the 1940s, producing some of the most militant unionists in Canada. Despite the good wages, the mines and smelters were dangerous places to work, with very high injury and death rates. The Depression had permitted the companies to have a free hand to create prosperity, but there were costs to be paid.

Sudbury had become a community sharply divided between the bosses and their workers. The management of the International Nickel Company was geographically insulated in Copper Cliff, where residential and social segregation were enforced rigorously. In Sudbury the professionals sought homes south of the tracks towards the lake. The ever more numerous hourly employees were crammed into overcrowded Sudbury or settled on the fringes on the east and west. During the decade, Sudbury became even more overwhelmingly working class than it had been earlier, for the vast majority of the increased population were wage earners who worked for the mining companies.

"What a week, what a week ... no news anywhere ... The Depression!" The *Sudbury Star* of 24 February 1932 captured something of the desperation as Sudbury headed into its worst year. The difficulties of the early 1930s lingered into the last five years of the decade, effectively crippling the city officials. The paradox was a booming mining industry and a bankrupt city.

Several institutional and administrative changes had followed the incorporation of Sudbury as a city in 1930. Whereas the mayor and aldermen had previously been elected at large, now only the mayor ran city-wide. The five mayors during the decade were Peter Fenton (1930–32), William Marr Brodie (1933–34), Wilfred Joseph (Bill) Cullen (1935–36), John Rudd (1937–38), and William (Bill) Laforest (1939–40). There were now nine aldermen instead of six, three from each ward: Ryan west of the CPR line (Elgin), McCormick east of Elgin and south of Elm, and Fournier north of Elm east of the tracks. The composition of the councils is revealing. Fournier ward returned three French Roman Catholics at every election, over half of them hourly employees. Ryan and McCormick returned no francophones and only four Catholics, a mere 13 percent of all the aldermen in the decade. Of that English group only four were hourly employees, one-quarter were professionals, and the rest, one-half of the total, were owners or managers of businesses (see Table 6.1). The single representative of the ethnic community, Anthony Gustiani, was a contractor who served in 1931. Throughout the 1930s the city's business was run by professionals and businessmen, usually Ontario or British-born English-speaking Protestants or French-Canadian Roman Catholics.

The list of aldermen reads like a who's who of Sudbury: Charles Carrington, Cecil Facer, George McVittie, H.M. Claridge, D.H. Andress, Percy Morrison, Frank Muirhead, Bill Laforest, Oscar Noel de Tilley, and J.F. Frank Lemieux. John Simpson, owner of the Plumbing, Heating and Sheet Metal Works, and Ed White, proprietor of Westbrooke Coal and Wood, each served on council for six of the ten years. Noel de Tilley, the assistant manager at Laberge Lumber, was one of three francophones who served for four terms. Stability marked the council, especially after 1932, and, with some notable exceptions, there was a consensus about most matters.

Fenton was the controversial populist mayor through the worst of the Depression. Though a people's mayor, he could be high-handed and slipshod. On assuming office in 1930 he promised a new town hall, a subway under the Elm Street tracks, improved water, sewage, and hydro services, and better fire protection. But he accomplished little except the incorporation of Sudbury as a city and the opening of a new jail. The city was allowed to annex the small built-up area west of Regent and south of MacLeod (on 1 January 1931), but an attempt to solve taxation problems with "equalized assessment" was divisive.

One immediate and beneficial result of the granting of city status was a greater participation in the electoral process. Since A.J. Samson had defeated Fenton in 1926, all succeeding mayors had been acclaimed for two years, and some council seats actually remained unfilled. In 1930, however, candidates in abundance ran for the city council – three for mayor and twenty-four for aldermen. One of the candidates for the mayoralty was Tom Travers, who had been mayor in 1916. Charging Fenton with incompetence, inefficiency, and excessive expenditures, he gathered wide support. Fenton ran an expansionary campaign with the slogan "Sudbury is a progressive city; we should be optimists and boosters, not pessimists and knockers."[45] The third candidate was Fred Korpinen, a communist from *Vapaus*; he received 69 votes. Travers got 1,278, and

Table 6.1
Occupations of Members of City Council, 1930–1940

Occupation	Number
Company owners and managers	14
Lawyers	3
Small retailers	3
Self-employed	2
Insurance	2
Chiropractor	1
Undertaker	1
Foremen and supervisors	3
Hourly employees	12
Other	1
Total	42

Fenton won with 1,373 in the largest turnout up to that time. Only two aldermen survived that first city election, and Fenton was returned in large part because a second term for mayors had become the norm in the 1920s. In 1931 he was faced with two crises: a cabal and the Depression.

It was common for aldermen to unite for a common purpose, but when the Catholics lined up against the Protestants in 1931, the effect was explosive. "Alderman Laforest, the Crusader" led four other Catholics: J.B. Ducharme, Paul Savard, A. Gustiani, and Bill Cullen.[46] As stated by Laforest, their objective, and the purpose for which they had been elected, was to make the management of the city's affairs more efficient. Nevertheless, they were suspected of a conspiracy. Using their majority, they first had the city treasurer, H.R. Grant, fired and replaced by A.J. McDonell. They charged R.H. Martindale, who managed the waterworks and the David Street power plant, with inefficiency, and found fault with William McMullen, the city engineer. When Grant was dismissed, the Lions Club protested in writing, and its spokesman, Dr. H.M. Torrington, stated to council, "It looks as if it were a straight question of the Catholics lining up against the Protestants."[47] Laforest and his "coterie of aldermen," according to the Sudbury Star,[48] continued their efforts throughout the year, and in December Laforest, listing himself as "gentleman," opposed Fenton for the mayoralty in the "hottest election Sudbury ha[d] known."[49]

According to Laforest, Fenton had promised to support a French-speaking candidate in the election. Instead, he ran for a third term himself, arguing there was a need for experience to combat the problems of the Depression. Laforest charged him not unfairly with "nepotism and profiteering," "reckless spending," and using "poor business methods."[50] There can be little doubt that this election was the "most intense and most bitter" in the history of the city. Fenton won by a margin of only twenty-one votes, which was lowered to thirteen in a re-count. Though the split was partly between Catholics and Protestants, the split between the French and the English was even more pronounced.[51]

The results of the aldermanic elections suggest that Fenton owed his re-election to the emotions stirred up by the religion and language issue, for only two of the nine sitting aldermen were returned. The ratepayers' associations in McCormick and Ryan, who had demanded "retrenchment and economy," elected slates of high-profile businessmen, none of them Catholics.[52] They included the lawyer W. Marr Brodie, two company owner-presidents, Charles Carrington and D.H. Andress, and a company manager, W.J. Barager. Their mandate was to straighten out the city finances and to control Fenton. The Depression made their job difficult.

A year earlier, at the end of 1930, Sudbury had begun to be touched by mounting unemployment. "We are out of work and starving," declared the leader of a delegation before council at the end of October. "What are we going to do?" Fenton met this "Red outbreak" with an emergency police squad of war veterans specially equipped with "50 batons."[53] He was also aggressive with the demonstrators of 1 May 1932, assuming the leadership in what he called "anti-Communist week in Sudbury."[54] Though Fenton castigated political agitators, especially when "foreigners" were involved, he usually showed compassion for the unemployed. That side of him was seen in a medical crisis a few weeks later.

Doctor's bills frequently went unpaid in the 1930s, and when a young "expectant mother ... left on the doorsteps of St. Joseph's hospital" was denied immediate treatment, Fenton ordered the doctors to treat her because "a doctor has certain obligations to fulfil, obligations that he undertook when he joined his profession."[55] The response of the medical profession was a declaration that "unless they are paid, or unless the city guarantees the accounts, they would no longer attend persons on relief."[56] Dr. Torrington stated, "Mayor Fenton's statement is absolutely wrong ... No doctor has ever been bound by oath to attend anybody"; he was supported by the Canadian Medical Association then meeting at the Royal York Hotel in Toronto. Fenton had pleased the unemployed, but he received poor marks for diplomacy and did little to solve the problem.

Though Fenton had some council support in this case, he often stood alone against his hard-nosed aldermen. When council imposed inquisitorial regulations on those seeking relief in July 1932, only Fenton mentioned how "keenly" the recipients felt the disgrace of the relief. Assistance was to be refused anyone with a car or telephone. In Alderman Brodie's opinion, a claimant with a car should "sell it and live on the money." Alderman Andress felt justified in his stand because "one man whose lights were cut off asked the treasurer how his wife was going to run an electric stove, washing machine, vacuum cleaner and radio with coal oil."[57]

To be fair, Sudbury had done more than most communities for the victims of the Depression, and at a very high cost. As soon as the "dire circumstances" of some citizens became known, the old jail was turned into a "flop house," which housed 4,142 guests in December 1930 alone.[58] By the end of January 1931, between 375 and 400 were being fed twice a day at soup lines. This was reduced to one meal a day on 16 March in an attempt to force the recipients to look for work, which did not exist. By the beginning of April, 1,693 married men were registered as unemployed, over 400 men were being fed, and 170 families were getting assistance. By the end of the month the city had served 102,329 meals at a cost of $6,591.52,[59] which had not been budgeted for. Alderman Laforest, as chairman of the finance committee, was blunt: "We must call a halt," and he forced a curtailment of all expenditures while unemployment increased, forcing even more to seek relief. With about two thousand on the city's doorstep by the end of the summer, council had no choice but to provide for them. Fenton, in deciding to run against Laforest that fall, declared, "No citizen would object to paying three mills more taxes to help the men out of work."[60] He appeared to be in a minority, and the following year the new council would not tolerate his erratic activities after his re-election.

Led by W. Marr Brodie, the 1932 council attempted to administer welfare on strict business principles by reorganizing the relief organization, which screened applicants carefully, required them to answer eighteen questions, and rejected transients. Yet as Alderman J.D. McInnes, chairman of the relief committee, told the Central Volunteer Relief Organization, over four thousand persons, about one-quarter of the "permanent population of the city," were on relief of one kind or another at a monthly cost of twenty thousand dollars.[61] Although the city was responsible for only one-third of that cost, it was a third it did not have. Taxes could not be collected, and debentures could not be sold. In desperation council again tried to eliminate as much welfare as possible and to be punitive with those who got it. "The city of Sudbury can't do any more," McInnes told an angry crowd in early September. Maurice Ouimet, the leader of a group of unemployed, shouted, "We can't wait longer. We're hungry and if you don't give us food we're going to get it ourselves. Our children have nothing to eat."[62] Mayor Fenton averted the crisis by delaying the cutbacks, and a worried province ordered the creation of a welfare board for Sudbury,[63] to be chaired by Alderman McInnes. He and Fenton soon clashed over relief when the mayor continued to administer as he saw fit, often granting welfare to those rejected by the committee. Actions like this became the main issue in the civic election that December. Laforest, who was temporarily out of politics, had become the district relief officer and was active in the "Back to the Land" movement. Alderman Brodie, who was a lawyer, took on Fenton and his "spending orgy" in 1932, defeating him decisively 3,138 to 1,591.[64] For the rest of the 1930s there were few places for men like Fenton. Sudbury was to be administered like a company.

With good luck and good management Brodie gave a new direction to municipal politics in Sudbury. The revival of the nickel industry in the summer of 1933 was the good luck he needed. On the management side it was retrenchment with a vengeance. The "dole" was abolished,[65] and he appointed businessmen to a new welfare board that made relief directly dependent on work done by the applicant. He then turned to the city employees, releasing several, including five firemen and three policemen, and reducing the salaries of others. The city sewage plant and incinerator, the next targets, were closed at a saving of a thousand dollars a month,[66] though he was opposed by several councillors and the board of health eventually forced council to reopen the sewage plant and incinerator. In the summer the soup kitchens were transferred to "private enterprise" at a significant saving. The city also began to deny such services as water and hydro to those who did not pay for it and to take court action against those who had not paid their taxes. In October there were still 546 heads of families with 2,124 dependents on relief.[67]

Despite appearances, Brodie was not heartless. The city was under enormous pressure from the provincial government and debenture holders. The province demanded economy from municipalities on the one hand, and then shuffled off an ever-increasing relief burden onto them, on the other. In an attempt to solve its own problems in October, the province decided to shift an additional monthly relief charge of $8,650 to Sudbury. Since this was "absolutely out of the question" to the city, Brodie stormed into Queen's Park and put his case so strongly that the provincial government agreed to "take complete charge" of the administration of relief in Sudbury.[68] Brodie had a good case, for two weeks later the city defaulted on the payment on the principal of bonds maturing that winter, though it continued to pay the interest. Sudbury could not bear the costs of relief and was in danger of going into receivership, already the fate of over thirty Ontario municipalities.

That no one could have done better than Brodie and his council was widely recognized. He was unopposed for 1934 and his whole council was returned. Despite council's efforts and the improved employment prospects, there was no way to avoid paying relief to the unemployed. In July 1934 there were 2,763 in Sudbury alone at a cost of $22,295.95.[69] A month later the bondholders filed suit against Sudbury and were only prevented from foreclosing by the intervention of the Ontario Municipal Board.[70] Under Brodie the city's debt was decreasing and expenditures were being controlled. That a sense of desperation prevailed, however, was demonstrated towards the end of 1934. When the apparent cause of the Depression was "traced to women in industry," five of the Sudbury council supported a resolution from St. Thomas asking for provincial legislation forbidding women to work in industry if their husbands were gainfully employed. There was no mistaking the belief that a woman's place was the home. Mayor Brodie took exception, noting that several Sudbury businesses were run by women, and it would be nonsense to expect them to leave when they married.[71]

By the end of the year Brodie and several of the men who had been with him on council for three years had had enough of "retrenchment" politics. Bill Cullen, a CPR dispatcher, was mayor in 1935 and 1936, and a thankless job it was to be. On 21 June the province forced Sudbury into receivership. Russell Merkel was named trustee and "all cheques, payrolls, and payments from city funds must be approved" by the Department of Municipal Affairs.[72] The order, which was not lifted until 1941, was totally unexpected and probably unnecessary, for North Bay, which was in worse circumstances, was left alone. Through careful debt management over the previous three years, Sudbury was almost unique in having improved its financial situation.[73] The action of the province was never fully explained, though its fear of creditors certainly played a part. No doubt W. Marr Brodie, the new vice-chairman of the Ontario Municipal Board (OMB), had a hand in it as well. He had been appointed because, in the words of Municipal Affairs Minister David Croll, he was "one of the most capable civil administrators in the province" and had done an outstanding job in "one of the most difficult municipal situations in the province."[74] One of his first tasks with the OMB was to review Sudbury's estimates and make recommendations. Perhaps he was protecting Sudbury from its creditors and from the numerous demands in the city for expensive services such as roads and sewers.

What is usually forgotten is that the booming nickel industry that was attracting thousands of people to Sudbury to find work was making no direct contribution through local taxes in Sudbury, where the majority of the people now lived. In 1935 the accumulated debt was over $3 million, tax arrears were over $561,000, and punishing expenditures on relief and welfare continued throughout the decade. In the summer of 1935 there were still over 2,500 on relief, though the number declined to 1,763 in April 1936. As late as 1940 over $79,000 was required for relief.[75] With full employment this might appear incongruous, but to Mayor Cullen there was a simple explanation. "The boom is a boomerang," he declared to a delegation of Canadian mayors in Ottawa seeking federal aid in November 1935, for it had created a national whisper campaign: "Go to Sudbury."

Neither Mayor Cullen nor any of his successors in the 1930s discovered a solution. The population rose dramatically from 20,079 in 1935 to 32,301 in 1940, a 61 percent increase,[76] compelling additional expenditures on health and sanitation, highways and streets, water and sewers, welfare, police, and fire protection. There were, in addition, demands for housing, schools, hospitals, and public transit. With much of the rest of the province still in the Depression, Sudbury's special needs received scant attention. The provincial trustee did permit the city to double its expenditures for health, sanitation, and police protection, and its highway and street budget rose from $38,737 to $140,446,[77] but the moneys had to be raised from the already overtaxed property owners. The increased costs were partially offset by the non-industrial construction of the later 1930s, but with no industrial property, the levy on individual property owners continued to be oppressive.

By the middle of the decade the city had reorganized most of its departments and services into efficient agencies. Although the distribution of electricity in the city had been notoriously inefficient, it had made a profit, which council diverted to the general revenue. On 1 January 1936, under pressure from the Hydro-Electric Power Commission of Ontario, the Sudbury Hydro Commission was created as an autonomous unit, with the mayor one of the commissioners. Under this new system the service was improved and extended; by 1941 it covered 99.3 percent of all households.[78] The residents of Sudbury were better served but the city council lost revenue. All the while, streets, water mains, and sewers had to be built for new subdivisions, for which there had been no overall planning. In 1937 Mayor John Rudd sought advice on town planning from A.J.B. Gray, the supervisor of the department of municipal affairs. Soon after, the city hired George Proctor, a Toronto expert in property assessment, with a view to equalizing assessments and improving taxation. The system recommended by Proctor was imposed a year later. There have been few greater failures in Sudbury municipal history. Shocked property owners appealed their assessments by the hundreds, over fifteen hundred of them successfully. His work rendered worthless, Proctor was fired in November 1939 at the height of the "scandal" and in the middle of the municipal election. Mayor John Rudd, not without reason, was soundly thrashed by Bill Laforest.[79]

Laforest, an aggressive alderman who showed considerable financial skill as chairman of the finance committee in 1930, 1936, and 1938, had lost to Fenton in the controversial 1931 election, but became a dominant public figure of the decade, both on and off council. Returned to council in 1936 and 1938, he was elected mayor in 1939 after losing yet another difficult election in 1937. That year Laforest appeared assured of victory until J. Frank Lemieux, a lawyer, entered the contest, splitting the French vote. Though Laforest carried Fournier easily, he was still regarded with suspicion outside.[80] That there were recriminations about Lemieux's running was to be expected, but Lemieux was not a crank candidate. He received substantial support in his campaign for a "Greater Sudbury," making him an apostle of the modern regional municipality.[81] Lemieux did not run for 1939, and Laforest had the landslide victory over Rudd.

Laforest's victory suggests that much of the religious and linguistic animosity that was obvious at the beginning of the decade had dissipated, though it had certainly not disappeared, especially the language division. Laforest had significant majorities in all wards except Rudd's own, McCormick, and even there Laforest did well.

The problems of municipal taxation in Sudbury continued for decades. Still at the mercy of the provincial trustee, the city continued to muddle through without any real blueprint to control its chaotic growth. Throughout 1939 the Sudbury Businessmen's Association petitioned the city for a planning board. On the advice of a consultant the creation of a Sudbury Town Planning Commission was finally recommended on 2 January 1940, just as the Second World War made planning essential in all matters.

When Julian Duguid of the *London Daily Telegraph* visited Sudbury in 1933, he found it "quite horribly familiar," so like all smelter towns:

> There were the same forlorn buildings against a background of dun hills, the same baked earth and slag heaps; all vegetation killed by sulphur fumes from the smelter. It was as if these houses knew they would be abandoned should the mines run out. Yet the inhabitants, I know, would account it blasphemy to speak one word against the place.[82]

Nothing that happened in Sudbury in the 1930s changed that image; in fact, it might even have been magnified. The increased smelting activity continued to blacken the rocks and stunt the trees. The expanding population caused a haphazard growth of cheap dwellings in a city that showed no capacity for planning and had little money for services. At the beginning of the decade Mayor Fenton had elaborate plans for improvement and alderman J.B. Ducharme talked about a "town planning commission,"[83] but all the schemes were shattered by the Depression.

Yet as Duguid noted, Sudburians loved their city, scars and all. In the 1930s it was still a very compact city. The post office at the corner of Elm and Durham was at the centre, a twenty-minute walk at most from anywhere within the city limits. All the main churches, banks, and stores were downtown, including the newly expanded Canadian Department Store, as Eaton's on Durham was then called. It was a rare shopper who did not spend a good part of the day there. Cochrane-Dunlop hardware store was frequently included in a typical week, as was

Silverman's, which was remodelled and enlarged just before Christmas 1935. Residents walked along Durham and Elm to the post office and then went northeast to the Borgia Market, often along the tracks, for fresh fruit, vegetables, meat, and fish. At the end of the day, loaded down with packages, they could take the streetcar home, but the system was "cold, unhealthy and crowded," especially at shift change time. "If any railway packed cattle into cars the way men are packed into those street cars," declared one user, "the humane society would get after them and bring them to court."[84] In 1932 the system went bankrupt and was taken over by the city. By 1940 the automobile had made it all but irrelevant, and by then the population had sprawled east of Sudbury along Howey and west on Copper Cliff Road.

Starting in 1935, a residential building boom was under way. Single-family dwellings dominated in the fringes, and apartment buildings were erected in the core. It was in this era that Howey Drive was settled. Development started on subdivisions to the west, south, and east of Minnow Lake, including one called Brodie in 1937, in memory of the former mayor, who had died on 6 May that year. Houses were also being built on the western and eastern end of Gatchell and in the large block south of Lorne. Moving farther south, development started in the Martindale area off Regent as well as on Maki Avenue.

The typical Sudbury house was a small one-storey family dwelling, with an average of 4.4 rooms, fewer than in any other Canadian city. The majority of the houses were valued at less than four thousand dollars, which was at the low end of the scale. Almost all of them had running water (97.6 percent), but only two-thirds had private toilets, and only slightly more than half (51.5 percent) had private baths, the lowest percentage in Canada.[85] About a third (31.8 percent) were heated by wood, the other two-thirds by coal. Electricity was becoming more popular for cooking, but wood and gas still dominated.

At the beginning of the decade half of all Sudburians owned their own houses, but by 1940 that percentage had fallen to 39 percent. The single men continued to live in the large boarding houses in the Donovan, but these were unsuitable for the young families, which were in greatest need. More and more people were forced to live in apartments. In 1930 there were only thirty-seven relatively small apartment blocks in Sudbury; by 1940 that figure had more than doubled to eighty, as new buildings went up, especially on Elm, Cedar, Pine, and Bloor. Some had pretentious names like Hampton Court, Dufferin Terrace, and Wembley Court, and they were expensive. In fact, there were only three places in Canada with higher average rents than Sudbury's: Halifax, Outremont, and Ottawa.[86]

More than accommodations were expensive in the thirties. The high wages meant inflated prices for almost everything. Although the differences were insignificant at the beginning, from 1933 onward the cost of almost all essentials was considerably above both the Ontario and the Canadian averages. Milk stayed two to three cents more a quart for the decade, eggs were two to five cents more a dozen, butter was one to three cents more per pound. For some reason coffee was always cheaper in Sudbury than in the rest of the country, though that was small consolation when coal averaged three dollars more a ton and oil was two to five cents more a gallon.[87] The amounts may not seem great, but they were 10 to 25 percent more than the rest of Canada was paying.

Because of the high prices, especially rent, people were forced into the outlying communities, where the most fortunate got into cheap company housing in places like Coniston or Falconbridge. Others lived in the "shack towns" in the Valley, where there were no by-laws. You could grow the essentials and keep cows, pigs, and chickens. Some even produced enough to sell at the Borgia Market, and they often came by in horse and wagon. Despite the arrival of the car, the horse still had its place on the streets and roads, especially for delivering milk, bread, coal, and wood.

During the spring thaw a horse sometimes provided the only means to travel the flooded and muddy roads. Junction and Nolin creeks overflowed almost every year, washing the roads into nearby basements. Though Sudbury did have twenty miles of paved streets by 1940, most were still gravel, and the roads in and out of the city were frequently impassable in the spring. There was little money for improvements in the 1930s. People lucky enough to be near the railway could avoid the roads, and often took the milk run from Coniston to Sudbury and places up to a hundred miles away.

Except for the very adventurous car traveller, the train was the only link between Sudbury and places outside the region, and almost all travellers spent some time at the train station on Station Street (now Elgin) or visited at least one of the establishments nearby like the Pacific Cafe or the Sudbury Hotel. The Prospect Hotel opened for that traffic in the 1930s. Those with more time crossed the creek to Elgin on their way to the still respectable King Edward or, after 1938, the stunning new art deco Coulson. With its "studied streamlined design," it offered "hot and cold running water" in every room. It also had "two commodious beverage rooms, one for women and one for men ... The men's beverage room is designed with utilitarian purpose the main object ... [The women's has] a pleasant combination of colours, with indirect lighting, and stainless steel furniture."[88]

After liquor and beer sales were legalized in 1934 the licensed beverage room became part of the Sudbury landscape. With such a high percentage of young single men, it was perhaps unavoidable that the tavern became the centre of many people's social activities, and Sudbury offered a wide range of choices, from the modern Coulson to the joints on the fringes. Long Lake Road, which began where the General Hospital is now situated, drew a steady stream of clients to "Chi Chi's" south of the bridge at Ramsey Lake. Farther along on Nepahwin, Madame Pigeau's Blue Lantern offered even more stimulation.

Ramsey Lake was the centre of the most exciting novelty of the 1930s, airplane trips. A Saturday flight over the Nickel Basin or to some wilderness lake for fishing was considered very daring. Several operators were in the area, and regular flights to Chapleau or Timmins were available at certain times of the year. The first to offer a scheduled service were Jack and Charles Austin, who flew their Waco seaplanes off Lake Ramsey to Toronto. From a modest beginning on 1 March 1934, Austin grew into a major regional carrier with fabled pilots like Rusty Blakey, who joined them in 1937. By that time, flying, especially in flying clubs, had become a passion with people like Baxter Ricard and the Northern Ontario Flying Club, which was agitating for an airport on its property off Garson Road. Until the 1950s, however, the only air service was provided by the seaplanes on Lake Ramsey – a clear indication of the limits of Sudbury's growth.

In Sudbury's collective memory the hockey championships of the 1930s are of first importance. Sixty years later the notions of Sudbury's sports prowess are based on those victories. They began when the 1932 Cub Wolves won the Memorial Cup and ended with a world championship at Prague in 1938 for a senior version of the Sudbury Wolves. In the intervening years Sudbury teams captured one national and several provincial titles. The 1932 victory of the Cub Wolves under their coach Sam Rothschild and their manager Max Silverman over the Winnipeg Monarchs has a mystique for Sudburians that cannot be matched. An all-star team of Falconbridge and Sudbury players, the team won the Northern Ontario title on the soggy natural ice of the Palace Rink at the end of February, and then left on its month-long quest, always the underdog against such teams as the Toronto Marlboroughs at Maple Leaf Gardens, the Ottawa Shamrocks, the Montreal A.A.A.s, and finally the Winnipeg Monarchs. The *Sudbury Star* secured a special radio licence to broadcast the Montreal games and the last Winnipeg game back to

Sudbury. When the final whistle was blown and the Cub Wolves had won by a single goal, people rushed out into the streets of Sudbury, shouting, singing, and dancing around bonfires. It was a scene matched only by the celebrations at the end of the Second World War. Rothschild and Silverman became local folk heroes, and one of the players, Hector "Toe" Blake, a hockey figure of national prominence.

Sudbury has never duplicated that victory of its local boys over the best in Canada. All subsequent teams were strengthened or dominated by "imports" who were attracted by the money of prosperous Sudbury. In 1935 the Cub Wolves lost in the Memorial Cup finals to the Winnipeg Monarchs. The next year the Sudbury Falcons, a senior team, lost in the Allan Cup finals to the Kimberley Dynamiters. The Frood Mine Tigers, which included some of Canada's top amateur players, captured the Allan Cup in 1937. Among the "imports" on the Tigers were three future National Hockey Leaguers, Bingo Kampman, Merv Chamberlain, and Mel Hill. More typical were men like Charlie Marshall and George Hastie. Marshall, who had played with the Moncton Hawks in their heyday, moved first to the Sudbury Falcons and then to the Frood Tigers for the playoffs. Hastie, a smart centre, came from the Hamilton Tigers and was still playing hockey in Sudbury in the 1980s. He scored the last goal against the North Battleford Beavers in the final of the Allan Cup at Calgary. He also scored the overtime goal that gave the Tigers the victory in the International Tournament for the "world title" held later in Toronto.

In 1938 Max Silverman took a pickup team to Europe for the world championships. Called the Sudbury Wolves, the core was made up of senior players from the Copper Cliff Redmen, along with several other senior and junior players. The team won thirty of thirty-two games and brought home a bronze statue as "world champions," though almost no one took European hockey seriously.

Hockey was not the only sport in town. The Falconbridge Falcons, stacked with Europeans, won a provincial soccer championship in 1932. Two years later the Sudbury Canoe Club Ladies Softball team won a provincial title without imports. Speed skating became popular after artificial ice was installed in Copper Cliff's Stanley Stadium in 1935, and several major talents moved to the region. Among them were Florence Hurd, the North American indoor champion, her brother Alex, and Frank Stack, several times Canadian champion. Prosperity also attracted a world-class marathon runner. The Lions Club brought Taavi "Dave" Komonen to Sudbury in January 1934 and then cheered him on to victory in the Boston Marathon of 19 April.

Lake Ramsey was the centre of year-round sports activities, including the Canadian Canoeing Association championships in August 1936.

The Sudbury Canoe Club, with its facilities at CPR Bay, was home to world champions Bill Beaton and Gib McCubbin and sponsor of the 1936 regatta. A tent city was erected at Bell Park from which spectators cheered locals Allan Eldridge and Jack McInnes to a junior tandem title. Beaton, then thirty-nine, was a member of the senior fours, which placed third.

The championships of the 1930s gave Sudbury its self-image as an important "sports city" that lasted for decades. It did not matter that most of the athletes were paid imports who were in Sudbury only because of the nickel boom. The worship of sports heroes became a ritual, and a sports background was regarded as useful training for public office. Harry Towns, manager of the Frood Tigers, was elected to city council in 1938. Bill Beaton was also on council and served as mayor of the city from 1941 to 1951. Even as late as 1966 Max Silverman was elected mayor, scoring another victory for the 1932 Cub Wolves.

Though sports were a prominent activity during the 1930s, their significance has been exaggerated, for church organizations and activities were undoubtedly more important to most people. The ethnic clubs, though they sometimes sponsored sports events, devoted most of their energy to political or social activities. There were numerous men's organizations and lodges, such as the Rotary, the Lions, the Kinsmen, the Foresters, the Knights of Columbus, the Masons, the Moose, and the Orangemen, with a multitude of goals. The Rotary Club worked for several years to establish a YMCA in Sudbury; the building on Elm was finally opened in 1937. Other groups raised money for the hospital, helped to create parks, and supported the underprivileged.

Quite rightly, Sudbury was regarded as a cultural slum in the 1930s. There was no live theatre, little music, less dance, and little demand for them. The folk art of the French Canadians and other ethnic groups was still considered quaint. The only theatrical experience that captivated everyone was the Hollywood movie. The *Sudbury Star* made a special effort to keep Sudburians informed about the stars, their clothes, their diets, their cars, and their mates. *Lights of New York*, the first completely talking film, was a "sensation" at the Grand Theatre in December 1929. At that time Sudburians had a choice of several movies at the Grand, the Capital, the Regent, and the Rio.

At the centre of all activities was William Edge Mason, the publisher of the *Sudbury Star*. He controlled the Grand Theatre, in which he showed the newest movies with the most advanced technology. Mason's influence in Sudbury during the 1930s cannot be overestimated. The *Sudbury Star* had a monopoly that was never challenged – nor was Mason's command over its point of view. In retrospect the paper looks outspoken because of the strong positions he took. He was pro-business, pro-British, anti-foreign, anti-union, anti-communist. Above all he supported the mining giants in all their activities. There were no "sulphur fumes" in Sudbury, and nickel was not being shipped to Germany. In 1935 Mason became even more influential when he acquired a licence to operate Sudbury's first and only radio station, CKSO. Mason did not limit himself to the media. He was president of the Sudbury Cub Wolves hockey team that won the Memorial Cup in 1932. He served as president of the board of trade and was chairman of the public school board.

Above all, Mason was a controversial public figure, much admired and much despised. To the businessman he was a hero, to the labourer a monster. Those who hated him had several delicious weeks in 1932 when he was on trial for arson. The Sudbury transit building had been torched on 6 September 1931 by John Slotinski, who swore, "[Mason] told me to make a good fire and I'd get $500."[89] Mason said the whole issue was blackmail, to force him to drop charges against Kero Koleff, a former manager. Slotinski was sent to Kingston for four years, and Mason was then charged with arson. The whole scene received front-page treatment in the *Star*. Mason, "the well known publisher and businessman," chose trial by jury. On 11 June 1932 the *Star* proudly announced, "W.E. Mason is honourably acquitted." For Sudburians it was an exciting diversion from the Depression, then at its worst. Like the Cub Wolves, Mason had emerged victorious and had become part of Sudbury's folklore.

By the time the Second World War broke out, the texture of life had changed for Sudbury and its residents. The relatively simple town of 1930 had matured into a crowded city that was overflowing into its hinterland. The main streets still had their familiar faces, but thousands of new people rushed by them into the jobs and stores that seemed to multiply with the passing months. The war was to bring even more dramatic changes. The faint remnants of the 1930s Depression rapidly disappeared with the full employment caused by the demands of wartime industries.

---

1   Julian Duguid of the *London Daily Telegraph*, quoted in the *Sudbury Star*, 8 November 1933.
2   *Census of Canada*, 1941, vol. II, 210.
3   Ibid., Table 48.
4   Frederick Simpich, "Ontario: Next Door," *National Geographic* 52, no. 1 (1932): 136.

5 *Sudbury Star*, 2 July 1932.

6 Ibid., 13 July 1932: "About 25 Finnish residents of Sudbury left at midnight last night for Soviet Russia ... " Ten had been born in Sudbury, some residents of up to twenty-five years. The only "agitator" was Mrs. Hilda Kratz.

7 Ibid., 9 December 1935.

8 Mary Stefura, "Ukrainians in the Sudbury Region," *Polyphony* 5, no. 1 (Spring/Summer 1983): 75.

9 *Sudbury Star*, 3 May 1930.

10 Ibid., 7 March 1931.

11 Ibid., 4 May 1932.

12 Ibid., 1 October 1932.

13 See Maurizio A. Visentin, "The Italians of Sudbury," *Polyphony* 5, no. 1 (Spring/Summer 1983): 33.

14 *Sudbury Star*, 30 October 1935.

15 *Census of Canada*, 1931 and 1941.

16 See F.A. Peake and R.P. Horne, *The Religious Tradition in Sudbury, 1883–1983* (Sudbury: Downtown Churches Association, 1983), 54–55.

17 *Sudbury Star*, 31 December 1929.

18 Ibid., 23 November 1929.

19 Leslie Roberts, "Sudbury Looks to the Future," *Maclean's*, 15 March 1931, 40.

20 *Sudbury Star*, 26 February 1930.

21 Ibid., 27 July 1932.

22 Ibid., 31 January 1934 and 2 December 1935.

23 Ibid., 25 October 1933.

24 Ibid., 18 November 1933.

25 Ibid., 13 December 1933.

26 Ibid., 22 May 1935.

27 Canada, House of Commons, *Debates*, 21 March 1934, p. 1690.

28 Ibid., 9 February 1938, p. 298

29 Ibid., 3 April 1939, p. 2519.

30 *Census of Canada*, 1941, vol. X, Table 3.

31 *Sudbury Star*, 10 December 1932.

32 Ibid., 30 December 1935.

33 See Vernon's *Directory*, 1930 and 1940, as well as *Sudbury Star*, 6 and 17 July 1935.

34 *Sudbury Star*, 17 November 1934.

35 *Census of Canada*, 1941, vol. VII, Table 9, p. 268.

36 *Census of Canada*, 1941, vol. VI. Men in Toronto earned $1,229, women $657. In Rockcliff the average man earned $3,698, the average woman $424.

37 Department of Labour Annual Report, quoted in *Sudbury Star*, 1 June 1932.

38 The Department of Labour in its annual reports, *Labour Organizations in Canada*, includes the following data for Sudbury:

Year	No. of Unions	No. of Members
1929	11	337
1930	12	150
1931	10	164
1932	9	87
1933	11	105
1934	9	76
1935	10	108

(continued)

Year	No. of Unions	No. of Members
1936	12	627
1937	13	118
1938	11	139
1939	10	302
1940	9	338

39 *Sudbury Star*, 23 June 1934

40 Ibid., 27 April 1935.

41 For additional information, see John B. Lang, "A Lion in a Den of Daniels: A History of the International Union of the Mine Mill and Smelter Workers in Sudbury, Ontario" (M.A. thesis, University of Guelph, 1970). Long's thesis, like that of Krats, is full of information not available elsewhere.

42 Horne, "Disappointment to Euphoria," 14–15.

43 Mike Solski and John Smaller, *Mine Mill: The History of the International Union of Mine Mill and Smelter Workers in Canada Since 1895* (Ottawa: Steel Rail, 1984), 102.

44 Quoted in ibid., 102.

45 *Sudbury Star*, 29 November 1930.

46 Ibid., 21 January and 25 April 1931.

47 Ibid., 28 January 1931.

48 Ibid., 8 July 1931.

49 Ibid., 2 December 1931.

50 See ibid., 2 and 5 December 1931.

51 The results, as reported in the *Sudbury Star* of 9 December 1931, were as follows:

Ward	Fenton	Laforest
Advance	31	35
Ryan	1,208	641
McCormick	920	389
Fournier	294	1,367
Totals	2,453	2,432

52 *Sudbury Star*, 18 November 1931 and 9 December 1931.

53 Ibid., 1 November 1930.

54 Ibid., 7 May 1932.

55 At city council meeting on Monday, 20 June 1932 (*Sudbury Star*, 22 June 1932).

56 *Sudbury Star*, 25 June 1932.

57 Ibid., 13 July 1932.

58 Ibid., 1 November 1930 and 7 January 1931.

59 Ibid., 2 May 1932.

60 Ibid., 2 December 1931.

61 Ibid., 5 March 1932.

62 Ibid., 7 September 1932.

63 Ibid., 19 October 1932. Alderman McInnis was the chairman of a committee of three councillors and three citizens. On 1 October there were 846 heads of family with 3,190 dependents on direct relief. Two hundred meals were being served per day, and 131 men stayed at the old jail every night.

64 *Sudbury Star*, 26 November and 7 December 1932.

65 Ibid., 11 January 1933.

66 Ibid., 22 February 1933.

67 Ibid., 11 October 1933.

68 Ibid., 18 and 28 October 1933.

69 Ibid., 4 August 1934.

70 Ibid., 29 August 1934.

71 Ibid., 17 October 1934. Those in favour of the motion were Carrington, White, Simpson, Cullen, and Noel de Tilley. There were two abstentions, and two were absent. The issue had arisen on 12 September, when the *Sudbury Star* announced, "Militant feminists get little sympathy from Sudbury women." According to Mrs. J.A. Laberge there might be exceptional women, "but if a woman had a home and children she owed her first duty to them and if she did that properly, generally speaking, she would have little time for an active career outside the home."

72 *Sudbury Star*, 22 June 1935.

73 In 1935 Sudbury's debenture debt was $231.66 per capita; North Bay's was $270.25. Two years later Sudbury's had dropped to $95.62 and North Bay's to $146.56; by 1940 Sudbury's was $67.24 and North Bay's $122.58 (Department of Municipal Affairs, *Annual Report of Municipal Statistics*, 1935, 1937, and 1940). The increase in Sudbury's population accounts for some of the drop in the average, but Sudbury also had a significantly greater drop in the actual debt.

74 *Sudbury Star*, 19 January 1935. Brodie died suddenly in May 1937.

75 Ontario, Department of Municipal Affairs, *Annual Report of Municipal Statistics*, 1934–40; and *Sudbury Star*, 16 September 1935 and 11 April 1936.

76 Ontario Department of Municipal Affairs, *Annual Report of Municipal Statistics*, 1936 and 1941.

77 Ibid.

78 *Census of Canada*, 1941, vol. IX, Table 11A, p. 58. For details see Gwenda Hallsworth, *A History of Hydro in Sudbury* (Sudbury: Sudbury Hydro-Electric Commission, 1985).

79 The results of the election for 1939, as reported in the *Sudbury Star* of 7 December 1938, were as follows:

Ward	Laforest	Rudd
Advance	13	7
McCormick	838	1,029
Ryan	1,296	946
Fournier	2,164	212
Totals	4,311	2,194

80 The results of the election for 1937, as reported in the *Sudbury Star* of 9 December 1936, were as follows:

Ward	Laforest	Lemieux	Rudd
Advance	7	5	6
McCormick	252	280	813
Ryan	519	590	975
Fournier	1,048	438	195
Totals	1,826	1,313	1,989

81 *Sudbury Star*, 9 December 1936. Lemieux and Bill Beaton ran against Laforest in 1940. The results were Laforest 3,467, Beaton 2,419, and Lemieux 1,059. Laforest led in all wards.

82 Quoted in the *Sudbury Star*, 8 November 1933.

83 *Sudbury Star*, 30 November 1929.

84 Ibid., 4 December 1929.

85 *Census of Canada*, 1941.

86 Ibid., 1941. For the apartments see *Vernon's Directory*, 1920 and 1940.

87 The averages are derived from the *Labour Gazette*, which published comprehensive tables every month. The specific comparisons were based on the July prices.

88 *Sudbury Star*, 22 December 1937.

89 Ibid., 6 February 1932.

CHAPTER SEVEN

THE 1940S

Graeme S. Mount

The 1940s in Sudbury were marked by contrasts. The first half was dominated by the anxiety and restrictions of the Second World War; the prosperous second half by euphoria. In the war years several Sudbury ethnic groups met with suspicion and repression; yet their relatives were greeted with enthusiasm in the later years. An ultra-traditional political bastion in 1940, Sudbury was later a hot bed of socialism and a victim in the Cold War struggle during the "Red Scare." The least unionized city in Canada in 1940, it had the largest local of mine and mill workers in Canada by 1950. Those unionized Sudbury men were among the highest paid in the country but lived in some of the poorest housing with inferior municipal services. A peaceful inland community far from the dangers of the war, Sudbury was the scene of an incendiary riot on VJ-Day that defies explanation.

Throughout the Western world the forties were dominated by war: the Second World War was followed by civil wars in Greece and China and the Korean War, not to mention the Cold War, which gave a new definition to international relations. Sudbury, in one way of another, was a participant in all those conflicts.

The Second World War hit Sudbury in several ways: economic, political, social, and personal, and it started immediately. Kathleen Ferguson of Copper Cliff and two of her children, Kathleen, nine, and Margaret, three, were passengers on the British liner *Athenia* when she was torpedoed on the first day of the war.[1] Sudbury men immediately lined up to enlist, and before the war was over, thousands of men and women were to serve. According to the Royal Canadian Legion, 489 young men from Sudbury died in action during the Second World War. One of them was Sudbury's flying ace, Theo Doucette, the first person born in Sudbury to win the Distinguished Flying Cross.[2]

The war required far more than men going off to battle, however, and the countless contributions of ordinary citizens were a measure of the community. INCO's eleven thousand employees joined other Canadians in registering with the authorities so that the federal government could make the most efficient use of the available manpower. Children saved their pennies for war savings stamps and certificates. Four dollars worth of twenty-five-cent stamps would return a five-dollar bill at the end of the war. Boys boxed during their summer holidays, charging admission to the fights, and sent the proceeds to the Red Cross. The Girl Guides held a bake sale and fishpond to raise money for the war effort. People of all ages played bingo to raise funds to buy cigarettes for servicemen. When the Sudbury Children's Aid Society sought homes for forty children evacuated from Great Britain, Sudburians responded with enthusiasm. In April 1941, 170 servicemen staged a mock occupation of Sudbury as part of their training, and by September of that same year Sudburians had salvaged sixty tons of scrap material for war purposes. The war also created opportunities for employment. A local factory that produced skis for soldiers at the front had all the orders it could handle. A sub-regional office of the Wartime Prices and Trade Board was located in Sudbury. The Sault Ste. Marie–Sudbury Regiment held a training camp at Minnow Lake during the summer of 1942. Some incidents brought the war especially close to home. One was the arrival of German prisoners of war on their way to their camp west of Sudbury, which caused excitement and apprehension, for there was the danger that prisoners might escape. Another was the air-raid sirens and blackout drills that reminded everyone that there really was a war.[3]

Sudbury's ethnic groups were very deeply affected by the war because most of their homelands had been overrun. On 21 September 1939, seventy people from Hungary met at All People's Church and declared their loyalty to Canada, regardless of whatever course of action Nazi Germany might force their homeland to adopt. The city's Polish community organized concerts to raise funds for the Red Cross to provide food and shelter to homeless Polish refugees in Europe.[4] A former student of the Sudbury High School, Joseph Zdyb, won the Polish Distinguished Flying Cross. The Croatian orchestra performed at a dance on 9 February 1940, while Yugoslavia was still neutral, and donated the proceeds to the Canadian Legion, which planned to buy educational and recreational amenities for servicemen. Croatians bought Victory Loan Bonds in substantial numbers, and other Yugoslav immigrants provided music for the Poles' concerts.[5] People of British and French extraction sang at wartime benefit concerts. In 1940 Northern Ontario Ukrainians paraded from St. Mary's Church to the Cenotaph, where they pledged their loyalty to the Allied cause and boasted that they had stifled communist Ukrainian elements. The Chinese community played a large role in the 1941 Victory Bond campaign,[6] and on New Year's Eve, 1941, published a full-page advertisement for the campaign in the *Sudbury Daily Star*, quoting Kipling and depicting Winston Churchill and Chiang Kai-Shek as the two great men who would lead the Allies to victory. Matters were awkward, however, for the Italians, Germans, Austrians, Czechs, and Slovaks living in Sudbury. They had to register as enemy aliens under the Defence of Canada Regulations, since their homelands were part of the German Reich at the moment of Canada's declaration of war. Failure to do so meant internment.[7]

All groups, in a way, had to fight their own war. Even before Finland was attacked by the Soviet Union in 1939, for example, Sudbury Finns had organized the Sudbury District Finnish War Aid Association, whose coffee parties proved particularly successful. With donations from one dollar a cup for coffee, the association raised twelve hundred dollars within a few weeks. Spectators also paid admission to a Sampo Hall ski demonstration in February 1940, with proceeds to the war effort. The same month, Mr. and Mrs. Arne Kasten of Broder Township hosted a chicken dinner for the benefit of the Finnish War Aid Society, and the society organized a benefit concert. The performers included a forty-voice Finnish choir. Before the fighting stopped, Sudbury's Finnish community had contributed seventeen hundred dollars to the cause. The Russo-Finnish War affected INCO and Sudbury directly, for the company had an operation at Petsamo and Kolosjoki in the part of Finland overrun by Soviet forces. There was general relief when Mrs. I.J. Simcox, formerly of Copper Cliff and wife of INCO's general manager at Petsamo, called early in December 1939 to say that all the Canadian employees and their families had reached Kirkenes, Norway.[8]

Within Sudbury the most divisive issue was the 1942 referendum in which Prime Minister King requested voters to release him from his promise not to introduce conscription for overseas service. Those who said "yes" numbered 8,180; the "no" forces mustered 4,949 votes. Though Sudbury as a whole voted overwhelmingly in the affirmative, French Canadians and Italians appeared the most reluctant. The largely English McCormick Ward voted "yes," 2,406 to 605. Ryan Ward, populated by the working class and immigrants from the Ukraine, Finland, Poland, and

Czechoslovakia, also voted "yes," 4,229 to 1,563. In Fournier Ward, with a majority of French Canadians, the vote was "no" by a margin of more than two to one. Copper Cliff also voted in the affirmative, 1,203 to 479, but those who cast their ballots at the Italian Hall polling station voted 365 to 193 in the negative. Sudbury's "yes" vote was less substantial than the nearly 84 percent "yes" vote across the province of Ontario, but French Canadians were more numerous here than in most parts of the province. Quebec voted "no" by almost 72 percent.[9]

Similarly, when the provincial Liberal government of Mitchell Hepburn asked the Ontario legislature to censure the federal Liberal government for its failure to prosecute the war with sufficient diligence, three of the ten nays came from northern ridings, and the Sudbury Liberal MPP, J.M. Cooper, joined six other northerners in absenting themselves at the time of the vote.

By that time Sudbury was in full wartime production and short of workers. Because of this the war created new jobs for women as well as men. Although women performed traditional volunteer activities such as knitting and sewing, collecting blankets and clothing, playing bridge to raise funds for war work, making food for charities and soldiers on leave, and canvassing for funds, they also entered fields previously reserved for men. On 20 April 1940, the *Sudbury Daily Star* carried an illustrated report: "The first group of Sudbury girls enrolled in the Women's Auxiliary Motor Service, designed to qualify women for men's work in a wartime emergency, had their first lesson in the care and operation of heavy motor vehicles at the McLeod Garage Thursday (April 18) night."[10]

Two months later twenty-eight women had completed the course and obtained the right to drive and repair cars, trucks, tractors, and ambulances. Other Sudbury women then undertook and completed the course. It was also deemed newsworthy that eighteen-year-old Anne Graf began to drive a truck for Burton Grocery and Meat Market, that women could become theatre ushers, and that CKSO's station identification was being announced by women. In fact, CKSO hired women for all but technical work. In the early years of the war, however, there were few jobs for women in Sudbury, and hundreds moved to places like Toronto to work in munition plants and other factories.[11]

When women were eventually hired for men's jobs at INCO, it was almost revolutionary. "WOMEN IN INDUSTRY – Replace men at INCO Plant" was the *Sudbury Daily Star*'s introduction to a photo series on 18 November 1942, though the *Star* stressed that this was a temporary measure, since women would return to their natural jobs at the end of hostilities. In addition to doing office work, women were employed soldering cables on batteries, operating ore distributors, repairing flotation cell equipment, piloting ore trains, operating heavy moulding equipment, and working on lathes.[12] The CPR followed suit and hired women as mechanics. Weare Holbrook even wrote a poem that appeared in the *Star* on 20 November 1942:

> *Oh, the girl I adore*
> *Isn't here any more –*
> *She's a welder at shop number three,*
> *She works night and day*
> *Getting overtime pay*
> *And she hasn't a moment for me.*
> *In vain do I wait*
> *By the Frood Mine gate*
> *And waiting I plaintively pine*
> *For vine-covered porch*
> *An acetylene torch*
> *And that little spot welder of mine.*

He might also have been waiting at the barracks gate, for by then Sudbury women had joined others in the Canadian Women's Army Corps, the Canadian Women's Auxiliary Air Force, and the Women's Royal Canadian Naval Service. The movement of women into non-traditional positions, though unsettling to many, was generally accepted as long as it was for the duration of the war only. "Women at the mines are carving a definite place for themselves and will continue to do so until the peace in reached," wrote the *Star* on 20 November 1942. "They are sacrificing for the good of the cause the subtle protection of femininity, but it should prove a phase of their life on which they can look back with praise and satisfaction." At the end of the war women were unceremoniously ordered back to their kitchens as men resumed their proper place in industry.

When the war was finally over on 15 August 1945, the relief in Sudbury, as in the rest of Canada, was profound. Far from any real danger during the fighting, Sudbury had suffered less than most cities and prospered more than most. Nevertheless, that night Sudbury exploded in its VJ-Day riot. The *Sudbury Daily Star* reported:

> Sudbury's riot was the only one in Canada to mark V-J Day. This morning it was estimated that at least $40,000 damage was done, and the figure may exceed this as the result of looting of supplies at the city's liquor, beer and wine stores and shattered plate glass windows said to

number 40. Constable Robert C. Ford, of the R.C.M.P., is
in hospital, two other police were slightly injured, and 28
men are under arrest.[13]

Because of wartime restrictions on immigration and the departure of men
and women to war, the population growth rate in Sudbury slowed down
for the first time since 1883. The 32 percent increase, from 32,203 to
42,410, was less than half the growth rate of any previous decade. Not
surprisingly, the basic demographic patterns did not change greatly,
though there were significant differences. Most of the trends established
earlier in the century continued, although residents of French extraction
overtook the British. Of the others, Ukrainians grew the most, Italians
came to outnumber the Finns, and Germans declined (see Table 7.1).

Because of these shifts in population there was a considerable change
in the relative size of the religious groups. Roman Catholics, who had
always been in a slight majority, increased by 12.5 percent in the 1940s to
make up almost 70 percent of the total. The United Church and the
Anglicans held their own among the Protestants, while the Presbyterians
declined slightly (see Table 7.2).

The city's population continued to be young and male. In 1941 slightly more than half the population was under the age of twenty-four; in
1951 slightly fewer than half were under twenty-four. In 1941 Sudbury
had 113.52 males for every hundred females, and in 1951, 113.45. This
was typical of all resource-based towns. Of the 14,142 men in the work

Table 7.1
Sudbury's Main Ethnic Groups, 1941–1951

Ethnic Group	1941	1951
British and Irish	13,379	15,502
French	10,772	16,060
German	1,299	845
Finnish	1,241	1,478
Italian	959	1,502
Polish	815	1,127
Ukrainian	1,617	2,571
Other European	897	3,195

Source: *Census of Canada*, 1951.

Table 7.2
Religious Groups in Sudbury, 1941–1951

Church	1941	1951
Anglican	3,094	3,210
Baptist	596	747
Eastern Orthodox	539	716
Jewish	232	184
Lutheran	1,431	1,971
Mennonite	13	7
Presbyterian	1,723	1,687
Roman Catholic	18,466	26,518[a]
United Church	5,685	6,880
Other	490	

[a] Includes Eastern Rite.
Source: Census of Canada, 1951.

force at the end of the period, the vast majority were hourly employees, over 8,000 of whom worked in mining and smelting alone. The city had few professionals, though there were 51 doctors, 100 mining engineers, and 403 retail proprietors or managers.

The census reveals that most Sudburians of the 1940s lived in expensive rental apartments or flats that provided less for the money than most cities in Canada. Most of the men would be classed as semi-skilled or blue-collar workers. Most married women "kept house," but if they worked outside the home, they earned less, on average, for their labour than most Canadian working women. Of the 3,083 women in the work force at the end of the decade, over half (1,583) were employed in the "service" industries, a quarter were clerks, and only 20 percent were professionals, half of them schoolteachers.

Sudburians were less likely to own their houses than most others in Ontario and, at 4.4 persons per household, were the most crowded. Fifteen percent of households lacked inside toilets, but most had telephones, refrigerators, radios, and electric or gas stoves. Over 40 percent had cars, 10 percent below the provincial average.

Throughout most of the 1940s INCO and Falconbridge were exceptionally prosperous and paid their men well. The importance of nickel as an essential war material was never more obvious, and the Cold War armaments race after 1945 kept the peacetime economy booming. The production figures tell the story (see Table 7.3).

The *Canada Year Book* of 1945 was illuminating: "Nickel is very important in war because of its strictly military uses, such as armour plate, gun forgings, gun recoil springs and bullet jackets, and for its use in industrial nickel steels for the production of war equipment."[14] The monopoly of the region remained secure until the end of the decade; in fact, about 90 percent of the world's nickel originated in the district mines, mostly INCO's. Falconbridge, according to D.M. LeBourdais, was at a significant disadvantage after Germany invaded Norway on 9 April 1940 and captured the company refinery at Kristiansand.[15] Eventually INCO took on the refining of Falconbridge matte until the end of the war.

Except for the slowdown at war's end in 1945 and 1946, INCO continued the expansion that had begun in the mid–1930s. In 1941 the company launched a $26-million expenditure that resulted in plant construction and mine development. INCO's internal newspaper, the *INCO Triangle*, reported the creation of five thousand new jobs between December 1939 and April 1944. In 1946 another $7 million was allocated for a pilot mill at Copper Cliff, where several new houses were being constructed for employees. In 1947, according to Robert C. Stanley, INCO's chairman and president, "Sales of nickel ... were the highest of any peacetime year except 1937."

Table 7.3
Quantities and Value of Nickel Produced in Canada, 1940–1950

Year	Quantity (lbs)	Value ($)
1940	245,557,871	59,822,591
1941	282,258,235	68,656,795
1942	282,211,803	69,998,427
1943	288,018,615	71,675,322
1944	274,598,629	69,204,152
1945	245,130,983	61,982,133
1946	192,124,537	45,385,155
1947	237,251,496	70,650,764
1948	263,497,163	86,904,235
1949	257,379,216	99,173,289
1950	247,317,867	112,104,685

Source: Canada Year Book, 1945, 1951, and 1952–53.

The *Triangle* announced with pride that INCO's underground development, almost all of it in the Sudbury basin, totalled 54,790 feet – more than ten miles.[16] Another $2 million was spent on houses in Levack, Creighton, and Garson in 1948 when a $5-million sulphur-recovery plant was under construction. As the decade came to a close, the company announced, first, an $18-million expenditure that would create over fifteen hundred new jobs, and then a breathtaking $50-million building program.

All this expansion was not without cost to INCO's employees who settled in the city. When the Rotarians were distributing pre-Christmas charity in 1943, they discovered considerable "ill health and squalid living conditions." A month later, Sudbury experienced a diphtheria epidemic, resulting largely, according to Dr. W.J. Cook, medical officer of health, from "poor housing conditions and overcrowding." In an editorial on 26 January 1944, the *Sudbury Daily Star* lamented the lack of adequate heat and ventilation in many homes. In part out of recognition of the enormous housing crisis, INCO planned a new company town called Lively to the west of Copper Cliff.[17]

Despite its successes, it was not all clear sailing for INCO, for in May 1946 the United States Department of Justice filed an anti-trust suit against the company. "It was charged that the United States subsidiary of International had been guilty of monopolistic practices, and the Department of Justice sought to have its rolling mills separated from the parent company."[18] After an expensive and protracted legal battle, INCO succeeded in 1948 in maintaining its company intact, but was forced to modify its marketing and pricing practices drastically, setting the stage for the end of its monopoly position over the next quarter century.

An equally unwanted opponent was the International Union of Mine, Mill and Smelter Workers, which achieved certification in 1944 at both INCO and Falconbridge, despite enormous hostility from multiple sources. Organizers had discovered in the 1930s that it was no simple matter to unionize the mine and smelter workers in Sudbury. All previous attempts had failed, and INCO had gone to inordinate lengths to prevent their workers from unionizing.[19] Time and circumstances, however, were on the side of Mine Mill. The war and full employment created a nationwide atmosphere in favour of unions. Eventually, both the federal and the provincial governments enacted legislation that eliminated several of the impediments to certification. In the meantime guerrilla warfare between INCO and Mine Mill produced victims and an animosity with few parallels. Determined to unionize Sudbury workers, Mine Mill, an affiliate of the Congress of Industrial Organizations (CIO), held several secret meetings in Sudbury in 1941. This led to the opening of a Durham Street office early in 1942, and the battle was joined. On 24 February the office was sacked in "broad daylight" by "a dozen goons," who beat two of the union workers so badly they were hospitalized.[20] The police arrested none of the well-known assailants, but they immediately apprehended Robert Carlin and Jack McCool, two Mine Mill officials, when they attempted to distribute a leaflet attacking INCO and identifying the "goons" as INCO shift bosses. The tone was set.[21] With the media controlled by W.E. Mason, the Mine Mill side of any story or incident received short shrift indeed.[22] Add to this the open denunciation by the churches and the judicious use of the courts by the company,[23] and the difficulties become obvious. The pressure from Mine Mill and the CIO was relentless, however, and INCO was faced with a worthy challenger.

As soon as Local 598 was chartered on 21 April 1942, INCO immediately organized and subsidized its own company "union," the United Copper Nickel Workers Union, christened the "Nickel Rash" by its opponents,[24] an indication of the rank and file support it received. In 1943 when the CIO endeavoured to organize a parade, supposedly on behalf of the 1943 Victory Loan campaign, the Sudbury police commission denied them permission. Magistrate McKessock opposed Mine Mill's application on the grounds that "there was no point in inviting trouble," and Judge E. Proulx said that whereas a Victory Loan parade might be justifiable, a union parade was unnecessary.[25] INCO clearly had allies throughout the city. One of the union organizers, Bob Miner, has described his problem in finding accommodation once he mentioned his name to prospective landlords.[26] No matter what the obstacles, Mine Mill continued to sign up members in increasingly large numbers. The high-handed methods of the company played into the hands of the union organizers.

Among the best known of the several organizers then in Sudbury was Robert H. Carlin, who had come to the city from Kirkland Lake in 1942. A wartime Mine Mill strike in the Kirkland Lake gold mines had been a spectacular failure,[27] but Mine Mill was already at work in Sudbury, which had far greater potential because its enormous work force was producing an essential component of the Allied war effort. Carlin has related how he came as a stranger to Sudbury and used his anonymity to promote the union. He called it "CIO" rather than "Mine-Mill" because the CIO's prestige among workers was higher, and he left CIO pamphlets by the toilets in a beer parlour. Then, unrecognized, he sat near the washroom door to watch the men's reactions as they emerged. One day he followed an apparently responsive individual onto the streetcar and to his home, where he introduced himself and discussed union activity.[28] Others, such as Miner, McCool, and James Kidd, fought for Mine Mill. The converts began sign up by the dozens, three thousand in one month alone.

The Ontario government, through its Ontario Labour Court, had made it all but impossible to prevent a certification vote at INCO, and in December 1943, 6,913 voted for Mine Mill and 1,187 for the Nickel Rash.[29] Of the 959 voting at Falconbridge and with only three spoiled ballots, 765 favoured Mine Mill ahead of the Falconbridge Workers' Council.[30] On 4 February 1944 Local 598 of the Mine Mill and Smelter Workers became the collective bargaining unit for INCO, and on 8 March 1944 for Falconbridge workers. The first contracts followed immediately. Because wages had been frozen by wartime regulations, Mine Mill was limited in what it could do for its members, but it made progress on grievance procedures, seniority, and time spent on the job.[31] Check-off (whereby union dues were deducted from paycheques), which was won in 1945, was but the first of a series of additional victories that marked the rest of the decade: paid vacations, medical benefits, improved working hours, and special holidays in addition to the higher wages, which already ranked with the highest in Canada. At the local level Mine Mill was a success.

Throughout the decade, however, the union was weakened by the constant infighting between Carlin and Kidd for leadership of Sudbury's Local 598.[32] Hovering over everything, however, were the issues of the Cold War and the anti-communist frenzy. As Canadian labour historian Irving Abella wrote some years ago, "No union had greater potential and failed so miserably, or secured larger gains and suffered larger losses in so short a time than did Mine Mill."[33]

The period from 1945 to 1950 was one of Soviet domination of Eastern Europe. The Soviet army occupied or seized control of eastern Germany, Poland, Bulgaria, Hungary, Romania, and Czechoslovakia, one after the other. During the Second World War the Soviet Union had been an ally, and the presence of communists among union leaders was of only marginal importance. Soviet and Western interests coincided, and a strike at INCO or Falconbridge would have been as damaging to Soviet interests as to Canadian or American. After the war, however, the Soviet Union appeared a threat. Nobody knew the extent of Soviet ambitions, but Igor Gouzenko's revelations of an elaborate spy network throughout Canada and the United States gave the impetus to a witch hunt. During the Soviet blockade of West Berlin through the winter of 1948–49, the world was threatened with another war. Suddenly, the presence of communists in Canadian unions, including Mine Mill, had become a matter of national concern.

To the local union leadership, communism was irrelevant. Even from the perspective of retirement in 1980 Carlin adamantly denied that communists had any influence in Local 598. More recently Mike Solski and John Smaller, in *Mine Mill: The History of the International Union of Mine,*

Mill and Smelter Workers in Canada Since 1885, were equally outspoken, blaming the whole crisis on external forces: "Compliance by the King government showed the subservience of Canadian policy makers to Cold War hysteria promoters U.S. Secretary of State (also INCO director) John Foster Dulles and the notorious Senator Joseph McCarthy."[34] In retrospect, a case can be made that there was a conspiracy to emasculate the Mine Mill union by all means possible, even though there was virtually no evidence that communism or communists had any influence or control over Local 598. It is a very complicated story involving Canadian and American governments, national and international unions, spies, infiltrators, deserters, lawyers, judges, clergymen, and the police. The ordinary Sudbury miner became a pawn in a game over which he had no control. In the end he and Sudbury suffered the humiliation of all pawns: to be sacrificed and cast aside.

In 1948 and 1949 the Canadian Congress of Labour (CCL) seized upon unsubstantiated criticism of an affiliated union's newly negotiated contract as a pretext to expel Mine Mill from the national organization. Thereafter CCL affiliates were free to raid Mine Mill with impunity. The raids, which began immediately, continued into the 1960s. Local 598 of the Mine Mill and Smelter Workers was left to face INCO and Falconbridge on its own; rendered less powerful to negotiate strong contracts for its members, it was there to all and sundry for the pickings.[35]

On 4 August 1943, the sitting Liberal MPP, James Cooper, went down to defeat along with most members of what was to be Ontario's last Liberal government until 1985. The local Conservatives had decided not to contest the Sudbury seat, probably because they did not want to divide the non-CCF vote.[36] The CCF candidate was none other than the Mine Mill organizer who had arrived recently in Sudbury, Bob Carlin. But the Conservative leader, George Drew, who insisted that Sudbury voters must have the right to vote Conservative,[37] imposed a Sudbury barrister, Harry Waisberg, when the local organization failed to find a candidate.[38] Carlin won handily, Cooper came second, and Waisberg was a very poor fourth, behind an Independent, William Beaton, the mayor of Sudbury. In that election the CCF won thirty-four seats, ten of them in Northern Ontario; the Conservatives had thirty-eight MPPs and formed a minority government. The Liberals lagged far behind with fifteen seats (see Table 7.4).

Carlin's local popularity was never more obvious than during the next provincial election, in 1945. Despite a widespread collapse of the CCF, Carlin won Sudbury Riding handily.[39] In the whole province the CCF kept

Table 7.4
Provincial Election of 1943, Results in Sudbury Riding

Candidate and Party	Votes Received
Robert H. Carlin, CCF	15,096
James W. Cooper, Liberal	7,583
William S. Beaton, Independent	1,521
Harry Waisberg, Progressive Conservative	1,061

Source: *Sudbury Daily Star*, 5 August 1943.

only eight seats and lost the role of official opposition to the Liberals. As an MPP Carlin supported several local projects, such as the establishment of a university in northeastern Ontario. His best efforts, however, were against INCO, speaking out against air pollution and calling for stricter government control over the company. In doing this, he found himself accused by Mines Minister Leslie M. Frost of threatening employment in Sudbury and failing to represent the true interests of the workers.[40] Eventually the CCF found it necessary to repudiate the opinions of Carlin, whose strong support of Mine Mill had become an embarrassment to the party: even the CCF was not immune to the purges of the Cold War. Asked on the floor of the legislature to dissociate himself from certain communists in the International Union of Mine, Mill and Smelter Workers, Carlin refused.[41] This happened during the 1948 pro-Soviet coup in Czechoslovakia, as the world wondered whether the Czech foreign minister, Jan Masaryk, had jumped from a window or been pushed. Under the circumstances, the CCF decided that someone else would have to be its candidate next time (in 1949). The voters, however, gave Carlin, who ran as an Independent, almost 3,000 more votes than Victor Whalen, the official CCF candidate. Mayor Beaton, who ran as a Liberal, was again soundly beaten. Unfortunately for Carlin, Welland Gemmell, the Progressive Conservative, capitalized on the CCF split vote and won by 292 votes.[42] Gemmell was appointed minister of mines by Leslie Frost, who replaced George Drew as premier of Ontario in 1949.[43]

Maintaining that he was never anything other than a socialist,[44] Carlin, as a matter of principle, repeatedly refused to dissociate himself from communists, communism, or even Soviet policy. That unwillingness to antagonize his communist allies and supporters rendered both him and the Mine Mill Union controversial, embarrassed their friends, divided their union, and lessened the union's influence.[45]

Though Sudbury had been branded a hot bed of radicalism by people inside and outside the community, the description was an exaggeration, and nowhere was that more obvious than at the municipal political level. Throughout the 1940s control was easily maintained by a handful of extremely traditional municipal politicians. One man, Bill Beaton, was mayor continuously from 1941 into the next decade. Five members of city council, Percy Morrison, Alex MacKinnon, Warren Koth, Kenneth McNeill, and Arthur Whissell, sat with Beaton for most of the years. Throughout the decade 88 percent of the positions were held by only thirteen men.

With Sudbury prosperous throughout the 1940s, it was perhaps to be expected that city council would do little more than go through the motions of municipal government. It ploughed the snow, built some roads, opened new subdivisions, and talked incessantly about plans that were rarely executed. For the most part, however, the councils of the 1940s let Beaton run the city's affairs, and he usually allowed nature to take its course. "No one disliked Bill Beaton," one resident explained. When asked what he did as mayor, the reply was revealing: "When you complained, Bill could talk you into thinking everything was wonderful. Only later did you realize that he had said nothing."[46]

Beaton holds the record with eleven consecutive years in office as mayor, and his name is still appropriately celebrated with the annual "Beaton Classic," a sports marathon requiring many physical skills. It is appropriate because Beaton remained "physically adventurous" throughout his life, and it was his athletic success that made him prominent.[47] Even when he was mayor, it was his "wide background in sport" that was considered his strength. The cult of the sports personality, of course, is not unique to Sudbury, but it is deeply entrenched there. Alex MacKinnon, who spent nine years on council in the forties and ran against Beaton for mayor in 1942, was as late as 1948 "best known in Sudbury for his outstanding hockey career" in the National Hockey League.[48]

With few exceptions, the elections of the 1940s belonged to Beaton. He won contests in 1940, 1942, 1948, and 1950 and was acclaimed in the others. When he defeated the respected incumbent mayor, William J. Laforest, in December 1940, the *Sudbury Daily Star* noted, "He is aggressive, even to the point of being scrappy, and will undoubtedly liven things up in civic circles, whether for better or worse remains to be seen."[49] The *Star* came to consider it something of both, but by the end of the decade it saw Beaton's "one man rule" as both inefficient and dictatorial.[50] In the early years, however, Beaton was mayor for all the people.

Realizing that Sudbury was a workers' town, Beaton supported Mine Mill's right to hold a parade in the spring of 1943. When the Sudbury Police Commission refused the union's request for a permit, Mayor Beaton let his disagreement with his fellow commissioners' decision be known. Winning the enmity of the *Sudbury Daily Star* with his stand,[51] Beaton also found himself under attack the same year from the *Sudbury Beacon*, Mine Mill's organ, for entering the provincial race as an Independent (socialist). According to the *Beacon*, Beaton was but a tool of W.E. Mason, deliberately dividing the labour vote in order to defeat Carlin.[52] The *Beacon* insisted that Carlin was the only CCF candidate in 1943.

In 1943, the year of Mine Mill's successes in the INCO and Falconbridge certification campaigns and of Carlin's election to the Ontario legislature, the union put forward a full slate of candidates for council, including mayor, three each for the public and separate school boards, and hydro commissioners. One Mine Mill organizer, J.P. McCool, won a seat in Ryan Ward by the slimmest of margins. Two other members of the slate, A.W. Stevenson and Mrs. D.W. Ward, were elected to the public school board, but the union's nominees were all rejected by the separate school supporters.[53] In attempting to explain such a poor showing in a "workingman's town," the *Sudbury Beacon* editorialized that too few of its members had made the effort to vote.[54] It was also possible that the voters felt there were limits to what Mine Mill ought to be allowed to do.[55] What is most likely was that the voters chose to keep their local politics separate from their workplace and their provincial government, as Mayor Beaton had learned on two occasions.

There were few other ripples on the local political scene in the decade. In 1944 the Sudbury Civic Reform Association, successor to the Mine Mill group, nominated nine candidates, six for aldermanic seats and three for the public school board. McCool retained his council seat easily, as he did until 1948. Another candidate, A.B. Baker, joined Stevenson and Ward on the public board, giving the reform slate three of the six seats.[56] Despite that victory, the local scene was little affected by the labour vote.

Sudbury's main preoccupation throughout the 1940s was the problem of growth. Though the politicians agreed that planning was essential, it was in fact ignored during the 1940s in spite of a promising beginning. J.D. McInnes, chairman of the newly appointed Town Planning Commission, had presented his first report to council on 15 March 1940. One of its recommendations was for the installation of parking meters downtown;[57] later that year, Sudbury became the first city in Canada to introduce such meters, albeit on a six-month experimental basis. The idea found favour with the merchants, who believed that too many people were leaving their cars downtown all day, without permitting the turnover that would allow other motorists to shop. At a charge of five cents an hour, the meters succeeded in encouraging motorists to leave the downtown quickly and also made a tidy profit for the city. This alone persuaded the politicians to keep them permanently.[58] The installation of parking meters seems to have been the one contribution of the Town Planning Commission. With no power or budget the commission unfortunately disappeared. As the 1940s progressed and the city became overcrowded and municipal services less and less adequate, the complaints about the need of planning increased, but the Beaton councils had no intention of handing any power or control to another body.

Early in 1943 Beaton and the city staff did draft an expansionary "10-Year Plan … of metropolitan proportion."[59] More a list of what the city wanted than a plan, it anticipated a subway or overhead crossing of the CPR line on Elm Street, an airport, an artificial-ice rink, the elimination of streetcars, a university, highway links to Toronto and Timmins, a house of refuge, new municipal buildings, and new roads and sewers. With the exception of the Elm Street crossing, the city did eventually achieve all these objectives, though the "Plan" was irrelevant, since all its recommendations had been made previously. One specific recommendation places the Plan in relief: "abolishment of the Canadian Senate."[60]

Beaton is usually given credit for two accomplishments: the elimination of the streetcars and the decision to construct the arena. Sudbury had two systems of public transit, the much-maligned Sudbury–Copper Cliff Suburban Electric Railway Company and the City Bus Lines. Though there is much nostalgia today about the streetcars and people nod and wink about the deals that led to the closing of the company, it had outlived its usefulness and was not providing good service. That was not entirely the company's fault, for it was shackled with obsolete, second-hand equipment and inadequate budgets. During the war it had been of exceptional value transporting workers to essential jobs, but with the onslaught of the automobile after the war and the obvious advantages of gas-powered buses, the Sudbury–Copper Cliff Street Railway Company came to an end. In 1950 the city purchased the City Bus Lines. When the streetcars made their last trips on 1 October 1950, the city had thirty-three buses on the roads.[61]

By 1949 it was not just the Sudbury urban transportation system that needed attention. The neglect of roads, sewers, the water system, and public services generally had taken its toll, and Beaton had made some enemies. He was re-elected in the December 1948 vote, but he was no longer untouchable, and several new faces appeared on council. The main issue in that election, however, was a referendum on the construction of a new civic auditorium. Sudbury was certainly lacking any similar facility, but it required a vote by property owners to authorize the $700,000 debentures. To Beaton and most other members of council, the construction of the building was a priority. The vote was as follows: yes, 2,870; no, 1,477. Much of the opposition was in Fournier Ward. "It is particularly appropriate that the project be endorsed by such a large majority," editorialized the *Star*. "After all, the property-owners of the city are the ones who are taking over the chief financial burden, as well as all of the responsibility."[62] Beaton immediately pressed ahead with the construction of what became the Sudbury Arena, and it was appropriate that a sports centre was his last major contribution. Another proposal to build a much-needed new library building received short shrift from Sudbury politicians, who knew their constituents.

Sudbury had derived enormous economic benefits from the industrial and commercial activity both during and after the war. Unemployment had virtually disappeared before the war started, and the city's welfare budget was minimal. In April 1940 INCO contributed $15,000 and its employees $3,000 to the YMCA's financial campaign. By the summer of 1940, there was a labour shortage. City tax collections jumped $100,000 in the period 1 January–15 June 1940 above their level of the previous year, and the CNR reported an increase of 40 percent in its summer freight traffic. Christmas sales set a new high record,[63] and important new businesses moved into the city. On 28 November 1940 "another beautiful new store ... by Birks, Ellis, Ryrie, [Jewellers]" was opened on Durham Street.[64] Sudbury banks reported higher bank clearings (more than $53 million) for 1940 than for any year since 1930.[65] By mid-1941 the city's collective finances had recovered so well that the services of the Ontario Municipal Board, which had been supervising them for five years, came to an end.[66] Customs revenues for 1941 set an all-time record, and Sudbury's municipal tax rate for 1942 was its lowest since 1931.[67]

Recording these developments as well as trying to influence them was the *Sudbury Daily Star*, owned by W.E. Mason. Also the proprietor of CKSO, the only radio station in town until CHNO opened in 1947, Mason truly was the city's media czar.[68] The people and causes he supported could expect pictures, long newspaper stories, and editorials, often on the front page; those he disagreed with could expect hostile editorials or no publicity at all. The Mine Mill Union made a virtue out of his opposition, as did Mayor Beaton, who may even have won his elections because of Mason's opposition. In fact, Mason's candidates repeatedly lost in federal and provincial elections. Mason had been Sudbury's leading "booster" since he started the *Star* in January of 1909. It was Mason who donated the land upon which the Sudbury Legion erected its building in 1947.[69] Had he lived, he might not have been so happy in 1965, when, because of dwindling numbers, the Legion sold the building to Local 6500 of the United Steelworkers of America. Mason worked tirelessly for charities like the Sudbury Red Cross, in organizations such as the board of trade, and in sports clubs. He undoubtedly would have enjoyed the following hockey story from Stockholm, Sweden, 16 February 1949. The *Sudbury Daily Star* explained:

> The Sudbury Wolves hockey team, headed by the redoubtable Maxie Silverman of Sudbury, were central figures Wednesday night in a swirling hockey-mad crowd which stormed the gates of Stockholm's mammoth Olympic Stadium. Egged on by virulent notices in the Swedish press, which labelled the Canadians as "dangerous men," the rioters got out of police bounds. Fourteen were injured in the mad scramble and were taken off in ambulances. The game with Sweden ended in a bitter 2-2 tie.[70]

It is sometimes forgotten that Mason was president of the Sudbury Hockey Club that won the Memorial Cup in 1932. For almost forty years he had published a Sudbury-centred newspaper that residents detested. His death on 22 June 1948 ended an important link with Sudbury's past. His successors sold the *Sudbury Daily Star* to the Thomson newspaper chain, thereby ending the local touch.

Under Mason, the *Star* prided itself on being "Northern Ontario's largest newspaper," and that same striving for regional importance influenced CKSO radio. In 1946 the station increased the power of its transmitter to five thousand watts so that it could reach listeners as far away as Mattawa and Timmins. When Mason died, his will stipulated that funds be set aside to establish the W.E. Mason Foundation, one of whose purposes was to support the construction of public buildings. In 1949 the foundation turned over land on Mackenzie Street, valued at about twenty thousand dollars, to the Sudbury Public Library Board, which was to use the land for a new library.[71]

The construction of public buildings and of homes continued during the war years and mushroomed in the second half of the decade.[72] Among the best-known structures were the Randolph Apartments downtown, Prince Charles Public School on Van Horne (which became École publique Jeanne Sauvé in 1985), the centre wing of the Sudbury General Hospital, and the third floor of the Wembley Public School. The Sudbury High School, which was declared a fire hazard in 1946, was replaced by a new building, opened in 1951.[73] Despite the war, church building also continued. St. Andrew's United Church managed to add an extension to its building on Larch Street (since demolished), and St. Paul's United Church opened on Regent Street in 1949. All People's United Church and Christ the King Roman Catholic were rebuilt after fires, and the Salvation Army opened a hostel on Larch Street.

By 1950 Sudbury had reached a crisis. There was no more space for buildings within the old city limits and unregulated development had been permitted both within and outside the town limits. Strip development was creeping out the Kingsway, up Notre Dame, along Lorne, and down Regent and Paris. Nodules were emerging in the Lasalle-Barrydowne area of what was already being called New Sudbury. Lo-Ellen Park to the south was in its infancy but growing.[74]

Don Forbes, a *Sudbury Daily Star* reporter, described what he had seen when he flew over the city with Nickel Belt Airways in January 1949:

> The mighty Sudbury district unfolds around the city like a map as the plane rises – first the smoke of the Coniston smelter, then the white farm fields along the old Garson road and of the Blezard Valley, finally the smoke of Falconbridge and from trains at Capreol coming over the horizon.
>
> Over the whole preside the three stacks of Copper Cliff, which look huge even from above. In the distance on all sides circle the dark rock of the outpost hills, beyond which signs of civilization lose themselves in the vastness of the district.
>
> From the ground, the Sudbury area seems densely settled and even on a map the many roads, towns and railroad lines give it the appearance of concentrated civilization. It is different from the air, however.

From above, the eye can take in the deserted areas lurking just behind the hills hemming in the roads and fertile valleys and the general impression is one of man's works making only a slight impression on the works of nature.

The close relationship of Sudbury and railroads is one of the first things noticed from the air. Dividing the city into four distinct communities, the C.P.R. main line and Sault Ste. Marie branch and the C.N.R. line cut dark paths between the closely packed buildings.

The January snow, of course, had covered most of "man's works" in the Sudbury district, but Forbes recognized a central feature of the district. As he circled overhead he was struck by the dense central city and the numerous tentacles of roads and rails reaching out from the core. It was, he decided, "like a huge sprawling octopus."[75]

1   *Sudbury Star*, 4 September 1939 and throughout the month. Note that on 1 December 1939 the *Sudbury Star* began to appear daily under the name *Sudbury Daily Star*.

2   There were frequent stories about Doucette in the *Sudbury Daily Star* throughout 1942 and 1943.

3   *Sudbury Daily Star*, 13 August 1940, 29 June 1940, 8 February 1941, 11 July 1940, 12 August 1940, 24 June 1942, 20 June 1940, 24 June 1940, 11 November 1940, 23 April 1941, 4 September 1941, 28 December 1943, 28 February 1942, 30 July 1942, 29 August 1940, 3 September 1940, and 25 October 1941.

4   Ibid., 22 September, 1 February 1940, and 31 July 1942.

5   Ibid., 22 May 1943, 9 February 1940, 7 March 1942, and 12 February 1940.

6   Ibid., 6 May 1940 and 4 June 1941.

7   Ibid., 16 October 1939 and 18 September 1940.

8   Ibid., 25 January 1940, 23 and 26 February 1940, 7 March 1940, and 2 and 29 December 1939.

9   Ibid., 28 April 1942.

10 Ibid., 19 January and 20 April 1940.

11 Ibid., 28 June, 12 September 1940, 24 July 1941, 29 May 1942, 11 April 1942, and 11 October 1941.

12 Ibid., 18 and 20 November 1942.

13 Ibid., 15 August 1945.

14 *Canada Year Book*, 1945, 315.

15 D.M. LeBourdais, *Sudbury Basin: The Story of Nickel* (Toronto: Ryerson, 1953), 168–69.

16 INCO *Triangle* 4, no. 1 (April 1944): 2, and 8, no. 1 (April 1948): 8.

17 The INCO expansion figures are found in Charles Dorion, *The First 75 Years: A Headline History of Sudbury, Canada* (Ilfracombe: Stockwell, [1958?]), 177–80.

18 O.W. Main, *The Canadian Nickel Industry: A Study in Market Control and Public Policy* (Toronto: University of Toronto Press, 1955), 122.

19 See Mike Solski and John Smaller, *Mine Mill: The History of the International Union of Mine, Mill and Smelter Workers in Canada Since 1885* (Ottawa: Steel Rail, 1984), chap. 5; Irving Abella, *Nationalism, Communism and Canadian Labour: the CIO, the Communist Party, and the Canadian Congress of Labour, 1935–1936* (Toronto: University of Toronto Press, 1973), 86; and John B. Lang, "A Lion in a Den of Daniels: A History of the International Union of Mine, Mill and Smelter Workers in Sudbury, Ontario, 1942–1962" (M.A. thesis, University of Guelph, 1970), 51–58.

20 Solski and Smaller, *Mine Mill*, 103.

21 Abella, *Nationalism, Communism and Canadian Labour*, 90; Lang, "A Lion in a Den of Daniels," 66; and Jim Tester, "The Shaping of Sudbury: A Labour View" (address to a public meeting of the Sudbury and District Historical Society, Sudbury, 18 April 1979), 25.

22 See, for example, *Sudbury Daily Star*, 24 April 1943 (editorial).

23 Bob Miner, *Miner's Life: Bob Miner and Union Organizing in Timmins, Kirkland Lake, and Sudbury*, ed. Wayne Roberts (Hamilton: Labour Studies Programme, McMaster University, 1979), 10 and elsewhere.

24 Lang, "A Lion in a Den of Daniels," 68; Tester, "The Shaping of Sudbury," 26; and *Sudbury Daily Star*, 11 November 1942.

25 *Sudbury Daily Star*, 16 April 1943.

26 Quoted in Miner, *Miner's Life*, 8.

27 Abella, *Nationalism, Communism and Canadian Labour*, 90; and Lang, "A Lion in a Den of Daniels," 65.

28 In July 1980, Robert Carlin taped a series of interviews with Anne Boyd. These tapes are available at the Sudbury Industrial Archives (SIA), J-N. Desmarais Library, Laurentian University. The information here is from the third tape, cited hereinafter as Carlin Tapes. Abella, *Nationalism, Communism and Canadian Labour*, 90, and Lang, "A Lion in a Den of Daniels," *passim*, also stress the importance of Carlin.

29 Lang, "A Lion in a Den of Daniels," 76.

30 *Sudbury Daily Star*, 21 December 1943.

31 Carlin Tape IV, 78–79.

32 See the correspondence between James Kidd and his brother Cleve (the Kidd papers) in SIA; also Lang, "A Lion in a Den of Daniels," *passim*.

33 Abella, *Nationalism, Communism and Canadian Labour*, 86.

34 Solski and Smaller, *Mine Mill*, 125.

35 Abella, *Nationalism, Communism and Canadian Labour*, 101–10; and Lang, "A Lion in a Den of Daniels," 149–73.

36 Lang, "A Lion in a Den of Daniels," 84.

37 *Sudbury Daily Star*, 21 and 22 July 1943.

38 Ibid., 23 July 1943.

39 Ibid., 5 June 1945.

40 Ontario, *Debates of the Legislative Assembly*, 28 October 1947, 1056–61.

41 Ibid., 11 March 1948, 163–69 and 16 March 1948, 295–96.

42 *Sudbury Daily Star*, 8 June 1948. The results in Sudbury Riding were as follows: Welland Gemmell, Progressive Conservative, 8,940; Robert H. Carlin, Independent-CCF, 8,648; William S. Beaton, Liberal, 6,959; Victor Whalen, CCF, 5,852; and J.M. Leduc, UE, 402.

43 *Sudbury Daily Star*, 7 December 1943.

44 Carlin, Tape V.

45 Abella, *Nationalism, Communism and Canadian Labour*, 91-98. See also the interchange in

the Ontario legislature between Carlin, then CCF-MPP for Sudbury, and Kelso Roberts, a Progressive Conservative MPP (Ontario, *Debates of the Legislative Assembly*, 11 March 1948, 163–69, and 16 March 1948, 295–96).

46 Interviews with D. Paul and A. Hastie, 12 May 1992.

47 This image is held by most people who recall the era. George Thomson, who arrived in town in 1939 to teach English at Sudbury Mining and Technical School, supplied this statement on 12 May 1992.

48 *Sudbury Daily Star*, 8 December 1942 and 4 December 1948.

49 Ibid., 3 December 1940. Beaton's first victory in 1940 was facilitated by a divided vote in the Flour Mill. Beaton received 2,875 votes, Laforest, 2,462, and E.A. Whissell, 1,431, with 867 of them in the Flour Mill. Laforest may have lacked the common touch.

50 See for example *Sudbury Daily Star*, 2 December 1950.

51 Ibid., 24 April 1943.

52 *Sudbury Beacon*, 10 August 1943; see also advertisement in the *Sudbury Beacon*, 31 July 1943.

53 *Sudbury Daily Star*, 5 December 1944.

54 *Sudbury Beacon*, 7 December 1943.

55 Lang, "A Lion in a Den of Daniels," 88–89.

56 *Sudbury Daily Star*, 5 December 1944.

57 Ibid., 16 March 1940.

58 Ibid., articles on 24 February 1940, 5 September 1940, 7 January 1941, 4 September 1941, and 4 May 1943; editorials on 26 February 1940, 8 and 17 January 1941, and 7 April 1943; advertisement of 14 August 1940.

59 Ibid., 25 February 1943.

60 Ibid. The CPR, which always refused to help pay for underpasses, was consistent. According to the *Sudbury Daily Star*, 14 December 1949, D.S. Thompson, CPR vice-president, told the city by letter that the "subway [underpass] will not greatly benefit the railway and that the contribution will not be made."

61 Nowhere is the story of the streetcars treated with more affection than in John D. Knowles and Nickel Belt Rails, *The Sudbury Streetcars: The Sudbury–Copper Cliff Suburban Electric Railway Company* (Sudbury: Nickel Belt Rails, 1983).

62 *Sudbury Daily Star*, 7 December 1948.

63 Ibid., 10 January 1940, 18 April 1940, 16 July 1940, 22 June 1940, 2 October 1940, and 24 December 1940.

64 Ibid., 27 November 1940. Birks had previously been in the Capital Theatre building.

65 Ibid., 2 January 1941.

66 Ibid., 30 July 1940 (editorial).

67 Ibid., 2 January 1942 and 21 March 1942.

68 He also owned the *North Bay Nugget*, situated in the same federal constituency as Sudbury, until the election of 1949.

69 Interview with George Grace, former managing editor of the *Star*, 22 May 1992.

70 *Sudbury Daily Star*, 17 February 1949.

71 Dorion, *The First 75 Years*, 206.

72 See, for example, *Sudbury Daily Star*, 3 August 1944, 2 November 1944, 2 October 1946, 26 November 1946, and 15 December 1949.

73 *Recollections 1908–1983* (Sudbury: Reunion 83, 1983).

74 *Sudbury Daily Star*, 30 September 1949, advertisement.

75 Ibid., 11 January 1949.

CHAPTER EIGHT

THE 1950S

O.W. Saarinen

"No community in Canada faces a brighter future than does this capital city of Northern Ontario,"[1] the *Sudbury Daily Star* pronounced on 25 April 1950. Subsequent events supported the forecast, for in Sudbury the fifties were years of growth, prosperity, and unbridled optimism, at least until 1958. The rising standard of living was fuelled by the continual expansion of the operations of local nickel producers in response to strong demand in the world nickel market. This growth attracted a much-enlarged unionized labour force that not only gave Sudbury its first industrial strike in 1958 but also made the city the site of one of the most spectacular inter-union rivalries and raids in Canadian history.

The economic buoyancy of the Sudbury Basin also began the slow process of fundamental change in the structure of local employment and population, particularly in Sudbury. The reshaping of the city went hand in hand with urban sprawl beyond the municipal boundary. The phenomenon was most notable in the adjoining townships and in the Valley to the north. In the short term this led to demands that the city boundaries be enlarged; in the long run it laid the foundation for regional planning and government. The decade ended with the successful expansion of the city through the amalgamation and annexation of surrounding areas and with visions for "continued economic growth" and a "new adventure and new experience."[2] As it had for the first half of the century, Sudbury throughout the 1950s continued to serve as the central urban node of the Sudbury Basin, but its influence throughout northeastern Ontario became even more pronounced in the decade.

The unprecedented expansion of the local mining industry during the fifties was directly linked to the decision by the United States government to encourage international competition and to break up monopolies as part of its policy to contain communism and promote global stability. The American decision had an immediate effect on the Sudbury economy because INCO had almost a monopoly of the "free world's" nickel supply and because American defence officials believed that nickel constituted "the world's most critical material." The Korean War (1950–53) brought this concern into sharp focus. As a consequence of the new policy, the United States allocated $789 million between 1950 and 1957 both to stockpile nickel and to diversify its suppliers of strategic metals through special purchase agreements.[3] According to the Royal Commission on Canada's Economic Prospects (1955), these American contracts were the most significant factor in Canadian nickel production at the time.[4]

After the outbreak of hostilities in Korea, INCO, under the direction of its chairman and president John F. Thompson, began an extensive development of new underground mines to replace the open pits, which were nearly exhausted. This program resulted in the beginning of regular production at Murray mine in 1950, the initiation of the Creighton project for the mining of lower-grade ores by inexpensive caving methods in 1951, the opening of the Stobie section of the Frood-Stobie mine in 1951, the introduction of oxygen flash-smelting of copper concentrates in 1952, the large-scale production of liquid sulphur dioxide by Canadian Industries Limited in 1952, and the perfection of a new process for recovering nickel from pyrrhotite while simultaneously recovering a high-grade iron ore.[5]

A five-year stockpiling contract to sell nickel and copper to the United States in 1953, combined with increased use of nickel for civilian purposes, led to the expansion of mining, promoted and increased the utilization of ores, and encouraged the search for new nickel supplies. After Henry Wingate became president of INCO in 1955, the company began mining at a far greater depth than ever before attempted locally. Above ground, an iron-ore recovery plant was constructed near Copper Cliff in 1956; its 194-metre stack was the world's tallest smelter chimney. Later that year, INCO announced that it would develop a nickel deposit in the Mystery-Moak Lake district of Manitoba. This assured the company of two reliable sources of nickel in Canada. In 1957 a new sulphuric acid plant was completed at Copper Cliff by Canadian Industries Limited. That year marked a high point for nickel producers in several ways. Production surpassed expectations at the very time that the military demand was less than the civilian demand for the first time since 1950. This was a portent of a soft market. The next year the International Union of Mine, Mill and Smelter Workers (IUMMSW) struck INCO for the first time.

Owing to the depressed state of the market and the end of stockpiling by the United States, the company easily waited out the strikers and dictated a contract. By the end of the decade, however, operations had returned to normal.

Throughout the fifties Falconbridge Nickel Mines grew from being a minor producer with an essentially European market into a major producer through its development of mines on the northern part of the Sudbury Basin and an aggressive sales campaign that broke INCO's monopoly in the United States. Much of the credit for this progress went to Horace Fraser, who was vice-president of Falconbridge at the time, but his success was made possible by the American decision to diversify its suppliers.[6] The expansion of the Falconbridge operations began slowly in 1951 when McKim mine joined Falconbridge as a source of ore for the Falconbridge smelter. In 1952 and 1953 the company signed large contracts with the United States for nickel and cobalt for a period extending to 1962. The 1953 contract proved to be the big breakthrough for Falconbridge. Under its terms the United States agreed to pay, in addition to the market price, a premium of forty cents a pound on the first 100 million pounds of nickel produced. Since the market price was set by INCO, the contract amounted to a $40-million subsidy to Falconbridge; this was enough to cover the estimated cost of the expansion needed to fulfil the contract.[7]

During the decade, Falconbridge purchased the M.J. Poupore Lumber Company (in 1952) and opened numerous mines, including Mount Nickel (between 1954 and 1957), Hardy (in 1954), East (in 1954), Longvack (in 1956), and Fecunis (in 1959). The symbol of the advances made by the company was the opening of its technologically advanced smelter in 1958. The year 1959 was noteworthy in that it marked the first time that production from the northern mines (Hardy, Longvack, and Fecunis) exceeded that from the southern mines (Falconbridge, East, and McKim). By the end of the decade Falconbridge's post-war expansion had exceeded expectations[8] and the company had avoided a confrontation with its workers.

There were other mining companies in the Sudbury Basin during the 1950s, though they were small by comparison. They were Milnet Mines, (1952–54), Nickel (East) Rim Mines (1952–58), Nickel Offsets (1953–57), Consolidated Sudbury Basin Mines (1955–57), and Lowphos Ore. The last was a subsidiary of the National Steel Corporation, which began the open-pit mining of iron ore at Moose Mountain near Capreol in 1959.[9] The reopening of the Moose Mountain mine was part of a new trend in the steel industry in North America towards using lower-grade iron ore.[10]

The significance of mining and mining-related employment during

The northwest corner of Durham and Larch has been the site of hotels for over one hundred years. These three photos show the location from the first decade of the century through the 1930s and into the 1940s. The Coulson Hotel, which still stands, was built in 1938, replacing the New American, which had burned in 1937.

Courtesy: Ray Thoms.

At the end of the 1940s Sudbury was one of the fastest-growing cities in Canada.
The streetcar, the Balmoral Hotel, and the post office were all to disappear within a
decade. Progress in the form of the automobile, the bus (centre left), and new
buildings would replace them.

Sudbury's city council changed in 1954 with the arrival of several new faces. Grace Hartman, centre, was to become the city's first woman mayor. To her left is Joe Fabbro, who would serve as mayor a record thirteen of the nineteen years between 1957 and 1975. From left to right: Pat Murphy, Sam Rothschild, G. Coe, Hartman, Fabbro, Vic Whalen, A. Gravel, K. McNeil, J. Cormack, and A. Theriault.

Local 598 of the International Union of Mine, Mill and Smelter Workers became a vital organization in Sudbury in the 1940s and 1950s. One of its activities was to run the Mine Mill Camp at Richard Lake. This group of children at a day camp in the early 1950s receives a nature lesson. Weir Reid, the controversial recreational director of the union, is on the right.

Nels Thibault moved through several offices in Local 598 of Mine Mill in the 1940s and 1950s to become national president of the union during the critical years between 1955 and 1960. He supported the 1958 strike and fought a losing battle against the United Steelworkers of America in the raids between 1959 and 1963.

Courtesy: Mike Solski/Sudbury Public Library.

The 1958 Mine Mill strike against the International Nickel Company is a pivotal event in Sudbury's history. On the eve of the strike, 23 September 1958, the men gathered at Mine Mill Hall to receive last-minute instructions (above). The following day the men were out in force at the Copper Cliff smelter.

Courtesy: Mike Solski/Sudbury Public Library.

Though the 1958 strike was without violence, the fight for domination between Mine Mill and the Steelworkers was marked by skirmishes, vandalism, brutality, and deceitfulness. Some old friends have never spoken since. Pictured here is a row that took place on 26 August 1961.

Courtesy: *Local 598 Mine Mill News.*

The role of women in the 1958 strike has been misrepresented by both sides. That the Mine Mill strikers had the support of women throughout is obvious from this picture of some of the 4,000 women who rallied to the strikers' support on 10 December 1958, shortly before the strike ended. The settlement was ignominious, however, and it became fashionable to blame the end on the "woman factor."

Courtesy: Mike Solski/Sudbury Public Library.

On 12 December 1958 a "back to work" meeting was orchestrated at the Sudbury Arena by several groups, though few of the 2,000 in attendance were members of Mine Mill. Mayor Joe Fabbro, centre left, spearheaded the move along with Mrs. Leola Breen. There is no evidence that Mine Mill "women" participated in the meeting despite the claims of the anti-union media or the later accusations of Mine Mill apologists.

Courtesy: Mike Solski.

In the 1950s and 1960s Sudburians began to build subdivisions on the previously
avoided blackened rock. Shown here is one of the earliest near Regent, looking
west to Copper Cliff and the Superstack. The regular formations on the horizon to
the right are the slag piles.

Courtesy: Gerald O. Tapper.

The typical Sudbury house was a small wood frame structure like those shown
burning here. Poor fire protection led to some of the highest insurance rates in
Canada. Urban renewal in the central city demolished acres of similar houses. This
fire in the 1960s was in the Gatchell district, home to immigrant populations such as
the Italians. Note the gardens.

Courtesy: Bob Keir.

Elm Street, looking east in 1973. The streetcars are gone and the Balmoral has been replaced by Zellers. The Nickel Range Hotel was demolished four years later. Much of the area on the east side of Elm in the background was the centre of Sudbury's urban renewal project, including a city centre shopping mall.

Courtesy: Inco Archives.

The original St. Andrew's Presbyterian Church on Larch Street, built in 1910
in the fashionable Gothic revival style, grew to serve Northern Ontario's largest
Protestant congregation as St. Andrew's United Church before it was closed on
22 September 1968.

Courtesy: Michael J. Mulloy.

When old St. Andrew's was demolished, the congregation decided to replace it with
an innovative "place of worship, of cultural activity, and of community dialogue." On
27 May 1973 the multifunctional St. Andrew's Place was officially dedicated.
Housing a sanctuary, a few shops, several study rooms and lounges in the tower on
the right, and senior citizen accommodations in the tower on the left, it has given
new meaning to the role of the inner-city church.

Courtesy: Michael J. Mulloy.

A clear indication of changing times is reflected by this picture of professionals
on strike. A long strike by secondary school teachers closed the schools for
months in 1980. The blue-collar worker in the smelter had been replaced by the
white-collar professional at Civic Square.

Courtesy: *Northern Life.*

Shown here at a performance in Sudbury in the early 1980s, Robert Paquette
was a member of the Sudbury group CANO before achieving stardom
as a single performer.

Courtesy: *Le Voyageur.*

Few groups were more active or visible in the 1970s than the Sudbury Franco-
Ontarian arts community. The old Ste. Anne's Parish Hall under the name "La
Slague" became the vital centre for cultural and musical activities. Several of the
largely volunteer participants are shown here. The theatre was upstairs; the
"Galerie du Nouvel-Ontario," in the basement.

Courtesy: Cédéric Michaud.

During the 1970s cross-country skiing became a Sudbury pastime, with numerous trails linking the lakes in and about the city, as this picture illustrates. Perhaps it was inevitable in the 1980s that an industrial city like Sudbury would virtually spurn skiing in the rush to become the "snowmobile capital of Canada."

Courtesy: Laurentian University.

Alex Baumann enthralled Sudbury and much of Canada when he captured two gold medals with two world swimming records at the 1984 Olympics. He is shown here at a victory celebration at Laurentian University.

Much of Sudbury's physical past has been replaced by modern buildings and
divided highways as the city rushes to become Toronto North. In the foreground
is the Civic Centre, which houses city and regional governments as well as the
Board of Education. The tower is a provincial government building. The area
beyond and to the right is the urban renewal district. Ste. Anne's, destroyed by an
arsonist in the summer of 1992, is in the centre background.

Courtesy: Regional Municipality of Sudbury.

Except that they work in hard rock, there is little in common between the miners
of the 1990s and those of a century earlier. Modern technology has changed the
industry almost beyond recognition.

Courtesy: Laurentian University.

The Inco Superstack has been a landmark since its erection in 1970. Controversial from the beginning, it is credited with virtually eliminating the pollution problem in Sudbury, on the one hand, and with spreading pollutants to far-flung regions of eastern North America, on the other. In the foreground are the "company houses" that once housed the middle management but that are now both privately owned and well maintained.

Courtesy: Gerald O. Tapper.

From its opening in 1984 Science North has symbolized the importance of tourism in the diversification of the Sudbury economy. The interactive displays attract a year-round clientele, while Lake Ramsey is an ideal setting for several activities. In the heart of winter the Snowflake Festival (above) has become popular, while in the summer (below) boat cruises on the *Cortina* depart from Science North regularly. The Sudbury Yacht Club is shown in the foreground.

Courtesy: Science North.

Table 8.1
Sudbury District Labour Force by Industrial Groups, 1951 and 1961

	1951		1961	
Industry	*Number*	*%*	*Number*	*%*
Total	40,326	100.0	55,254	100.0
Agriculture	1,529	3.8	794	1.4
Forestry	2,140	5.3	1,538	2.8
Mining and quarrying	11,134	27.6	16,316	29.5
Manufacturing	8,146	20.2	7,251	13.1
Construction	2,923	7.2	3,089	5.6
Transportation, communication, and utilities	3,867	9.6	4,805	8.7
Trade	3,851	9.6	6,987	12.6
Finance, insurance, and real estate	537	1.3	1,136	2.1
Community business and personal service	5,634	14.0	9,302	16.8
Public admin. and defence	n.a.	n.a.	2,548	4.6
Other	500	1.2	1,465	2.7

Source: Statistics Canada, *Census of Canada*, 1951 and 1961.

the fifties is shown in Table 8.1. Between 1951 and 1961 employment in the district grew from about 40,300 to more than 55,000, an increase of 37 percent; the mining component increased from 27.6 percent to 29.5 percent. The regional economy was still primary or extractive. Manufacturing was the second-most-important economic activity. Much of this manufacturing, however, was related to mining, for it included concentrating, smelting, and refining. The significance of manufacturing declined substantially in both absolute and relative terms. Whereas in 1951 manufacturing accounted for slightly more than 20 percent of the labour force, by 1961 the proportion had dropped to just over 13 percent. In the Sudbury Basin proper, the share of direct employment by INCO and Falconbridge declined from more than 40 percent in 1951 to 36 percent in 1961.[11] On the other hand, employment in trade rose, owing in part to the increased importance of Sudbury as a retailing and wholesaling centre for the new community of Elliot Lake, created between 1956 and 1959.

The rise of the mining industry was paralleled by the emergence of the International Union of Mine Mill and Smelter Workers (IUMMSW) as a powerful and militant union. After the Canadian Congress of Labour (CLC) expelled the IUMMSW in 1949, it granted the jurisdictional rights of the mine, mill, and smelter workers of Canada, including those employed by INCO and Falconbridge Nickel Mines, to the United Steelworkers of America (USWA). The first attempt by the USWA to raid Mine Mill Local 598 in 1950 failed. Within Mine Mill, the battles of the union with the CCL and the Co-operative Commonwealth Federation (CCF) led in 1951 to Nels Thibault replacing Robert Carlin as regional director for District 8 in Eastern Canada. In the same year Thibault's promotion resulted in the 1951 election of Mike Solski as the president of Local 598.[12] Solski was returned by acclamation in 1953, 1955, and 1956. Under the leadership of Thibault and Solski, Mine Mill engaged in an active program of unionizing the service workers of the city under the banner of the General Workers' Union, Local 902. Union halls were built in Sudbury, Garson, Chelmsford, Coniston, and Creighton. The union also made important social and cultural contributions to the region by establishing a summer camp for its members and their families at Richard Lake in 1951, hiring Weir Reid as a recreational director in 1952, supporting numerous local fund-raising drives, and sponsoring cultural events. Even in those matters, the Cold War intervened. The union sponsorship of a planned visit by the Royal Winnipeg Ballet in 1954 was cancelled through American intervention. The union also met problems when it tried to have its criticism of local institutions reported in the local media.[13]

In 1955 the union members in Mine Mill became the first in Canada to be granted total autonomy within an international union. This autonomy was followed by increased efforts by the Steelworkers to penetrate Mine Mill in Canada. These efforts culminated in the elimination of Mine Mill as a union force in the Elliot Lake area. The position of Mine Mill was further weakened by an economic depression in the non-ferrous metals industry in 1957. It was against that backdrop that negotiations began with INCO for a new contract. On 15 March 1958, INCO announced that it was laying off 1,000 employees at Sudbury. Despite strong protests from Mine Mill and a rebuke from Kelso Roberts, the attorney-general of Ontario, INCO laid off 300 more employees while negotiations were taking place. On 23 May the company made its final offer of a two-year contract with no wage increases. When Mine Mill rejected the offer, INCO reduced the work week to thirty-two hours. After attempts at conciliation failed on 24 September 1958, Local 598 struck INCO. Thus began the first in a series of strikes that were to become a way of life for those employed in the Sudbury mining industry. Unfortunately for the union, the strike was called at a time when the company had a large inventory. The job action continued without incident until December, at which time a "back to work" movement supported by Mayor Joe Fabbro, Mrs. Leola Bleen, several religious leaders, but few strikers' wives contributed to a resumption of negotiations.[14] On 22 December 1958 the Mine Mill workers ratified a humiliating contract that provided for wage increases of only 6 percent over three years. INCO's use of accumulated inventories and mass layoffs as collective bargaining tools had proved to be an enormously effective corporate tactic.[15]

The humiliation of Mine Mill set the stage for an internal reform movement in the union. Spurred by dissatisfaction with financial management and the desire for affiliation of the local with the Canadian Labour Congress, calls were made for a change in leadership. The need for reform was actively supported by the Roman Catholic Church through the person of Alexandre Boudreau, an economics professor at the University of Sudbury, who formed the Northern Workers' Adult Education Association and conducted local, adult leadership courses for miners.[16] Boudreau's desire for change was based on his belief that the local leaders of Local 598 were communists. In the executive elections of 10 March 1959, the Solski slate was defeated by the reformers, led by Don Gillis, who ran on a platform of affiliation with the Canadian Labour Congress. The goal of the Gillis administration was twofold: full internal control of union finances by the local membership and open warfare against communism. These policies brought the administration into a confrontation with the national executive of the IUMMSW headed by Nels Thibault. Other actions taken by Gillis included the controversial firing of Weir Reid, the recreation director, who bore the brunt of the anti-communist zeal of the reformers, and the hiring of Allistair Stewart, a chartered accountant and former CCF member of Parliament for Winnipeg, to audit the books of Local 598. After a month of detailed investigation, Stewart presented a report critical of Mine Mills' bookkeeping procedures; the report did not, however, contain any allegations of illegal actions.[17]

With a critical situation brewing in Sudbury, Thibault resigned as national president to contest the presidency of Local 598 in an election scheduled for 17 November 1959. This election became a major topic of discussion at the Catholic Social Life Conference held in Sudbury in October, at which time Mayor Joe Fabbro asked the residents of the region to prove their opposition to communism. Boudreau claimed that the election represented "a last ditch fight between Christianity and Communism." Thibault was subsequently defeated in a huge turnout of members.[18] As the decade ended, the stage was set for a raid on Local 598 by the Steelworkers.

The increased employment in the mining industry during the fifties resulted in a large growth in population throughout the Sudbury Basin. That growth was reinforced by improvements in the transportation and communication systems, which made Sudbury more important as a distribution centre for northeastern Ontario. Meanwhile there were demands for improvements in public services. As early as 1950 Mayor W.S. Beaton observed that growth in the Sudbury area had "caused it to far outstrip those facilities provided by the provincial and federal governments such as public buildings, local offices of government service and especially education, highways, hospitals, airport, and encouragement to industries."[19]

The population changes in the Sudbury area from 1951 to 1961 are shown in Table 8.2. During this period the Sudbury Census Metropolitan Area grew by more than 58 percent, the fourth-highest rate of metropolitan growth in Canada after Calgary, Edmonton, and Saskatoon. The increase in population was due partly to natural increase (at 2.9 percent a year, one of the highest in Ontario) and partly to a positive net migration of more than twenty thousand for the entire Sudbury district.[20] The region continued to attract new migrants from 1951 until 1958. The migration process also changed the ethnic composition of the regional population. The most notable change was the increase in the proportion of Italians and Germans, while the percentage of British, French, and Ukrainian groups also declined (see Table 8.3). Though much of the population continued to live in ethnic enclaves, there was a considerable increase in the number of Italians in the Gatchell and Robinson Lake neighbourhoods of the city.

As the population grew, old landmarks disappeared, among them the Central Public School across from the CPR station in 1950, the Kingsway and Copper Cliff arches in 1950 and 1952, the streetcars in

Table 8.2
Sudbury Census Metropolitan Area Population Growth, 1951–1961

Year	Population	Growth Rate (%)
1951	80,543	33.9 (1951–56)
1956	107,889	18.0 (1956–61)
1961	127,446	58.2 (1951–61)

Source: Statistics Canada, *Census of Canada*, 1951, 1956, and 1961.

Table 8.3
Population by Ethnic Origin in the Sudbury Area

| Ethnic Origin | City of Sudbury | | | | Sudbury Metropolitan Area | |
| | 1951 | | 1961 | | 1961 | |
	N	%	N	%	N	%
British	15,502	36.6	26,748	33.4	37,084	33.5
French	16,060	37.9	27,340	34.1	40,012	36.1
Ukrainian	2,571	6.1	3,881	4.8	4,942	4.5
Italian	1,502	3.5	6,343	7.9	8,080	7.3
Finnish	1,478	3.5	2,994	3.7	na	na
Polish	1,127	2.7	2,302	2.9	2,845	2.6
German	845	2.0	3,211	4.0	4,215	3.8
Netherlands	284	0.7	677	0.8	1,064	1.0
Scandinavian	389	0.9	910	1.1	1,192	1.1
Other	2,652	6.2	5,714	7.3	11,260	10.1
Total	42,410	100.00	80,120	100.0	110,694	100

Source: Statistics Canada, *Census of Canada*, 1951 and 1961.

1950, the Joduin icehouse near Lake Ramsey, the meat section of the City Market in 1951, the old Balmoral Hotel in 1957, and, most regrettably of all, the post office building at the corner of Elm and Durham streets in 1959. Meanwhile new public buildings were appearing in and around the city. Among them were the Sudbury General Hospital in 1950, at the time the city's highest building, the Sudbury-Algoma Sanatorium in 1952, and the Sudbury Memorial Hospital in 1956. These facilities made Sudbury the dominant medical centre for northeastern Ontario. There were also new social and cultural buildings: the Sudbury Arena was built in 1951 on the site of the former Central Public School, the Sudbury Public Library in 1952, and the Pioneer Manor Home for the Aged and the Community Y in 1953. The same decade saw the formation of the Sudbury Male Chorus in 1951, the Sudbury Symphony Orchestra in 1953, and both the Sudbury Philharmonic Society and the Karl Pukara Accordion Orchestra in 1957.[21]

Other changes were due to commercial development. In the downtown, chain stores were enlarged (Kresge's in 1950 and 1959) and new stores added, such as Canadian Tire in 1953 and Zellers in 1958. The

Empire, Lasalle, and Plaza cinemas were built during this decade, a modern Sudbury Hydro building went up in 1957, and a new federal post office building was built in 1958 on Elm Street. Grocery shopping habits were changed by the increased use of cars, which forced the large grocery chains to seek strategic locations near the periphery of the downtown, where there was more space for parking. Loblaw's, for example, moved to Frood and Elm in 1950, A & P chose Elm and Lansdowne in 1951, and that same year, Dominion built at Riverside and Regent. All of these changes, though, paled in comparison to the opening of the New Sudbury Shopping Centre in 1957, the most significant commercial innovation in decades. Built by Principal Investments of Toronto, it was located on twenty-eight acres of land in McKim Township at the corner of Lasalle Boulevard and Barrydowne Road, with parking for more than two thousand cars. An immediate success, the shopping centre tilted the centre of gravity of the city to the northeast. The attraction of the shopping centre led to the immediate decline of the city downtown as a magnet for shoppers.[22]

As the population grew, older regional schools had to be expanded and new ones built. In 1951 alone, Sudbury High School, St. Charles College, and the St. Elizabeth School of Nursing moved into new quarters. They were followed by Marymount School of Nursing in 1953, Chelmsford High School in 1955, Nickel District Collegiate and Vocational Institute and Marymount College in 1956–57, Lively High School in 1957, Levack High School in 1958, and Lockerby Composite School in 1959.[23]

The most noteworthy educational event of the decade, however, was the evolution of Le Collège du Sacré-Coeur into the University of Sudbury/Université de Sudbury. Under rights granted by the original charter of 1914, the board of directors of the Jesuit college decided in 1956 to transform the institution into a university. The University of Sudbury was subsequently approved by the Province of Ontario in 1957, and in the same year Le Séminaire de Hearst became an affiliate of the fledgling institution. Plans to construct the university beside the existing college on Notre Dame Avenue were dropped and a search undertaken for a permanent site elsewhere. In the meantime evening courses leading to a B.A. were offered by the University of Sudbury in scattered locations in the city. In 1958 the university acquired temporary accommodations in the Empire Building (formerly the Grand Theatre) on Elgin Street. A board of regents was formed, which included such prominent men as Benjamin Avery, J.N. Desmarais, H.J. Fraser, P.J. McAndrew, George Miller, R.D. Parker, S. St. Aubin, and A.J. Samson. Under an agreement with the Engineering Faculty of the University of Toronto, engineering courses were started in the fall of the year. Early in 1959 the Reverend Émile Bouvier assumed the position of president of the University of Sudbury, replacing the Reverend A. Raymond.[24]

By that time the Northern Ontario University Association had been formed under the leadership of the Reverend E. Lautenslager of the United Church in Sudbury. The purpose of the association was to create a Protestant university or college within a federated university which would also include the University of Sudbury.[25] There was heated debate about both the nature of such a university and its location. North Bay in particular was determined to be the site and was supported by the Northeastern University Committee, which had been formed in 1958 to help the Roman Catholic Fathers of the Resurrection create a federated university in that community.[26] All the while the University of Sudbury was in serious financial difficulty because of the provincial government's policy of not funding denominational universities. It was within this context that talks began between the University of Sudbury, the Northern Ontario University Association, and the Northeastern University Committee to discuss the feasibility of forming a federated bilingual university in Northern Ontario.[27] After many charges of foul play and a series of complex manoeuvres involving church leaders, politicians, and corporations, Laurentian University of Sudbury was established in 1960, making the city the centre of post-secondary education in northeastern Ontario.[28]

Sudbury's regional importance in health and education was aided considerably by advances in transportation and communications. The decade opened with the construction of the Union Bus Depot by Local Lines Ltd. in 1950, the opening of the Lorne Street underpass, and the creation of Sudbury Bus Lines by Paul Desmarais in 1951. It was from this modest beginning that Desmarais later rose to the top rank of the Canadian "Establishment."[29] During the decade, Sudbury's links with southern Ontario were expanded with the opening of the Sudbury–Parry Sound stretch of Highway 69 in 1952 and the beginning of work on the Gravenhurst section in 1956.[30] In 1952 Sudbury Airport was opened, and in 1954 TransCanada Airlines began regular flights to Sudbury.[31]

Changes also occurred in the city core. In 1958 the CNR stated its intention of moving its downtown station in the Borgia Street area to a new site in Neelon Township,[32] thus paving the way for a renewal study in the downtown core, which had declined after the opening of the New Sudbury Shopping Centre. As the decade drew to a close, proposals were made to rationalize the internal transportation network in the city by building an inner by-pass around the downtown as well as a freeway linking Highway 17 East to Brady Street over the rocky Kingsway plateau.

The function of the city as a central place was profoundly influenced by the arrival of television and French broadcasting. In 1953 CKSO-TV, owned by George Miller, W.B. Plaunt, Sr., and J.M. Cooper, became Canada's first privately owned commercial television station, and introduced Sudburians to Kay Woodill, Judy Jacobson, Trudy Manchester, Bill Kehoe, and Basil Scully, all of whom became household names. In 1957 the Sudbury area acquired a third radio station, after CKSO and CHNO, with the all-French CFBR, owned by Baxter Ricard.[33] These changes in the communications field brought about a substantial weakening of the *Sudbury Daily Star*'s influence on public opinion.

The opening of the New Sudbury Shopping Centre in 1957 symbolized a trend away from the compact city that was already well under way. In fact, while the Sudbury Census Metropolitan Area increased in population by more than one-half during the decade, that of the city of Sudbury remained constant, as shown in Table 8.4. New urban development took place largely outside of the city limits in isolated pockets and along the main highways. Much of the basis for this indiscriminate urban sprawl was the high population densities in Sudbury and the resulting high cost of land. One 1951 study reported:

> The growth of the city has now reached such proportions that the gross density of population is approximately 20 persons per acre, a degree of crowding greater than exists in any Canadian city of the same order. Little usable land remains to be developed, other than rocky escarpments and some low lying areas.[34]

The congestion was confirmed in 1953 by the Dominion Bureau of Statistics, which reported that with "42,410 jammed in 9,450 units," Sudbury was the most crowded city in Canada. More than one-third of the housing units in the community were officially designated as "overcrowded," that is, having more than one person for each room.[35] Sudbury was in a crisis and unable to absorb the population increase brought about by the expansion of the mining industry. The move from the inner city to the suburbs was led by young families attracted by single-family houses with spacious lots at reasonable prices.[36]

A glance at Map 8.1 (page 202) reveals three patterns of urban expansion beyond the city limits during the fifties. The first pattern was an urban sweep into McKim and Neelon townships. In McKim, residential

Table 8.4
Population of Selected Municipalities in the Sudbury Region,
1950–1959

Year	City of Sudbury	McKim Twp.	Neelon & Garson Twp.	Waters Twp.	Drury, Denison, & Graham Twps.	Rayside Twp.	Hanmer Twp.	Balfour Twp.	Dowling Twp.
1950	47,054	10,788	4,994	852	522	1,051	844	658	292
1951	50,222	11,707	5,872	997	597	1,338	862	630	194
1952	46,059	12,700	7,195	1,166	776	1,460	969	687	267
1953	46,043	14,196	8,790	1,188	855	1,723	1,114	800	564
1954	46,631	15,721	10,020	1,214	998	2,371	1,241	1,069	844
1955	47,057	16,841	10,748	1,298	1,121	2,740	1,419	1,243	1,270
1956	47,245	17,751	11,674	1,444	1,205	3,100	1,562	1,448	773
1957	47,701	19,098	12,109	1,616	1,369	3,491	1,733	1,550	933
1958	47,773	19,857	12,822	1,733	1,534	3,818	2,323	1,614	972
1959	48,355	20,476	12,822*	1,798	1,511	4,055	2,763	1,658	1,039
1950–59 increase (%)	2.8	89.8	156.7	111.0	189.4	285.8	227.3	152.0	255.8

Source: Department of Municipal Affairs, *Annual Report of Municipal Statistics* (Toronto: Department of Municipal Affairs, 1950–1959).

growth was intensified around Ramsey Lake and on the flat plain beyond the Flour Mill neighbourhood.[37] East of the city, the growth followed the old Coniston Road beyond the Minnow Lake area, while to the south the growth spread along Long Lake Road into Lockerby. The residential cluster north along Lasalle Boulevard was known as New Sudbury. To the west of the city, expansion stopped at the INCO boundary. By the end of the decade, new residential development had doubled the population in McKim Township. In the meantime subdivisions were springing up rapidly in the western part of Neelon Township, especially between Barrydowne and Falconbridge Road north of Highway 17 East and from Minnow Lake to Moonlight Avenue along Bancroft Drive. These new subdivisions caused the population of the township of Neelon and Garson to increase by more than 150 percent in the fifties.

The second pattern was the spread of residential activity into the more peripheral townships situated south and west of the city. The western thrust occurred in Drury, Denison, Graham and Waters townships, while the southern penetration reached into the unorganized township of Broder. Unlike the more urban development found in McKim and Neelon, the spread of population in these outer townships had a more recreational and rural character. This was especially true of the many Finnish settlements found in these districts.

The third trend was the rapid conversion of agricultural land in the Valley into residential subdivisions, notably along Highway 69 north from McCrea Heights to Capreol and along Highway 541 from Azilda to Levack. The availability of agricultural land for settlement purposes was promoted by the unprofitability of milk and potato production and the desire of farmers to supplement their incomes by working in the mining industry or by subdividing their farms.[38] During the fifties the townships of Dowling, Balfour, Blezard, Rayside, and Hanmer all recorded significant population increases, ranging from 152 to more than 285 percent. Unfortunately, this unregulated sprawl lacked many municipal services, such as water and sewage disposal. Eventually the chaotic growth led to a crisis that overwhelmed the local municipal officials and forced the province to impose regional planning and government in the 1970s. Nevertheless, some orderly development did take place in Sudbury, in the INCO and Falconbridge company towns, and on the RCAF townsite near

Map 8.1: Sudbury Area Subdivision Applications, 1946–1959

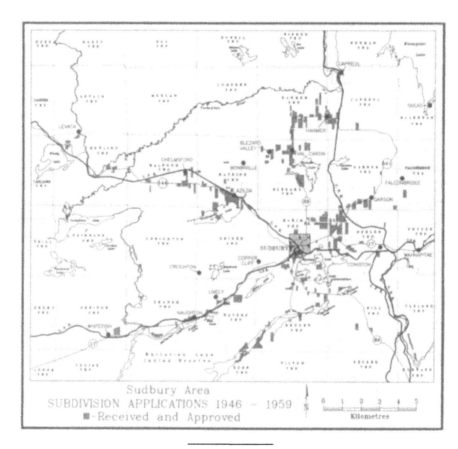

Sudbury Area
SUBDIVISION APPLICATIONS 1946 – 1959
■ Received and Approved

Hanmer. Compact residential construction in the city took place in the Beaton, Alexandra Park, Lakeview, Northern Heights, Marymount, Holditch, and Park Ridge subdivisions. The newer residential zones, many with winding streets, served as a welcome change to the traditional gridiron face of the city. Outside the city, company townsites were expanded and new ones created.[39] In 1950 INCO continued to build houses in Levack, and work was begun at Lively. This planned town on eleven hundred acres near Creighton mine in Waters Township consisted of 450 homes, built in a variety of architectural styles, with all the normal urban amenities. Incorporated as a town in 1953, Lively quickly achieved the standard three thousand population typical of company towns in the Sudbury area. Construction was simultaneously started on the RCAF townsite for the employees of the Pinetree Line radar defence station south of Hanmer. Another company-sponsored development was the erection of housing in the Improvement District of Onaping in 1956. Built to serve the needs of Falconbridge Nickel Mines in the Hardy and Levack mines area, this community reached a population of approximately one thousand by the end of the decade.[40]

The acute problems resulting from urban sprawl and the continued presence of a "one-basket" economy after the Second World War gradually brought about the realization of the need for more planning. Urban planning in the Sudbury region had begun in 1947 with the formation of the joint McKim, Neelon, and Garson Planning Area. This was followed in 1948 by the formation of the Sudbury and Suburban Planning Area.[41] The boards set up to serve these planning areas found it difficult to promote and to implement effective measures because of the rapid unregulated development immediately after the war. An important step was taken in 1950 when the consultants John Bland and Harold Spence-Sales recommended that a planner be hired and a Sudbury planning department be created. Their study included several proposals, such as the renewal of the deteriorating downtown core, the removal of the CPR and CNR connecting rail lines through the heart of the city, the construction of an inner ring road, an underpass at the junction of Riverside Drive and Elgin Street, and the creation of more public open spaces.[42]

In 1953 both the township of McKim and the township of Neelon and Garson were designated by their councils as planning areas. Despite many earlier calls for planning, it was not until 1954 that Sudbury itself was designated as a planning area and the first planning board came into existence.[43] The city, under pressure from the province to hire a planning director and to create a separate planning department, took a step in this direction in August 1955, when it hired Arnold Faintuck, an architect, as a planner for the Sudbury Area Planning Committee, which consisted of representatives from Sudbury, McKim, and Neelon and Garson. Faintuck and Oryst Sawchuk, a local architect and planner, began to promote orderly planning based on their studies at the University of Manitoba. Repeating many of the proposals in the earlier report by Bland and Spence-Sales, they called for the construction of an outer ring road circumscribing the built-up part of the city, the delimitation of twenty-nine neighbourhoods framed around the four communities of New Sudbury, Minnow Lake, the Central City, and Lockerby, and the establishment of a university campus and stadium off Notre Dame Avenue.[44]

Within the city, a temporary freezing by-law restricting all building outside the main commercial areas to single-family houses was given approval by the Ontario Municipal Board (OMB) in 1955. This interim measure was designed to give the city a measure of planning control until an official plan was completed.[45] At the same time, a comprehensive fourteen-part program covering subjects ranging from zoning to transportation was set up by Faintuck and E.W. Thrift. In the meantime studies were begun on a proposed by-pass south of the eastern approach of Highway 17 along the Kingsway to link Brady and Lorne streets.[46] In September 1957, Faintuck resigned and was replaced by Klemens Dembek, who had been born in Poland and trained at the University of Manchester in England. Dembek identified the absence of controls on land use as the main planning problem and criticized the sprawling and unregulated development that ignored long-term costs.[47] In order to combat this problem, Dembek, Sawchuk, and Prof. Gordon Stephenson of the University of Toronto began to lay the groundwork for an urban renewal study and redevelopment scheme. It was thought that such a study, to be financed by the two senior levels of government, would serve as the foundation for an official plan.[48] Another proposal was that the land bounded by Brady, Minto, Larch, and Drinkwater be acquired for a new city hall. In 1959 an urban renewal study was finally authorized; undertaken by Gordon Stephenson, it received federal approval later in the year. In August 1959 an important step was taken when the province approved Sudbury's first official plan. In October a new city zoning by-law was approved by the OMB.[49]

As a result of the accelerated population growth in the Valley, a tentative move towards planning in this area first began in 1954 with the formation of the Rayside Township Planning Area. The Onaping and Balfour planning areas followed in 1956 and 1957 respectively. As the provincial government became aware of the scattered subdivision activity in the Valley, the Department of Planning and Development attempted to encourage a broader form of area planning. These attempts eventually bore fruit, and in September 1959 the Valley municipalities requested the province to establish a joint planning area for the entire valley.[50]

Environmental planning also emerged during the late fifties.[51] In 1956 the Sudbury and District Health Unit was formed to provide health and inspection services in the Sudbury Basin and beyond. This was followed in 1957 and 1959 by the creation of the Junction Creek and Whitson Valley Conservation Authorities. These authorities were established to deal with the costly problems of the flooding that occurred annually in the city. Previously, the northern and central parts of the city had acquired a Venetian look each spring as Junction Creek overflowed its banks. Economic planning also started in 1957, when an industrial commission for the Sudbury district was established with a mandate to attract new industrial ventures to the region. After receiving its charter in October 1958, the commission hired the Battelle Memorial Institute from Columbus, Ohio, to study Sudbury's potential. The report of December 1959 suggested twenty-eight different avenues of possible economic development for the future.[52]

Some of the most bitter controversies throughout the 1950s concerned the boundaries between Sudbury and the adjoining municipalities. Though these battles were partly connected with urban sprawl, they were more intimately linked to the way in which the mining operations of INCO and Falconbridge Nickel Mines were assessed and taxed.

The rationalization of municipal boundaries in the Sudbury Basin began in a subdued fashion in January 1951, when the OMB granted Sudbury permission to annex 171 acres from McKim Township in the Gilman and Prete streets subdivision areas.[53] Later that month, Sudbury requested permission to annex all of McKim Township except the towns of Copper Cliff and Frood. The official intent of the annexation was to increase the city's population by some eleven thousand and to add an additional twenty-six square miles to the city's tiny four and a half square miles. The request set in motion a series of amalgamation and annexation requests to the OMB that were to remain unresolved throughout the decade. At the board hearings on that 1951 petition, Sudbury supported its position with the claim that the lack of municipal sewers in the Minnow Lake area was causing pollution in Lake Ramsey, the source of the city's water supply.[54] INCO argued that the territory in McKim Township lying west of Highway 69 and situated north and west of the city limits should not be annexed because it was unsuitable for building. The only reason the city wanted to annex this area, in INCO's view, was to give the municipality the opportunity to apply a profit tax to Murray and

McKim mines. The OMB delayed making a formal decision on the boundary issue until 1953, at which time it announced that the situation was so confused that it needed more information. The question was resolved temporarily in the second half of 1954, when Sudbury withdrew its application for the annexation.[55]

Various proposals for both amalgamation and annexation were discussed by local politicians throughout 1955, and a request was made to the provincial government to study the issue. This led to the release of a provincial report in the spring of 1956 that visualized a federation of thirty-three Sudbury-area municipalities with a combined population of some 123,000. Disappointed with the report, Sudbury responded with two further studies that called for the annexation of up to fourteen communities into a single municipality. The province rejected Sudbury's request and abandoned its own proposal.[56] The next action was taken in August 1956, when Sudbury applied to the OMB for the amalgamation of several nearby municipalities, including the towns of Coniston, Copper Cliff, and Frood Mine. A preliminary hearing was held in November to discuss the application in more detail. While the hearing was still pending in 1957, the OMB gave some recognition of the land crisis in Sudbury by granting the city permission to annex ninety-two acres of McKim Township for the purpose of the Northern Heights land assembly scheme.[57]

In 1957 the situation was entirely altered when the Ontario Supreme Court ruled that INCO's iron-ore plant buildings west of Copper Cliff were not assessable for the purposes of municipal taxation.[58] This judgment effectively eliminated the benefits of annexation. The vexing issue of mining taxation policy, however, which had been festering for half a century, had already forced the provincial government to devise other means of dealing with the inequity. For the city of Sudbury, which did not have any mines within its boundaries, a "provincial grant in lieu of mining tax" had been introduced earlier. Under the provisions of this grant policy, the city was to receive $100,000 annually with the understanding that such a grant would be forthcoming for ten years. In 1951 a new system of payment was worked out on the basis of $25 for every miner and smelter worker who lived in the city but worked elsewhere. This amount was increased to $40 in 1956, for a total provincial grant of $227,600, but since smelter workers were excluded, the reality was a significant decrease. In response to complaints, the government in 1959 reinstated the smelter workers, and increased the grant to $45, which resulted in additional mining grants to the Sudbury region of $184,000.[59]

The mining revenue payments introduced by the province in the 1950s were strongly criticized by the local municipalities because they placed mining communities in a unique and unfair position compared to other towns. According to the *Sudbury Daily Star*, the citizens of Sudbury were being penalized financially because they lived in a modern community shackled by anachronistic legislation. It was claimed that Sudbury was "a city without a city's birthright."[60] A special accounting study produced for the city in 1956 concluded that under normal conditions Sudbury would have received about $434,000 from industrial assessment; thus the mining revenue payments from the province were the equivalent of only 52 percent of the revenue that Sudbury would have received as a typical Ontario industrial town.[61] The unfairness of the system was emphasized in other studies, which claimed that the small revenue payments were the cause behind the low levels of municipal services in Ontario mining communities.[62]

The mining assessment and tax structure lay very much at the root of the financial and boundary problems of the region's mining municipalities. From a provincial perspective, the amalgamation and annexation issue before the OMB raised important policy implications regarding the future treatment of mining communities. The main OMB hearings dealing with Sudbury's amalgamation and annexation request were held in February and October of 1958. As the OMB observed in its final decision, the real purpose of the application was to obtain additional revenue for the city through the acquisition of mining properties within its boundaries. In its wisdom the OMB ordered that on 1 January 1960 the town of Frood Mine and the township of McKim be amalgamated with Sudbury and that the west half of Neelon Township be annexed (see Map 1.2). Specifically excluded from the amalgamation were the towns of Copper Cliff and Coniston and the townships of Creighton, Snider, Falconbridge, Waters, Broder, and Dill.[63] Though the decision was based in part on the importance of regional water supplies and sewage disposal, it was obvious that the mining industry had more influence than municipal politicians. Despite the setback, Sudbury, with a population of about seventy-five thousand, began the 1960s as Ontario's sixth-largest city.

Municipal politics in Sudbury were essentially concerned with the promotion of growth, and simply moved from one short-term expedient to another with no thought to planning. Nevertheless, when W.S. Beaton was elected mayor for the eleventh consecutive time in 1950, it was clear that the council and the city were undergoing changes. In that year, Dr. Faustina Kelly Cook, a Sudbury-born francophone, and Grace Hartman, a former high school trustee, were elected Sudbury's first women aldermen. Cook served one term on council, but Hartman was to have a long and distinguished career in municipal politics.[64] In the outlying INCO towns of Coniston and Levack, the seeds of political change were sown when, for the first time, contests for the mayoralty were held in 1950. In Coniston the tradition of acclamation for mayor had continued since the town's incorporation in 1933.[65] In the 1952 elections, however, W. Kilimnik became the first Coniston mayor who was not an INCO executive.

In Sudbury, Beaton's reign was finally broken when he was toppled in December 1951 by Dan W. Jessup, a local grocer. To ensure better monitoring of the finances of the growing city, a board of control was introduced in 1952; as well, numerous planning initiatives were considered. In December 1954, after serving three terms as mayor, Jessup was brought down by Léo Landreville, a prominent lawyer. Much of the interest in that election centred on the "new-deal" candidates, backed by the union, who failed to win any seats.[66] Landreville continued as mayor until he was appointed to the Supreme Court of Ontario in September 1956. It was during his tenure that the Northern Ontario Natural Gas Company was awarded the local franchise to distribute natural gas in the city. The propriety of Landreville's part in the tendering process later led to public inquiries by the Law Society of Upper Canada and the Government of Canada,[67] which ultimately forced the former mayor to resign from the bench. Though Sudbury voters had previously rejected the idea of a two-year term for municipal councils, by 1956 they had changed their minds. Joseph Fabbro was the first mayor with a two-year mandate and he was re-elected in 1958. Fabbro had served as an alderman from December 1952 until 1956, at which time he became mayor after Landreville's resignation. Meanwhile, political activity in the adjoining townships of McKim and Neelon and Garson remained closely associated with amalgamation and annexation issues and internal problems related to water, sewers, roads, subdivisions, and education.[68]

Provincially, the Sudbury region was represented by Progressive Conservatives for most of the decade; federally, by Liberals.[69] The CCF lost much of its support because of the intense factionalism in the union movement in the fifties. On 22 November 1951, Welland S. Gemmell, a store owner from Whitefish, defeated Léo Landreville to retain his seat in the Sudbury riding for the provincial Progressive Conservatives. In 1952 Gemmell was appointed minister of lands and forests. When the next election was held, on 9 June 1955, the Sudbury riding had been divided in two. In Sudbury itself, Gerald J. Monaghan, owner of a local service station and a city politician, replaced Gemmell, who had died the preceding year. Monaghan lasted until 11 June 1959, when he was succeeded by the flamboyant Elmer Sopha, who became the only Liberal MPP from the Sudbury region during the fifties. In Nickel Belt, the other riding created in 1955, Rhéal Bélisle, a wholesaler and farmer and a former reeve of Rayside Township, won for the Conservatives and was re-elected in 1959. At the federal level, the Sudbury area was a Liberal bastion, and there were no safer seats in Canada. On 10 May 1953, in the first election of the decade, a pharmacist, David R. Mitchell, became the Sudbury riding's federal member. Mitchell was re-elected in 1957 and survived the Diefenbaker landslide of 31 March 1958. In the 1953 election, J. Leo Gauthier, a lumber dealer, easily won the Nickel Belt riding for the third time; he was re-elected in 1957. When Gauthier retired in 1958, Osias J. Godin won the seat handily for the Liberals.

When the voters rejected two-year terms for elected officials in 1950, they also rejected the idea of competitive Sunday sports. In 1956, when they changed their minds about the two-year term, they also revised their opinions about Sunday sports. The vote on sports was almost predictable, since it was taken at a time when interest in sports was at an all-time high. Enthusiasm was generated by the erection of new facilities, such as the Sudbury Arena and a community YMCA with a gymnasium, and improvements to Queen's Athletic Field, where three tennis courts were built to replace the courts at Memorial Park.[70] In addition, local athletes enjoyed considerable success at various provincial, national, and international meets. The spirited competition between the Sudbury High and Technical schools on the high school front also attracted much attention.

The main stimulant to the regional sporting scene was the opening in 1951 of the Sudbury Arena. The arena replaced the old Palace Rink, which had been demolished in the late thirties; in the interval Stanley Stadium in Copper Cliff had been used for much of the hockey and skating in the area.[71] The arena ushered in a new era, not only for the sports-minded but also for those who sought a greater variety of entertainment. In 1953 the arena enabled the city to host the Macdonald's Brier Tankard, the first national curling championship held in Northern Ontario.[72] It was also used for the Ice Cycles, the Water Follies, religious meetings, public skating, school hockey, bingos, and political rallies.

Of course, the main attraction was hockey. On 21 November 1951, a record crowd of five thousand saw the Sudbury Wolves defeat the Sudbury Caruso Miners 7–0.[73] These two teams belonged to the newly formed Northern Ontario Hockey Association (NOHA) Southern Group

Senior "A" League, which included the Soo Greyhounds and the North Bay Black Hawks and later the Soo Indians and the Pembroke Lumber Kings. When the Sudbury Caruso Miners folded in 1952, the Sudbury Wolves continued, winning two championships in three seasons.[74] The peak of interest in hockey was reached in the spring of 1954, when the Wolves defeated the Soo Greyhounds for the local title and then went on to defeat the Abitibi Eskimos, Owen Sound Mercurys, and Matane Red Rocks and advance to the Allan Cup finals against the Penticton Vees. The Wolves, coached by Max Silverman, eventually lost a thrilling and controversial seven-game series and the accompanying right to represent Canada at the World Championships.[75] Many of the Wolves players remained in Sudbury and distinguished themselves in a variety of careers. Senior hockey then underwent a period of decline owing to a series of controversies over such matters as salaries.[76] In 1959 Sudbury became part of the Eastern Professional Hockey League, which included teams from Montreal, Sault Ste. Marie, Trois Rivières, Kingston, and Hull-Ottawa; the league, however, folded after NHL games began to be shown on television. Baseball suffered a similar fate. The Nickel Belt Baseball Association, which comprised the Sudbury Shamrocks, Frood Tigers, Copper Cliff Redmen, Creighton Indians, Garson Greyhounds, and the Coniston Red Sox, managed to draw up to eight thousand spectators during the early 1950s for games played at Queen's Athletic Field. By 1959 the baseball scene too had collapsed, unable to withstand the competition from newer sports and other activities.

Other sports of note during the decade were fastball, paddling, football, skiing, basketball, and soccer.[77] Fastball emerged after the decline of baseball on the diamond fields. No doubt because of Beaton's influence, paddling remained prominent, as evidenced by the success of Don Stringer in Canadian and North American competitions. In the 1956 Olympics held in Australia, Stringer placed seventh in the 10,000-metre singles. He thus followed the discus thrower Roy Pella, who had previously represented Canada and the Sudbury region in the 1952 Olympics. In football the Sudbury Hardrocks were organized in 1951–52, with the intent that a separate football league in Northern Ontario would eventually be created. By 1954 the Northern Ontario Rugby Football Union was officially recognized. Through the efforts of Ellis Hazen and Henry Moser, skiing grew in popularity as the decade progressed. Hazen was instrumental in forming the Nickelteen Ski Club, and Moser was active in developing downhill skiing facilities at Levack. In basketball the Sudbury Merchants won the Canadian Senior "B" championship in 1956. Another favourite pastime for many ethnic groups was soccer.

In many ways, the 1950s were years in which Sudbury emerged as a metropolis and regional capital. This was the decade that witnessed the city's expansion far beyond the modest four and a half square miles that had contained it since 1893. That the expansion did not grow farther or faster was in large part a result of resistance by the nickel industry, which, though prepared to offer jobs to Sudbury's citizens, was not anxious to have them tap company coffers for necessary municipal services. It was the extension of this same attitude towards the community at large, particularly on INCO's part, that led to the first of many bitter strikes in the nickel industry and a change in union representation.

Along with population growth, the 1950s saw the emergence of many buildings and institutions that were the foundation upon which Sudbury was to build itself into a regional metropolis that dominated not only the Sudbury Basin but much of northeastern Ontario as well. This was the decade that saw the establishment of CKSO-TV, three hospitals, and Laurentian University. In sports, modern facilities like the Sudbury Arena gave the community the possibility of competing not only regionally but nationally. The city's physical growth was paralleled by a commitment to planning, tentative at first, but becoming more powerful with each passing year. By the late fifties, Sudbury gave evidence of being a much different city than it had been a decade earlier, with modern buildings, an efficient transportation network, and a higher level of services. The city's history should record that in this decade planners like Arnold Faintuck, Klemens Dembeck, and Oryst Sawchuck had a greater long-term influence on the city than politicians like Dan Jessup and the disgraced Léo Landreville.

1 *Sudbury Daily Star*, 25 April 1950.

2 Ibid., 26 December 1959 and 16 November 1959.

3 Val Ross, "The Arrogance of INCO," *Canadian Business* 52, no. 5 (May 1979): 122; and Jamie Swift, *The Big Nickel: Inco at Home and Abroad* (Kitchener: Between the Lines, 1977), 30.

4 Royal Commission on Canada's Economic Prospects, *Final Report* (Ottawa: Queen's Printer, 1955), 92.

5 Much of the information for this section on INCO has been derived from the International Nickel Company of Canada Ltd., *Annual Reports* (Toronto, 1950–59).

6 The development of Falconbridge Nickel Mine is in O.W. Main, *The Canadian Nickel Industry: A Story in Market Control and Public Policy* (Toronto: University of Toronto Press, 1955), 122.

7   See John Deverell and the Latin American Working Group, *Falconbridge: Portrait of a Canadian Mining Multinational* (Toronto: Lorimer, 1975), 45–46.

8   Falconbridge Nickel Mines Ltd., *Annual Reports* (Toronto, 1950–59).

9   Information regarding these companies has been obtained from the Financial Post, *Survey of Mines 1950–1960* (Toronto, Financial Post).

10   Robert Stephenson et al., *A Guide to the Golden Age: Mining in Sudbury, 1886–1977* (Sudbury: Department of History, Laurentian University, 1979), 64–95.

11   Battelle Memorial Institute, *Economic Development Opportunities for the Sudbury Area, Ontario* (Columbus: Batelle Memorial Institute, 1959), 12; and O.W. Saarinen, "A Geographical Basis for Regional Planning in the Sudbury Area" (M.A. thesis, University of Western Ontario, 1966), 70–71.

12   The history of the IUMMSW is traced in John B. Lang, "A Lion in a Den of Daniels: A History of the International Union of Mine, Mill and Smelter Workers in Sudbury, Ontario, 1942–1962" (M.A. thesis, University of Guelph, 1970); and Robert A. Stephenson, "'To Strike – or Not to Strike?' An Examination of the International Union of Mine, Mill and Smelter Workers' Strike in Sudbury During 1958" (honours B.A. thesis, Department of History, Laurentian University, 1978). See also *Sudbury Daily Star*, 6 November 1951.

13   The role of the IUMMSW in promoting the socio-cultural development of the Sudbury area is well documented in Lang, "A Lion in a Den of Daniels."

14   The events of 1958 are covered in *Sudbury Daily Star*, 17 March 1958, 24 September 1958, 12 December 1958, and 19 December 1958.

15   Wallace Clement, *Hardrock Mining: Industrial Relations and Technological Changes at Inco* (Toronto: McClelland & Stewart, 1981), 306–7.

16   Alexandre Boudreau was a former Canadian consul in Boston. He had experience with UNESCO and in the field of adult education and had taught previously at Laval University and the University of Ottawa. Boudreau was hired by the University of Sudbury as director of the university's Extension Division. See *Sudbury Daily Star*, 15 September 1958 and 2 October 1959.

17   *Sudbury Daily Star*, 11 March 1959 and 1 June 1959.

18   The events linked to this election are covered in the *Sudbury Daily Star*, 10 October 1959, 23 October 1959, and 18 November 1959.

19   *Sudbury Daily Star*, 25 April 1950.

20   Ontario Department of the Provincial Secretary, Registrar General's Branch, *Vital Statistics* (Toronto: Queen's Printer, 1950–59).

21   For newspaper coverage of the change, see *Sudbury Daily Star*, 25 April 1950, 29 September 1950, 25 May 1951, 25 August 1958, 29 April 1959, 14 October 1950, 9 December 1952, 13 January 1956, 7 June 1952, 25 September 1952, 14 March 1953, 29 October 1953, 29 March 1957, and 14 May 1957. See also Metro Kozak, "Sudbury," in Helmut Kallman, Giles Potvin, and Kenneth Winters, eds., *Encyclopedia of Music in Canada* (Toronto: University of Toronto Press, 1981), 898–99.

22   For a review of the commercial developments, see *Sudbury Daily Star*, 31 May 1950, 8 July 1959, 25 August 1958, 3 April 1957, 17 June 1958, 23 November 1950, 30 April 1951, and 27 November 1957.

23   Ibid., 20 September 1951, 10 September 1951, 18 September 1951, 26 October 1953, and 14 March 1957. Refer also to *INCO Triangle*, February 1959, 13.

24   The history of Laurentian University is outlined in Gwenda Hallsworth, *A Brief History of Laurentian University* (Sudbury: Laurentian University, 1985). For related newspaper coverage, see *Sudbury Daily Star*, 17 December 1959, 6 May 1957, 5 September 1957, 19

November 1957, 19 February 1958, 6 May 1958, 14 March 1958, 14 May 1958, and 22 January 1959.

25 Hallsworth, *A Brief History*, 11; and *Sudbury Daily Star*, 12 December 1958.

26 *Sudbury Daily Star*, 5 December 1958 and 19 February 1959.

27 Ibid., 12 December 1959.

28 Hallsworth, *A Brief History*, 17.

29 *Sudbury Daily Star*, 22 May 1950, 15 September 1951, and 19 September 1951; and Peter C. Newman, *The Canadian Establishment*, vol. 1 (Toronto: McClelland and Stewart/Bantam, 1977), 43–87.

30 *Sudbury Daily Star*, 19 August 1952 and 10 July 1956.

31 Ibid., 16 August 1952 and 30 January 1954.

32 Ibid., 24 February 1958.

33 Ibid., 20 October 1953 and 9 December 1957.

34 John Bland and Harold Spence-Sales, *A Report on the City of Sudbury and Its Extensions* (Sudbury: City of Sudbury, 1950), 5.

35 *Sudbury Daily Star*, 5 June 1953.

36 Ibid., 8 January 1954.

37 The growth of McKim Township is traced in "McKim Grew Rapidly as Sudbury First Burst Seams 10 Years Ago," *Sudbury Daily Star*, 4 August 1953; and "Tiny Dot That Was Sudbury Junction Nearly 80 Years Ago 'Swallows Up' McKim Township from Which It Sprang," *Sudbury Daily Star*, 31 December 1959.

38 Ontario Department of Municipal Affairs, Community Planning Branch, *The Sudbury Area: Factors of the Regional Environment* (Toronto: Department of Municipal Affairs, 1960), 24; and *Sudbury Daily Star*, 4 February 1958.

39 *Sudbury Daily Star*, 8 January 1954.

40 For residential activity in the downtown, see *Sudbury Daily Star*, 25 April 1950, 24 August 1951, 6 January 1950, 17 November 1952, and 20 October 1950. Refer also to Ontario Municipal Board, *Order 668*, 1952, and *P.F.M.* 3109-55, 20 October 1955.

41 The early history of planning in the area is traced in Ontario Department of Municipal Affairs, Community Planning Branch, *Sudbury Area* (Toronto: The Department, 1960). See also O.W. Saarinen, "Planning and Other Development Influences on the Spatial Organization of Urban Settlement in the Sudbury Area," *Laurentian University Review* 3, no. 3 (February 1971): 47ff.

42 Bland and Spence-Sales, *A Report on the City of Sudbury*, 1–23.

43 *Sudbury Daily Star*, 1 December 1950, 3 June 1954, 21 August 1954, and 29 September 1954; and Ontario Department of Municipal Affairs, *The Sudbury Area*.

44 *Sudbury Daily Star*, 3 February 1955, 12 August 1955, 1 September 1955, and 7 November 1956. See also Arnold Faintuck and Oryst H. Sawchuk, "A Plan for Sudbury" (M. Arch [C.P.] thesis, University of Manitoba, 1955), 40–45.

45 *Sudbury Daily Star*, 3 August 1955 and 12 October 1955.

46 Ibid., 23 November 1956.

47 Ibid., 29 June 1957, 27 August 1957, and 25 October 1957.

48 Ibid., 19 November 1957, 23 November 1957, 10 December 1957, and 31 January 1958.

49 Ibid., 14 March 1958, 30 September 1958, 21 January 1959, 6 November 1959, 23 November 1959, 22 October 1959, 11 March 1958, 27 June 1959, 26 September 1959, 6 November 1959, and 22 October 1959.

50 Ibid., 11 March 1958, 27 June 1959, and 26 September 1959.

51 For a review of these environmental iniatives, see *Sudbury Daily Star*, 20 November 1957, 19 September 1959, 29 March 1950, and 26 September 1959.

52 Ibid., 5 June 1957, 14 July 1959, and 26 December 1959.

53 Ibid., 16 and 17 January 1951; and Ontario Municipal Board, *P.C.F.-4756*, 16 January 1951.

54 Ibid., 24 January 1951 and 15 August 1951.

55 Ibid., 17 August 1951, 6 June 1954, and 6 November 1954.

56 Ibid., 26 May 1956 and 19 July 1956.

57 Ontario Municipal Board, *P.F.M.-5847*, 12 August 1957.

58 *Sudbury Daily Star*, 13 February 1957.

59 Ibid., 16 January 1958 and 13 March 1959.

60 Ibid., 1 August 1954.

61 Clarkson, Gordon & Co., *City of Sudbury Report in Connection with Amalgamation Proceedings* (Sudbury: City of Sudbury, 1957), 18–19.

62 Mining Tax Reform Committee, *Modification of Mining Taxation in Ontario* (Sudbury: Regional Municipality of Sudbury, 1977), 4. Refer also to J.R. Winter, *Sudbury: An Economic Survey* (Sudbury: Laurentian University Press, 1969), 56.

63 Ontario Municipal Board, *P.F.M. 5143-6*, 12 November 1959, 5, 16–20; and *Sudbury Daily Star*, 16 November 1959.

64 *Sudbury Daily Star*, 5 December 1950.

65 Ibid., 29 November 1960.

66 Ibid., 4 December 1951, 13 November 1951, and 7 December 1954.

67 Hon. I.C. Rand, *Inquiry Re: The Honourable Mr. Justice Léo Landreville* (Ottawa: Queen's Printer, 1966).

68 *Sudbury Daily Star*, 3 February 1955.

69 This summary of provincial and federal elections in the Sudbury area has been derived in part from Pierre G. Normandin, ed., *The Canadian Parliamentary Guide* (Ottawa: 1950–60), and *Biographies de la région de Sudbury/Biographies of the Sudbury Region, Version préliminaire/Preliminary edition* (Sudbury: Département d'histoire, Université Laurentienne/Department of History, Laurentian University, 1980).

70 *Sudbury Daily Star*, 29 October 1953; and *INCO Triangle*, August 1958, 15.

71 *Sudbury Daily Star*, 7 June 1952.

72 *INCO Triangle*, February 1953, 10.

73 *Sudbury Daily Star*, 22 November 1951.

74 A review of hockey activity in the 1950s is given in *Sudbury Daily Star*, 2 July 1955.

75 Ibid., 17 May 1954.

76 Ibid., 15 April 1958 and 15 July 1955.

77 For a review of the other ports, see *INCO Triangle*, September 1956, 5; November 1953, 13; February 1960, 7, 11; and April 1956; and *Sudbury Daily Star*, 4 September 1954.

CHAPTER NINE

THE 1960s

Gwenda Hallsworth
and Peter Hallsworth

The 1960s were the era of Pierre Trudeau and Quebec separatism, the women's movement and the peace movement, the Vietnam War and civil rights protests. These were years of turbulence, both nationally and internationally, and inevitably, the reverberations were felt in Sudbury. Though the city changed in every decade, in the 1960s the changes were especially dramatic. No institution, organization, or group was left untouched by the combination of local, national, and international circumstances.

The mining companies were faced with aggressive world-wide competition at the very time that labour relations were deteriorating. The decade began and ended with hitherto unparalleled labour unrest, but whereas at the start of the 1960s workers had been pitted against workers, by the end of the decade the workers were united against the corporations. In the decade, an expanded city forced local politicians to cope with an enlarged, inadequately serviced territory with insufficient revenues at the very time that the demand for services had skyrocketed. Urban transportation, for example, could no longer be left to chance. Similar revenue shortages and increased demands for service were experienced by hospitals, schools, colleges, universities, churches. Outside the city, the regional towns and villages were finding it increasingly difficult to cope with their problems, and the Ontario government decided that the nickel region would follow a new course. By the end of the decade, Sudbury was becoming the political, educational, and health centre of the region.

Sudbury's lifeblood during the sixties was the mining industry. When world demand for nickel rose, economic activity in Sudbury increased;

when the market for nickel was sluggish, the mining companies decreased production and laid off workers. The demand for nickel rose dramatically during the decade, partly because of a great demand for stainless steel in home appliances, but also because of the war in Vietnam, especially after 1965, with the full-scale participation of the United States. In that year, the *Sudbury Star*[1] reported, "The employment picture at present is the best since 1957."[2]

During the 1960s, both INCO and Falconbridge expanded their operations. INCO increased production at established mines like Creighton, which was deepened to 2,180 feet, and opened new mines at Little Stobie, Totten, McLennan, Kirkwood, Coleman, Copper Cliff North, and Copper Cliff South. The Iron Ore Recovery Plant at Copper Cliff was completed in 1964, a new mill at Frood Stobie went into operation in 1966, and construction began on an $85-million refinery in 1969. In addition, INCO began mining operations abroad in Indonesia, New Caledonia, and Australia. At the same time, Falconbridge reported record earnings, which were limited only by production shortages. Throughout the decade labour relations took on a totally new character as several strikes were combined with high labour turnover and a shortage of miners and tradesmen. Because of the increased world demand for nickel, the emergence of competing producers, and shortfalls in local productivity, Sudbury's share of the world supply dropped from a high of 95 percent in 1950 to 66 percent in 1968 and was predicted to fall to 51 percent by 1975.[3]

Despite the local prosperity of the decade, this was a difficult time for the labour movement. The legacy of the first strike at INCO, in 1958, was years of bitter internecine struggle.[4] In November 1959, after Don Gillis defeated Nels Thibault for the presidency of Local 598 of the International Union of Mine Mill and Smelter Workers (IUMMSW), which at the time represented workers at both Falconbridge and INCO, relations between the local and national executives degenerated into acrimony and backbiting. In February 1960 the national executive issued a charter creating a new local, Number 1025, for employees of Falconbridge, a move strenuously opposed by Local 598, which was led by Gillis. Gillis won that battle in the short term when the Ontario Labour Relations Board (OLRB) refused to certify the new local. Fresh from that victory, Local 598 then withheld its per capita payments to the national office, which made up more than 50 percent of the national's income. The two sides took their battle to the courts with applications for injunctions and counter-injunctions. More trouble arose in May 1960, when 70 percent of the labour force walked out in a wildcat strike at Falconbridge over the issue of the compulsory wearing of safety glasses. Elections for District 2 of the union[5] again pitted Mike Solski and Gillis slates against one another, further aggravating the situation.

The national union's troubles within the labour movement at large dated back to 1949, when it was expelled from the old Canadian Congress of Labour for bad unionism and raiding, and to 1950, when it was expelled from the American Congress of International Organizations (CIO) because of its alleged domination by communists.[6] Its application for re-affiliation with the Canadian Labour Congress (CLC) was rejected in January 1960, and the IUMMSW remained a maverick, not to say pariah, in the Canadian labour movement.

Riven by these internal and external disputes, the IUMMSW was in a very poor position to fight a takeover bid by the United Steelworkers of America (USWA), which had set its sights on the Canadian mining industry, with the tacit support of the Canadian Labour Congress. In 1961 the USWA launched a determined campaign to capture the Sudbury labour force in a raid that generated considerable ill will and put Sudbury on the front pages of newspapers across the country. Matters came to a head on 10 September 1961, when violence erupted during a mass rally at the Sudbury Arena with CLC officials in attendance, and the police had to clear the arena with tear gas.

INCO capitalized on the situation by refusing to bargain with Local 598, citing uncertainty within the union and the dispute between it and the USWA. Meanwhile the USWA continued to gain strength. In November 1961, a USWA official, Tony Mancini, claimed that 45 percent of local membership had been signed by the Steelworkers; in the same month the union applied for bargaining rights at INCO. In December the USWA won a membership vote at INCO's Port Colborne plant and was duly certified by the Ontario Labour Relations Board (OLRB).[7] In January 1962 Mine Mill's attempt to stave off the Steelworkers and prevent a vote in Sudbury was turned down by the OLRB, which scheduled a ballot between 27 February and 2 March 1962.[8] Voting in large numbers took place without incident.

After Mine Mill failed to substantiate its charges that the vote had been fraudulent, the OLRB eventually ordered a count, which took place on 11 June 1962. It was extremely close (7,182 for USWA TO 7,167 for Mine Mill). Thirty-six ballots were questioned by Mine Mill, and both sides claimed victory, but matters were going badly for Mine Mill. It suffered its second defeat in Port Colborne in two months when it was replaced as the representative of civic workers by the National Union of Public Service Employees. In March the national office expelled for life Gillis and five other officers of Local 598 for having collaborated with the USWA.[9] A vote in April at INCO's operations at Thompson, Manitoba, resulted in an easy victory for the Steelworkers.[10] Then, on 15 October, after several hearings and adjournments, the OLRB ruled that the results of the June ballot count were valid and announced the certification of the USWA as the bargaining agent at INCO. This certification, for all practical purposes, marked the end of the IUMMSW at INCO, although it struggled on for another five years. Steelworker Local 6500 was formed in November 1962; its first president and all but two of its new officers were former Local 598 officers who had served under Gillis.[11]

The Steelworkers' raid on Falconbridge, however, was not successful, and in July 1962 USWA withdrew its application for certification because the hearing showed clearly there were a large number of forgeries among the applications. Mine Mill thus continued as bargaining agent at Falconbridge, and in 1964 it began a campaign to win back certification at INCO. It succeeded in gaining sufficient support to warrant a new certification vote, which was ordered by the OLRB in October 1965. The vote, held in December 1965, gave the Steelworkers an easy victory – 8,194 to 6,099. On the other hand, a further attempt by the Steelworkers to take over at Falconbridge failed in August 1965.[12] They did, however, succeed in organizing the Falconbridge office and technical employees in September 1966.[13] By then the IUMMSW was effectively beaten, and in February 1967 the two unions signed an agreement to end their raiding upon one another, clearing the way for a possible merger.[14] In a vote held in April the membership of the USWA approved the merger, which was opposed, however, by Local 598. Appeals to the courts resulted in Local 598 at Falconbridge winning the right to exist independently, despite the disappearance of the national IUMMSW. Local 598, now known as the Sudbury Mine Mill and Smelter Workers Union, defiantly continued as the representative of the mine and smelter workers at Falconbridge.[15] As in all wars, the victims nursed their grievances for the rest of their lives and carried the scars to their graves. The union wars of Sudbury made very deep scars indeed.

The change to the Steelworkers did not bring an end to the violence; rather, it was the beginning of an era of labour unrest previously unknown in Sudbury. In September 1962, before the Steelworkers' certification was confirmed by the OLRB, INCO laid off 2,200 workers, citing large stockpiles and increased competition.[16] Negotiations between the new Local 6500 and INCO dragged on through early 1963 until a three-year contract was signed on 10 July. In 1963 nickel production picked up, and in early 1964 INCO rehired its laid-off employees and began to hire new workers. The demand for nickel, and thus for labour, continued to rise during 1965 and 1966, so that when the collective agreement expired in July 1966 the union was in a much stronger position than it had been in since the mid-1950s. During the negotiations, a wildcat strike at Levack in July spread immediately until all 17,000 INCO workers were in an illegal walkout. When violence erupted on the picket lines, a special squad of the

Ontario Provincial Police was brought in to maintain order – with helicopters, dogs, and mace. The armed-camp atmosphere lasted for three weeks before the workers returned to their jobs. In mid-September they again went out on strike, legally this time. In view of the increasing competition and high demand for nickel and reduced stockpiles, not to mention the war raging in Vietnam, INCO quickly offered an acceptable three-year contract with raises equivalent to 25 percent over the term of the agreement, thus making Sudbury workers among the highest paid in the province.[17]

When the three-year contract expired at INCO in 1969, the workers again went out on strike, determined to retain their position among the best-paid industrial workers in Canada. This strike lasted from 10 July to 14 November 1969; meanwhile Mine Mill was on strike against Falconbridge from 21 August to 22 November 1969. Despite the bitter dispute between them in the preceding years, the two unions supported each other on the strike issues. The eventual settlements again favoured the unions, since the companies were still trying to meet the unprecedented demand for nickel. While there was some grumbling in the local business community about the excessive power of unions and the unreasonable increase in wages, most workers considered their gains to be a revenge for their defeat in 1958. For Sudbury, however, the industrial wars produced an uncertainty previously unknown, for the city was forced to cope with a pattern of industrial unrest based on three-year contracts. While employees of the mining companies had high earnings and began the cycle of saving to cushion themselves for the anticipated strike, approximately 5,000 workers in subsidiary industries were laid off and an estimated 2,500 mine workers left town to seek employment in other booming mining towns like Elliot Lake.

The union activities of the 1960s thus created in Sudbury an uncertain, tense atmosphere. The struggle between the two unions for control directed the energies of workers against workers instead of against the companies, and the community became a hostage in the struggle.

One aspect of the increasing influence of labour in Sudbury during the 1960s was the growing strength of the New Democratic Party (NDP), formed in 1961 from an alliance between the old Co-operative Commonwealth Federation (CCF) and labour. Although the new party attracted supporters who were not in the labour movement, and some members of the labour movement supported other parties, the fact is that in the 1960s the Sudbury area proved fertile ground for a party that prided itself on being the voice of labour. For that reason Sudbury voters did not always follow provincial or national political trends.

During the decade, there were two provincial general elections and four federal general elections as well as a by-election in the Sudbury riding. The provincial general elections, both won by the Progressive Conservatives, were held in 1963 and 1967. In 1963 there were two provincial ridings in the region, Sudbury and Nickel Belt. In Sudbury, lawyer Elmer Sopha, who had represented the Liberal Party since 1959 and was a popular local figure, had little difficulty in holding the seat in both elections. In 1967 the NDP candidate in Sudbury improved his party's share of the vote and helped to pave the way for NDP victories in the next decade. In Nickel Belt, the Conservative candidate, Gaston Demers, won the seat in both elections, but in 1967 his majority was reduced when the NDP candidate, Don Scott, placed second. The NDP's base in the riding was built upon in the next decade, when the NDP candidate was elected. In 1967 a third riding was created, Sudbury East, which was immediately captured by Elie Martel of the NDP, who held the seat until he was succeeded by his daughter, Shelley Martel, in the election of 1987.

At the federal level, D.R. Mitchell, the member for Sudbury, who was first elected in 1953, held the seat in the election of 1962, which resulted in a Progressive Conservative minority government, and in the 1963 and 1965 elections, both of which produced minority Liberal governments. In the 1967 by-election, held after Mitchell's death, Bud Germa of the NDP swept to victory, only to fall victim to "Trudeaumania" the following year when Jim Jerome regained the seat for the Liberals. In Nickel Belt, in 1961 and 1963 O.J. Godin of the Liberals managed to keep the seat he had first won in 1958; he was defeated by Norm Fawcett of the NDP in 1965. Like Germa, Fawcett was a casualty of the Liberal sweep of 1968, when he was replaced by Gaetan Serre.[18]

The 1960s were the last decade in which the provincial and federal governments were to have comparatively little influence on Sudbury. Locally, however, there were significant developments in government that had far-reaching effects. During the decade city council attempted to cope with the multitude of problems it had inherited when it amalgamated with McKim Township, Frood Mine, and part of Neelon Township in January 1960. Councils also tackled some of the continuing problems that had not been solved earlier. Their efforts met with varying degrees of success, and some of the problems remained to challenge politicians in the next decade.

With amalgamation, a new structure for city council was created, consisting of a mayor, four controllers, and twelve aldermen. The addition of thousands of new voters in new wards broke the rhythm that had determined winners and losers for decades, and several new faces and different types of aldermen emerged on the scene. The incumbent mayor, Joe Fabbro, who was unable to survive the changes, lost to a former alderman and member of the board of control, Bill Edgar, a public school principal. Two years later Edgar was succeeded by a former reeve of McKim, Bill Ellis. Fabbro returned for 1964 and 1965 but was defeated by Max Silverman in a vigorous and bitter contest between two colourful personalities. With Silverman's death on 6 October 1966, the deputy mayor, Grace Hartman, became Sudbury's first and only woman mayor. During Canada's centennial in 1967 Mayor Hartman served with charm and style, but those were not enough to carry her through the fall elections against Fabbro, who began an eight-year reign as mayor.

In 1956 the city of Sudbury, supported by the township of Neelon, had applied to the Ontario Municipal Board (OMB) for amalgamation with surrounding municipalities in order to tackle four serious problems: sewage disposal, the deterioration of Lake Ramsey as the city's water supply, the need for a proper planning area, and, finally, and what in many ways was most important, the low proportion of non-residential assessment. The OMB eventually imposed an amalgamation, effective 1 January 1960, which incorporated McKim Township, Frood Mine, and the western half of Neelon Township into the city.[19] That decision saddled Sudbury with a large unserviced residential territory but deliberately excluded the towns that were at the heart of the city's application: Copper Cliff, Creighton, Frood Mine, and Falconbridge. These were all company towns with large industrial operations, and in deciding to exempt them from amalgamation, the OMB had complied with the wishes of INCO and Falconbridge, which did not want their property taxed.

As a result of the flawed amalgamation, the city increased in area from five to fifty-four square miles and became the sixth-largest municipality in area in the province.[20] Whereas the old city had a comparatively small area with a high population density, the annexed parts had only pockets of intense development, which, for financial reasons, had not been serviced adequately.[21] Within the original city of Sudbury, for example, 100 percent of the houses had water and 99 percent were connected to sewers. The original city also had 71 miles of road, of which almost 38 miles had pavement and storm sewers. In the new areas there was no water and no sewers and 63 of the 91 miles of road were unpaved.

Nevertheless, even though the OMB decision did not meet all the city's needs, amalgamation still had some benefits. The problems of sewage and pollution of Ramsey Lake were solved in this decade with the building of a five-mile rock tunnel collector sewer and the Kelly Lake Sewage Treatment Plant.[22] Between 1960 and 1969 the city spent over $16 million on sanitary sewers and sewage treatment, more than doubled the miles of drains, constructed eighteen lift stations, and fully serviced all built-up parts of the enlarged city.[23]

The problem of the water supply, however, was not tackled seriously until a study in 1966 forced the city to take action.[24] For seventy years the source of Sudbury's water had been Ramsey Lake, supplemented by two deep wells at Second Avenue and Falconbridge Highway. The study recommended that the amount of water drawn from Ramsey be limited to six million gallons (27 million litres) a day, but the average in the 1960s was seven million (32 million litres), and on some days it exceeded nine million (40 million litres). In addition, the treatment plant at Ramsey was inadequate, for although it provided screening, chlorinating, and fluoridating, it failed to remove unpleasant odours and tastes. A comprehensive report in 1968 gave eight alternative schemes for the city water supply; council adopted the one with the Wahnapitei River as the main source and Ramsey as a secondary source, a full treatment plant on the Wahnapitei River, and a partial treatment plant on Ramsey; the cost was $4,050,000.[25]

The amalgamation also made more co-ordinated planning possible, since the newly acquired areas were included in the city of Sudbury's first official plan, which had been adopted in 1958,[26] and it did result in an increase in revenue from provincial grants under the Mining Tax Act.[27] But it also led to a significant increase in costs, especially in education and public works outside the old city. Before amalgamation the city had spent an average of $700,000 a year on construction and $360,000 on maintenance. After amalgamation, if the same ratios held, it should have spent $1,600,000 a year on construction until 1964 and $800,000 on maintenance. In fact, the expenditure on construction averaged only $515,000 a year, and owing to the inherited miles of substandard roads, maintenance costs increased to $1,100,000 in 1963.[28] The result was that instead of solving the city's taxation problems, amalgamation intensified them, leaving Sudbury in a much more serious financial situation than any other municipality of a similar size in Ontario.

As early as 1964 the city submitted a brief to the Ontario government on its financial problems,[29] noting that although the city's taxes were 20.7 percent higher than the average for twenty Ontario cities, fewer municipal services could be provided. The city attributed its problems to the absence of rateable assessment on the mining industry, the lack of secondary industry, the difficulty and cost of construction owing to the large amount of rock, low overall population density (although there were some pockets with very high density), and the need of the newly amalgamated areas for all services. There was one other notable observation with significant implications. Sudbury, it was claimed, was no longer a mining town with a highly transient population but had become a complex commercial city. If the city had more money, it would be spent on an improved sewage system, flood control, expanded waterworks and schools, as well as new public buildings, expanded police and fire services, and better roads, libraries, parks, and recreational facilities. The brief did not suggest any specific solutions to these problems, nor did the province take any action. The imposition of partial amalgamation had left the city a hostage with inadequate financing and unresolved problems.

A 1966 study by Laurentian University economist J.R. Winter described the difficulties in more detail. Property taxes and debenture debt had risen rapidly since amalgamation, but the tax base had not grown in step with the debt and the city's expenditures on services were lower than they should have been because of the lack of revenues. The tax base was inadequate because the region's largest industry, mining, was exempt and the mining taxes in lieu were quite inequitable. As Winter pointed out, metropolitan Sudbury was economically and sociologically a single unit and so should have been a single unit politically, but areas that should logically have been in the city were, in fact, independent, and the continued existence of company towns was a glaring, inequitable anomaly in mid-twentieth-century Canada.[30]

Just how serious this problem was for the city became evident in March 1967, when the city's five-year capital plan was presented to the board of control. The plan called for $80 million in debentures, but because this was an impossible figure for the city to raise, the application to the OMB was for the amount of $33,047,857, less than half the desirable total. Even this amount would double the per capita debenture debts by 1971 and increase the percentage of debenture debt to rateable assessment from 15.35 to 37.6 percent.[31]

Much of the money was required for water and sewerage; yet concentrating on these projects had an adverse effect on road and street work. There was a constant need for reconstruction and arterial connections, and in 1968 the public works department reported that it would be years before the main streets would be brought up to standard, although good progress had been made on improvements of the Kingsway, Barrydowne Road, Regent Street South, and Ramsey Lake Road.[32] The construction of the Brady Street underpass, which began in 1961, proved a boon in eliminating the long delays for both pedestrians and vehicles at the Riverside Drive level crossing, which had been a serious inconvenience to Sudbury commuters for years.

A 1965 study[33] considered through traffic to be only a minor problem and did not therefore recommend construction of highway by-passes, although it supported a proposal originally made in 1959 for a connecting link for Highway 17 that would allow motorists travelling east and west to pass easily through the city. There was also a recommendation for a Brady Street expressway, to be built in two stages, 1965–70 and 1970–75, at a total cost of $26,271,000. This proposal was never acted on.

The matter of public transportation and how it should be paid for was debated constantly throughout the period and, like so many other problems, it was still unresolved at the end of the decade, the reason in this case being because city council was unwilling to provide a publicly owned bus system. Before amalgamation, the franchise for the bus service in the city had been held by Sudbury Bus Lines; three other companies, Nickel Belt Coach Lines, Local Lines, and Frood Bus Lines, operated to points outside the city. After amalgamation, the first council allowed the three companies to continue operating in the districts they had served before amalgamation. In a plebiscite held in 1963, the voters rejected a proposal to award a city bus franchise to Laurentian Transit, which was an amalgamation of Nickel Belt Coach Lines and Local Lines.

In 1964 G.P. Henderson, general manager of the St. Catharines Transit System, who was hired to review the Sudbury situation, recommmended a unified system with fourteen routes, whose anticipated annual deficit of $44,000 would be financed by the city. In July 1965 council called for tenders on the basis of the Henderson report but received only one submission, from Sudbury Bus Lines. Negotiations dragged on for several months until, in February 1966, the board of control recommended that council award an unsubsidized franchise to Laurentian Transit. Put to another plebiscite in March, the idea was again rejected by the voters. At the end of March Sudbury Bus Lines discontinued its service and Laurentian Transit took over its routes. After further negotiations with Laurentian, council finally asked the OMB for permission to grant that company a franchise for three years. After public hearings in December 1966, the OMB approved the franchise, to be effective 1 January 1967. According to the terms of the franchise, Laurentian Transit was to receive no subsidy and was to meet certain service criteria; council could terminate the contract on 120 days' notice if service proved to be inadequate.[34] As a result of all these changes and uncertainty, at the end of the decade there was widespread demand for a publicly owned transportation system, a demand met only in 1972.

During the 1960s efforts were made to improve the quality of other services in Sudbury, although many of the proposed plans, like those for public transportation, were not brought to fruition until the 1970s. For example, as the decade closed, city hall was still crowded into the former Bell Telephone Exchange building, with little prospect for change. After an inquiry conducted by the Ontario Police Commission recommended that a new police building be erected, the city put up the new building as a centennial project, a reasonable decision, if not the most popular in all quarters.[35]

The same inquiry that recommended a new police building also argued that twenty extra constables should be hired. The fire department was also asking for a larger staff: in 1964 it had only 56 permanent firemen and 108 volunteers. One of the difficulties of protecting Sudbury was illustrated in 1962, when a large bush fire broke out within the enlarged city boundaries. This particular type of fire hazard was partially solved when the city signed an agreement with the provincial Department of Lands and Forests, by which the department assumed responsibility for preventing and controlling bush fires in an area of 14,093 acres within the city. Even so, fire protection was still inadequate. In 1969 Sudbury suffered its worst fire when the New Sudbury Shopping Centre partially burned, with a loss of over $1.6 million.[36] As a result of all this, Sudbury had the highest rates of fire insurance in the province.[37]

In addition to inadequate staffing, the fire department laboured under the handicap of trying to save substandard frame housing. Housing in Sudbury was also in short supply owing to a lack of serviced land, the costs of new construction,[38] and a severe shortage of rental accommodation. In 1962 it cost $1,900 to service a lot for a new bungalow, but that rose to $3,200 in 1968; meanwhile, construction costs rose 25 percent between 1962 and 1967.[39] Though rental space increased during the 1960s with the building of town houses on Centennial Drive and highrise apartments on Ramsey View Court, there was still a shortage of rental accommodation.

In 1964 the Central Mortgage and Housing Corporation (CMHC) Act was amended to make long-term, low-interest loans available to non-profit organizations for the purpose of constructing low-rental housing. To take advantage of this program, the provincial government established the Ontario Housing Corporation (OHC), and locally, the Sudbury Housing Authority was set up to manage, maintain, and supervise OHC units. The city's first public housing project was Cabot Park, which consisted of eighty-four family units. Among other public housing projects was the first senior citizens' complex on Kennedy Street; later other units were made available as part of the city's massive downtown urban renewal project.[40] Even so, the decade closed with the city still in a housing crisis that was to continue well into the 1970s.

As the decade began, everybody knew that the redevelopment of the central downtown business district was essential if the district was to retain its predominant position as the commercial, business, government, entertainment, and cultural centre of the region. In 1960 Sudbury's downtown core displayed evidence of its origins as a mining town, with the rail lines going through the centre of the city, the rickety Borgia Street Market, and the old Queen's Hotel, which was still a favourite spot for hookers and heavy drinkers. The move of retail business out to the suburbs had begun with the opening of the New Sudbury Shopping Centre in 1957, and as the 1960s began, this trend showed every evidence of accelerating.

In 1959 the Sudbury Planning Board authorized an urban renewal study, and by 1961 the city had a specific plan for urban renewal of the downtown.[41] It was, however, 1966 before the plans[42] were approved by all levels of government. Urban renewal was to be the largest single public undertaking in Sudbury's history, and also the biggest and most comprehensive scheme of urban development ever to receive both federal and provincial support. The estimated cost of the project over nine years was $15 million, of which the federal government would pay 50 percent and the province and the municipality 25 percent each. Known as the Borgia District, the project covered 59.8 acres and was to include public and private housing, as well as a major commercial development. The agreement between the city and the developer, Marchland Holdings of Toronto, signed on 24 July 1968, provided for 177 units of rent-geared-to-income housing (including 50 for senior citizens), 800 units of private housing, a shopping mall, a department store (Eaton's), a supermarket (Bonimart), a Holiday Inn, office space, and multi-level parking for 750 cars. The demolition of the old CNR freight sheds, the Queen's Hotel, and more than twenty other buildings began in the fall of 1968, and the new construction began early in 1969.

City council's debates on urban renewal were often acrimonious. Many believed that Marchland had been given a monopoly on downtown development,[43] especially after council rejected another large commercial development on seven acres of CPR property at the corner of Elm and Elgin streets. Submitted by Marathon Realty, the real estate arm of CPR, this project was considered a threat to the Borgia development to which council was so deeply committed. One Marathon Realty project, however, did go ahead: in 1967 development began on a fifty-five-acre industrial park on CPR property on Lorne Street.

In keeping with the efforts to improve the quality of life in the city, determined attempts were made to improve the environment. The Junction Creek Conservation Authority, which had been formed in 1957, began many new projects in the 1960s. In 1964 and 1965, Junction and Nolin creeks were covered over, thereby ending the long-standing practice of allowing city sewage on its way to Kelly Lake to travel fully exposed through the downtown. For the Authority, 1966 was its biggest year yet with programs designed for flood control, the establishment of conservation areas, and plans to protect parkland and watersheds and to provide facilities for leisure activities. INCO also played a part in improving the environment: under district agriculturalist T.H. Peters, the company conducted experiments, with some success, in restoring vegetation to areas that had been denuded.[44] In 1969 plans were made by INCO to build a "Superstack," which, though it would not solve the problems of emissions, did eventually improve the air quality in the immediate Sudbury area.

In Sudbury, the enormous challenges facing the municipal government were made even more difficult by the constant growth of the population. Although the population did decline by about 1,220 between 1961 and 1964,[45] between 1964 and 1967 it increased again and by 1971 stood at 90,515, compared to 80,120 in 1961.[46]

There were several reasons for these trends. Like much of the rest of North America, the birth rates in Sudbury declined in the 1960s. No doubt the arrival of "the pill" in 1960 was a contributing factor, though evidence is fragmentary. That said, the birth rate was still higher in Sudbury than in the province as a whole, although the downward trend common elsewhere was also obvious in Sudbury (see Table 9.1).

Sudbury's higher-than-average birth rate can be accounted for by the city's young population. In 1961 the median age in the city of Sudbury was 26.3, compared to 29.3 in Ontario, and in 1971, 24.4 in Sudbury and 28.2 in Ontario.[47] Moreover, throughout the decade more than 61 percent of the population was Roman Catholic.[48] This group may not have been influenced by liberalizing trends in family planning as quickly as the non–Roman Catholic section of the population.

If the birth rate is one reason for the expansion of Sudbury's population in the 1960s, the second, and more important, was immigration into the community. Between 1957 and 1971, 9,138 immigrants settled in Sudbury, causing a slight change in the ethnic composition. The largest group to arrive between 1957 and 1971 was the Italians, followed by the British, and the Finns.[49] Overall, however, the proportions changed little (see Table 9.2). In this table, Finns were included with "Other European," but in 1961 there were 2,994 people of Finnish descent in Sudbury, the sixth-largest ethnic group.

Although the net number of immigrants to the region grew during

Table 9.1
Number of Live Births per 1,000 Population, 1962–1967

Year	Sudbury	Province
1962	32.8	24.6
1963	29.4	24.1
1964	27.2	23.2
1965	25.8	21.0
1966	22.8	19.0
1967	22.5	17.8

Source: Maury O'Neill and Peter Andrews, *Sudbury Statistical Summary*
(Sudbury: Department of History, Laurentian University, 1986), 24.

the decade, the pace slowed down between 1961 and 1964, largely because of the economic recession. In addition, housing was in such short supply that many who did come to town could not stay. In 1962 the Sudbury Canada Manpower Centre, which provided about 40 percent of the average of 500 persons who were hired each month by INCO, reported that 80 percent of new employees left within six months and that 25 percent of these did so because of the lack of housing.[50] It was only after the middle of the decade, when industry's fortunes improved and the housing stock grew, that immigration rose again (see Table 9.3).

The mining industry continued to provide the largest number of jobs for men. In 1961, 40 percent of all men worked in the industry, and in 1966, 41 percent.[51] Nevertheless, a trend towards less dependence on mining for employment opportunities was beginning to be obvious in the 1960s. The growth in population meant there were more jobs in trade, services, and public administration. The combined percentages of these three categories increased from 32.9 percent in 1951 to 42.9 percent in 1966.[52] Since a large proportion of the population was of school age, there was a need for more teachers. Jobs were also created by the new university and the demand for hospital and social services.

For those responsible for providing health care and education, the 1960s were a challenging decade. In those years, Sudbury became the medical centre of northeastern Ontario. The Sudbury and District Hospital Council, a non-profit volunteer organization formed in 1961, with representatives from all hospitals, was set up to co-ordinate activities.[53] A brief prepared by this body illustrated the shortage of the

Table 9.2
Population by Ethnic Origin in the City of Sudbury, 1961 and 1971

	1961		1971	
	N	%	N	%
British	26,748	33.38	30,570	37.08
French	27,340	34.12	28,940	31.97
Ukrainian	3,881	4.84	3,860	4.26
Italian	6,343	7.92	8,405	9.28
German	3,211	4.00	2,930	3.24
Polish	2,302	2.81	2,035	2.25
Scandinavian	910	1.14	880	0.97
Netherlands	677	0.85	660	0.73
Russian	268	0.33	85	0.09
Jewish	148	0.18	225	0.22
Other European	7,049	8.80	295	0.33
Asiatic	453	0.57	1,065	1.18
Aboriginal	182	0.23	360	0.40
Other	608	0.76	7,210	7.96
Total Population	80,120		90,520	

Source: Census of Canada, 1961 and 1971.

Table 9.3
Population Change, Sudbury and District, 1961–1967

1961–64	CMA[a]			District of Sudbury
	City	Excl. City	Incl. City	
Natural increase	5,498	2,071	7,569	11,623
Net migration	-6,718	-1,318	-8,036	-11,885
Actual change	-1,220	753	-467	-262
1964–67				
Natural increase	4,289	1,369	5,658	8,113
Net migration	2,011	-275	1,736	5,487
Actual increase	6,300	1,094	7,394	13,600

[a] Census Metropolitan Area.
Source: Ontario Housing Corporation, The Sudbury Housing Market (Sudbury: The Corporation, 1968), 48.

hospital facilities needed to serve the present and future population. The dire situation in Sudbury hospitals was central to the study. By 1960 the Sudbury General Hospital, which had been built in 1950, contained 326 beds in a building designed for 190. All hospitals had waiting lists. For those needing elective surgery there was a six-month wait. Of particular significance was the fact that only 55.47 percent of patients were actually from the city of Sudbury.[54] Before the end of the decade, the Sudbury and District Hospital Council launched a capital building campaign with a goal of $10 million. An additional $20 million would be supplied by government grants. Three existing hospitals (Algoma, the Sudbury General, and the Memorial) were to be renovated and expanded and the old St. Joseph's Hospital was to be closed and replaced by a new facility known as Laurentian Hospital.[55] In 1967 the regional nature of health care was reinforced when an Ontario Department of Health task force recommended that local health units be amalgamated to form new comprehensive units, each headed by a full-time medical officer of health. Of the twenty-nine units formed thoroughout the province, one was the Sudbury Health Unit, with Dr. J.B. Cook as medical officer of health and Miss F. Tomlinson as director of nursing.[56] In an even more significant change in 1968, the Ontario Department of Health designated Sudbury as the regional health centre for northeastern Ontario.[57]

The expansion in health care led to the arrival of doctors and other health professionals from many countries, particularly the United Kingdom. Such were the improvements in health care and medical facilities that helped a Sudbury surgeon, Dr. Paul Field, perform, in 1968, the first successful aorta-coronary by-pass operation in Canada, at the Sudbury Memorial Hospital.[58] Since then, the hospital has successfully performed many such operations. This, as much as anything, illustrated the improvements in health care in the decade.

There were also changes in the training of nurses. In September 1967 Laurentian University admitted the first students to a baccalaureate program in its school of nursing. Then in October 1969, the two existing nursing schools, St. Elizabeth, which was founded in 1911, and Marymount, which opened in 1951, were replaced by the Sudbury Regional School of Nursing, which became part of Cambrian College in 1973. These changes meant that nursing schools were no longer run by religious institutions and that nursing education acquired an academic basis.[59]

If the 1960s saw great changes in public health, even greater changes occurred in education. Several forces were at work, not the least of which was a burgeoning school population. In the public primary schools, the number of students rose steadily, from 6,564 in 1960 to 6,967 in 1968. In the 1960s, as the population moved to newer suburbs, the public board could not build schools fast enough and on occasion children were transported by bus from New Sudbury to older schools downtown.[60] At the secondary level, enrolment in grades 9 to 13 throughout the Sudbury metropolitan area rose from 4,957 in 1961 to 8,943 in 1967, an increase of 80.4 percent.[61] One result was that the expansion of the school system that had begun in the 1950s continued in the 1960s: additions were built onto existing schools, and new schools were opened, including Lasalle Secondary School in 1962, Garson-Falconbridge Secondary School in 1963, and Lo-Ellen Park Secondary School in 1963. In 1969, as a result of considerable lobbying by the French community for a secondary school of its own, the Sudbury High School Board opened L'École secondaire Macdonald-Cartier Secondary School. In 1971 the words "Secondary School" were quietly dropped from this name.[62]

As new schools were built, new teachers had to be hired. During the 1960s, when it was difficult to recruit enough teachers, a high percentage of teachers each year were new to the profession. In an attempt to solve the chronic problem of recruitment, representatives from the board of education visited teachers' colleges and tried to persuade new teachers to start their careers in Sudbury. Recruiters referred to the process as going to the "cattle auction." Boards also advertised abroad for qualified teachers and sometimes even sent representatives overseas on hiring expeditions.[63] In earlier years, particularly in the primary schools, teachers were hired after completing just one year at teachers' college, and so during this decade large numbers were involved in upgrading either by working part-time towards a degree at Laurentian University or by attending Department of Education courses during the summer. Yet many teachers still found time to supervise extra-curricular activities after school, mainly music, sports, and conversational French.

Within the schools there was great ferment concerning the curriculum. In 1961 the province implemented the "Robarts Plan," which divided secondary school students among three programs: arts and science; science, technology and trades; and business and commerce.[64] Later in the decade, it established the Committee on Aims and Objectives of Education in the Schools of Ontario under the co-chairmanship of Emmett M. Hall and Lloyd Dennis. Among the members of the committee was Ernie J. Checkeris, a long-time Sudbury school trustee. The *Hall-Dennis Report*, which was released in 1968, suggested many radical changes in the education system.[65] But even before then, changes and experiments had been taking place in Sudbury schools. By the mid-point of the decade all public schools had television sets and educational television programs were watched by students in classrooms. Sudbury's first senior public school (consisting of only grades 7 and 8) opened in 1965 at Churchill Public School. A number of schools experimented with such things as "total language approach," "ungraded schools," "team teaching," "new math," and "experimental science programs." Eventually some schools were wholly non-graded and used the school library as a focal point.

In the separate school system, this period saw growing interest in different schools for French and English students. In 1962 a school inspector, Onésime Tremblay, commented that "the separation of the two linguistic groups can be effective only if it ensures homogeneous entities." Gradually, mixed schools were converted to unilingual schools, and when St. Thomas school was replaced, two new schools were built, one for anglophones and one for francophones. By the end of the decade, the separate school board had only seven mixed schools, compared to twenty-eight for anglophones and forty for francophones.[66]

In the 1960s Sudbury was not unique in experiencing ballooning school enrolment, new schools, expanding teaching staffs, and new programs, and by mid-decade, it had become clear locally, as in the province, that it was difficult to maintain quality and efficiency under the existing system of 1,600 public boards. In 1967 the Department of Education announced that as of 1 January 1969 these boards would be consolidated into 100 large boards. In retrospect, this reorganization was the most dramatic change in Ontario education since the 1840s. By the end of the decade, the various public and high school boards in the Sudbury area were amalgamated into a single public board of education that covered the region from French River to High Falls.[67]

Changes had also taken place in the separate system. In 1960 the Sudbury Separate School Board took over the former boards of McKim and Neelon townships. The number of trustees increased from six to twelve, and there was one French and one English administrator. By the end of the decade, the Sudbury Separate School Board and twenty-four smaller boards in the district became one unit, with twelve elected trustees and 24,376 students, of whom 10,043 were English and 14,333 were French. By the end of the decade Sudbury had become the regional centre for education, just as it had for hospitals.

At the post-secondary level, Sudbury was also expanding its regional influence through Laurentian University of Sudbury and Cambrian College. When the university first opened in 1960, it contained the non-denominational University College as well as two federated religious colleges, the Roman Catholic University of Sudbury and the United Church Huntington University. In 1963 the Anglican Thorneloe University also became federated with Laurentian. In 1964 the university moved from its temporary quarters downtown to the first buildings on its new campus off Ramsey Lake Road. Construction continued for the rest of the decade. Although at first the university had offered courses only in the arts and sciences, the range of programs increased with the opening of schools of nursing, physical and health education, social work, translating and interpreting, and commerce and administration. Graduate studies were introduced in 1969. The number of full-time students rose from 100 to over 2,000 in the ten-year period with a similarly large increase in the number of part-time students too.[68] The fact that nearly 90 percent of the students came from Northern Ontario was a clear indication that there had been a need for a northern university.

Cambrian College began operations in 1966 in the former Sacred Heart College building on Notre Dame, which had closed its doors in 1967 after being in existence since 1913. In the early years under its first principal, John Koski, Cambrian College served the districts of Algoma, Manitoulin, Sudbury, and Nipissing with campuses in North Bay and Sault Ste. Marie as well as Sudbury.[69] The opening of Cambrian filled an educational gap in the area by offering post-secondary courses in business and industry as well as courses leading to careers in social services. In 1968 property was acquired north of Lasalle Boulevard for a permanent campus, for it was obvious that the temporary quarters would soon be inadequate. Site preparation began in 1969 for the first buildings.[70]

The rapid growth of the new universities and colleges throughout the province led to the same problem in obtaining qualified teachers as in the elementary and secondary schools. Sudbury's two post-secondary institutions had to recruit staff actively from Canada and abroad. This was a particularly difficult task for Sudbury because of its unappealing reputation outside the region.

The participation of several religious denominations in the formation of Laurentian was an indication of the continuing importance of churches in the life of Sudburians, though the post-war boom in church membership during the 1950s was followed by a period when many long-held and accepted beliefs were being questioned. For several reasons, doubt, cynicism, and uncertainty became prevalent. Throughout Canada churches attempted to make their services more appealing but to little avail. With the exception of the more fundamentalist and conservative churches, there was a decline in both attendance and membership.[71] In Sudbury, the membership of St. Andrew's United Church, which had been 2,236 in 1958, dropped to 1,829 in 1963; part of the reason for this decline was that some members had moved to newer churches in the suburbs, St. Peter's in Lockerby and St. Stephens in New Sudbury. Despite the creation of new congregations, the decline in total members was real. In 1968 a portion of St. Andrew's Church was declared unsafe; this led to the eventual decision to construct a multi-use building during the 1970s. Other churches were also built or rebuilt during the decade, including a new Jewish synagogue, Shar Hashomayin, on John Street, in 1961, and a new citadel by the Salvation Army in 1967.[72]

Sudburians' interest in sports continued unabated throughout the 1960s. For both spectators and participants, leisure activities were dominated by sports. In the 1960s the municipal government played a larger role in providing facilities for recreational purposes, and the schools began to emphasis a wider range of sports. The arts, on the other hand, did not receive as much support from the local authorities, and music and drama were mainly provided by enthusiastic amateurs. Some talented people made interesting contributions to the arts and crafts in the city, and the schools encouraged music and drama both in class and as extra-curricular activities.

Team sports had long been enjoyed in Sudbury, a tradition that continued during the decade; hockey, football, softball, fastball, and soccer were particularly popular. Some teams achieved success at the Northern Ontario and provincial levels, though there were few national successes. The Park National Hotel team represented Eastern Canada in the World Fastball championship at Clearwater, Florida.[73] New Canadians from Europe sparked an interest in soccer. Two successful teams were the Italia Flyers and the Sudbury Polish White Eagles; despite the name, a large number of players on the latter team were Irish. In 1964 the Italia Flyers, who represented Eastern Canada, reached the finals of the Dominion Challenge Cup before being defeated. In 1969 the White Eagles won the Ontario championship.[74] Although soccer did not attain the popularity of hockey and baseball among children in the city, the game was played by a number of teams, often coached by emigrants from Europe, where soccer was more popular than in Canada. A number of people also attained prominence in a variety of individual sports, including canoeing, wrestling, badminton, and basketball.[75] These activities were capped by the Kiwanis Club's annual selection of the Sportsman of the Year.[76]

The growing interest in organized sports was demonstrated by a group of volunteers who formed Sudbury Sports Central, headed by a full-time executive director, to promote amateur sport.[77] There was also an improvement in school programs, especially for girls, and in 1964 for the first time a field meet was held that enabled successful girls to move on and participate in the Northern Ontario Secondary School Association Championships.[78]

The city's Parks and Recreation Department[79] ran a variety of programs and encouraged neighbourhood playground associations to maintain rinks in winter. During the summer the department offered programs for children in the various neighbourhoods or at day camps. The department also developed Bell Park, Bell Grove, Moonlight Beach, and Camp Sudaca, following a master plan prepared by Mitchell Associates.[80] Although the city made some efforts to make Sudbury a pleasanter place to live, the amount spent on recreation by the municipality was low compared to other cities. In 1964 at $3.78 per capita it was the second lowest in Ontario.[81]

The Junction Creek Conservation Authority (JCCA) was also active during the decade. With city backing it bought a property off Bancroft Drive at a cost of $100,000. The purchase was intended to give the public access to Minnow Lake and a "wide assortment of outdoor facilities." Similarly, property costing $785,000 was acquired in New Sudbury for "active and passive recreation." A stadium and field for various sports and facilities for winter and summer activities, including nature trails, were planned.[82] The JCCA also helped to develop the Laurentian Lake Conservation Area on the southeast shore of Lake Ramsey. In addition to providing picnic tables and fireplaces, the JCCA planted a considerable number of trees. In 1968 twenty thousand trees were planted by two thousand students.[83] Concern for the environment was becoming more widespread, and in 1968 the province created the Environmental Health Studies and Service Branch of the Department of Health. That year, Sudbury was the first site chosen for a study of the effects of long-term exposure to industrial air pollution.[84]

The cultural diversity of the people in Sudbury has always been an important facet of life in the city. Various groups have organized schools for their children and provided musical and dramatic entertainment based on their particular culture. One result of the large number of Italians who came to Sudbury during the decade was the expansion of the Caruso Club, which was the social focal point for many. Finnish theatre has had a long history in the area, but the 1960s saw a decline in interest, probably because second- and third-generation Finns were less fluent in the language and their ties with Finland were weaker. In 1967 various Finnish groups united to produce *Tukkijoela* (On Timber River), which was virtually the last true Finnish theatre produced in Sudbury.[85] Other ethnic groups, perhaps influenced by newcomers, organized schools, choirs, and instrumental groups. A German choir under Ilse Jakelski was founded in 1966. Three Ursuline Polish nuns taught at the Polish school connected with St. Casimir's and the Ukrainians organized the Lunalysenko Choral Ensemble.[86]

Special occasions encouraged various ethnic groups to celebrate in a spectacular manner. The 25th Finnish Grand Festival attracted five thousand visitors to Sudbury in 1964, and Finns from all over North America enjoyed a week of cultural and athletic events.[87] Many festivals were held in 1967 when Canada celebrated its centennial. The Sudbury Centennial Celebration Committee was headed by R.N.H. Beach with W.E.W. Cressey as part-time co-ordinator. One long-term benefit of the centennial was the Sudbury Centennial Museum Society's purchase of the Bell Rock Mansion and grounds for $65,000 from the Nickel Lodge of the Masonic Order. The lodge returned $5,000 as a donation to the projected museum and art gallery. The building was eventually given to Laurentian University to house its Museum and Arts Centre.[88] At least one centennial project that became an annual event was a display of food, arts, and crafts by various ethnic groups.[89]

Cultural activities were not confined to ethnic groups, however. In the French community, both Sacred Heart College and the University of Sudbury presented plays performed by students. The Catholic Church was even more directly involved in the cultural life of francophones. At Ste. Anne's Church, there was a youth cultural centre run by Père Albert Regimbal, s.j., and the diocese newspaper *L'Information* was influential until 1968, when *Le Voyageur* began publication. On the English side, the Sudbury Little Theatre Guild continued to be active during the 1960s. The guild, in existence since 1948, presented plays, held workshops, and sponsored the Sears Drama Festival for high schools as well as professional performances featuring such actors as William Hutt and Douglas Campbell. It also competed with other Northern Ontario theatre groups for a chance to enter the finals of the Dominion Drama Festival (DDF).

Until 1957 Northern Ontario drama groups had competed in the southern Ontario "zone" of the DDF, but that year the guild, headed by Peg Roberts, applied successfully for the creation of a new zone consisting of groups from Northern Ontario and Northern Quebec. This became the Quonta Region and the fourteenth zone of the DDF. During the 1960s, the guild continued to flourish and to present high-quality performances by some splendid local actors and actresses, including Jerry "Sparkle" Markle, Judy Erola, Helen Grenon, Bert Meredith, Rita Dennis, and Ken Gardner. An outstanding and popular theatrical production called *A Taste of Sudbury*, written by Marie Gardner and Gordon Merriam and directed by Mickey Merriam, was one the highlights of the centennial celebrations. The enormous interest in theatre in the 1960s helped lay the groundwork for the establishment of a professional theatre in the next decade.[90]

The Sudbury secondary schools became more active in theatre during the decade. The first Regional High School Art-Drama Festival was held in 1961. Members of the Sudbury Little Theatre Guild assisted with school productions, such as *Oklahoma* (presented by Sheridan Technical School) and *Oliver* (presented by Lockerby Composite). Like theatre, the musical and artistic life of the city still depended to a great extent on amateurs. In 1967 the Sudbury Philharmonic Society celebrated its tenth anniversary. The founder and director was a professional musician, Eric Woodward, who came from England, but the performers were mainly amateurs. During the sixties the cultural life of the city was also enhanced by painters like Nellie Keillor Lowe and Ivan Wheale.

During the decade the municipality provided some facilities for recreational activities but did little to enhance the cultural life of Sudbury. Efforts to improve the cultural amenities of the city were hampered by inferior physical facilities and the lack of adequate funding to improve them, and a reverse snobbery that shunned anything except sport. The public library had half as many professional librarians as national standards deemed appropriate, and the stock needed to be doubled to obtain a satisfactory collection.[91] One improvement was the opening of the first branch library in 1966 in the New Sudbury Shopping Centre. During the decade, changes began that in the 1970s led to professional theatre, more concern with the environment, and better and more diverse recreational facilities.

The 1960s were an exciting decade for Sudbury. After a slow start, the mining industry boomed thanks to a heavy world demand for nickel, and the population went up accordingly. The unions that had begun the decade in great turmoil seemed to have worked out a modus vivendi among themselves and, at the same time, established a reputation for militancy vis-à-vis the companies. The expansion of Laurentian University, the founding of Cambrian College, the creation of new regional school boards, and Sudbury's emergence as a regional health centre strengthened the city's claim to be the most important urban centre in northeastern Ontario.

Sudburians began to take more pride in their city and to put more emphasis on the quality of their lives. Urban renewal in the downtown core and recreational, sporting, and cultural activities begun in the 1960s gradually started to transform the bleak and ugly mining city that was once Sudbury.

Despite all that had been accomplished, the basic problems of the Sudbury area, which resulted from the structure of local government and the terms of its financing, remained unresolved at the end of the decade. The ineffective, ill-considered amalgamation that had been imposed on the community in 1960 by the Ontario Municipal Board had avoided the real issue, which was that the whole Sudbury region was really one community. The OMB ruling had served only to compound the existing problems. By the end of the decade, everyone knew something had to be done. Thus, on 13 February 1969, the province appointed J.A. Kennedy, chairman of the OMB, to report to the minister of municipal affairs upon the structure, organization, and method of operation of the municipalities in the Sudbury area and to suggest what reorganization of local government would be required by anticipated future development. The whole process had started once again.

1 Note that, effective 13 October 1961, after moving into its new building, the *Sudbury Daily Star* became the *Sudbury Star*, the name it had carried almost from its establishment until it went daily in December 1939.

2 *Sudbury Star*, 30 October 1965. See also *Canadian Annual Review* (Toronto: University of Toronto Press, 1961–66); Falconbridge Nickel Mines Ltd., *Annual Reports* (Toronto: 1960–69); International Nickel Company of Canada, *Annual Reports* (Toronto: 1960–69); INCO *Triangle*, April 1968 and March 1969; *Northern Life*, 28 December 1968 and 27 November 1969; and *Sudbury Star*, 8 March 1965, 3 January 1966, and 13 December 1966.

3 *Northern Miner*, 27 November 1969, 54. See also Robert Stephenson et al., *A Guide to the Golden Age: Mining in Sudbury, 1886–1977* (Sudbury: Department of History, Laurential University, 1979), 34.

4 The principal source for this section is John B. Lang, "A Lion in a Den of Daniels: A History of the International Union of Mine, Mill and Smelter Workers in Sudbury, Ontario, 1942–1962" (M.A. thesis, University of Guelph, 1970).

5 The IUMMSW divided Canada into two districts: District 1 was all of Western Canada to the Manitoba-Saskatchewan border; District 2, the rest. District 2 was further subdivided into five subdistricts. In 1960 Sudbury alone made up subdistrict 2, and it was by far the largest, with about 16,000 members. The other four subdistricts had a combined total of about 4,000. See Frank Southern, *The Sudbury Incident* (Toronto: York Publishing and Printing, 1978).

6 *Sudbury Star*, 14 November 1961.

7 Ibid., 15 January 1962.

8 Ibid., 2 February 1962.

9 Ibid., 16 March 1962.

10 Ibid., 2 May 1962.

11 Ibid., 29 November 1962.

12 Southern, *The Sudbury Incident*, 152, 154, 165.

13 Falconbridge Nickel Mines Ltd., *Annual Report* (Toronto, 1966).

14 *Sudbury Star*, 9 February 1967.

15 Southern, *The Sudbury Incident*, 183.

16 International Nickel Company of Canada Ltd., *Annual Report* (Toronto, 1962).

17 International Nickel Company of Canada Ltd., *Annual Report* (Toronto, 1966).

18 Caroline M. Hallsworth, *Federal, Provincial and Municipal Elections in Sudbury* (Sudbury: Sudbury Public Library, 1981).

19 Ontario Municipal Board, *P.F.M. 5143-56.*

20 E.G. Higgins and F.A. Peake, *Sudbury Then and Now: A Pictorial History of Sudbury and Area, 1883–1973* (Sudbury: Sudbury and District Chamber of Commerce, 1977), 115.

21 Sudbury (City), *1964: The Year of Dilemma: Submitted to the Hon. J.P. Robarts and the Government of the Province of Ontario by the Mayor's Committee on Sudbury's Financial Problems* (Sudbury: The City, 1964), 11–13.

22 D.S. James, "A Study of the Effects of Amalgamation and Annexation of the City of Sudbury and Adjoining Municipalities" (B.Comm. thesis, Queen's University, 1964), 28–29.

23 Sudbury (City), Public Works Department, *Special Report, 1969–1970.*

24 Sudbury (City), *Report on City Water Supply 1967.*

25 Sudbury (City), Public Works Department, *Report* (January–February 1969).

26 D.S. Cuomo, "The Evolution of the Planning Process in the Sudbury Area: The Roles of the Principal Actors" (B.A. thesis, Department of Geography, Laurentian University, 1980), 19–21.

27 James, *A Study of the Effects of Amalgamation*, 33–35.

28 Sudbury (City), *1964: The Year of Dilemma*, 11–13.

29 Ibid., 1.

30 J.R. Winter, *Sudbury: An Economic Survey* (Sudbury: Sudbury and District Industrial Commission and Laurentian University, 1967).

31 *Sudbury Star*, 4 March 1967.

32 Sudbury (City), Public Works Department, *Report* (1968).

33 M.M. Dillon Ltd., *Sudbury Area Transportation Study* (Sudbury: M.M. Dillon, 1965).

34 *Sudbury Star*, 21 December 1966.

35 Ibid., 30 November 1966.

36 Higgins and Peake, *Sudbury Then and Now*, 120.

37 Sudbury (City), *1964: The Year of Dilemma*, 11.

38 Chamber of Commerce, Civic Square Affairs Committee, *The Housing Problem of Sudbury* [Sudbury: The Chamber 1968].

39 Ontario Housing Corporation, *The Sudbury Housing Market* (n.p.: The Corporation, 1968), 71–80.

40 Donald E. McCullough, "The Evolution and Distribution of Public Housing in the City of Sudbury" (B.A. thesis, Laurentian University, 1972), 4, 21.

41 Sudbury (City), Planning Board, *Renewal in the Nickel City: An Urban Renewal Study for Sudbury, Ontario* (1961).

42 Sudbury (City), Urban Renewal Commission, *Borgia Area Urban Renewal Project Study* (1966), 4 vols.

43 *Sudbury Star*, 8 May 1969.

44 *INCO Triangle*, June 1961 to September 1964.

45 Ontario Housing Corporation, *The Sudbury Housing Market* (Toronto: The Corporation, 1968), 43.

46 Maury O'Neill and Peter Andrews, *Sudbury Statistical Summary* (Sudbury: Department of History, Laurentian University, 1986), 24.

47 Ibid.; and Sudbury (City), *1964 : The Year of Dilemma*, 11.

48 O'Neill and Andrews, *Sudbury Statistical Summary*, 33.

49 Ontario, Ministry of Culture and Recreation, Multi-Cultural Branch, *Immigration to Ontario by Country of Last Permanent Residence, 1957–1971, Part I* (Toronto: The Ministry, 1976).

50 Ontario Housing Corporation, *The Sudbury Housing Market* (Toronto, 1962), 71.
51 Ontario Housing Corporation, *The Sudbury Housing Market* (1968), 15.
52 Ibid., 14.
53 Jeannette Bouchard, *Seven Decades of Caring/Sept décennies de soins* (Sudbury: Laurentian University Press, 1984), 52.
54 Sudbury and District Hospital Council, [*Brief*] [n.p., 1966?], 6.
55 Ibid.
56 Ibid., 51.
57 Ibid., 52.
58 Mary C. Shantz, *Sudbury: Book of Lists*, typescript (Sudbury: Sudbury Public Library, n.d.).
59 Bouchard, *Seven Decades of Caring*, 52.
60 Sudbury Public Schools, *Superintendents' Annual Reports* (1960–68).
61 Ontario Housing Corporation, *The Sudbury Housing Market* (1968), 36.
62 Interview with G.W. Thomson, former director of education, 9 May 1992.
63 Interview with George W. Thomson, 30 March 1992.
64 A.K. McDougall, *John P. Robarts: His Life and Government* (Toronto: University of Toronto Press for the Ontario Historical Studies Series, 1986), 56–57.
65 Provincial Committee on Aims and Objectives of Education in the Schools of Ontario, *Living and Learning: The Report of the Provincial Committee* (Toronto: Ontario Department of Education, 1968).
66 Sudbury District Roman Catholic Separate School Board, *One Hundred Years of Catholic Separate Schools of Sudbury* (Sudbury: The Board, 1984).
67 Higgins and Peake, *Sudbury Then and Now*, 118.
68 Gwenda Hallsworth, *Le Beau Risque du Savoir/"A Venture into the Realm of Higher Learning"* (Sudbury: Laurentian University, 1985).
69 In 1972 North Bay and Sault Ste. Marie became independent colleges.
70 Higgins and Peake, *Sudbury Then and Now*, 115.
71 F.A. Peake and R.P. Horne, *The Religious Tradition in Sudbury 1883–1983* (Sudbury: Downtown Churches Association, 1983), 64; and Graeme S. Mount and Michael F. Mulloy, *A History of St. Andrew's United Church, Sudbury* (Sudbury: The Church, 1982), 79.
72 Peake and Horne, *The Religious Tradition in Sudbury*, 59, 60–61, 67.
73 Frank Pagnucco, *Home Grown Heroes: A Sports History of Sudbury* ([Sudbury]: Miller Publishing, 1982), 35–36.
74 Ibid., 121–22.
75 For information on these people, see ibid.
76 Shantz, *Sudbury's Book of Lists*. In the 1960s, the winners were as follows: 1960 – Erroll Gibson; 1961 – Alex MacPherson; 1962 – Maurice LaFrance and Gertie Dekardine; 1963 – Matti Jutila; 1964 – Bob Leduc; 1965 – Tom St. Jean; 1966 – Antero Rauhanen; 1967 – Richard Pagnutti; 1968 – Ed Taylor; and 1969 – Marcel Clements.
77 Higgins and Peake, *Sudbury Then and Now*, 115.
78 Pagnucco, *Home Grown Heroes*, 161–62.
79 Higgins and Peake, *Sudbury Then and Now*, 117.
80 *Conservationist* 5 (January/February 1969): 173.
81 Sudbury (City), *1964: The Year of Dilemma*, 14.
82 *Conservationist* 1, no. 2 (August 1965): 7; and 1, no. 6 (March/April 1966): 1, 4.
83 *Conservationist* 4, no. 1 (May/June 1968): 8.
84 Bouchard, *Seven Decades of Caring*, 50.

85 Irene "Mickey" Merriam, "Finnish Theatre in the Sudbury District" (honours thesis, York University, 1976), 26–27.

86 *Polyphony* 5, no. 1 (Spring/Summer 1983): 55, 80, 85.

87 *Sudbury Star*, 30 July 1964.

88 Ibid., 14 January 1967.

89 *Centennial Scrapbook.*

90 Personal files, Peg Roberts; J.E. Miller, *The History of the Sudbury Little Theatre Guild, 1948–1962* (Sudbury: J.E. Miller, 1962); and Merriam, "Memoirs of a Director," 11.

91 Sudbury (City), *1964: Year of Dilemma*, 13.

CHAPTER TEN

THE 1970s

Dieter K. Buse

"One of the main reasons for the existence of Sudbury, an ugly mining town of 80,000 persons, and Copper Cliff, a company town of 3,450, is the International Nickel Company of Canada, the US controlled producer of 65% of the world's nickel supply and employer of 16,000 men," wrote the *Toronto Star* in 1968.[1] Twelve years later, in an article headed "Strike-ridden Sudbury – the bitter lesson," the *Edmonton Journal* continued to paint a grim picture of the community: "In 1980 Sudbury's gears are in reverse ... The city is staggering and being rendered sterile ... this is a falling and failing city."[2]

Despite the persistence of the negative image, much changed in Sudbury during the 1970s. Population, pollution, work patterns, economic conditions, physical appearance, transportation, governmental structures, and cultural opportunities were all altered fundamentally during the decade. Even though Sudbury remained dependent upon trends and policies beyond its control, the source of that dependence had changed from a single reliance on the mining industry to a dual dependence on mining and government. But even while losing its traits as a mining centre and undergoing a transformation towards a middle-class distribution and service centre, Sudbury's image remained unchanged and its dependency constant.

At the beginning of the 1970s Canada and Ontario were in the midst of a mini-recession, but in Sudbury the economy was booming. In 1971, in an article entitled "Sudbury: INCO expansions help maintain record growth," the *Financial Post* detailed the projects INCO and Falconbridge had under way and added: "Sudbury is a vital growing centre bent on redevelopment, economic prosperity, education and improving the appearance of the city."[3]

By 1980, after a decade of layoffs, mini-booms, strikes, cutbacks, and more layoffs, Sudbury might have been a ghost town. Instead, it weathered the worst recession since the Second World War as well as any Ontario city. Though the total population had declined, the bankruptcy rate was no worse than elsewhere in the late 1970s. Sudburians shared the general Canadian economic problems of inflation, uncontrolled government spending, and staggering interest rates. As the mining industry declined in importance in the local economy, Sudburians experienced the same problems as other Canadians.[4] How Sudbury came to conform to the Canadian pattern is not easy to explain, but it appears that Sudbury had gone through an economic transition. Though still heavily tied to mining and smelting, the city had evidently begun to live by other means as well.

The changes in Sudbury's economy can be seen in the changes in occupational patterns. In 1971 mining, with 18,000 workers, accounted for 23 percent of the 76,480 jobs in the Sudbury district. Construction accounted for 8 percent, manufacturing – including smelting – for 13 percent, and trade, finance, and real estate for 14.5 percent. Community, business, and personal services were growing quickly and were already 19.5 percent. Fewer than 1 percent of the labour force worked in farming, fishing, or forestry.

Since some of the jobs in construction, communications, transportation, trade, and business services were directly related to the mining industry, the *Financial Post* could write in 1971, "Sudbury remains basically a mining town with the two nickel companies providing 50% of the employment."[5]

The 1981 census confirmed that the importance of INCO and Falconbridge in the labour market had lessened dramatically. From 1971 to 1981 the two companies had reduced the number of miners and smelter workers they employed by about ten thousand. As a result, there was a decline in the ratio of men to women in the labour market. In 1971 it was four to one; by 1981 it was less than two to one. When more jobs become available for women, it is usually because of a shift away from the extractive and manufacturing industries to services, administration, and small business. That is exactly what happened in Sudbury, and the result was an increase in clerical and service jobs. The number of federal government employees, for example, nearly quadrupled from 1971 to 1981, and by the latter date a majority were women.[6]

Further evidence that Sudbury was no longer primarily a mining community was the increase in the number of small businesses, especially boutiques and specialty stores, which rose by about 30 percent according to *Vernon's City Directory*. Employment also increased in the communications industry. Most important was the expansion of jobs in education, medicine, and government. By 1981 more than 10,600 people were working for the eleven largest employers in those fields. If the social services organizations, the communications industry, and other lesser employers are counted, this sector of the economy had surpassed the mining and smelting totals. The old view of Sudbury as a "one-industry town" reflected more the old image than the changing reality.[7]

Ultimately the employment levels in mining and smelting were determined by the nickel market. As the Vietnam War consumed planes and tanks, bullets and steel plating, speeded-up production became the order of the day. At the same time, the automobile industry was still using large quantites of nickel for its flashy, chrome male dreams.

During 1970 and 1971 both INCO and Falconbridge attemped to make up for production losses due to the strike in 1969 by raising production. Those were years of bonuses, overtime, and deaths.[8] In 1970 INCO's output was one and one half times that of 1968. In the same year mining deaths averaged one a month. The inquests blamed poor training by the company and the circumvention of safety regulations by workers eager to produce for the bonus pay. In 1971 INCO's Sudbury work force hit a high of over twenty thousand, which it never again surpassed. By 1972, as the end of the three-year contract came nearer, the union, fearing that part of INCO's production was intended not for the market, which was moderating, but as a stockpile against another strike, tried to limit overtime, talked slowdown, and generally helped restore the eight-hour working day.

In 1973, as the market for nickel moderated, so too did INCO's output, and by the next year the bubble had burst. In 1974 INCO laid off fifteen hundred workers and shut down the smelter for a month of "repairs." Nickel sales were under pressure because INCO had lost what had been almost a world monopoly. Owing as much to INCO's poor management as to lessening demand, French and Japanese producers were able to enter the market and undersell INCO. Faulty planning had caused INCO to invest heavily in Third World sources of ores. Those projects proved expensive, sucked away cash flow, and did not bring the expected high returns, as increasing fuel costs undercut their viability.

After a nine-day strike in 1975 was settled by negotiation, a small burst of increased work time ended in 1977 with three thousand layoffs. "There is a burning rage and it is fastened deep within the psyche of community consciousness,"[9] declared Elmer Sopha, the eloquent former Liberal MPP. By this time Sudbury's workers were mostly men with established families and a long-term investment in the region. The young and single in search of a fast buck had been weeded out by the shutdowns, layoffs, and slowdowns. The established workers thought about their long-term security. Despite the knowledge that INCO had a thirteen-month stockpile, had laid off three thousand workers, and had closed for six weeks, in September of 1978 the Steelworkers voted 6,319 to 4,141 to strike INCO. That strike over grievances and retirement permitted INCO to rid itself of its high inventory.[10] When the workers returned, however, approximately one thousand jobs had been saved by the strike and the negotiated settlement that ended it. The number employed did drop from fourteen thousand to eleven thousand as a result of attrition and some early retirements, but there were no further layoffs. After the strike some overtime started again but not on a large scale, and through 1980 the production rate remained stable with summer shutdowns.

The work pattern, which is demonstrated here with INCO data but was similar at Falconbridge, showed a boom-and-bust cycle: strike, overtime, slowdown, speed-up, strike, mini-boom, layoffs, strike. In this sector the labour force continued to typify a resource community dependent upon external markets and a few companies. Other strikes in the growing service sector, by newspaper and telephone employees, illustrated the difficulties of resisting technological change, while those by teachers reflected the fullness of the public purse.[11]

Some aspects of work patterns and the layoffs and strike of 1977–78 require special comment. The layoffs resulted in the establishment of the Select Committee of the Ontario Legislature, which revealed not only INCO's economic vulnerability but also the need to diversify the economy of Sudbury.[12] Comments on the strike varied widely. When the work stoppage began in 1978, the former NDP leader, Stephen Lewis, ranted, "Sudbury has succumbed to madness. The decision by a majority of the nearly 12,000 Steelworkers ... has achieved a new pinnacle of irrationality and intransigence."[13] The local *Northern Life* saw the situation more realistically: "[INCO] is either purposely or clumsily inciteful [*sic*]."[14] Community leaders blamed the company more than the workers as estimates emerged that a six-month strike would cost the region $58 million. The local community rallied to the side of the strikers by publishing newsletters, forming wives' and citizens' support groups, and collecting money. Mine Mill also collected money and food for the strikers, symbolically ending the bitter feud that stretched back to the 1940s. The mayor and councils of city and region spoke in favour of the workers, demonstrating that they too wanted an end to the dependency upon the mining giants. Coming so soon after the layoffs, the strike made everyone aware that a new economic basis for Sudbury was a necessity.

That necessity became evident also from changes in the nature of the workplace during the 1970s. Not only were the service sectors – medical, educational, social – growing dramatically, but mining and smelting had been mechanized and rationalized. Those changes are described in Wallace Clement's *Hardrock Mining*. Underground ramp mines, scoop trams, and jumbo drills replaced mucking and jacklegs. Owing to mechanization, the miner was transformed from a skilled craftsman – driller, blaster, or slusher – to a semi-skilled machine tender. Supervisors could observe workers more closely in enlarged and centralized work spaces. Above ground Clement noted "a strong tendency ... particularly evident since the early 1970s, to move from mechanized production to automated production ... The consequences for labour are just as significant ... Much of the bull work has been eliminated, but so has much of the craft production; they have been replaced in many instances by dial watching and patrol duty."[15] Maintenance work increased substantially, but its few hundred jobs could not make up for the halving of the work force in a decade.

During the 1970s the changes in the local economy were paralleled by changes in the population. Whereas the population was growing in 1970, it soon slowed down and by 1976 it had stopped. When the Regional Municipality of Sudbury was formed in 1973, it contained 162,700 residents; that number rose to a peak of 167,000 in 1977. By 1981 the number had dropped to 159,000, the losses having occurred primarily in the city of Sudbury.[16] From a high of 99,309 in 1972 the city had declined to 91,829. That 4.5 percent loss between 1976 and 1981, which was the largest in any large Canadian city, moved Sudbury from sixteenth to twentieth in the country.[17]

This change in the size of the population was accompanied by a dramatic transformation of the population by age and sex. Before the 1970s Sudbury had the typical demographic make-up of a mining town.[18] Even in 1976 Sudbury's population continued to illustrate

> at least three significant differences from that of Canada and Ontario. The Sudbury district had a much larger

proportion of younger people ... Secondly, persons 55 years and older represented a much smaller proportion of the total population. And, finally, in the latter group, males outnumbered females, a situation which was usually the reverse in the rest of the population.[19]

By 1981 those differences were nearly gone.

In 1971, 43.4 percent of the males and 45.3 percent of the females were under 20 years of age. In 1981 the comparative figures had fallen to 36.7 percent and 35.2 percent. In 1971, 4 percent of the males and 4.4 percent of the females were over 65. By 1981 the comparative figures had risen to 5.4 percent and 5.9 percent. If the numbers are taken another way, in 1971 more than half the people in the Sudbury region were under 25, whereas by 1981 half the people were over 30. Another demographic change was in the composition of the population by sex. In the Sudbury area in 1971 the ratio of men to women in the age groups 20–24 and 25–29 was 120 and 115 to 100. Only in the over-70 age group did women again outnumber men. But by 1981 men were outnumbered by women in the age groups 20–25, 26–35, and 36–45.

These shifts in the composition of the population were due to trends in the local economy. At the beginning of the decade labourers in their twenties had come in search of the high wages in the mining industry. The youthful nature of the population was reinforced by the lower than average age at death of miners and smelter workers. In addition, few middle-class people stayed in Sudbury after they had retired, because of the lack of social services, such as nursing homes. During the 1970s the number of young male labourers had declined dramatically as a result of production slowdowns and the mechanization and rationalization of the mining and smelting industries. In the meantime, the community expanded its social services, making it more attractive to an older population. By 1981, as well, Sudbury was part of the national trend to smaller families, so that there were comparatively fewer young people around.

Other aspects of Sudbury's population showed fewer alterations. The ethnic composition changed only slightly over the decade. In the region the population remained roughly one-third French, one-third British, and one-third other, though in the city the British increased and the French declined. The older immigrant groups in the city also fell slightly: Italians from 9.3 percent to 8 percent, and Germans from 3 percent to 2 percent. The influx of Vietnamese, Chinese, East Indians, Pakistanis, and others, however, kept the balance similar to 1971.

Though Sudbury may have been special among larger Canadian cities in its three-sided ethnic balance, as the decade opened the manner in which the ethnic groups clustered together within the city repeated the patterns of other Canadian cities. For example, the French constituted the great majority in the Flour Mill area and in the towns of Azilda, Val Caron, and Blezard Valley. The Italians were heavily concentrated in Gatchell, whereas the Ukrainians remained along King Street and Howey Drive and the Poles along the Kingsway. During the 1970s these ethnic concentrations were lessened as many of the second generation moved to other districts and were assimilated.[20] This process was symbolized by the physical decay evident in some of the ethnic halls.

Within Sudbury, concentrations of population developed along Paris Street, Notre-Dame, Lasalle, and Barrydowne, nearly all coinciding with highrises or apartment blocks close to new shopping districts. Overall, New Sudbury and the southern part of the city gained in relation to the northwest and eastern sections of Sudbury as well as the downtown, where urban renewal removed many people. In the region some of the outlying towns of two thousand to four thousand people (Val Caron, Val Therese, Hanmer, and Garson) grew while other similar-sized towns (Falconbridge, Copper Cliff, Coniston, Levack-Onaping, and Blezard Valley) all lost more than 5 percent. In the long run the city of Sudbury suffered an even greater population loss than the region's towns, especially the French-Catholic ones, since its birth rate was much lower.[21]

The dispersal of the population, especially by the destruction of the downtown ghettos and boarding houses, did not change the relationship between where people worked and where they lived. Except in the small towns at the edge of the region like Levack-Onaping, Capreol, Lively, and Falconbridge, the majority of people did not work in the area where they lived. Thousands came from the Valley to Sudbury and Copper Cliff, while many Sudburians still travelled the traditional routes to mines and smelters east and west of the city.[22]

If the demographic trends hinted at an older population and new workplaces, Sudbury's social organizations also underwent alterations. "New" groups, in particular those of ethnic origin, women, and native peoples, organized to obtain public hearings. Some social institutions remained unchanged, though: the seventy-two churches of 1981 were still one-third Catholic (24), one-sixth United Church (13), and one-tenth Anglican (7), the same pattern as in 1971. Religion as a private commitment continued to be important for about half the population. Though only a few churchmen of the main denominations were active in public affairs, the public activities of many ethnic groups were often based in their religious organizations.

In 1981 the largest ethnic group in the Sudbury region was the francophones with 34 percent of the total population.[23] However, this group remained very under-represented in the political councils, the social institutions, and the cultural forums of Sudbury.[24] And there were more serious problems. Despite their significance locally, francophones were still a minority in the province and were threatened by assimilation as well as uncertain legal rights.[25] The local francophone leadership attempted to gain a more visible and audible presence, a share of power, and a redressing of ancient inequities, but it was outside events that spurred this re-evaluation and attempt at assertiveness.

The problems of the Northern Ontario French population have always been related to education and the Catholic Church. Owing to the refusal of the Ontario government until the late 1960s to support French-language instruction beyond the ninth grade, there was no public secondary school in the Sudbury area until L'École Secondaire Macdonald-Cartier opened in 1969. Le Collège du Sacré-Coeur had long provided secondary education but for a substantial fee. Those who could not afford Le Collège were faced both with the mental and educational difficulties of shifting to English instruction in midstream and with the threat of assimilation. As a result, most francophones dropped out of school. In the mid-1970s the percentage with a doctorate, a university degree, some university education, or even Grade 13 remained at approximately one-half the provincial average.[26]

This situation would not have been possible without the active cooperation of the Catholic Church, which, as in Quebec, preferred to control the higher education that existed and to dominate a traditionally minded population. During the 1950s and 1960s the church had openly participated in the break-up of Mine Mill, a union with radical tendencies but also one that acknowledged the large French element among its membership. Part of the executive was always French, and in addition to providing recreational and cultural activities for all members during the fifties, the union published its newspaper partly in French. The clergy's part in helping to destroy Mine Mill embittered many miners.[27]

During the 1970s the secularized children of many of these men sought a separate Franco-Ontarian identity by designing their own flag and by creating a separate culture. By 1970 the folk-rock group CANO was performing songs written by Sudbury's Robert Paquette, and the Théâtre du Nouvel-Ontario (TNO) was producing Franco-Ontarian plays.[28] "For the traditional leadership of the community the new theatre was a scandal. The group's anti-clerical attitudes, its marijuana parties and its use of *joual* French was disturbing."[29] The songs and plays, which represented a hybrid culture – American, Quebec, northern, lower class – dealt with the problems of being French in a Northern Ontario English environment.

Whereas CANO, Robert Paquette, and those involved in the TNO, such as André Paiement or Robert Marinier, attained cultural prominence during the 1970s, their successes were short-lived. The TNO lived on at La Slague, and *La Nuit sur l'Étang* (Night on the pond), a cultural and musical showcase of francophone talent, first presented in 1973, became an annual tradition at Laurentian University. But by 1980 most of the early groups had been dissolved or had moved away. For the most part their assertion of the French fact separate from the church had failed to create an alternative culture. Within a decade, the successors of these groups were back in the church basements or tied to the Centre des Jeunes, which was founded in 1950 by Père Albert Regimbal, one of the staunchest anti–Mine Mill clergy, and which was headed during the 1970s by Monique Cousineau, a "dynamic ex-nun."[30] The revolution had been tamed.

Yet the French fact had changed. Though the francophone cultural community had re-established its ties to the Catholic Church by the end of the 1970s, its dependence upon the finances of the state had also become evident. Despite the fact that the francophones were not directly represented at any level of government, the elite of the community was successful in obtaining money from the federal and provincial governments for its projects.[31] In 1978 a local CBC French station was set up. Whereas until 1969 there had been no French secondary schools, in 1980 there were four.

Meanwhile, university students and professors as well as journalists and professionals were agitating to obtain or expand educational, cultural, social, judicial, and medical services in French.[32] Such services became fully available in some institutions such as the university, hospital, and courts, the latter a first in Ontario.[33] Spoken French also became more readily accepted in Sudbury restaurants and stores. Businesses like Bell Telephone no longer openly practised linguistic discrimination, though few encouraged bilingualism.[34] The fact remained, however, that a French-speaking person needed to know English to live and work in an area officially designated as bilingual but an English-speaking person did not need to speak French.

Despite many surface changes, by the end of the 1970s the French community remained in a situation similar to that of the late 1960s. The threat of assimilation continued owing to the predominance and pervasiveness of American culture in Canada, to intermarriages in which the predominant language became English, to the lack of French-language higher education in commerce, science, and technology, and above all to the reliance of the traditional elite upon the conservative institution of the church, a reliance now reinforced by the dependence of this class on the state. Neither of those institutions in the past had offered much help against discrimination, though the church had encouraged and perhaps ensured the survival of the language. The government, through its support to the service sector, enlarged the local French-speaking middle class of lawyers, doctors, journalists, and professors.

At the same time as the emergence of a francophone white-collar group that might be the basis of long-term improvement in social standing and economic well-being, the francophones were being threatened by the educational system. Simultaneously with the expansion of French secondary schools, the government of Ontario began to foster French immersion classes for anglophone children. In 1974, after surveying the community, the Sudbury Board of Education established French immersion in three schools: Alexander, George Vanier (in Lively), and Lindsley (in Onaping). That year there were fifty-four pupils, taught by three teachers; in the following years the program expanded. By 1981 the fear was being expressed openly that the products of that schooling would soon be displacing francophones in the government positions that required bilingualism.[35]

Those of British descent in Sudbury continued to support a few clubs which still showed evidence of ties to an earlier homeland, though both the Orange Hall and Empire Club were defunct by 1977. Since Sudburians of British background dominated the social life of the city, they had little need for separate and special organizations. With some notable exceptions, they dominated the English-language service clubs, such as the Elks, Moose, Masons, Royal Canadian Legion, the YMCA, and the YWCA; controlled the boards of the hospitals and charitable and education organizations; and generally ran the socially oriented sports clubs like the Sudbury Curling Club and the Idylwylde Golf and Country Club. Indeed, the exclusive membership of the Idylwylde at the beginning of the decade made it the second home of the business and professional elite. When the Idylwylde applied for public funds in 1979, it was compelled to open its membership to the general public.

During the 1970s the "other" ethnic groups showed a remarkable assertiveness. Threatened by biculturalism and bilingualism, which gave advantages to French-speakers, and sustained by large federal government subsidies, the other ethnic groups embraced "multiculturalism." In April 1971 a two-day conference of Northern Ontario ethnic groups proposed the establishment of a multicultural centre.[36] In 1973 a multicultural advisory council was set up, and in 1978, after a feasibility study funded by the federal government, the Sudbury Multicultural Centre finally opened; its purpose was to co-ordinate the activities of ethnic groups, promote interracial and religious harmony, and contribute to an understanding of the world's multitude of cultures and customs.[37] The Multicultural Centre served as the meeting place primarily of the smaller and newer immigrant groups, such as Indians, Pakistanis, West Indians, and Chilians.

The older and larger immigrant groups, mainly from Europe and in their second and third generation, co-operated with this organization but worked primarily through the Sudbury Folk Arts Council, which in 1978 comprised nineteen ethnic groups. The Italians, Finns, Poles, Ukrainians, Serbs, Croatians, and Greeks already had their own clubs or churches, where they continued their earlier separate social and cultural endeavours. The Italians often gathered at the Caruso Club, which had a new hall, while the Finns met at Sampo Hall or Voima Club. The Ukrainians, like the Finns, had two halls to match their pro- and anti-left political positions.

As elsewhere in Canada, the main contribution of the ethnic associations was to provide an instant community for immigrants of the same group. The number and variety of these establishments also made Sudbury a special city where food fairs, ethnic dancing or singing, and cultural displays provided introductions to other ways of life. During the 1970s Sudbury was spared the ethnic strife that arose in cities like Toronto, Montreal, and Vancouver, perhaps because some local members of the ethnic community worked for the city administration or belonged to the professional elite as architects and lawyers.[38]

Two ethnic groups that had an influence on the community far out of proportion to their numbers were the Italians and the Scandinavians. With two regional chairmen (Joe Fabbro and D. Dozzi), a mayor (Fabbro), and numerous councillors, the Italians were over-represented politically for their 8 percent of the population. The Scandinavians' cultural and political presence also seemed out of proportion to their 1 percent of the population. The popularity of cross-country skiing made their social clubs highly visible. The Germans and Dutch, who with 4.4 percent and 1.25 percent of the population respectively were the third- and fifth-largest ethnic groups, seemed the least prominent, though the former had a language school and an active association similar to those of the Finns, Croatians, Italians, and Ukrainians.

During the 1970s women made their presence known throughout Canada, and Sudbury proved to be no exception. Though Grace Hartman had served as mayor in the 1960s, women remained severely under-represented on city council and in most other public offices. During the 1970s only two women, Mary Conroy and Sandra Korpela, were elected to council, the latter ousting Andy Roy, a veteran politician who had made discriminatory remarks about women. The school boards had always had some women trustees, but otherwise women had played a very secondary role in institutions, except on the volunteer boards.

Of more immediate concern to many women was that in 1971 Sudbury women were paid approximately one-third of the average for men and that only one-third of women were working outside the home, 10 percent lower than the Canadian average.[39] Employment opportunities continued to remain limited for women throughout the 1970s. By 1976 the participation rate for women had increased to only 39 percent in Sudbury, compared to over 45 percent for the country. The mentality of the male mining community lingered on.

In reaction to this situation, and inspired by events in the United States and elsewhere, a local women's movement emerged. Its leaders advocated personal liberation (an end to the bra and abortion on demand) and equality in legal rights (equal pay for equal work and an end to sexual discrimination). Despite some internal disagreement about methods and purposes, by the mid-1970s when the rhetoric had calmed, significant results appeared. By 1976 there was an abortion referral service, Women Helping Women, and in 1978 a rape crisis centre opened.[40] That same year a women's studies program was set up at Laurentian University. In 1979, after the Northern Ontario Women's Conference, a group of seventeen participants formed Women in Action with the intention of setting up a women's centre. By 1981 the centre was in operation, with literature available on women's situations and problems. Government grants were obtained to run houses for battered women, to study employment opportunities, and to make women aware of their potential to work in a variety of trades. By the end of the decade, however, the various women's organizations and their leaders were surviving on government subsidies or working at jobs dependent upon government support. The great burst of activity had gained positions for the leaders, but the women's employment rate stayed under 40 percent; with the downturn of the economy, unemployment rose more sharply among women than among men.[41]

Another group faced with difficulties and discrimination in Canadian society, including Sudbury, were natives. Eighty percent of those not on reserves were living on welfare, many had serious drinking problems, there was a high suicide rate, and the average life expectancy was forty-six, compared to the Ontario average of seventy-three.[42] During the 1970s, inspired in part by trends elsewhere, Sudbury's native population took steps to improve its situation.

In 1973 a group of natives, with assistance from the federal government, founded the Indian Friendship Centre, where a native counsellor helps natives adjust to city life.[43] The Sudbury school board began to teach elementary schoolchildren about native languages, art, songs, and customs. In 1970, when government grants were increased to aid access to higher education, Laurentian University began to offer courses in native studies, including the Ojibway language and culture. Some of the courses were taught by natives. Publicity by the American Indian Movement helped, and new projects were created that tried to acknowledge the value of native communal living arrangements. For example, in 1975 the Sudbury branch of the Canada Housing and Mortgage Corporation gave a loan to develop group homes for native children, who had frequently not survived reformatory school when mixed with whites.[44]

By the end of the decade some improvements could be recorded in increased native participation in education, as well as in the popularity of Indian art, the election of working natives as chiefs of bands, plus a new pride and self-reliance among many native youths. As with the women's movement, however, most of the advances depended upon government aid. In 1975 native leaders pointed out that of the seven thousand federal civil servants dealing with native affairs only 10 percent were natives; each time an issue such as this became controversial, the government threatened to withdraw funds for projects in native communities.

For all groups in Sudbury, including natives and women, post-secondary education became more accessible. Laurentian University and Cambrian College, two of the main educational institutions that were officially bilingual but whose administration had remained predominantly English, expanded during the 1970s. The university grew in enrolment and staff until 1973, after which it stabilized at around 3,000 full-time students and 250 faculty members. Laurentian continued to provide an opportunity for upgrading by teachers, homemakers, and managers and gave the local middle class a larger cultural and intellectual world. Most important, it provided higher education for the sons and daughters of working-class families who could not afford to study in southern Ontario. Cambrian College, also with over 2,000 students, provided another cultural centre as well as apprenticeship and technological training. During the decade the provincial government financed the expansion of both institutions. Laurentian added an Olympic-sized swimming pool and a second science building and enlarged its residences, and Cambrian built a new complex at the northern edge of New Sudbury and by 1980 was completing a gymnasium and auditorium.

What marked Sudbury's social organizations and institutions during the 1970s was their variety, made possible not only because a multitude of existing churches, service clubs, unions, and ethnic groups remained active during the decade, but because new groups began to appear. Some of the issues and events, such as civil rights, student demonstrations, Vietnam protests, and environmentalism, that had made the late 1960s an era of radicalism continued into the seventies in Sudbury. Newer social organizations, especially women's groups, native centres, francophone cultural endeavours, and a variety of more radical causes such as Amnesty International, *The Mucker* (a community newspaper), and Project Ploughshares (an anti-war group), gave Sudburians greater possibilities for self-expression. Is it valid to speculate that the multiplicity of social groups helped overcome the class differences created by wealth and occupation?

The effect of the economic booms and busts of the 1970s as well as INCO's rationalization program on the everyday lives of Sudburians was starkly revealed by the housing market and apartment vacancy rates. During the late 1960s and into the early 1970s, Sudbury experienced its greatest housing shortage ever. In 1969, when the five-month INCO strike ended, all the boarding houses were full and apartments or houses for rent seemed nonexistent. In July 1970 the classified advertisements in the *Sudbury Star* listed only six apartments and three houses for rent. At 0.3 percent Sudbury had the lowest vacancy rate in Canada when the first statistics were gathered in 1970.[45]

The manager of the local branch of the Ontario Housing Corporation, which had a waiting list of 3,800 people seeking a place in 481 rent-geared-to-income units, commented, "The housing situation is hurting INCO worst. They bring in men from all over but many only stay for a few months because there is no place to house their families."[46] Among the direst conditions were those at the so-called INCO Hilton, a workers' sleep camp run by Crawley-McCracken next to a graveyard in Lively. The grounds became a sea of mud whenever it rained. In March 1971 *The Mucker* exposed the conditions and Sudbury East MPP Elie Martel commented upon them in the legislature.

Socially concerned persons, however, knew that the transient workers, their families, and anyone on low incomes, indeed, even middle-class wage earners, suffered more than INCO and other firms. Even newly arrived university professors had to wait for the newspapers to come off the presses and then rush to find the few houses or apartments advertised for rent. In August 1970 the *Sudbury Star* reported that a woman and four children were living in a station wagon.[47] Eventually they received a temporary home in a church basement and later in a rent-geared-to-income apartment, thanks to the efforts of Mort Paterson, a

United Church minister, and Ann Morrison of the women's liberation movement.[48]

Meanwhile, shady entrepreneurs took advantage of the crisis. In 1971 there was a public outcry concerning a housing scheme known as Whitson Gardens, established by Ross Shouldice, a realtor who took low down-payments and arranged financing such that at the end of the first five years the "owners" would owe more than at the beginning. He eventually lost his realter's licence, and many of the badly built town houses stood as empty monuments to the folly of building on swamps.

After INCO announced its first layoff in January 1972, the situation was quickly reversed. By the end of 1973 Sudbury had an apartment vacancy rate of 10 percent. In a review of the housing situation that year, the *Sudbury Star* noted, "Like all mining towns, Sudbury's housing market rises and falls according to the length of the lines at the mines' employment offices."[49] Sudbury was again first in Canada, only this time with the highest vacancy rate.

In the early 1970s builders were far behind and were sometimes doing slipshod work in a seller's market; by 1973 construction starts of new housing had caught up with the demand. In 1970, 995 new units were begun; in 1971, 2,694; in 1972, 1,685; and in 1973, 933; but in 1974 the number dropped to 449 before going back up to 922, 1,053, and 1,285 in 1975, 1976, and 1977.[50] By 1973 house prices had levelled off, and the *Sudbury Star* commented that the empty apartments were providing a "field day for tenants." Because of a new mini-boom and a short strike before the great economic bust of the late 1970s, the vacancy rate for apartments dropped to 1.2 in 1977, since no new ones had been built.

Within a month of the introduction of province-wide rent controls in 1976, the Sudbury rent review board had received 1,700 applications for hearings against rent increases. One of those cases is enlightening. In July 1976, Nickel Belt MPP Floyd Laughren argued against rent increases after a woman bought a group of apartments from INCO and sought to raise the rents by 50 percent. Since the previous landlord had been making a profit, Laughren thought the rents should not be raised. The new owner argued that the costs of refinancing should be borne by the tenants. When Laughren asked for the rationale behind such an unjust move, the woman (Mrs. Carpenter) replied: "The rationale ... was part of the free enterprise system. The company is simply making a good deal and looking for some return on the investment."[51] Within a few years, as the larger INCO layoffs and then the long strike of 1978–79 led to a decrease in population, the same woman complained publicly that after she had invested all her savings and gone to all the governments for aid, no one seemed able to help her. She had a 23 percent vacancy by December 1977 and 84 percent by

1979. *Northern Life* reported in March 1979: "Mrs. Carpenter doesn't want charity. But she says there is something wrong with a system [!] which can break a small investor who has supplied a needed service to the community."

By the end of the 1970s, a balance between housing supply and demand had begun to be established in Sudbury as the economy drifted despondently at the national level and continued to go downhill locally. One reason was the sharp increase in the number of publicly funded housing units – from four hundred in 1970 to more than four thousand by 1980. Another was the beginning of the second phase of urban renewal, which included non-profit housing.[52] Through government intervention the substandard and hovel-like housing of the early 1970s had been improved and the high rents stabilized.

If the state of the housing stock was one indicator of the quality of life in Sudbury during the 1970s, a second was the nature of the environment. Responding to an increasing public awareness that the environment and the human body were being dangerously affected by industrial contamination, the Ontario legislature passed the Air Pollution Act in 1967. Later, the government announced a schedule for INCO's emissions: 5,200 tons a day by 1 July 1970; 4,400 tons by 31 December 1974; 3,600 tons by 31 December 1976; and 750 tons by 31 December 1978.[53] By 1972 the company had erected the largest free-standing stack in the world to dissipate the emissions. During the 1970s INCO and Falconbridge cut their daily sulphur dioxide emissions to one-third of their highest (1970) level. As a result, the official Ontario pollution index began to record consistently lower rates for Sudbury than for Hamilton or Toronto.[54] These were major developments in the history of the community's environment.

In INCO's case, however, such actions and the favourable publicity that resulted were always combined with a threat. If stringent pollution controls were insisted upon, production – and hence jobs – would be cut. Frequently these threats were taken seriously by the local business community as well as the provincial government, which knew the company had already reduced its labour force. In mid-decade, when INCO requested that the 1976 level of emissions be extended into the 1980s, the *Sudbury Star* questioned whether pollution standards were hurting INCO's production.[55] When the government later issued a new pollution order, INCO succeeded in obtaining permission to continue at the 3,600-tons-a-day level until 1980.[56] The NDP MPPS from Sudbury protested what they and the unions found to be coercion by the company and co-operation by the government against the interests of the public. By 1980, despite the progress that had been made locally, the two companies, combined, were still putting nearly *one million tons* of emissions into the atmosphere each year and were the largest source of acid rain in North America.

Though Sudbury's air had improved significantly during the 1970s, the decades of high emissions had left their mark on the soil.[57] In 1975 Dave Balsille, chief of air quality for the Ministry of the Environment in the northeastern region, reported on a sampling since 1970 which showed that soils were contaminated within a five-mile radius of the smelters; that is, plant growth was restricted.[58] What had happened to humans remained unclear. By then the federal government knew what the cost of re-vegetation and reclamation would be, for it had commissioned a secret study in 1974, which inadvertently became public in 1977.[59] The study estimated the damage to the environment of Sudbury at $465 million a year. Those costs were an estimate of economic losses, health costs, and the expenditures on reforestation. By the time that the report appeared, Sudbury was in the midst of the 1977 cutbacks. As the discussion moved from rhetoric to analysis, it also moved to who would pay. In 1980 the president of INCO asked the "Fifth Estate" television program, which was going to broadcast an interview with him, to delete his comment that the public should pay for the pollution clean-up.[60] The issue had become whether the polluters or the public would finance the clean-up, a perfect illustration of Sudbury's dual dependency.

In the end the public paid. With federal and provincial funds, the regional government initiated a program in 1978 to reclaim the barren lands that had been such an eyesore.[61] Using local students' labour during the summer months, the program, which entailed the liming of acidic soils, grassing, and tree planting, reclaimed more than twenty-five hundred acres of land within three years. Where there had been only barren outcroppings of rock and thin, eroded soil, the newly planted grasses and bushes began to retain moisture and reverse the destructive cycle. Most of the work was done on the strip that had been laid bare by deforestation and smelter fumes, that is, beside the main east-west, north-south arteries and the airport road.

In spite of significant environmental improvements in the area during the 1970s, the great majority of non-residents, especially southern Ontarians, still thought of Sudbury as a wasteland, a "moonscape" or a "dump."[62] That image was reinforced in the national media. The string of poplars along the Trans-Canada Highway near Copper Cliff could not hide one of the largest industrial complexes in the world, and in some places the blackened, bare rocks and protruding headframes continued to dominate the horizon. A walk along parts of Elgin or Durham streets could just as well have been in the Bronx. And yet Civic Square and St. Andrew's Place could match or outshine the new developments in comparable cities.

Almost unnoticed was the slow emergence of a modern, comfortable, and attractive city in the 1970s. Whether the declining population and limited tax base would be able to sustain the attempt to give the city and region a new face would only be known by the end of the century. In 1970 all the two-lane roads leading into Sudbury were still dotted with ten-test shacks. They were evidence of the housing difficulties in boom times, as well as the lack of zoning and planning outside the city's core. By 1981 these shacks had been converted into typical North American bungalows or had been bulldozed to make way for four-lane thorough-fares. Only a person who had known Sudbury in the earlier years when landscaping was considered a private luxury and all the roads were joined chaotically and were generally inadequate for the traffic, could understand how significant the 1970s have been to Sudbury's development. In 1980 Sudbury was still an underdeveloped city but a substantially improved one.

In 1970 the downtown of Sudbury, especially its main streets of Durham, Elm, and Elgin, still looked as it had decades earlier. "In fact," reported the *Financial Post* in late 1971, "82% of the 271 buildings in the heart of the city were substandard."[63] The brick façades were worn, and occasionally a gaping hole between two buildings revealed where fire had taken away one of the rotting structures. For a city approaching 100,000, Sudbury's downtown was a motley collection of men's clothing stores, credit institutions, car dealerships, and beer parlours. It reflected the spending habits of the young, male population. Typical of the city's appearance was the city hall, which was still accommodated in over-crowded quarters in the former Bell Telephone Exchange building. City council meetings were held in the public library auditorium.

By 1970, however, a new Sudbury was emerging just north of Elm in the old Borgia district. The first phase of the urban renewal begun in 1969 was taking shape. Across from the new mall stood the domed Ukrainian Orthodox Church and, just beyond it, respectable public housing with rents geared to income. This first phase of urban renewal moved the shopping and entertainment centre east and north, away from the railway tracks. Later, a second phase added highrise apartments and extended the mall. Combined with the modernization of the road system around the city's core (the construction of the Brady Expressway, also known as Fabbro's Folly in honour of the mayor, the widening of Notre Dame, and the extension to Laurie Street) as well as a couple of striking office buildings (IBM and Royal Trust Tower), urban renewal had laid the basis for a rejuvenation of the downtown.

The eastward shift of the downtown continued with St. Andrew's Place, a complex that received national attention during its conception and construction. In August 1973 the *Financial Post* asked, "When is a church not a church?" and answered, "When it is in Sudbury."[64] When, under the leadership of Charles Forsyth, St. Andrew's United Church, which occupied a piece of prime real estate between Memorial Park and the business district, needed to replace its dilapidated church building, it chose not to move or try to finance a traditional building. Instead, it decided on a plan that would make it more integral to the community. With financing from the Central Mortgage and Housing Corporation, it built a structure that combined apartments, commercial space, an old-age home, and a multi-use space:

> It comprises a 10-story block containing 107 apartments for elderly people, with a street level restaurant and service centre; a six-story block ... The sanctuary, sandwiched in between these two taller buildings, seats 450 in spacious splendour and is also available as a concert hall for the community ... There are tapestries, carved doors, paintings and sculptures, as well as stained glass – almost all of which were commissioned locally.[65]

The decisive element in the revamping of Sudbury's downtown was the new Civic Square, a series of matching pre-cast off-white buildings facing the city's central park. The project was conceived in the early 1970s and built in stages. The focal point of the complex, which took in more than a city block, was the new city hall, a triangular building with the long side completely glassed. A luxurious council chamber allowed the citizens to see and hear the council's deliberations in comfort; parking was provided underground. The main triangular building was complemented by a diamond-shaped building to the west that housed further city administration, the board of education, and the reference collection of the public library. In 1977 the provincial government agreed to build another matching diamond-shaped complex on the north side. The buildings faced northwest onto a large courtyard containing a pool and fountains. The matching Bell Telephone building and fire hall, which both opened in 1976, gave the whole area a strikingly unobstructed but unified appearance. The central building contained a space ideal for displays and larger public meetings. This complex captured the eye from the railway overpass that had provided the main southern access to the downtown since 1974. With broad avenues on all sides and white colouring, the Sudbury Civic Centre seemed to represent a new innocence as the city sought to rebuild not only its physical self but also its image.

Among the noteworthy architectural additions of the 1970s were some stylish churches, especially Our Lady of Perpetual Help, which was built in the shape of a great ark. The largest building that was started in the seventies, and which opened in 1982, was the federal government's income tax processing centre. The off-white building had a basically square shape but with one front corner cut away and stepped-back upper storeys; the impression at night was of a delicate pattern of lights. The other major improvements included downtown office buildings (such as Scotia Tower and the City Centre addition) that gave Sudbury the semblance of a rising skyline. The low, squat, and mainly squalid buildings that continued to stretch along Elgin Street and the railway tracks remained a contrast to the newer downtown edging towards the Paris Street–Notre Dame arteries.

The physical appearance of the city was also helped by improved shopping facilities. By 1974 the rebuilding of the New Sudbury Shopping Centre added a large Sears store and mall, and in 1981 the south end of the city acquired a large shopping mall. Commercial development was especially strong along Paris and Regent streets, where the population had increased and there were high disposable incomes.[66]

Two results were evident from these commercial developments. Many streets and stores in Sudbury became indistinguishable from business strips all over North America: the franchising of Sudbury caught up with the continent. After you had taken your car to Midas, you could enjoy "international" cuisine at McDonald's and Kentucky Fried Chicken, before you relaxed at the Holiday Inn. The other result was a general upgrading in the appearance of grounds, store fronts, and design. By 1980 Sudbury looked more like other Canadian cities of its size than it had in 1970. Most of the transformation of Sudbury into a service centre, however, was fuelled by government grants and funding; in some years, in fact, the value of public buildings constructed exceeded the value of commercial construction.[67]

If, in economics and work, the 1970s were marked by an increase in governmental intervention, so too in politics the decade opened with a demonstration of state power when Prime Minister Trudeau invoked the War Measures Act in October 1970 against an "apprehended" insurrection in Quebec. In Sudbury this affront to civil rights was both protested and applauded. Many local events, however, depended upon ignorance and deviousness and had little to do with the larger trends. Sudbury's news events were as varied as the city's work patterns. Their tragic and humorous qualities, which illustrated universal human foibles in a northern setting, could provide material for many theatre pieces. A tragic incident was the accidental crossing of nitrogen and oxygen lines during a hospital extension, which may have resulted in more than twenty deaths in 1974.

In these years Laurentian University often served as a source of amusement and gossip in Sudbury. It began with the Leandre Page incident. Page, who taught French language and literature and had great rapport with the students, had come to Laurentian's French Department with high recommendations from the University of Windsor. In addition, he was a founding editor of the *Laurentian University Review*. His career seemed assured until a suspicious colleague made inquiries about his credentials. Despite public reassurances from university administrators, it became evident that Page had no academic credentials, at least not those he claimed. Further investigations revealed that Page, under another name, was being sought by Interpol. According to rumour he had had a successful career as an imposter, having once been an archbishop in Rome. The immigration authorities were also looking for Page, who had escaped them by faking a heart attack. Other, minor episodes at the university, such as the attempts to fire the director of the school of engineering, led to publicity and highly unacademic letters in the newspapers. Hearings on closing the school of nursing and later the school of translators as well as the departments of anthropology, philosophy, and geology were also grist to the gossip mills. In 1970 sit-ins by students and staff to remove a president received national publicity. In 1979 francophone students who wanted a special lounge used similar tactics when they blocked the elevator of the administration tower. Another incident involving Laurentian students was at least partially responsible for the city's getting a much-needed and greatly expanded public bus system in 1972. A number of students on their way to L'École Normale on the private bus line, which was owned by Paul Desmarais of Power Corporation, had to be taken to hospital after the bus stalled and the exhaust leaked into the bus, causing serious illness among the passengers.

And then there was the tornado of 20 August 1970. A grand piano, it was reported, was blown into Lake Ramsey; window glass was embedded in a wall twenty feet away; trees were mowed down; the Superstack, with workers at the top, danced a jig. These were some of the stories that spread around Sudbury in the aftermath of a storm that put Sudbury on television screens around the world. The tornado tore a strip a quarter mile wide from Lively to Field (near Sturgeon Falls to the east), and as it passed the York Street area it ripped roofs off churches and houses, moved buildings off their foundations, and killed four people.

Some sporting events were as spectacular as the wind storm, and their fame faded as quickly. More important than all the scoring and cheering appeared to be a trend towards individual and "thinking" sports as opposed to professionalized and "body" sports. Throughout North America the 1970s witnessed the emergence of jogging, the expansion of cross-country skiing, and the revival of bicycling. Sudbury followed those trends. By 1977 marathon running and light athletic clubs, such as Northland and Voyageur, were well established. The local cycling club was formed in 1974: in 1977 Gary Trevisiol led the team to a national championship.

Throughout much of the decade, sports headlines were dominated by swimming, as the Baumann brothers, especially Alex, set Canadian and then international records. Baumann's world records in butterfly and breaststroke events made him the Canadian Athlete of the Year in 1980. The Laurentian University Olympic-sized pool, non-existent in 1970, made the achievement possible and underscored the relationship between sports and facilities, as well as Sudbury's dependence on the public purse. Soccer also gained in popularity, and though there was no professional team in Sudbury, the local leagues and a university team greeted this sport enthusiastically. It took a place beside the old standards, hockey and football, though the latter were no longer idolized. Perhaps in compensation, Laurentian University's basketball and volleyball teams collected numerous national championships.

As in sports, variety and expansion marked the Sudbury cultural scene. By the end of the 1970s there was theatre, music, art exhibits, and dance performances to suit nearly every taste. But there were two notable omissions within this cultural coming of age. After the demise of Wolfe's Books, bookstores remained backward, hardly distinguishable from the book sections of drugstores or airport shops. A short-lived experiment, the Book Mine, tried to combine co-operativism and feminism and to serve as a general meeting place for leftist intellectuals. It sold an alternative literature and political materials in English and French. By the time it closed, a similar French venture, Prise de Parole, had also been reduced to a mere ordering depot. The second great void in Sudbury was related to the cinemas. Though at least seven new movie theatres opened during the 1970s, the offerings remained the same: American-style violence, male chauvinism, and Hollywood spectaculars. That Canada, Europe, and the rest of the world had had a movie renaissance during the 1970s was not known except at the semi-private showings at La Slague or the university film club. After all the debate about the censorship of *The Tin Drum*, not even the cut version came to Sudbury. This type of selective censorship outside Toronto, Montreal, or Vancouver by the American distributors constantly worsened. In the early 1970s at least a few English-Canadian films, such as *Going Down the Road,* and some French-language films, such as *Mon Oncle Antoine* and *La Vrai Nature de Bernadette,* were shown at a downtown cinema. These disappeared, and Sudburians continued to hear of prize-winning Canadian films but could only see ones like *Porky,* a sexist view of the world produced with Canadian subsidies but distributed by American companies. The cultural dominance by the United States contrasted sharply with what Mine Mill and ethnic groups had offered in the 1950s and 1960s.[68]

In theatre Sudbury continued a tradition of the Little Theatre Guild and other amateur groups, often competing successfully at the Kiwanis Festivals. In 1971 the Sudbury Theatre Centre hired Tony Lloyd as its first artistic director, and under his leadership the town began to enjoy live professional theatre.[69] Though the centre concentrated on mainstream pieces and plays using small casts, after a financial fiasco with a production of Brecht's *Three Penny Opera,* the subscription membership blossomed. In 1980 the group began to raise money for a building of its own, which was opened in 1982, thanks to large government subsidies.[70] The new physical home did not inspire the theatre to present more experimental works, but at least this group, like its French counterpart, produced some plays based on Canadian themes and issues.[71]

Dance and opera remained underdeveloped, though in music Sudbury was maturing. Two groups were largely responsible. Northern Lights Festival Boréal, an annual festival, established in 1971 and subsidized by the provincial government, offered a variety of music, from jazz to Latin American, previously not much acknowledged in Sudbury. Because it was one of the few functioning bilingual organizations in Sudbury, local groups like CANO and Robert Paquette and outsiders like Barde appeared at it. Canadian artists, including Valdy, Sleazy Waters, and Connie Kalder, were emphasized at the festival, which usually offered three days of crafts, food, and music. Using the Bell Park amphitheatre beside Ramsey Lake, the festival drew youthful participants from across the country, who enjoyed the swimming and dancing, and the grass, which was not always sat upon at these events.

The other main musical development was related to the symphony. At the beginning of the decade classical music was played primarily in private groups and the churches.[72] Incorporated in 1975 with Metro Kozak as conductor of the more than fifty-five musicians, the Sudbury Symphony Orchestra by 1981 had become the centre of a large musical network. It had some permanent members who were simultaneously instructors in the Cambrian College or the Laurentian University music programs that began in September 1978. Many instructors were also part of Laurentian's Huntington Conservatory of Music, which gave concerts at the local museum, contributed to the St. Andrew's Place concert series, and made skilled staff members available to the public to raise awareness of this art form.

These musical offerings were complemented by performances in the hotels such as the Coulson or Brockdan, which presented local performers like Paul Dunn and which had sent Stompin' Tom Connors to national fame. Simultaneously rock festivals filled the Sudbury Arena and Bell Park amphitheatre. The earlier workers' culture, centred on pubs such as the International, Frood, and Plaza Hotels, was dying out.

An important contributor to the variety and interest of Sudbury's cultural life was Laurentian University's Museum and Arts Centre (LUMAC), which brought many collections of art, both modern and traditional, from across the country. Its own collection, which was especially strong in original native and Inuit prints, was housed in the converted Bell mansion. LUMAC also gave display opportunities to many members of the local art and crafts community.

These examples illustrate that Sudbury's cultural scene gained in depth and variety. The increase in the number of FM radio stations from one to four and in the number of television stations from two to four, as well as cable, did not lead to an improvement in quality. But for a city of its size, Sudbury probably offered as much selection as could be expected in North America, where the main beneficiaries of government and corporate donations are the big cities.

In the 1970s Sudbury's political and social make-up underwent a transformation. Contemporaries noted the shift towards a community providing the social services for northeastern Ontario. But where had all the miners gone? And what of their children? Were they the new middle class of teachers, small business owners, social service professionals, and government employees who increasingly made up the largest sector of the work force? Though there are no definitive answers to such questions, it appears that the disappearance of jobs in mining and smelting was compensated for by a growth in government jobs.

Sudbury, whose situation as a natural transportation entrepôt was improved by the completion of Highway 144 to Timmins in 1970, evolved in the 1970s into the social service centre for northeastern Ontario.[73] Expanded hospitals, nursing homes, and psychiatric and other health facilities served the whole region.[74] An even larger area was served by the enlarged government and educational institutions. The 1980 edition of the directory of social services included lists of public and semi-public agencies that were either new or expanded and ranged from legal clinics to boys' reform homes, from burn centres to Children's Aid Societies.[75] A layer of middle-class jobs helped to diversify the Sudbury economy. In addition, a range of low-level managerial and secretarial jobs was added in the late 1970s as Sudbury received some political patronage in the form of government buildings and parts of ministries.

The layoffs of 1977 and the strike of 1978–79 led to a recognition by the business elite, the growing professional middle class, and civic officials that Sudbury needed not only economic diversification but an improved image, and that these changes could only come about through the involvement of the whole community. Using public moneys, the novel organization Sudbury 2001 tried to enlist ideas from the public. Some small industries emerged, though not all of them were successful.[76] One group of businessmen invested in an Angora goat farm. Not long after the first herd of goats was purchased in Texas, it was discovered that 2001 had paid for them but had not received ownership. A squabble emerged between the directors and a Mr. Schaffernicht, who claimed the goats as his. In the end it was a mess with a bad smell.

The local government too, in an effort to make the region less dependent on mining, established the Sudbury Regional Development Corporation in 1974. By the early 1980s some results were evident: more small, secondary industries had been established, while others, such as lumber companies and machine works, had been weaned off INCO. Development grants and subsidies fuelled the new and expanded businesses.[77] Science North, which was conceived in 1980 by a $200,000 study funded by INCO, illustrated the pattern.[78] Slowly the image of Sudbury received a touch-up, though, as shown above, the ugly stereotype remained. The *Financial Post* rightly entitled a special supplement on 11 October 1980: "The New Sudbury: Ontario's best-kept secret."

Just as urban renewal initiated the transformation of the city's buildings, so regional government brought an improvement to traffic arteries, planning, and zoning. The imposition of new governing structures by the Ontario government illustrated the need for outside intervention to end the petty fiefdoms of the towns surrounding the large city and the chaos in services and zoning. As well, even though by 1971 the community could at long last tax mining facilities such as INCO, larger regional structures were needed in order to create a more orderly and equitable system of tax collection and expenditure.[79] Yet, the way regional government came about and its attempts at economic diversification again demonstrated the region's dependence on Toronto. After a lengthy report by the chairman of the Ontario Municipal Board, the government of Ontario imposed a two-tier system of regional government on Sudbury and its surrounding towns in 1973. Copper Cliff lost its independent existence and became a ward of the city. The company town that had represented INCO's independence from and domination over Sudbury disappeared.

In the new two-tier system of government the city of Sudbury and six area municipalities were combined into one region administered by a council (see Map 10.1). That council, with nine representatives from Sudbury and one from each surrounding municipality, became responsible for regional roads, that is, the main thoroughfares and arteries. Policing, fire protection, water, sewers, and solid waste also became the region's responsibility. Moreover, the muddle of planning in the area

Map 10.1: The Regional Municipality of Sudbury, 1973

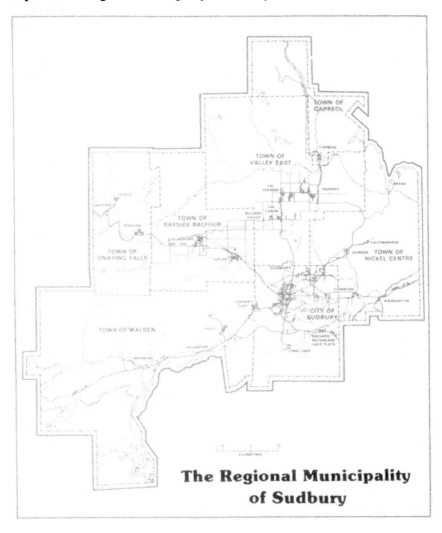

The Regional Municipality of Sudbury

ended, and as demanded by the provincial government in 1975, a general plan for future development of sewers, roads, and services was drawn up.[80] It sought to control urban sprawl, to minimize the cost of public services by rationalization, to improve the transport arteries, to improve municipal services through proper planning, and to aid economic development by means of industrial parks. One analysis of the workings of regional government, however, concluded, "Twelve years later regional government in Sudbury is accepted yet controversial."[81] The bickering between the city and the towns continued, the developers outflanked the planners in the battle over strip commercialization, and professionals replaced populists on many councils. The writer noted, however, "The level of services across the region has reached the median the province deemed desirable for all Ontarians," and he excused some shortcomings by pointing out that the restructuring had been "designed for a society expected to grow, not decline."[82]

The tax base was broadened, and municipal spending increased nearly threefold, but just as important were the diversification and planning studies that demonstrated how Sudbury stood in relation to other communities. By showing how disadvantaged it was, the region laid the groundwork for increased government funding and projects.[83] In the push to diversify, the province of Ontario and the federal government not only subsidized private enterprises but responded to the desperate cries for help, which were well orchestrated by local and provincial politicians in response to layoffs, foreign ownership, and rationalization. Later Floyd Laughren, the veteran NDP member of the provincial legislature for Nickel Belt, conceded, "In serving the constituency, we sometimes give an impression of problems being greater than they really are."[84] The taxation data centre, provincial buildings, and Science North were testimonials to their efforts and to the new dependency.

When Sudburians wanted to obtain employment, reduce pollution, improve housing, create transport links, regulate working conditions, or provide cultural opportunities, they turned increasingly to the various levels of governing institutions. The expectation grew that, with few exceptions, government could and should supply the funds, rules, direction, and enforcement necessary for diversifying the economy. The same thing was happening in other parts of the country and the province, but the phenomenon was especially marked in Sudbury.

Regulate, plan, zone, subsidize became the key words during the decade in which the term "Corporate Welfare Bums" was coined. Even companies wanted and received handouts, sometimes to repair the damage they had done to the landscape. In the short term the infusion of government funds worked in Sudbury. Any comparison of the building and transport chaos, the high death rates in the mines, the extreme air pollution, or the shortage of housing at the beginning of the decade with the improved situation at the end must lead to the conclusion that intervention helped to even out the extremes of the business cycles and to mitigate the severe social consequences of uncontrolled development. During the 1970s, the city began to rely on the public purse and government intervention as undirected free enterprise came to an end. By the end of the decade even the Liberals and Conservatives were arguing about who could obtain more of the patronage pie for the region. In an advertisement the MP for Nickel Belt pointed out that in the year since "re-election of the Liberal government, Nickel Belt has reaped the benefits of that commitment through federal grants such as: $310,000 for community services, $680,000 for senior citizens, $575,000 for cultural groups, $720,000 for student employment plus a tremendous $14.4 million for economic incentives ... And we've only just begun."[85] What was left largely unconsidered was what the purpose of government grants was and what would happen if public funds became scarce.

During the crucial transformation of the city and region two important Sudburians died. Until August 1971 Weir Reid, a former Mine Mill stalwart, had held court at his home, where he had inspired a new generation of social activists. On 3 May 1971 *Time*, which he identified with "crapitalism" and the "whoreoisie," devoted nearly a full page to the person it termed "the last angry socialist." In its obituary the *Sudbury Star* argued that he "could certainly have achieved the trappings of public honour had he chosen a more conventional road" than "constant opposition to the 'system.'"[86] Seven years later the city lost Joe Fabbro, the ebullient, eleven-term mayor and a second-generation Italian whose family had run a corner store, supplementing its income by bootlegging. Fabbro was a superb politician, and part of his success was that no one knew precisely where he stood. He retired to a mini-mansion overlooking Lake Ramsey, and caused raised eyebrows over his "investments." These characters embodied the Sudbury that had disappeared, a rough, iconoclastic, and interesting place not yet absorbed into the mainstream of Canadian urban life.

---

1   *Toronto Star*, 11 December 1968.
2   *Edmonton Journal*, 19 September 1980.
3   *Financial Post*, 9 October 1971.

---

4   A *Globe and Mail* article of 21 April 1982 pointed to what had happened to the Canadian economy under Pierre Trudeau as he began his fourteenth year in office: a sixfold increase in government spending, inflation at 12.5 percent from 4 percent, unemployment at 9 percent, a 2,000 percent increase in the budgetary deficit; and Canada had moved from being the second-richest country in the world to the thirteenth or fourteenth.

5   *Financial Post*, 9 October 1971.

6   Statistics Canada, Federal Government Employment in Metropolitan Areas, cited in Maury O'Neill and Peter Andrews, *Sudbury Statistical Summary* (Sudbury: Laurentian University, 1986), 60 (from 292 in 1970 to 1,041 in 1980). The percentage of women members in unions increased from 6.8 in 1971 to 18.7 in 1981. See O'Neill and Andrews, *Sudbury Statistical Survey*, 62.

7   For an example of the stereotype, see Jamie Swift, *The Big Nickel: Inco at Home and Abroad* (Kitchener: Between the Lines, 1977), 120.

8   See Royal Commission on the Health and Safety of Workers in Mines [Ham Commission], *Report* (Toronto, 1976), Table D7; and Swift, *The Big Nickel*, 123–34.

9   Cited in Jamie Swift, "No More Sudbury Saturday Nights: The Inco Layoffs," *This Magazine*, March 1978, 30. ("Sudbury Saturday Nights" refers to a song by Stompin' Tom Connors.)

10 Compare Deirdre Gallagher, "Inco: Steelworkers Historic Strike," *Canadian Labour* 24 (1979): 9–12, and François Ribordy, "La grève du nickel à Sudbury (Ontario) en 1978–1979," *Revue de l'institut de sociologie* 2 (1980): 195ff.

11 *True North* in October 1974 reported on the hundred-day strike over technological change at the *Sudbury Star*: "One incident stood out like a sore thumb during the 100 days on Mackenzie St. Betty Meakes, wife of *Star* publisher J.R. Meakes, screamed 'Jew boy' at striking Rick Winston as he walked the picket line. The slur was made in front of a handful of witnesses and reported to the Sudbury Human Rights Commission. The commission investigated but was unable to extract an apology." For more on the telephone strikes, see Joan Kuyek, *The Phone Book: Working at the Bell* (Kitchener: Between the Lines, 1979), which drew heavily upon her experiences in Sudbury. For more about teachers' walkouts, strikes, and high wage settlements, see *Sudbury Star*, 1, 12 and 18 December 1973, 6 February 1980, and 2 May 1980; and the *Globe and Mail*, 16 April 1980 ("Longest Teachers' Strike in Ontario Ended by Intervention of Minister of Education").

12 Select Committee of the Ontario Legislature on Inco and Falconbridge Layoffs, *Report* (Toronto, 1978).

13 *Toronto Star*, 1 September 1978.

14 *Northern Life*, 6 September 1978.

15 Wallace Clement, *Hardrock Mining: Industrial Relations and Technological Change at Inco* (Toronto: McClelland & Stewart, 1981), 163.

16 These and following figures based on *Census of Canada*, 1971, 1976, and 1981; the summaries in the Regional Development Corporation's *The Regional Municipality of Sudbury: A Community Profile* (1971ff; published annually); and O'Neill and Andrews, *Sudbury Statistical Summary*, 21–34.

17 *Globe and Mail*, 31 March 1982.

18 The German weekly *Die Zeit* summarized the situation on 7 October 1969: "Much Nickel, Too few women: Sudbury or Social Problems in a Canadian Frontier City." The lengthy essay commented on the problems of housing, pollution, chauvinism, strip tease dancers, large beer halls, the high incidence of rape, the cultural void, and INCO's

disdain for the unions.

19 Regional Municipality of Sudbury, *Economic Diversification and Impact Study* (Sudbury: Regional Municipality, 1977), Section III, 16.

20 Above and following based on Bill Nelson et al., *Atlas of the Regional Municipality of Sudbury* (Sudbury: Sudbury 2001, 1980), 14–16; and Sudbury Public Library's "ethnic collection" of clippings from local newspapers.

21 See summary of 1981 census in *Sudbury Star*, 21 March 1983: "Latest Census Shows Growth in Sudbury's Fringe."

22 Above based upon Bill Nelson et al., *Atlas of the Regional Municipality of Sudbury*, 33, derived from census data.

23 O'Neill and Andrews, *Sudbury Statistical Summary*, 30. Francophones made up 34 percent of the regional population; the British, at 23.9 percent, were the next-largest group. In the city of Sudbury itself, the British continued as the largest group, with 37.71 percent of the population; francophones were second, at 29.06 percent.

24 Summary of report by R. Carrière in *Laurentian University Gazette*, April 1982.

25 Sheila McLeod Arnopoulos, *Voices from French Ontario* (Kingston: McGill-Queen's University Press, 1982).

26 Ibid., 179.

27 Ibid., 104–14.

28 G. Gaudreau, ed., *Le Théâtre du nouvel-Ontario: 20 Ans* (Sudbury, 1991), 13ff.

29 Arnopoulos, *Voices from French Ontario*, 28.

30 Ibid., 69, 112ff.

31 In 1973 Prise de Parole, a newly established publishing house, obtained $1,500, the Théâtre du Nouvelle Ontario, $8,800, and the Centre des Jeunes, $15,000.

32 *Le magazine Macleans* (January 1971) had a special article on the problems of Sudbury, which included industry, housing, and traffic, but it emphasized the lack of services in French. By the mid-1970s the Association Canadian-Français de l'Ontario and many individuals were making their demands known. See *Sudbury Star*, 10 April 1974, 16 October 1974, 1 March 1976, 1 June 1976 ("Lalonde Pickets Court House"), 2 September 1976 (translation problems), and 29 September 1976 (ACFO listing of missing services).

33 A resumé in the report by Pierre Savard ("Arts with a Difference" [September 1977, copy in Sudbury Public Library's "ethnic collection"]) lists the bilingual and French services that emerged during the 1970s.

34 Arnopoulos, *Voices from French Ontario*, 108.

35 See the advertisement from the *Globe and Mail* (1981) cited in Arnopoulos, *Voices from French Ontario*, 71, claiming that unilingual English-speaking persons were becoming second-class citizens.

36 *Sudbury Star*, 24 November 1971.

37 For background of the centre and its funding problems and for some pro-ethnic propaganda, see *Northern Life*, 22 September 1992 (Lifestyle supplement).

38 The ethnic tolerance may also have been due to the trade union movement under the Mine, Mill and Smelter Workers, which respected various ethnic groups and encouraged egalitarian participation. See Mike Solski and John Smaller, *Mine Mill: The International Union of Mine, Mill and Smelter Workers in Canada Since 1895* (Ottawa: Steel Rail, 1984), 99ff.

39 This and following based on 1971 and 1981 census figures; see also O'Neill and Andrews, *Sudbury Statistical Summary*, 52ff.

40 *Northern Life*, 3 March 1982.

41 O'Neill and Andrews, *Sudbury Statistical Summary*, 55.

42 These and following figures from *Sudbury Star*, 5 May 1975.

43 This section is based on the newspaper clippings in the Sudbury Public Library's "eth-nic collection." Important articles appeared in the *Sudbury Star* on 27 September 1973, 26 March 1974, 9 and 27 September 1974, and 5 May 1975. In November 1971 a local judge, George Collins, could still speak of "just another stupid Indian," although later he apologized.

44 *Sudbury Star*, 28 June 1975.

45 Central Mortgage and Housing Corporation, *Vacancy Rate Survey*, April 1978, Table II.

46 *Sudbury Star*, 1 August 1970.

47 Ibid., 1 August 1970.

48 On 26 July 1971 the *Sudbury Star* presented a similar tale under the heading "When 9 Must Live in 300 sq. ft., It's Despair" and pointed to "a family dwelling" that had "no sanitary facilities, no water, no plumbing fixtures and no heating system." The hospi-tals had difficulty obtaining interns, even though they offered them room and board.

49 *Sudbury Star*, 22 August 1973.

50 Figures from *Sudbury Star*, 20 July 1973, 1 November 1974, 24 February 1976, and 18 March 1977.

51 Ibid., 29 July 1976.

52 See for example *Sudbury Star*, 22 February 1978, and *Northern Life*, 10 December 1980.

53 *Sudbury Star*, 14 July 1973. It is important to compare that with what was achieved: about 3,000 tons a day in 1978 and government demands that the emissions be reduced to 1,770 tons a day by the end of 1982. The 750 tons a day proposed for 1978 was not achieved until the 1990s.

54 See also a report on the community prepared by the Economic Council of Canada in 1973. The report showed that among eleven Canadian cities studied by the council, Sudbury had the best air quality during 1973. Using what the report termed "impact units of pollution," the ECC found that Sudbury's air had improved sharply since 1971, when 16.1 impact units were found; in 1973 it was down to 6.7 (*Sudbury Star*, 27 November 1974).

55 *Sudbury Star*, 20 September 1977

56 See *Sudbury Star*, 3 December 1977; and *Globe and Mail*, 31 July 1978.

57 One of the most extreme examples is described in T. Pawlick, *A Killing Rain: The Global Threat* (Vancouver: Douglas & McIntyre, 1984).

58 *Sudbury Star*, 24 April 1975.

59 Ibid., 6 December 1977. The 137-page report was entitled "The Sudbury Pollution Problem."

60 Reported in "The Problem at Inco," *Canadian Heritage*, April 1980, 18.

61 See Regional Municipality of Sudbury, *Land Reclamation* (Sudbury: 1980) (summary brochure), which outlined work done and plans for six hundred acres of plantings pro-posed for 1981.

62 In an editorial rebutting similar remarks, *Northern Life* on 2 December 1981 admitted, "Most of the world believes Sudbury is a dump."

63 *Financial Post*, 9 October 1971.

64 Ibid., 18 August 1973.

65 Ibid., 18 August 1973.

66 See Nelson et al., *Atlas of the Regional Municipality of Sudbury*, 19.

67 See Sudbury Regional Development Corporation, *A Community Profile* (1977–81).

68 For an illustration of what had changed, see J. Tester, ed., *Sports Pioneers: A History of*

the Finnish-Canadian Amateur Sports Federation 1906–1986 (Sudbury, 1986); and Solski and Smaller, *Mine Mill*, 111–21.

69 In 1971–72, 359 persons subscribed and 3,200 tickets were sold; in 1980–81, 2,500 subscribed and 28,000 tickets were sold (*Northern Life*, 13 January 1982).

70 Sudbury East Liberal MP and Minister of Mines Judy Erola (a former amateur actress) and Sudbury Liberal MP Doug Frith obtained $500,000 from the federal government; the provincial government at the urging of Conservative MPP Jim Gordon contributed $780,000, and the city of Sudbury donated $300,000 (*Directions '81* [a *Northern Life* supplement], 6 May 1981).

71 Historical overview in the *Toronto Star*, 19 April 1986.

72 The history of the Sudbury Symphony is summarized in *Northern Life*, "The Tabloyd," 13 September 1982.

73 This is also the view of O.W. Saarinen in "Sudbury (1945-1983)," in *To Our City / À notre ville* (Sudbury: Centennial Foundation, 1983), 41–45.

74 In 1962 a survey by the Canadian Medical Association revealed that Sudbury had the lowest ratio of doctors to population in Canada (1 to 1,062). In 1971, 139 doctors served 158,000 (1 to 1,112) and hospital space was in chronically short supply. See *Sudbury Star*, 25 March 1971 and 8 April 1971. With the stabilization of the population and the increase in specialists together with $22 million allotted to hospital expansion in 1971, the situation improved dramatically.

75 A summary of the public inspection reports of provincial institutions appeared in *Northern Life*, 16 December 1981. The review covered the courts, jails, youth reformatory, sanatorium, retirement homes, detoxication, and halfway houses, children's aid, hospitals, and educational institutions.

76 *Northern Life*, 13 January 1982.

77 David Lewis, in *Louder Voices: The Corporate Welfare Bums* (Toronto: Lewis and Samuel, 1972), tried to demonstrate that the corporations were not only paying less and less taxes but were receiving huge handouts. In its 1980 annual report the Sudbury Regional Development Corporation (p. 9) listed the subsidies obtained from the federal and provincial governments to help local companies expand ($400,000 in grants and $500,000 in loans to create seventy-eight jobs).

78 An advertising supplement to the *Financial Post*, 26 September 1981, presented only the benefits of the expenditures.

79 The pre-1970 situation is described in O.W. Saarinen, "Planning and Other Development Influences on the Spatial Organization of Urban Settlement in the Sudbury Area," *Laurentian University Review* 3, no. 3 (February 1971): 38ff, esp. 49.

80 *Official Plan for the Sudbury Planning Area* (revised 1978) builds on the city's official plan of 1970.

81 Carl M. Wallace, "Sudbury: The Northern Experiment with Regional Government," *Laurentian University Review* 17, no. 2 (February 1985): 97; compare *Northern Life*, 12 January 1983, which points out that, despite all the personal and policy conflicts, 116,000 people received municipal water and sewer services between 1973 and 1982 compared to 150,000 a decade later.

82 Wallace, "Sudbury," 98–99; compare Sudbury Regional Council, *Report of the Regional Government Study Committee* (November 1980), which found that "the majority of respondents favoured the status quo in terms of the form of representation on regional council" and that the aldermen and the public wanted more spending on job creation and senior citizens' homes and less on welfare and arenas.

83 See ABT Associates Research of Canada, Ltd., *Economic Diversification and Import Substitution Study for the Sudbury Region* (Cambridge, Mass., 1978). Available in Sudbury Public Library.

84 *Report on Business Magazine*, March 1987, 70.

85 *Direction '81*, 6 May 1981, 15.

86 *Sudbury Star*, 4 August 1971.

CHAPTER ELEVEN

THE 1980s

C.M. Wallace

The 1980s began with an obituary. Sudbury was a "falling and failing city" that had reached the inevitable fate of resource towns.[1] Even the *New York Times* wrote, "Canadian Mining Town Hits Bottom."[2] Less than ten years later, with most of North America in a recession, Sudbury was unimaginably prosperous. The city basked in the praise of a *Chatelaine* article that ranked it as one of the ten best places in Canada in which to live.[3] Not for the first time experts trekked to the community for clues to this apparent abnormality. Sudbury was a mining town that defied logic, at least in the view of observers who were bound by volumes of clichés. There are examples galore of the superficial. The visit of the Apollo astronauts to Sudbury in 1971 is invariably described as a trial walk on a moonscape. In reality, "the idea was to use the area's 1.8-billion-year-old meteorite crater as a teaching tool to study lunar impact sites."[4]

Sudbury's uniqueness was again demonstrated in the 1980s. Circumstances, politicians, location, and timing go far to explain the "miracle of Sudbury" in the decade. The decentralization policies of upper levels of government identified Sudbury as a target area for ministry relocation, and the city was represented by several aggressive politicians who capitalized on the movement. As part of image rebuilding in the face of world-wide criticism, the corporations demonstrated a community awareness previously unnecessary and initiated high-visibility projects, such as Science North. The environmental movement generated a decade of activity by governments, companies, academics, and students that miraculously disguised a century of neglect. The decline in population that had begun in the early 1970s was also reversed, and the dominance of the blue-collar work force was ended as professionals and clerical workers grew by the thousands in the service sector that replaced mining as Sudbury's staple industry. The result, according to Peter Newman, writing in *Maclean's* of 1 April 1991, was "Sudbury's Sunny Renaissance."

Nothing in Sudbury's history compares to the gloom and despair of the early 1980s. After a century of largely uninterrupted growth, the city experienced reversals at every turn. The community had been failed by nickel, a glittering false idol. Inco's[5] cherished monopoly had crumbled almost as rapidly as the garish chrome-covered cars that had characterized that world. The trail that led to Sudbury was by-passed in the rush to industrial plastics and Third World nickel. Inco and Falconbridge, despite the carnage, were well into a restructuring that eventually helped them to survive, but for a city addicted to unending development based on an expanding industrial work force, the outlook was grim.

To make matters worse, shortly after the Steelworkers struck Inco on 1 June 1982, the company suspended operations indefinitely because of soft markets, regardless of negotiations. Nine long months later the plants were still shut down. Falconbridge also ceased production. By September of 1982, 26.9 percent of the Sudbury work force was unemployed and soup kitchens had returned. Sudbury acquired a new title: "Unemployment capital of Canada."[6] In a sense things were actually worse than they seemed. At full production Inco and Falconbridge employed fewer than half the 25,700 employees of the early seventies and had plans for further cuts. Even after Inco started up again in the spring of 1983, it was obvious that the mining industry alone could not regenerate the Sudbury economy (see Table 11.1).

Adding to the gloom of lost jobs was the decline in total population – by the hundreds. After almost reaching 100,000 in 1976, it declined

Table 11.1
Employment by Inco and Falconbridge, 1981–1984

Year	Inco	Falconbridge
1981	13,598	4,034
1982	11,106	2,717
1983	10,641	2,637
1984	9,213	2,682

Source: *Key Facts, Sudbury* [1984].

steadily: 91,829 in 1981, 91,102 in 1983, 88,717 in 1986.[7] The city lost more than jobs and income; it sacrificed its status and position in the Canadian hierarchy to cities it had vaulted over in earlier years. That was the lay of the land in the mid-1980s, but the pronouncement of Sudbury's demise was both exaggerated and premature. The "renaissance" had been maturing in the darkest of years and was about to flower.

The change in the mining industry was but one of several elements in the overall revitalization of Sudbury, yet it was important. The strike of 1978–79, which is usually considered the turning-point, merely marked the inevitable. Labour-intensive heavy industry was in a world-wide decline as the international marketplace forced companies to adopt technological and managerial creativity. The strike of the late 1970s, which was a reaction against such alterations, certainly could not stop automation, mechanization, and computerization. When Inco resumed production on 4 April after the 1982–83 shutdown, it was finally equipped to resume its place as premier nickel producer in the world. By 1989 it surpassed all previous years with a profit of $753.4 million (U.S.) and Falconbridge showed a profit of $357 million. Though these were not duplicated in the early 1990s owing to declining prices, the record production of nickel had been by a work force that was almost unrecognizable.[8] Gone were the thousands of miners and smeltermen who had filled the roads morning and night since the war. The 6,800 employees at Inco's Sudbury operation and the 2,171 at Falconbridge, including managerial, technical, and clerical personnel, made up only 16.3 percent of the total for the district, down from 35 percent in the seventies. The blue-collar workers formed but a declining segment of the whole.[9]

Despite the diminished work force, the mining companies remained a major contributor to the regional prosperity. In 1990 Inco added $925 million to the local economy in wages, services, and mine and plant development, and it was still the largest single employer.[10] There was no escaping, however, the relative diminution of the role of the companies in the Sudbury region. In the fall of 1964 Mayor Joe Fabbro had greeted newcomers to Sudbury at a banquet with a local truth: "Inco calls the shots around here, and don't ever forget it."[11] Almost thirty years later, his successor, Jim Gordon, seemed to be saying the same thing with these words: "Inco is the bedrock, the underlying strength in this community." But he said more: "We finally have an adult relationship." The old paternal, authoritative style of management was gone,[12] and with good reason. The bedrock had been submerged under several layers of ground cover.

Long before the mining companies began their rejuvenation, decisions had been made that anticipated the Sudbury renaissance. As early as the 1950s planners and politicians at several levels had seen the need for diversification of the local economy and the improvement of services up to a minimum provincial standard. In a series of incremental moves the process that made Sudbury what geographers call the "central place" in northeastern Ontario got under way. Laurentian University, Cambrian College, and L'École Normale provided advanced education at the local level for the first time. Concurrently, Sudbury was designated as the northeastern Ontario health service centre. An undreamed of quality of medical service and specialization developed, culminating in treatment facilities, such as the burn and heart centres at Memorial Hospital. Both the General and Laurentian hospitals added air ambulance pads as part of their regional mandate. Transportation generally was improved by a connecting highway to Timmins in 1970, an upgraded airport and terminal in 1974, and a rebuilt Highway 69. Recognizing the advantages of the central location, numerous companies, including Bell Canada, moved their regional headquarters to Sudbury, as did banks, insurance companies, and drug and wholesale grocery distributors. Most of this had taken place before the 1980s.

In the 1970s both federal and provincial governments, realizing that the Sudbury economy was fragile, began to intervene with short-term job-creation projects and the permanent transfer of government departments, whole or in part. The first such major addition was the provincial government office tower in the Civic Square Complex, at a cost of over $12 million. This paled in comparison with the federal government Taxation Data Centre, begun in 1979 at a projected cost of over $30 million and completed in 1982 well over budget. This stunning, multi-layered structure, which appears to cascade towards Notre Dame Avenue at Lasalle, was acquired, for the most part, by MP James Jerome, a Trudeau Liberal who represented his constituents well. That building was then surpassed by Science North, a $35-million showpiece for the combined efforts of Inco, Falconbridge, and the municipal, provincial, and federal governments. Shaped like a giant snowflake and located strategically on the shores of Lake Ramsey, it was officially opened by Queen Elizabeth II on 4 October 1984 and has become the symbol of Sudbury's diversification and survival.

The floodgates had been opened for Sudbury. All the hospitals added to their buildings as well as their services; this expansion was capped when Princess Diana opened the Cancer Treatment Centre in 1991. Cambrian College built residences for the thousands of students of Northern Ontario who wanted its programs. Laurentian University added new science facilities and a students' centre, but its crowning achievement was the $12-million J.-N. Desmarais Library, which provided the students with facilities that matched the best in Canada and included modern archives for the regional collection. The province of Ontario transferred the Ministry of Northern Development and Mines to a $21-million building in the centre of the city and then erected a $52-million building on Laurentian campus to house the Ontario Geological Survey, the Miners' Health and Safety Centre, and the Ontario Research Directorate. Meanwhile, a combination of governments spent more than $50 million on Inco property to build an underground laboratory for the study of neutrinos – whether or not they exist. Though the cynical began to refer to Sudbury as the "pork barrel capital of Canada," Sudburians considered the expenditures their due.[13]

The buildings altered far more than just the physical appearance of the city, for they brought jobs by the thousands, practically all of them white-collar. The annual payrolls in 1990 tell the story: Cambrian College – $41.6 million; Taxation Data Centre – almost $38 million; Laurentian University – $36.8 million; General Hospital – $34.2 million; Laurentian Hospital – $31 million; Memorial Hospital – $22.2 million; Ministry of Northern Development and Mines – $21 million; Algoma Hospital/Network North – $12 mllion; Cancer Treatment Centre – $6.6 million; Cecil Facer Youth Centre – $5.6 million; Science North – $2.9 million.[14]

Though the flight from heavy industry to services was discernable in 1980, the effect of government intervention was to accelerate the economic diversification through job transfers. In the process it caused a social transformation in the city that matched the "greening" of the terrain. The blue-collar component of the population, though still prominent, had been surpassed by the nurse, the teacher, the clerk, the doctor, the salesperson, the business person, and, above all, the civil servant. The 1991 census confirmed what had happened. As the mining work force dwindled, the population of Sudbury rose to 92,884, or 4.7 percent over the 1986 count, and the region did even better, up 5.9 percent to 157,613.[15] The changed population altered the texture of life in Sudbury in numerous ways, some unexpected. The "strike" in Sudbury was usually associated with miners, mill men, or smeltermen. In the 1980s it was white-collar workers who walked the picket lines. The secondary school teachers closed the system from 6 February to 1 May 1980, the longest teachers' strike in Canadian history. The workers of the *Sudbury Star* spent most of 1984 on the line. In 1985 the university clerical staff was out for a month, and university professors and librarians struck Laurentian twice, for a week in 1985 and a month in 1988. Cambrian teachers had several strikes.

Nurses and social workers had very bitter strikes. At Charterways, the bus drivers closed the company down and forced it out of town. Not a year passed without a work stoppage of one kind or another. On the other side of the coin, Ron Macdonald, a former president of Local 6500 and staff representative of the Steelworkers, was elected president and chairman of the Sudbury Regional Development Corporation.

Another obvious indication of the changed nature of Sudbury in the 1980s was in housing. New subdivisions were opened in all districts of the city, but what distinguished them was the quality of the buildings. The 900-square-foot (91-square-metre) garage-less bungalow with one bathroom that had been the staple of the market up to the 1970s had been replaced by expensive multi-level designer houses for the upwardly mobile. There were even very exclusive lakefront and peninsular houses for the especially affluent doctors, lawyers, and entrepreneurs. As executives and senior civil servants were transferred into the city, at company and government expense, the market responded both in quality and price. This was but one reflection of the metamorphosis taking place, and it was this sort of change that visitors noticed.

There was also a noticeably different taste in the community for personal possessions and activities. The boutique moved into Sudbury to take its place with Mark's Work Warehouse. The skiers and bikers had the Outside Store. Although live theatre in both French and English and the Sudbury Symphony Orchestra had been in bud in the 1970s, they flourished in the 1980s. The Sudbury Theatre Centre, in particular, erected a stunning new building for its more than four thousand subscribers, the envy of theatre companies across the country. The university and colleges provided a steady diet of national and international guests and performances, and the university's arts museum in the Bell property finally became a vital centre for the arts. This is not to suggest for an instant that the renaissance in Sudbury had gone high-brow, for it was anything but the case. The traditional social activities in the halls and arenas, especially among the ethnic clubs, were unaffected by the recent invasion, and sports events and activities remained a Sudbury staple.

The highlight of the decade in sports came in 1984, when Alex Baumann gave Sudbury and Canada several glorious moments at the 1984 Olympics. Two gold medals and the world records propelled him to national prominence, and he carried his Laurentian University and Sudbury origins proudly, even after he became a marketing vehicle for several corporations. While not as spectacular, Laurentian's ladies' basketball team won seven national titles, which made it the team of the era. The 1983 Labatt's Brier, held in Sudbury, introduced Canadians to Ed Werenich. Curling and the Brier may have peaked that year as the

"Wrench" and his team became national celebrities and world champions.

Sudbury's infatuation with sports and the attending publicity led the community to sponsor the second World Junior Track and Field Championships in the summer of 1988. Though the games were an athletic and production success, they attracted much less interest than expected and left debts in the hundreds of thousands. Business people, the university, and the city were left holding the proverbial bag, and the empty stands at the Laurentian sports complex stood as a monument to that folly. That Sudbury was a "jock" town was another of the national images with its down side. The team of Sudbury, after all, was the Sudbury Wolves, and they did not win a single playoff at any level in the 1980s.

Two explanations are usually advanced for Sudbury's rejuvenation in the 1980s. The first credits government intervention, as mentioned above; the second attributes the honour to local boosters and politicians. Both arguments have some validity, for Sudbury was indeed fortunate in its political leadership at both the senior and local levels. Judy Erola inherited Jim Jerome's mantle, and as minister of mines in the final Trudeau cabinet she made Sudburians both grateful and proud, especially with the grants to Science North. Doug Frith, a former alderman like Jerome, and a former regional chairman, was also in the federal cabinet, keeping his eye on Sudbury. Provincially, the former and future mayor Jim Gordon sat for the Conservatives during their last days in power, and the former alderman Stirling Campbell served as a Liberal through Peterson's later years. Sudbury, therefore, had representatives on the government side during the crucial years when grants and decisions favoured the city.

It took strong local efforts, however, to direct the benefits to Sudbury rather than elsewhere, and claims are put forward for regional chairman Tom Davies and the regional council, Mayor Peter Wong and the city council, the Sudbury Regional Development Board, the Sudbury 2001 organization, the Chamber of Commerce, and individuals like Michael Atkins, who made *Northern Life* and *Northern Ontario Business* models of local boosterism. Oiva Saarinen has argued that Tom Davies's influence was decisive, especially during the 1982 layoffs:

> The Chairman of the Regional Municipality of Sudbury immediately instituted a dynamic response mechanism to deal with the short and long-term future of the community. This response consisted initially of an intense networking

process involving the entire citizenry. An evaluation stage followed which recognized the need to reduce the problem to more manageable proportions. This culminated in the formation of a focused mission statement involving eight sectorial recommendations linked to mining, government business, industry, finance, health, agriculture and education training. The statement priorized 300 proposals into 38 concrete recommendations. A "Team Sudbury" approach was then developed involving intense liaison with senior provincial and federal officials and proposed programs and sources of funding. This strategy helped to cushion the short-term blow of the 1982 layoffs and laid the framework for the successful longer-term planning undertaken by the SRDC and the Corporate Plan of the city of Sudbury.[16]

What Saarinen has described in this case was not so much the creative leadership of one individual as the advanced level of the professional government services that were being provided to the community of Sudbury by its municipal institutions under regional government.

Despite enormous criticism of the two-tier system, regional government had improved the quality of services throughout the area, including the city, which contributed the most. Water and sewer lines had been extended to communities such as Valley East that would never have got them otherwise. Roads were upgraded and maintained, and fire and police protection met the Ontario standards. Long-term planning at all levels of government had become crucial, and both local politicians and developers found their ability to manoeuvre restricted. That of course was exactly what J.A. Kennedy had in mind when he called for an "official plan," which he conceived as the "touchstone" to a better society. After it was implemented in 1978, most but not all of the unregulated development was eliminated.[17]

Though planning in Sudbury reached back into the 1950s, it took the official plan to solidify the disparate strands. The chief city planner, Klemens Dembek, deserves much credit for the creation of the "new" Sudbury, and Narasim Katary, the regional planner who later joined the Ontario Municipal Board, brought a creative intellectual sensitivity to both growth and redevelopment, especially during the early 1980s. "Let's keep what we have and let's improve the quality of life for citizens," he told residents in 1985. "We have to make life more liveable." Twenty years from now, he said, Sudbury "will look like a nice recreational city."[18] Despite Katary's idealism the planners and local politicians were frequently at cross-purposes with the municipal engineers and inspectors, who were more attuned to developers. When in 1992 the court ordered residents out of Galaxy Towers, public confidence was severely shaken in the professionals. Notwithstanding the assurances from officials, construction codes had been ignored, the building was declared unsafe, and the limitations of the system were obvious.

The planners and engineers were but part of a professional bureaucracy that came to manage the affairs of Sudbury and the region. It was that expertise that enabled Davies, Wong, and others to respond to the crises. While politicians "whooped and hollered," the employees of the city and region carried out their mandate in an increasingly professional manner. The days were long gone when the populist mayors like Bill Beaton or Joe Fabbro could run the council and the city. In the December election of 1982 Mayor Maurice Lamoureux was defeated by the former city engineer, Peter Wong, who ran on the need to have a trained professional as chief executive. Wong's council, for the most part, was also made up of professionals. The odd hockey player or local yokel still got elected, but they rarely stayed for more than one term. School principals like Bob Fera, doctors like Ricardo De la Riva, teachers like Stirling Campbell, administrators like Jim Marchbank, and businesswomen like Diane Marleau changed the face of city council. Since they also sat on the regional council, it too improved, and most of the war lords from the 1970s were gone.

Davies and Wong gave remarkable stability to municipal government in Sudbury throughout most of the 1980s, and Sudbury's recovery might have been less dramatic without them. Sudbury voters, however, grew tired of Wong's "efficiency," which in 1991 saw the city not only with no debts but with a surplus of $939,000 on an expenditure of $63.28 million for 1991.[19] In the December election of 1991 they returned to the excitement of Jim Gordon, who offered both to reclaim government from the bureaucrats and not to raise taxes.

The two-tier system of government suffered its worst growing pains when Gordon was mayor from 1976 to 1980. The first regional chairman, Don Collins, who had been imposed by Toronto, was driven from office by bureaucrats and politicians.[20] A successor, Delky Dozzi, died in office. The various mayors and councils in the seven municipalities continued the paralysing civil war that had inspired the province to combine them under one government in the first place. "Fear of the large, the powerful is really a manifestation of the basic human urge for self-preservation," Kennedy had written in 1970. "But, nowhere has it appeared more pronounced, more deep-rooted" in Ontario than Sudbury.[21] Ten years later little had changed, for on 8 April 1981 regional council voted to ask the province to abolish the "bureaucratic nightmare"[22] of the upper tier. The province curtly rejected the plea.

Far from dying, however, the issue returned again and again. The *Sudbury Star* described one enlightening discussion of a proposed study: "Last night's debate on one-tier government broke into three camps – some didn't want a study carried out under any circumstances; some favoured the study but not the one-tier government; and still others wanted to see if the study would make one-tier government feasible on economic grounds."[23] A "longtime regional government basher," Gilles Pelland, mayor of Rayside-Balfour, took the lead: "The only type of government we should have is one where we can turn back the clock and put in the old system."[24] Mayor Howard Armstrong of Valley East, who dared to disagree, provoked Pelland's wrath. "Mayor Pelland is like a bull-dozer," Armstrong remarked ruefully. "If you agree with him, you're a good guy. If you don't, you're a son-of-a-bitch."[25]

Personalities, issues, and emotions had become hopelessly intertwined, and the frustration was evident. With the city of Sudbury at a disadvantage on regional council, Mayor Wong demanded change: "It's important for us to look at rep by pop on regional council. We're paying two-thirds of the bill and getting one-third of the vote ... We get people on there who pay only 1.6 per cent of the bill, they get 5 per cent of the vote, and 20 per cent of the discussion."[26]

Prosperity and time plastered over most of the grievances in the later 1980s, though the two-tier system remained controversial. The departure of the old pre–two-tier warriors like Pelland, however, opened the councils to new faces who were more interested in Sudbury as one of the "smaller centres, where community spirit and good clean family values prevail." It had become, as *Chatelaine* proclaimed in April 1991, one of the ten best Canadian cities to live in.

The railway lines still cut through the centre of Sudbury, as they did in the 1880s, and image problems continue to haunt the city, despite the *Chatelaine* article. Sudbury is no longer a rail town, or a mining town. Nor, for that matter, is it devastated by industrial pollution. Popular images, however, have very long lives and are usually based on realities. A century of mining and smelting has indelibly marked the landscape, the community, and its people. Modern Sudburians try to obscure that past by "greening" sections of the blackened Shield and tearing down old buildings. This is part of an ongoing process to obliterate its heritage in the rush to become Toronto North. It was, after all, this "new sophistication"

that caused *Chatelaine* to observe, "Sudbury has long since relinquished its dependance on mining, attracting government offices, plus numerous educational companies and institutions, creating a new service-oriented economy."[27] Even the image has changed. From being a world symbol of industrial carnage, it has become a model of "environmental recovery" and the recipient of numerous awards, including a United Nations commendation. Sudbury begins its second century as the unchallenged capital of northeastern Ontario. It has transcended its roots to become a complex metropolitan regional centre. There is about Sudbury, according to the *Globe and Mail*, a "sweet smell of success."[28]

1   *Edmonton Journal*, 19 September 1980.
2   *New York Times*, 14 August 1982.
3   *Chatelaine*, April 1991.
4   *Globe and Mail*, 17 November 1992.
5   The International Nickel Company, in existence since 29 March 1902, had been known for years as INCO. In 1976 the company was officially renamed Inco. See *Sudbury Star*, 29 March 1992.
6   Sudbury had the highest rate in the country well into 1983. This quotation is from *An Economic Report on Northern Ontario*, a supplement to the *Financial Times*, 11 April 1983, 6.
7   *Census of Canada*, 1981 and 1986; and *Key Facts, Sudbury* [1984].
8   *Sudbury Star*, 30 March and 3 April 1991. Inco had reported losses of $1.3 billion in the first three years of the 1980s (*Sudbury Star*, 7 March 1992).
9   *Sudbury Star*, 27 April 1991 and 7 March 1992.
10 Ibid., 27 April 1991. The figures were as follows: wages and salaries, $490 million; bonuses, $30 million; pensions, $75 million; local supplies and services, $321 million; and local taxes, $19 million.
11 The author was at the banquet. Other speakers had lectured on the virtues of Christian capitalism.
12 Quoted in *Northern Life*, 29 March 1992.
13 Stated by M. Stevenson, 14 May 1992.
14 *Sudbury Star*, 27 April 1991.
15 Ibid., 28 April 1992. The 1986 census gave the following information on occupations in Sudbury:

	Male	Female
All occupations	39,405	29,955
Managers and admin.	3,865	1,940
Teaching	1,230	2,440
Health	630	2,605
Social, arts, and religion	2,950	1,515
Clerical	2,580	10,845
Sales	3,170	2,910
Service	3,920	5,995

(continued)

	Male	Female
Primary	5,285	195
Processing	1,360	195
Fabrication and Repair	3,690	300
Construction	4,464	80
Transport	2,355	510
Other	3,915	400

16 Oiva Saarinen, "Creating a Sustainable Community: The Sudbury Case Study Example" (unpublished manuscript, 1990), 13. See Regional Municipality of Sudbury, *Towards Economic Diversification in Sudbury Region*, 26 November 1982, and *Strategic/Corporate Plan of/by/for the City of Sudbury* (Sudbury, 1987). See also Oiva Saarinen, "Sudbury: A Historical Case Study of Multiple Urban-Economic Transformation," *Ontario History* 82, no. 1 (March 1990): 53–81.

17 J.A. Kennedy, *Sudbury Area Study*, 27 May 1970, 5.

18 *Sudbury Star*, 30 May 1985, but see "Planning a City," *Sudbury Star*, 5 November 1988, which discusses the views of Hans Huch, the regional planning director.

19 *Sudbury Star*, 20 May 1992.

20 See C.M. Wallace, "Sudbury: The Northern Experiment with Regional Government," *Laurentian University Review* 17, no. 2 (February 1985): 87–101.

21 Kennedy, *Sudbury Area Study*, 27 May 1970, 5.

22 *Sudbury Star*, 30 December 1989.

23 Ibid., 28 March 1985.

24 Ibid., 27 March 1985.

25 "Political Smoke Hides Real Issues" (editorial), *Sudbury Star*, 28 March 1985.

26 *Northern Life Weekender*, 2 March 1985.

27 *Chatelaine*, April 1991.

28 *Globe and Mail*, 17 November 1992.

BIBLIOGRAPHY

General
*Biographies de la Région de Sudbury/Biographies of the Sudbury Region, Version
préliminaire/Preliminary edition.* Sudbury: Département d'histoire, Université
Laurentienne/Department of History, Laurentian University, 1980.
Nelson, Bill, et al. *Atlas of the Regional Municipality of Sudbury.* Sudbury: Sudbury
2001, 1980.
O'Neill, Maury, and Peter Andrews. *Sudbury Statistical Summary.* Sudbury:
Department of History, Laurentian University, 1986.
Shantz, Mary, and C. Anderson. *Sudbury ABC.* Sudbury: Reference Department,
Sudbury Public Library, 1972.

Bibliographies
Jones, Richard. *An Annotated Bibliography of the Sudbury Area.* 2nd ed. Sudbury:
Sudbury Public Library, 1972.
Stelter, Gilbert A., and John Rowan, comps. *Community Development in
Northeastern Ontario: A Selected Bibliography.* Sudbury: Department of History,
Laurentian University, 1972.
Stephenson, Robert, et al. *Sudbury Mining Area: A Selected Bibliography.* Sudbury:
Department of History, Laurentian University, 1978.

Newspaper Indexes
Index to the Sudbury Star. Sudbury: Department of History, 1980–1983. A
computerized index by decade of the *Star* between 1910 and 1980. 2 vols.
Rowan, John. *Sudbury Journal August 1891 to May 1918: Index.* Sudbury: John
Rowan, 1970.

Books
Arnopoulos, Sheila McLeod. *Voices from French Ontario.* Kingston: McGill-Queen's
University Press, 1982.
Bouchard, Jeannette. *Seven Decades of Caring/Sept décennies de soins.* Sudbury:
Laurentian University Press, 1984.
Bray Matt, and Ashley Thomson, eds. *At the End of the Shift: Mines and Single-
Industry Towns in Northern Ontario.* Toronto: Dundurn Press, 1992.
Cadieux, Lorenzo. *Frédéric Romanet du Caillaud: "Comte" de Sudbury.* Montreal:
Éditions Bellarmin, 1971.
Christ the King: 60th Jubilee, 1917–1977. Sudbury: Christ the King Church, 1977.
Clement, Wallace. *Hardrock Mining: Industrial Relations and Technological Change at
Inco.* Toronto: McClelland and Stewart, 1981.
Deverell, John, and the Latin American Working Group. *Falconbridge: Portrait of a
Canadian Mining Multinational.* Toronto: Lorimer, 1975.
Dorion, Charles. *The First 75 Years: A Headline History of Sudbury, Canada.*
Ilfracombe: Stockwell, [1958].
Evans, Robert. *An Eye on Everything.* Sudbury: Laurentian University Press, 1966.
Collection of columns from the *Sudbury Star.*
Gaudreau, G., ed. *Le Théatre du nouvel-Ontario: 20 Ans.* Sudbury: TNO, 1991.

Geldart, Winston J. *For Want of a Nail: The Story of Cochrane Dunlop Hardware Ltd.* Toronto: Privately published, 1966.

Hallsworth, Caroline M. *Federal, Provincial and Municipal Elections in Sudbury.* Sudbury: Sudbury Public Library, 1981.

Hallsworth, Gwenda. *Le Beau Risque du Savoir/"A Venture into the Realm of Higher Learning."* [Sudbury: Laurentian University, 1985.]

———. *A History of Hydro in Sudbury.* Sudbury: Sudbury Hydro-Electric Commission, 1985.

Havel, J.E. *Les Citoyens de Sudbury et la Politique sur l'information, le comportement politique et les partis" Sudbury.* Sudbury: Laurentian University Press, 1966. Also published in English as *Politics in Sudbury: A Survey of Mass Communication, Political Behaviour and Political Parties in Sudbury.* Sudbury: Laurentian University Press, 1966.

Higgins, E.G. *Twelve O'Clock and All's Well: A Pictorial History of Law Enforcement in the Sudbury District, 1883–1978.* Sudbury: Sudbury Regional Police Association, 1978.

Higgins, E.G., and F.A. Peake. *Sudbury Then and Now: A Pictorial History of Sudbury and Area, 1883–1973.* Sudbury: Sudbury and District Chamber of Commerce, 1977.

Historic Sudbury: I. Sudbury: Sudbury and District Historical Society, 1979.

Howard-White, F.B. *Nickel: An Historical Review.* Toronto: Longmans, 1963.

Howey, Florence R. *Pioneering on the C.P.R.* [Ottawa: Mutual Press, 1938.] Reprinted as *Sudbury Minus One.* [Sudbury: Sheridan Technical School, 1968.]

Kelly, Michael C., et al. *Inventory and Guide to Historic Buildings in Sudbury.* Sudbury: Department of History, Laurentian University, 1978.

Knowles, John D., and Nickel Belt Rails. *The Sudbury Street Cars: The Sudbury-Copper Cliff Suburban Electric Railway Company.* Sudbury: Nickel Belt Rails, 1983.

LeBourdais, D.M. *Metals and Men.* Toronto: McClelland and Stewart, 1957.

———. *Sudbury Basin: The Story of Nickel.* Toronto: Ryerson, 1953.

Main, O.W. *The Canadian Nickel Industry: A Study in Market Control and Public Policy.* Toronto: University of Toronto Press, 1955.

McCharles, Aeneas. *Bemocked of Destiny: The Actual Struggles and Experiences of a Canadian Pioneer, and the Recollections of a Lifetime.* Toronto: William Briggs, 1908.

Miller, J.E. *The History of the Sudbury Little Theatre Guild, 1948–1962.* [Sudbury, 1962.]

Miner, Bob. *Miner's Life: Bob Miner and Union Organizing in Timmins, Kirkland Lake, and Sudbury.* Edited by Wayne Roberts. Hamilton: Labour Studies Programme, McMaster University, 1979.

Mount, Graeme S. *The Sudbury Region.* Burlington: Windsor, 1986.

Mount, Graeme S., and Michael F. Mulloy. *A History of St. Andrew's United Church, Sudbury.* Sudbury: St. Andrew's United Church, 1982.

Nelles, H.V. *The Politics of Development: Forests and Hydro-Electric Power in Ontario, 1849–1941.* Toronto: Macmillan, 1974.

Pagnucco, Frank. *Home Grown Heroes: A Sports History of Sudbury.* [Sudbury]: Miller Publishing, 1982.

Peake, F.A. *The Church of the Epiphany: A Century of Anglican Witness.* Sudbury: Church of the Epiphany, 1982.

Peake, F.A., and R.P. Horne. *The Religious Tradition in Sudbury 1883–1983.* Sudbury: Downtown Churches Association, 1983.

Prusila, Sheila, et al. *Vintage Schools: A Preliminary Survey of Schools Operating in the Sudbury Basin, 1883–1930.* Sudbury: Sudbury Board of Education, 1981.

Solski, Mike, and John Smaller. *Mine Mill: The History of the International Union of Mine, Mill and Smelter Workers in Canada Since 1895.* Ottawa: Steel Rail, 1984.

Southern, Frank. *The Sudbury Incident.* Toronto: York Publishing and Printing Co., 1978.

Stephenson, Robert, et al. *A Guide to the Golden Age: Mining in Sudbury 1886–1977.* Sudbury: Department of History, Laurentian University, 1979.

Sudbury and District Historical Society. *Industrial Communities of the Sudbury Basin: Copper Cliff, Victoria Mines, Mond and Coniston.* Sudbury: The Society, 1986.

Sudbury District Roman Catholic Separate School Board. *One Hundred Years of Catholic Separate Schools of Sudbury.* Sudbury: The Board, 1984.

Sudbury Public Library, Centennial Committee. *Sudbury Authors: Sudbury People Telling Sudbury's Story/Ils racontent notre histoire: Sudbury raconté par les Sudburois.* Sudbury: Sudbury Public Library, 1983.

Sudbury Secondary School. *Recollections 1908–1893.* Sudbury: Reunion 83, 1983.

Swift, Jamie. *The Big Nickel: Inco at Home and Abroad.* Kitchener: Between the Lines, 1977.

Tester, Jim. "The Shaping of Sudbury: A Labour View." Address to a public meeting of the Sudbury and District Historical Society, 18 April 1979. Available at Sudbury Public Library.

Thompson, John F., and Norman Beasley. *For Years to Come: A Story of International Nickel of Canada.* Toronto: Longmans, 1960.

Thrope, T. *A Review of the Logging and Pulp Operations in Sudbury District during the Years 1901–1950.* Sudbury: Ontario Department of Lands and Forests, 1950.

To Our City/À notre ville. Sudbury: Sudbury Centennial Foundation, 1983.

Young, Scott, and Astrid Young. *Silent Frank Cochrane: The North's First Great Politician.* Toronto: Macmillan, 1973.

Articles

Beach, Noel. "Nickel Capital: Sudbury and the Nickel Industry, 1905–1925." *Laurentian University Review* 6, no. 3 (June 1974): 55–74.

Brandt, Gail Cuthbert. "The Development of French-Canadian Social Institutions in Sudbury, 1883–1920." *Laurentian University Review* 11, no. 2 (February 1979): 5–22.

Bray, R.M. "The Province of Ontario and the Problem of Sulphur Fumes Emissions in the Sudbury District: An Historical Perspective." *Laurentian University Review* 16, no. 2 (February 1984): 81–90.

Devereux, H.E. "Sudbury: The Last Eight Thousand Years." *Polyphony* 5, no. 1 (Spring/Summer 1983): 17–20.

Gervais, Gaetan. "Les Franco-Sudburois, 1883–1983." *Polyphony* 5, no. 1 (Spring/Summer 1983): 21–29.

Krasib, Ljubo. "Croatians of Sudbury: Mobility of the Immigrants, 1880s to 1940s." *Polyphony* 5, no. 1 (Spring/Summer 1983): 59–70.

Krats, Peter V. "'Suomalaiset Nikkelialuella': Finns in the Sudbury Area, 1883–1939." *Polyphony* 5, no. 1 (Spring/Summer 1983): 37–48.

Lewis, Gertrud Jaron. "German-Speaking Immigrants in the Sudbury Region." *Polyphony* 5, no. 1 (Spring/Summer 1983): 82–85.

Moses, Dorothy, and Dina Abramson. "Jews in Sudbury." *Polyphony* 5 no. 1 (Spring/Summer 1983): 113-15.

Radecki, Henry. "Polish Immigrants in Sudbury: 1883–1980." *Polyphony* 5, no. 1 (Spring/Summer 1983): 49–58.

Ross, Val. "The Arrogance of Inco." *Canadian Business* 52, no. 5 (May 1979): 44–55.

Saarinen, O.W. "Ethnicity and the Cultural Mosaic in the Sudbury Area." *Polyphony* 5, no. 1 (Spring/Summer 1983): 86–92.

———. "Finns in Northeastern Ontario with Special Reference to the Sudbury Region." *Laurentian University Review* 15, no. 1 (November 1982): 41–54.

———. "Municipal Government in Northern Ontario: An Overview." *Laurentian University Review* 17, no. 2 (February 1985): 5–25.

———. "Planning and Other Development Influences on the Spatial Organization of Urban Settlement in the Sudbury Area." *Laurentian University Review* 3, no. 3 (February 1971): 38–70.

———. "Sudbury: A Historical Case Study of Multiple Urban-Economic Transformation." *Ontario History* 82, no. 1 (March 1990): 53–81.

Stefura, Mary. "The Process of Identity: A Historical Look at Ukrainians in the Sudbury Area Community." *Laurentian University Review* 15, no. 1 (November 1982): 55–64.

———. "Ukrainians in the Sudbury Region." *Polyphony* 5, no. 1 (Spring/Summer 1983): 71–81.

Stelter, Gilbert A. "Community Development in Toronto's Commercial Empire: The Industrial Towns of the Nickel Belt, 1883–1931." *Laurentian University Review* 6, no. 3 (June 1974): 3–53.

———. "Origins of a Company Town: Sudbury in the Nineteenth Century." *Laurentian University Review* 3, no. 3 (February 1971): 3–37.

———. "The People of Sudbury: Ethnicity and Community in an Ontario Mining Region." *Polyphony* 5, no. 1 (Spring/Summer 1983): 3–11.

Visentin, Maurizio A. "The Italians of Sudbury." *Polyphony* 5, no. 1 (Spring/Summer 1983): 30–36.

Wallace, Carl M. "Sudbury: The Northern Experiment with Regional Government." *Laurentian University Review* 17, no. 2 (February 1985): 87–101.

Theses

Blaine, Richard Paul, "The Settlement of the Sudbury Region." M.A. thesis. Toronto: University of Toronto, 1952.

Cuomo, D.S. "The Evolution of the Planning Process in the Sudbury Area: The Roles of the Principal Actors." B.A. thesis. Sudbury: Department of Geography, Laurentian University, 1980.

Dennie, Donald. "Sudbury 1883–1946: A Social Historical Study of Property and Class." Ph.D. thesis. Ottawa: Carleton University, 1988.

Dubé-Quibell, Lola. "Le Conseil municipal de Sudbury, 1893–1914." Thèse de Maîtrise ès Arts. Sudbury: Université Laurentienne, 1983.

Eldridge, Bruce. "The Sudbury–Copper Cliff Suburban Streetcar System: A Study of Urban Transit." B.A. thesis. Sudbury: Department of History, Laurentian University, 1980.

Ellis, D. "A Regional Study of the Sudbury District, Ontario." B.A. thesis. Toronto: University of Toronto, 1946.

Faintuck, Arnold, and Oryst H. Sawchuk. "A Plan for Sudbury." M.S. thesis. Winnipeg: University of Manitoba, 1955.

Forster, Dorothy M. "Entertainment in Sudbury, 1920–1930." Undergraduate essay. Sudbury: Department of History, Laurentian University, 1985.

Goltz, Eileen. "The Exercise of Power in a Company Town: Copper Cliff, 1886–1960." Ph.D. thesis. Guelph: University of Guelph, 1989.

———."Genesis and Growth of a Company Town: Copper Cliff, 1886–1920." M.A. thesis. Sudbury: Laurentian University, 1983.

Hallsworth, Gwenda. "'A Good Paying Business': Lumbering on the North Shore of Lake Huron, 1850–1910 with Particular Reference to the Sudbury District." M.A. thesis. Sudbury: Laurentian University, 1983.

Harris, Judith E. "Well-being in Sudbury, 1931–1971: A Social Indicator Analysis." M.Sc. thesis. Guelph: University of Guelph, 1978.

Horne, Ronald P. "Disappointment to Euphoria: A History of the International Union of Mine Mill and Smelter Workers in Sudbury, 1936–1944." Honours essay. Sudbury: Department of History, Laurentian University, 1981.

Jalava, Mauri Amiko. "Radicalism or a 'New Deal'?: The Unfolding World View of the Finnish Immigrants in Sudbury, 1883–1932." M.A. thesis. Sudbury: Laurentian University, 1983.

James, D.S. "A Study of the Effects of Amalgamation and Annexation of the City of Sudbury and Adjoining Municipalities." B.Comm. thesis. Kingston: Queen's University, 1964.

Kelly, Michael C. "By Divine Right: Sudbury as a Regional Metropolis, 1900–1910." M.A. thesis. Toronto: University of Toronto, 1984.

Kesik, John Lawrence. "A Linguistic and Religious Study of Sudbury Town Council, 1893–1930." B.A. thesis. Sudbury: Department of History, Laurentian University, 1985.

Krats, Peter V.K. "The Sudbury Area to the Great Depression: Regional Development on the Northern Resource Frontier." Ph.D. thesis. London: University of Western Ontario, 1988.

———. "'Sudbury Suomalaiset': Finnish Immigration Activity in the Sudbury Area, 1883–1939." M.A. thesis. London: University of Western Ontario, 1980.

Lang, John B. "A Lion in a Den of Daniels: A History of the International Union of Mine Mill and Smelter Workers in Sudbury, Ontario, 1942–1962." M.A. thesis. Guelph: University of Guelph, 1970.

Martin, J.P. "Sudbury: étude économique et humaine de la ville et de son bassin." Ph.D. thesis. Paris: University of Paris, 1971.

Mason, R. Frank. "The Vulnerable Gowan Gillmor: St. Paul of Algoma." Honours essay. Sudbury: Department of History, Laurentian University, 1988.

McArton, A.W. "Impact of Railway Expansion on Economic Growth of the Sudbury, Ontario, Area." M.A. thesis. Norman: University of Oklahoma, 1966.

McCullough, Donald E. "The Evolution and Distribution of Public Housing in the City of Sudbury." B.A. thesis. Sudbury: Laurentian University, 1972.

Merriam, Irene "Mickey." "Finnish Theatre in the Sudbury District." Honours thesis. Toronto: York University, 1976.

Saarinen, O.W. "A Geographical Basis for Regional Planning in the Sudbury Area." M.A. thesis. London: University of Western Ontario, 1966.

Stephenson, Robert A. "'To Strike – or Not to Strike?' An Examination of the International Union of Mine Mill and Smelter Workers' Strike in Sudbury During 1958." Honours B.A. thesis. Sudbury: Department of History, Laurentian University, 1978.

Topham, Judith "Sudbury: Growth and Development, 1920–1940." Honours essay. Sudbury: Department of History, Laurentian University, 1981.

Government Documents and Special Studies

Batelle Memorial Institute. *Economic Development Opportunities for the Sudbury Area, Ontario*. Columbus: Batelle Memorial Institute, 1959.

M.M. Dillon Ltd. *Sudbury Area Transportation Study*. Sudbury: M.M. Dillon, 1965. Available at Sudbury Public Library.

Ontario, Department of Lands and Forests. *A History of the Sudbury Forest District*. Toronto: The Department, 1967.

Royal Commission on the Health and Safety of Workers in Mines [Ham Commission]. *Report*. Toronto, 1976.

Royal Ontario Nickel Commission. *Report*. Toronto: King's Printer, 1917.

Sudbury 2001. *Proceedings [of a] Conference on Economic Development April 6, 7, 8, 1978*. [Sudbury: Sudbury 2001, 1978.]

Winter, J.R. *Sudbury: An Economic Survey*. Sudbury: Sudbury and District Industrial Commission and Laurentian University, 1967.

Other

Many other studies of Sudbury available in French are published by La Société historique du Nouvel-Ontario (c/o the University of Sudbury), or are found in *La Revue du Nouvel-Ontario*. The *Inco Triangle* and Falconbridge's *Falcon* are also good sources for a study of Sudbury. A great deal of very specialized material on the city and the region is listed in Gwenda Hallsworth, Ashley Thomson, and Lionel Bonin, *Bibliography of Northern Ontario, 1966–1991/Bibliography de l'Ontario du nord, 1966-1991* (forthcoming).

INDEX

Printed in the USA
CPSIA information can be obtained
at www.ICGtesting.com
JSHW012019140824
68134JS00033B/2774